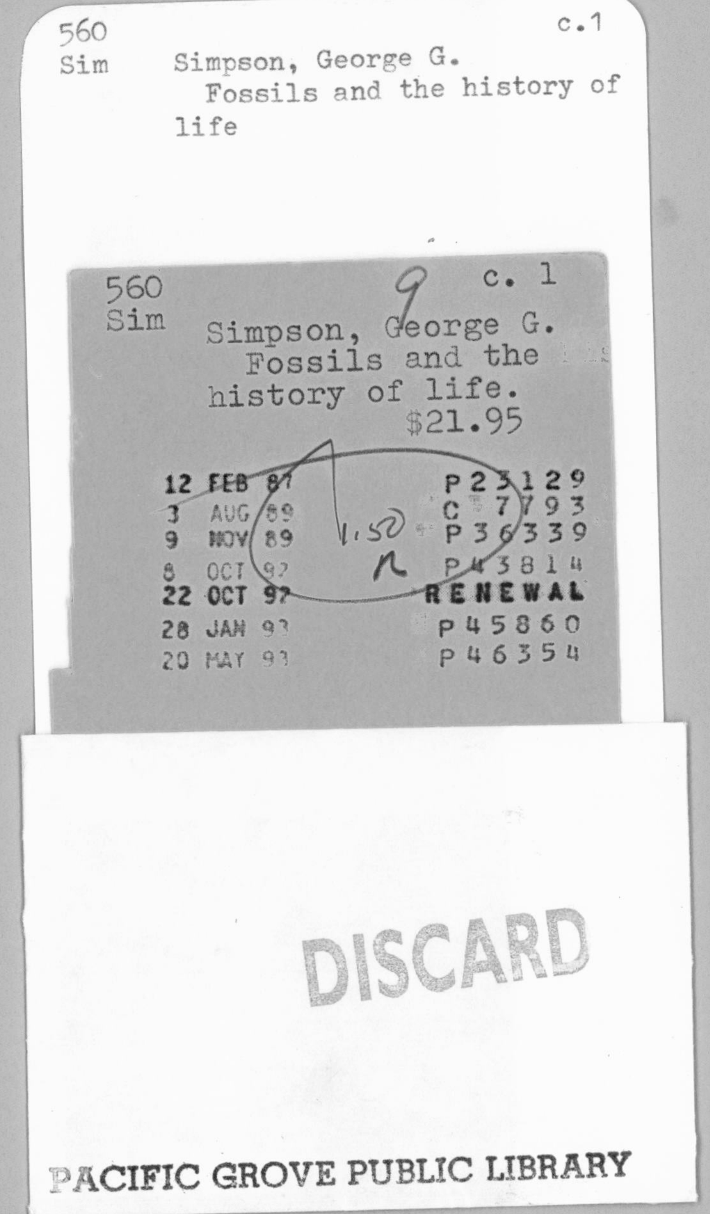

560
Sim
c.1
Simpson, George G.
Fossils and the history of life
560
Sim
c. 1
Simpson, George G.
Fossils and the history of life.
$21.95
12 FEB 87 P23129
3 AUG 89 C 7793
9 NOV 89 P36339
8 OCT 92 P43814
22 OCT 92 RENEWAL
28 JAN 93 P45860
20 MAY 93 P46354
DISCARD
PACIFIC GROVE PUBLIC LIBRARY

Fossils and the History of Life

FOSSILS AND THE HISTORY OF LIFE

George Gaylord Simpson

SCIENTIFIC
AMERICAN
LIBRARY

An imprint of Scientific American Books, Inc.
New York

Library of Congress Cataloging in Publication Data:

Simpson, George Gaylord, 1902–
Fossils and the history of life.

Bibliography: p.
Includes index.
1. Paleontology. I. Title.
QE711.2.S55 1983 560 83-4423
ISBN 0-7167-1564-3

Printed in the United States of America

Scientific American Library is published by Scientific American Books, Inc., a subsidiary of Scientific American, Inc.

Distributed by W. H. Freeman and Company,
41 Madison Avenue, New York, New York 10010.

2 3 4 5 6 7 8 9 0 KP 1 0 8 9 8 7 6 5 4

This book is dedicated to memories of four of the many good friends and inspiring colleagues who are no longer with us:

THEODOSIUS DOBZHANSKY

JULIAN HUXLEY

BRYAN PATTERSON

ALFRED ROMER

CONTENTS

PREFACE

The history of life on the earth cannot fail to interest us: we are an outcome of that history, and we live our lives among millions of other species that, although unlike ourselves, are outcomes of the same history. The subject is extremely complex. Hundreds of books and thousands of articles have been written about it. No one book can do more than sample and exemplify its many aspects. The most direct evidence for the history of life is provided by fossils, so this book is centered on their study, the science of paleontology, but it does make some relatively short excursions into closely related aspects of some other scientific specialties.

An idea owed primarily to Gerard Piel, publisher of *Scientific American*, is that there should be books about various more or less specialized sciences, written by specialists in each one, but written without the assumption that the reader will necessarily have previous technical knowledge about the subject. This book has been written with that purpose. It may interest other paleontologists, but it was written primarily for students, for scientists in fields other than paleontology, and for other intelligent adults who do not yet know much, if anything, about fossils and the history of life but who would like to.

As so often in the past, my wife, Anne Roe, has both encouraged and helped me in the long task of writing this book, interrupted as it was by illnesses and other problems. Although she is professionally a psychologist, her long association with me has made her also a more than amateur paleontologist and evolutionary biologist, just as mine with her has given me some understanding of psychology and its contrasts with other sciences.

The labor of transcribing my difficult handscript, with scratchings-out, insertions, rewritings, and rearrangements, as well as the bother of such errands as getting xerox copies made, has been undertaken at various times by three admirable and helpful young women: Bonnie Finkler, who typed almost all the text; Lindy Flynn, who did the same for almost all the extensive captions of figures; and Mary Petti, who helped me catch up from time to time when the work piling up in my study-office-library-laboratory got ahead of me.

My colleague at the University of Arizona, Everett H. Lindsay, Jr., encouraged me and gave me needed help on some technical aspects of the determination of geological time. Otherwise, I have not explicitly or directly consulted with colleagues, but it will be obvious that I owe them an enormous debt for knowledge obtained from their publications and often also from correspondence and conversation. Many of them are named in the text. If I tried to acknowledge all such assistance, however, it would take another book and a list of sources starting some time not later than 400 B.C. and continuing through 1983.

Although there is no dissent among paleontologists about the fact of evolution or the objective nature of the fossil record, there is healthy discussion about some details of the interpretation of those facts and about preference in methods of their classification. Where those differences seem to me important enough and interesting enough to merit consideration in such a condensed account as this I have stated the issues involved. I have also stated my own opinion when it is not neutral. It hardly needs to be added that no one else is responsible for my opinions or my statements about them.

This book was written during part of my half-time commitment as a Professor of Geosciences at the University of Arizona, in facilities provided by myself, and with the use of the library of the Simroe Foundation, which is supported only by Dr. Roe and me. Since I retired from the University of Arizona as of 30 June 1982, the University and my colleagues there were not involved in the completion of the publication. No grants or other institutional aid were involved.

GEORGE GAYLORD SIMPSON
Tucson, Arizona
March 1983

Fossils and the History of Life

INTRODUCTION: THE FASCINATION OF FOSSILS

Our home planet, Earth, has existed as a consolidated, separate body for at least four and a half billion years. (That is even more impressive written out as 4,500,000,000, but a scientist or a mathematician can whittle it down to 4.5×10^9.) There is now evidence that life existed on Earth as very simple, very primitive, very tiny organisms as early as 3,500,000,000 (or 3.5×10^9) years ago.

Surely there can be no history more dramatic, more fascinating, and more meaningful than the history of life through a span of time so enormous as to be almost incomprehensible in comparison with our brief human lifetimes. We have learned much about that history, and literally every day more is being learned. Thus in contemplation we can expand our perspective to include not only our mortal scores of years but also the earth's billions of years.

The history of life began obscurely, and so far it has culminated in the millions of kinds of living organisms around us—and in ourselves. Some aspects of the history can be inferred from the forms of life that exist at present, but much cannot. If we had no other evidence or record, our knowledge of this history would be without dates and—as we now know—it would completely lack many of its most significant and extraordinary events. Fortunately, many of those events have left a record, incomplete indeed but becoming ever clearer and fuller as investigation of it continues and expands.

The primary record of the history of life is written in the successive strata of rocks as in the pages of a book. In continuation of the metaphor, fossils may be called the writing on those pages. They are the remains or traces of organisms living at successive geological times. These are the primary subject of this book, and something will be said about the many aspects of the origins, study, and significance of fossils. They represent once living things and should be seen as such. They must be put in their sequence in time. They were influenced by, and bear witness to, geographic and geological changes on the earth. They are basic materials for the study of many factors of organic evolution. In special ways, they have both utility and profound meaning for us humans. Their study will be found to overlap broadly with both the earth sciences and the life sciences, combining historical geology and historical biology into one great synthesis.

We all know about the recipe that starts, "First catch your rabbit." Here at the beginning of this book it may similarly be said, "First find your fossil." That is the favorite occupation of most of the active students of fossils. Many years ago (in fact only a few years short of half a century ago) I expressed my enthusiasm for this pursuit in a way that I still endorse, although I cannot now quite so actively follow it:

> *Fossil hunting is far the most fascinating of all sports. It has some danger, enough to give it zest and probably about as much as in the average modern engineered big-game hunt, and the danger is wholly to the hunter. It has uncertainty and excitement and all the thrills of gambling with none of its vicious features. The hunter never knows what his bag may be, perhaps nothing, perhaps a creature never before seen by human eyes. It requires knowl-*

edge, skill, and some degree of hardihood. And its results are so much more important, more worth-while, and more enduring than those of any other sport! The fossil hunter does not kill; he resurrects. And the result of this sport is to add to the sum of human pleasure and to the treasures of human knowledge.

That is where the fun and the sport are, but I feel that I must add one more quotation from myself, written when I was older and somewhat more sober but no less enthusiastic:

The historian of life takes not only knowledge of fossils but also a tremendous array of pertinent facts from other fields of earth sciences and of life sciences and weaves them all into an integral interpretation of what the world of life is like and how it came to be so. Finally, he is bound to reflect still more deeply and to face the riddles of the meaning and nature of life and of man as well as problems of human values and conduct. The history of life certainly bears directly on all these riddles and problems, and realization of its own value demands investigation of this bearing.

CHAPTER 1

THE SCIENCE OF PALEONTOLOGY

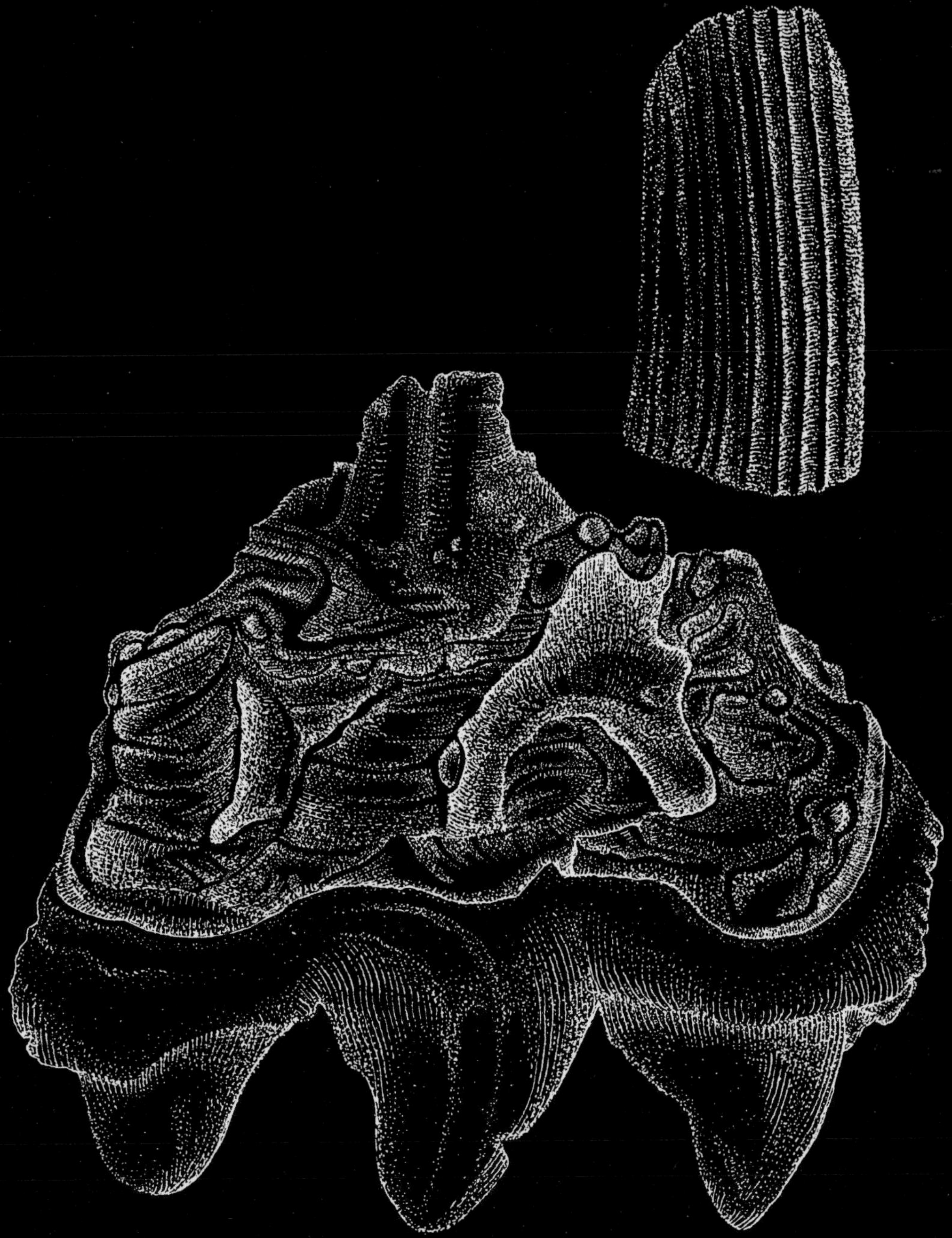

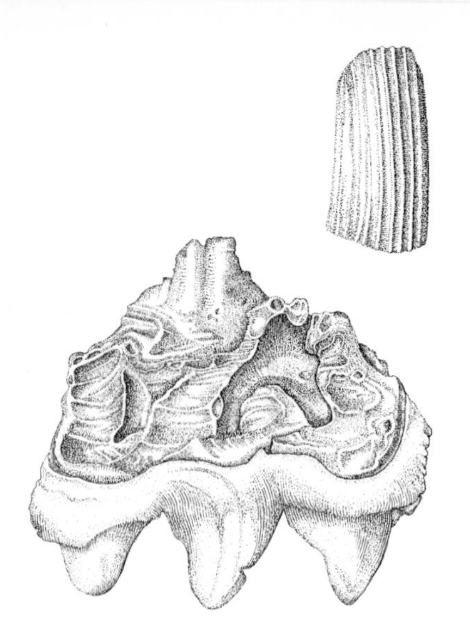

A drawing of two fossils from the same deposit. The larger specimen is what remains of one molar tooth of an American mastodon. After death the animal's remains were scattered and this tooth was separated from the jaw. It has been gnawed and has grooved marks left by the teeth that gnawed it. The gnawing was done by an extinct giant beaver known as Castoroides. *The specimen above right is a fragment of the enormous incisor such as made the grooved marks on the mastodon tooth.*

Paleontology is the science of discovering and studying the fossil record and from it deciphering the history of life. Although this science had much earlier roots, it received its present name (and full recognition as a science in its own right) in 1838, when the great British geologist Charles Lyell coined the name from classic Greek roots meaning "science of ancient life." (Lyell wrote the word *palaeontology,* and most of the British still do; but Americans and many others use *-e-* in place of the digraph or ligature *-æ-*.) The term has been adopted, with slight linguistic changes, in almost all the nonideographic literary and scientific languages.

Most people who are not professional paleontologists or archaeologists confuse those two professions. The words are similar in literal meaning (*paleontology* means the study of ancient life, and *archaeology* means the study of antiquities), but in modern usage the two terms are quite distinct. Archaeologists study not fossils but artifacts, which are any things made by humans. Nowadays they do not even insist that the artifacts always be antique. I have just read an archaeological report on artifacts only a few years old found in a dig in Harvard Yard.

The word *fossil* long antedates the word *paleontology. Fossilis,* from the verb *fodere* ("to dig"), was a Latin adjective early applied to anything that had been dug up. From it was derived a late Latin noun, *fossilium,* which was adopted into English by way of French as *fossile,* or *fossil,* still with the meaning of anything dug up, including minerals, crystals, rocks of various kinds and shapes, and also (but not particularly) the things we now call fossils. Nevertheless it was a long time before it was generally recognized that some of what were being called fossils were records of the history of life—or even that life has had a history.

It is enlightening for the history of science, and illustrative of the dependence of insight on the preconceptions and biases of an era and a culture, that it was a long, slow, and difficult feat to comprehend that the original designation "fossil" included two radically different classes of things. For example, Konrad von Gesner, who in 1558 published some of the earliest figures of fossils in a printed book, recognized that some looked almost exactly like living organisms, but he made no distinction between those and others that were quite unlike such organisms. He pictured both a living crab and a fossil crab, and he labeled the latter as a petrified crab ("ein steininer Meerkrebs" in his caption), and yet did not suggest that it had been a living animal before it was petrified.

When all the "fossils" or "petrifactions" known in the sixteenth to eighteenth centuries were considered, many naturalists found no clear line of separation in the series from those that looked exactly like organisms, such as Gesner's petrified crab, to those at the other extreme, such as quartz crystals, which bore no resemblance to any known organism. The existence of plantlike and of animallike fossils was well known, but it was explained away in several different ways, depending on the philosophical views of the explainer. To a Platonist, such fossils had never been alive but were images of organisms engendered in the earth by a molding force, a *vis plastica.* An Aristotelian would agree that they were not the remains of once living organisms but would argue that they had grown in the

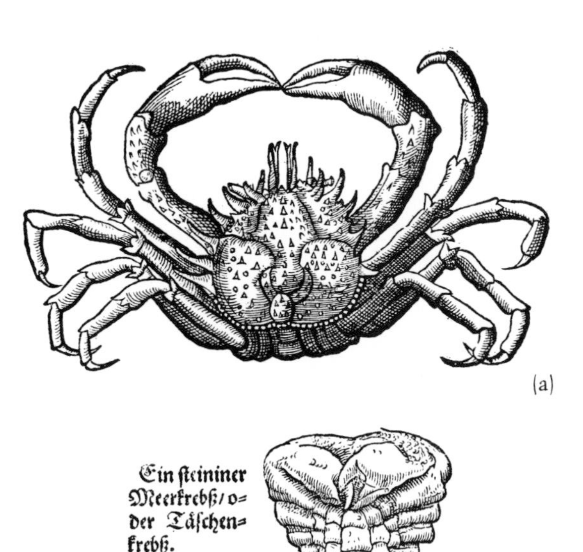

(a) *A living crab figured as such by Conrad Gesner in this woodcut printed in 1565.* (b) *A fossil crab figured by Gesner in the same work. He recognized the resemblance of this fossil to a living crab and in German called it "A petrified sea-crab or common-crab," but in his day this fossil was not considered as ever having been a live crab.*

(a)

(b) (c)

Like the fossil crab, this is also a woodcut from Gesner (1565), but it shows fossils in which he saw no resemblance to petrifactions of formerly living animals. His "Belemnitae" (a), *still called belemnites from the Greek word for "darts," were then commonly called "thunder stones." They are now known to be a sort of internal skeleton of marine animals related to squids. The objects in* (b) *and* (c), *called "Asterias" by Gesner because of their somewhat starlike shapes, are segments of stalks of crinoids, stalked echinoderms sometimes called sea lilies. Living stalked crinoids had not yet been discovered in Gesner's lifetime.*

A fossil sea urchin (echinoid) as figured by Corutus and Chioccus in a 1622 catalogue of a museum in Verona. This is an "easy fossil," so obviously like some living echinoids that its true nature could hardly be mistaken. By this time, such easy fossils were already being recognized as remnants of animals once alive.

Georges Cuvier (1769–1832). Although others had studied fossils before him, Cuvier is generally considered the founder of paleontology as a distinct science. He was most broadly important for establishing three of the basic principles of the history of life: (1) the pattern of that history is multiple, not unilineal; (2) when ancient rocks and their fossils are put in the sequence of time, the fossil faunas are found to have changed markedly in the course of geological time; and (3) many (or most) of the species found as fossils became sequentially extinct.

rocks from seeds (perhaps fallen from stars) or that they had originated by spontaneous generation in the rocks, as many living organisms were then believed to arise.

Even in those times, however, a number of philosopher-naturalists could hardly avoid recognizing that what have recently been called "easy fossils" were remains of ordinary, once living organisms. These were mostly marine shells, well preserved, similar to or identical with species still living, and usually found in unconsolidated sediments near the sea. The usual and, for a time, increasingly popular way of explaining away such fossils was to assume that they were once living organisms that had been buried as a result of the Noachian deluge (Noah's flood).

Within the then strict limitations of knowledge of nature and in the spirit of the times, the Zeitgeist in Europe, there was not much to choose among those three interpretations of organism-like fossils. With our now enormously increased objective knowledge and our more naturalistic Zeitgeist, all three are found equally inane, although one still has some nonscientific or antiscientific adherents. The view that was based on a literalist exegesis of the Bible did have one virtue: it recognized that certain fossils were the remains of true, natural organisms. This was a necessary, but not yet a sufficient, basis for the eventual understanding of such fossils as part of the record of the history of life.

General recognition of the organic nature of fossils (in the present sense of the word) was achieved slowly and can hardly be ascribed to any one person. Here just two of many contributions to this end may be cited as deserving of special remembrance. One was made in 1667 by a Dane variously known as Niels Stensen (in his paternal language), Nicolaus Stenonis (in Latin), and Nicolas Steno (in English), who suggested that fossils were organic in origin. Within a year of that same date the English polymath Robert Hooke independently published the view that animallike fossils are in fact the remains of animals. These worthies also looked for some historical significance in fossils, but they somewhat vaguely considered that significance to be involved in the Noachian deluge.

Three further steps were still necessary before the real historical significance of fossils could be grasped and a true science of paleontology could eventually emerge. These steps, too, were achieved only gradually, by many workers and with considerable stumbling.

The next of these essential steps was the recognition that the rocks containing fossils, and therefore the fossils themselves, were not contemporaneous but had been deposited in a definite and usually determinable sequence. Steno had taken a first, quite limited step in this direction, but it was well into the nineteenth century before this concept was well understood and generally accepted. Definite espousal and demonstrations of rock and fossil sequences were made more or less simultaneously by William Smith (especially in 1815) in England, Giovanni Battista Brocchi (especially in 1814) in Italy, and Alexandre Brongniart (especially in 1811) in France.

Those same great geologists were also pioneer paleontologists, and, at the same time that they were establishing the principle of sequence, they were establishing the next necessary general principle for a history of life. This principle is that different fossils appear at different places in the sequence and that characteristic suites of fossilized organisms lived at different times in the past history of the earth. This idea had been stated by Georges Louis Leclerc, Comte de Buffon, as early as 1778 but in a hypothetical way, and it remained for naturalists of the next generation to demonstrate it objectively. Best known of these was Cuvier, the French founding father of vertebrate paleontology (whose name is so splendid that I cannot forbear giving it in full: Baron Georges Léopold Chrétien Frédéric Dagobert Cuvier). Brongniart's significant work published in 1811 was a joint production with Cuvier. Cuvier's single most important work in this connection, however, was published in 1825 under a grandiloquent title (translated here from French), "Discourse on the Revolutions of the Globe and on the Changes That They Have Produced in the Animal Kingdom."

Charles Darwin (1809–1892). The usual pictures of Darwin show him as a rather sad-looking, heavily bearded old man. In this portrait by George Richmond, now at Down House, where Darwin lived for many years, he is a man about 30 years old with solid accomplishment already in hand and world fame in his future. His account of The Voyage of the Beagle *had been published, and he was working on the three volumes of geological observations that he made on that voyage. He was starting private notebooks on evolution that would much later become* The Origin of Species. *He was also marrying his cousin Emma Wedgwood, with whom he would live happily ever after.*

Cuvier was aware that, while some fossils represented animals more or less similar to those of today, others were quite different from anything now known alive. He considered three hypotheses that could explain those facts: (1) the strange animals revealed by fossils might still be living in unexplored regions; (2) they might somehow have been metamorphosed into living counterparts; or (3) they might have become extinct. Although Cuvier held that local faunas had also changed in the "revolutions of the globe," he opted for the third hypothesis: the animals represented by the strangest fossils had simply become extinct. Incidentally, Thomas Jefferson, whose life (1743–1826) broadly overlapped that of Cuvier (1769–1832) and who interested himself in such matters, as he did in practically everything, opted with religious fervor for the first of Cuvier's hypotheses. Jefferson piously believed that God would not have permitted any of His creations to become extinct.

Although, as always happens in such matters, he had less clear and less convincing forerunners, it was Charles Darwin who conclusively settled these questions in 1859 in the book we usually call *The Origin of Species* (although its whole title is *On the Origin of Species by Means of Natural Selection, or the Preservation of Favoured Races in the Struggle for Life*).

All three of the Cuvierian hypotheses are correct. Each applies to some, but in each case to different, fossils. In accordance with the first hypothesis, there have been some plants and animals originally known only as fossils and later discovered alive in somewhat out-of-the-way places. Among the most interesting examples is a creature that was named *Burramys parvus* by the late, great paleontologist Robert Broom from some fossil bones he found in 1894 in a region in Australia called Burra by the aborigines. The fossils of *Burramys* indicated a little marsupial so different from any other known that for many years there was controversy about its proper classification. Then in the Australian winter of 1966 one was found alive and well (also friendly) and living in a ski hut in the rugged, but

The first known skeleton of the large ground sloth named Megatherium *("big beast") by Cuvier. It was found near Luján, west-southwest of Buenos Aires in what is now Argentina, and in 1789 it was sent to Spain by the Viceroy of Buenos Ayres. In Madrid, the bones were reassembled more or less as in life (in this case, rather less than more), the first time this had been done for an extinct mammal. Drawings made in Madrid were forwarded to Cuvier in Paris and published in 1812 in Cuvier's monumental work on* Ossemens Fossiles *("fossil bones"), from which this figure has been taken. Cuvier correctly determined that this strange beast was a sloth of sorts and remarked that the only known sloths, including the much smaller and different living ones, were all from the New World. This was a biogeographic and evolutionary clue, the full significance of which was not understood for more than a century after this figure was published. The skeleton itself can still be seen in Madrid, somewhat (but still not completely) revised from Cuvier's awkward representation of it.*

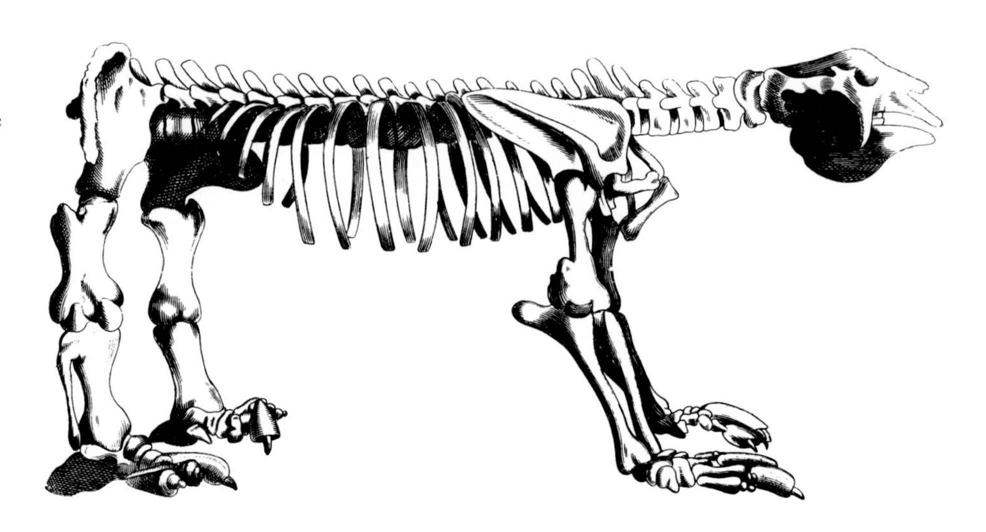

A modern restoration of Megatherium *painted by Charles R. Knight. The two animals in the foreground to the right are contemporaries of* Megatherium*: glyptodonts, large extinct armored relatives of armadillos.*

not notably high, Australian Alps. It died in less than a year, and it was mourned as the last of its race (as the last of its genus, in fact), but eventually others were discovered to be fairly common in their habitat, which is a difficult one for humans. (I have petted one of these charming creatures.)

Such discoveries of supposedly extinct animals are fascinating, but they have been few, and of course they decrease as the whole world and its animals become better known. Thus, the first of Cuvier's hypotheses is sometimes applicable, but it is not at all a general solution of the problem.

The Cuvierian hypothesis that many of the strange animals known only from fossils have become extinct is also correct, and it is much more important and widely applicable. It is now clearly established that the vast majority of species of organisms that have ever lived became extinct and now have no living descendants. Just why they became extinct is a different matter—a matter to which some further attention will be given here, although there is rarely any really good answer to that question, sometimes for the reason that there are too many possible answers. In any case, extinction is a normal, usual, and important part of the statistical history of life, and it requires study as such.

Cuvier's hypothesis numbered (2) above is that of evolution, which was established by Darwin and later investigators as unquestionably playing a major role in the history of life. In many respects, it is both the most interesting and the most important feature of that history. With the addition of this point, the whole basis had finally been laid for a science of paleontology and for the study of the history of life on a firm set of major principles, both geological and biological. As Darwin saw in 1859, a great deal then remained to be learned and much needed to be better understood. Now a great deal more has been learned and much is better understood. The search and the thinking were never more intense than now, and this will go on indefinitely.

So the word *fossil,* which originally meant anything dug up, has come to mean just the remains and traces of ancient organisms viewed as records of the history of life. It has been said that the expression *fossil fuels,* lately becoming so familiar, is the only survival of the original, broader meaning of the word, but that is not correct. The fossil fuels are fossils within present definitions of the word. Coal consists of the remains of ancient organisms (plants). Petroleum, natural gas, and the other hydrocarbons in or from geological deposits are trace fossils, in the sense of being substances derived from ancient organisms—but not from dinosaurs, as some advertisements seem to indicate.

There are so many different kinds of fossils as to be an almost bewildering array, not just in their biological classification but also in what is preserved and how it is preserved. As we can see from looking at the world around us, the great majority of organisms eventually leave no individual evidence that they ever existed. If an organism is to become a recognizable fossil, some part of its structure (or some result of its activities) must outlast such universally destructive factors as decay and erosion. With some exceptions, these relics must also be buried in a

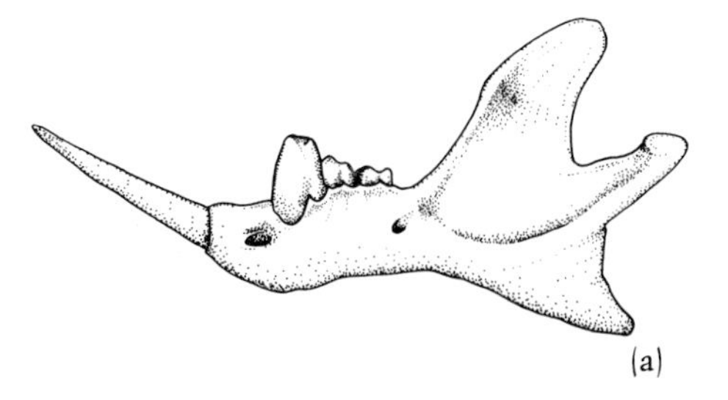

(a)

(b)

Literally a living fossil: (a) *The left lower jaw of a small marsupial, found as a fossil by Robert Broom in 1894 and recently etched out of its matrix by W. D. L. Ride. This apparently extinct animal was a theretofore unknown marsupial and was described and named by Broom in 1895 as an extinct genus and species,* Burramys parvus. *In 1966, a living animal of this species was found in a ski hut in the so-called Australian Alps, and later others were found alive in that region.* (b) *A photo of* Burramys parvus *taken to live in the Taronga Zoo near Sydney, Australia.*

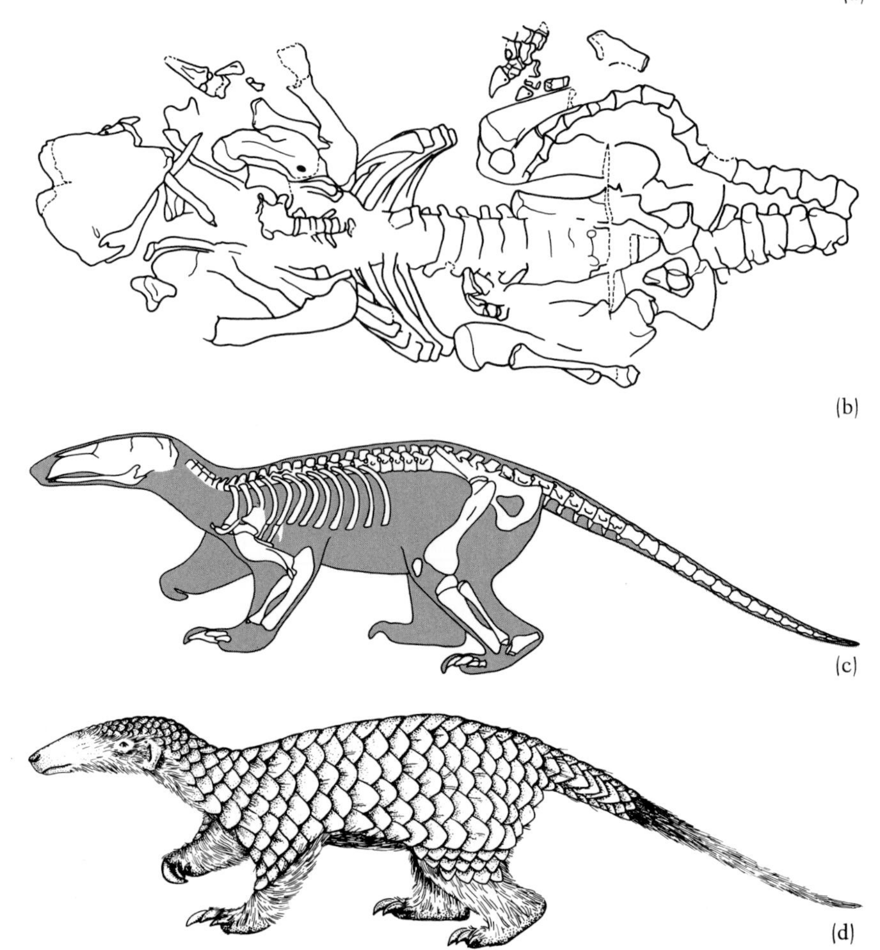

The resurrection of a fossil: (a) *Photograph of a nearly complete skeleton as it was buried in a deposit of lignite in the Geiseltal of Germany some 45 million years ago during the middle of the Eocene epoch. The skeleton is distorted and crushed which makes it difficult to distinguish the different parts in the photograph. The skull is to the left, and the tail, mostly twisted forward, lies with its base to the right.* (b) *A diagram of the bones showing their distorted positions as found.* (c) *A drawing depicting the preserved bones as they were positioned when the animal was alive. The gaps between the legs and toes and that between the head and neck allow spaces for bones not clearly preserved. An outline shows the contour of the living animal. Study of the skeleton indicates that the animal was certainly related and probably ancestral to the scaly anteaters or pangolins, which now live only in tropical Africa and southeastern Asia as far east as Bali. The fossil differs enough from the living species of the genus* Manis *to represent a different genus and species, named* Eomanis waldi. (d) *A restoration of* Eomanis *as it probably looked when alive. All living pangolins are covered with scales. Although these scales have no bony tissue and would not ordinarily be preserved in fossils, remains of them were found in another specimen of the Eocene genus, thanks to the remarkable preservation of usually not fossilizable materials in this deposit. The life restoration of* Eomanis *thus is covered with scales much as are the living species of the genus* Manis.

sediment that becomes a stratum in a stratigraphic sequence. They must also remain recognizable while that sediment undergoes various geological changes.

In view of these factors, it is obvious why the vast majority of animal fossils consist only of hard parts: shells, bones, teeth, the tough integuments of such animals as insects and crustaceans. There are exceptions: In Siberia and Alaska, some mammoths, an extinct species, have been preserved virtually whole by freezing and incorporation in permafrost. In arid regions, a few other mammals of extinct species have had their skins and some other soft parts preserved by simple desiccation outrunning complete putrefaction. Such exceptions are relatively recent, their ages counted in thousands rather than millions of years. There are also some fascinating but rare older exceptions to the rule of hard parts only. For example, in the middle Eocene, more than 45 million years ago, in what is now the Geiseltal in West Germany, there were swamps and lagoons in which vegetable matter, now converted into lignite (soft coal, *Braunkohle* in German), accumulated. Thousands of individual animals of innumerable different species, both invertebrate and vertebrate, were also buried in that accumulation. The deposit in its depths was evidently antiseptic, and many of the animals were preserved whole, some of them in such detail that the cell structure of muscles and other soft tissues can now be studied microscopically. Another famous exception, this one from the mountains of British Columbia, dates from the middle Cambrian, about 530 million years ago. At that time, this area was covered by a sea, and occasionally animals living on less deep bottoms were carried down into stagnant depths by submarine mud slides. There, more than 120 species of them, all invertebrates (vertebrates did not evolve until millions of years later) and most of them soft-bodied, were preserved in amazing detail.

Trace fossils are those that reveal the former presence and activities of animals but not the animals themselves. Among invertebrates they include such things as trails, tubes, borings, and worm casts. For such trace fossils the species that made them can hardly ever be exactly determined, but they do often provide information on the general ecology and makeup of ancient animal communities because they indicate various kinds of animals alive and in place when they were made. Fossil feces, known as coprolites, from invertebrates and vertebrates alike, are common fossils in some places. The most abundant trace fossils of vertebrates are the footprints and trackways of amphibians, reptiles, and mammals. Those of early reptiles, including dinosaur tracks like those long known from the Connecticut Valley, are especially abundant.

Most trace fossils are, in a sense, petrified behavior made while the animals were still alive and not, like other fossils, as aftermaths of death. This gives them a special interest, and their study has long been (and still is) one of the active specializations within the general field of paleontology. That is especially true of the study of vertebrate footprints and trackways, which by the middle of the nineteenth century had been given its own name: *ichnology*, based on the classical Greek word *ichnos* ("footprint" or "track"). For these tracks, too, the species

Dinosaur tracks and deduced (but not known) animals that made them. The tracks—trace fossils—were found in the Triassic beds of the Connecticut Valley, in which tracks of many different kinds have been found. The two sets of tracks here shown in much reduced size were not found together but were evidently made by members of the same species. Those on the left include impressions of the hind feet (large), front feet, long heels (in outline), and the ends of bones of the pelvis (single, heart-shaped imprint). These impressions were made when the animal was squatting down, not in motion. The tracks on the right were made by one animal walking on its hind legs and thus represent the left foot (in front) and the right foot (behind), the distance between them being a single stride. Such tracks were named Sauroidichnites barrattii *in 1837 by the pioneer New England paleontologist Edward Hitchcock. Although convenient for reference and for distinguishing them among the very numerous kinds of trace fossils, such naming of them has no standing in technical zoological literature since the names are not based on any actual remains of the organisms that left the traces. The restorations shown here, made by Richard Swann Lull, are reasonable inferences from the characteristics of the tracks but are based on no direct evidence. Lull considered these to have been herbivorous dinosaurs less than six feet in total length, relatively small and primitive in comparison with most of their later descendants or relatives, the Ornithischia, one of the two orders of dinosaurs.*

Cambrian sandstone showing the tracks of large worms that crawled across the wet sand, as well as an overall ripple pattern caused by the waves.

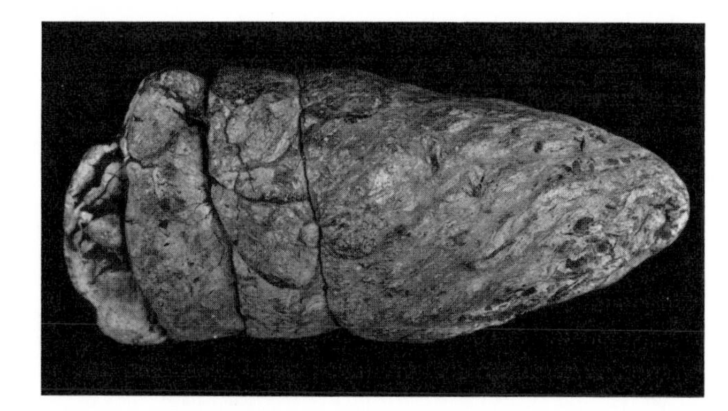

A coprolite, the fossilized dung of some prehistoric animal.

Dinosaur tracks made in the late Jurassic about 135 million years ago in what was then soft sand and is now hard rock. They were found in 1938 and subsequently excavated by Roland T. Bird along the Paluxy River near the town of Glen Rose southwest of Fort Worth, Texas. There are two quite different tracks. The large ones, made by almost elephantine feet, were those of a four-footed sauropod dinosaur, similar to Brontosaurus *and among the largest land animals that ever lived. The somewhat smaller but still impressive tracks, clearer to the left, are three-toed and were made by the hind feet of a bipedal carnivorous dinosaur. A section of these tracks was later excavated and installed under the skeleton of a* Brontosaurus *in New York's American Museum of Natural History.*

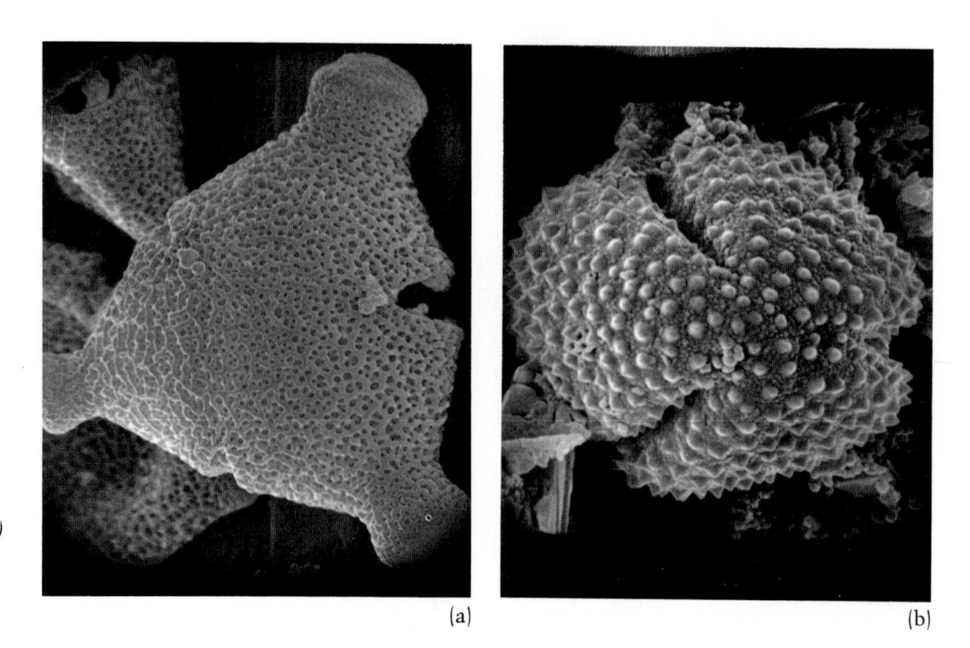

Scanning electron miscroscope (SEM) micrographs of pollen of two genera of plants. These exemplify some of the innumerable, well-marked differences that characterize pollen from different taxa and that make it usually possible to identify the genus and often the species of a plant from pollen alone. This has added enormously to knowledge of the distribution of fossil and Recent plants, both in space and in time, and it is the basis of the relatively new discipline of palynology in paleontology and botany. (a) *A Recent pollen grain of a species of the genus* Ceiba, *a tropical American tree that yields kapok and is sometimes called the "silk-cotton tree." (The bits seen in the background are broken parts of other pollen grains of the same tree.)* (b) *A pollen grain of a species of the genus* Artemisia. *Species of this genus (usually* A. tridentata*) are the familiar sagebrush so characteristic of the American Southwest (but not usual in the deserts). Outside of the tropics, the genus is practically world-wide in the northern hemisphere, various species ranging over the United States and into Canada, around the Mediterranean (where* A. absinthium, *or wormwood, is used in making absinthe), and eastward and northward even into Siberia. The particular pollen grain shown here was found in the nest of a Pleistocene packrat (*Neotoma *species). Surprisingly, such nests may last for thousands of years, and pollen from them is providing data on changes in flora and in climate.*

Various pollen grains differ greatly, not only in form and surface details but also in size. Of the two shown here, that of Ceiba, *here enlarged only 900 times, is much larger than that of* Artemisia, *which is enlarged 5,800 times.*

can rarely be determined with certainty, but much can be learned about them—for example, whether they were dinosaurs, whether they were four-footed or bipedal, and about how large they were.

Plants also have softer and harder tissues and organs—softer especially in leaves and flowers, harder in the woodier parts of stems and trunks—but on the whole their preservation as fossils is different from that of animals. Fossil wood is common enough, but leaves, although flimsier than wood, are even more abundant and widespread as fossils. Flowers, more evanescent, are generally rare as fossils.

Spores and pollen are mostly microscopic in size and do not have hard or skeletal parts in the usual sense. Until relatively recently (about the 1940s), it was not realized that they are nevertheless extremely abundant as fossils. At first they were studied mainly in geologically recent sediments, but intense and widespread activity has pushed such study back for hundreds of millions of years, far into the Paleozoic era, which ended about 225 million years ago. Spores and pollen, which are single reproductive cells of various sorts, are extraordinarily abundant in nature, much more so than any other recognizable products or parts of plants. Their comparatively common preservation as fossils is further due not to hardness in the usual sense but to their having complex outer layers or cuticles that are both tough and chemically resistant. These cuticles are also varied and characteristic in form, and many of them can be identified fairly closely, usually to genus and often to species. They thus give good records of floras at particular places and times, and they are especially helpful in deciphering ecological factors and events in the history of life. Their study has become a particularly active specialty, to

(a)

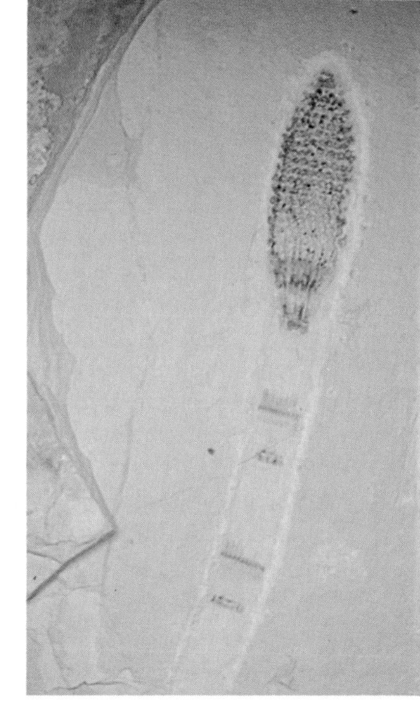

(b)

(c)

Fossil plants. (a) *Fossil leaves some 60 million years old. The top leaf is a poplar and the bottom is from a* Caesalpinia, *a tropical genus of trees and shrubs that include Brazilwood.* (b) *A fossil horsetail,* Equisetum winchesteri, *middle Eocene in age, from Wyoming's Green River Formation.* (c) *Partial remains of a flower and some other broken bits of vegetation preserved as thin, patterned carbon on thin-bedded, fine-grain sediment in what is now the People's Republic of China. The latter part of the fossil record of plants consists largely of such specimens as these.*

such a point that it has acquired a separate name as a science: *palynology*. (*Palyno*, in classical Greek, meant "to sprinkle," as with flour—or, presumably, as with pollen.)

As sciences advance, becoming more complex, they also tend to become more narrowly specialized and to proliferate names for their various specializations. Sometimes these seem unduly esoteric, and some of them are doubtless unnecessary; but they can serve at least two useful purposes. They may focus attention on fields of knowledge and research that are especially active now and promising for the future. They may also make reference to such fields more concise and precise. Two terms that serve both purposes for special aspects of paleontology have already been introduced here: ichnology and palynology. This is by way of introducing another: taphonomy.

The term *taphonomy* is derived from the classical Greek *taphos* ("burial") and *nomos* (literally "law," but sometimes used in modern compounds in the sense of "science"). (*Taphology* would be a better term, but *taphonomy* has become usual.) In a limited sense, taphonomy includes circumstances and events involving an organism that became a fossil from its death to its burial. In a more extended sense, taphonomy includes everything that has happened to a fossil from the death of the organism until the time when whatever remains of it is on a paleontologist's work table ready for study. Thus there are three different phases in taphonomy: first, from death to burial; second, the vastly longer phase during which it remains buried; finally, its discovery, collection, and preparation for study. Taphonomy can be seen, then, as a drama not only of death but also of resurrection.

If we think of a community of all kinds of organisms living together in one region at one time in the past and then consider what information about that community may now be directly available to us, it is obvious that such information is greatly less than for any such community now extant. Much of that loss occurs during the phases subsumed in taphonomy, and post-mortem information loss is often stressed in studies of taphonomy—or even considered as synonymous with taphonomy. There are, however, reasons for a different approach to taphonomy and to the fossil record.

The study of taphonomy is based on the preservation of information in the fossil record and not its loss. That record is a sampling of past life, and the samples are biased. Studying the history of life on the basis of samples is not only justified and highly informative, but also necessary. If we had a complete record—an obvious impossibility—dealing with it would overwhelm all the paleontologists and all the computers in the world. That our samples are biased is also obvious. The point here is that, to make reasonable interpretations of the history of life, we must recognize the presence of bias, judge the kinds and extents of biases, and make allowances for them. That is a major function of taphonomy and is one of the reasons for the growing attention to that aspect of paleontology.

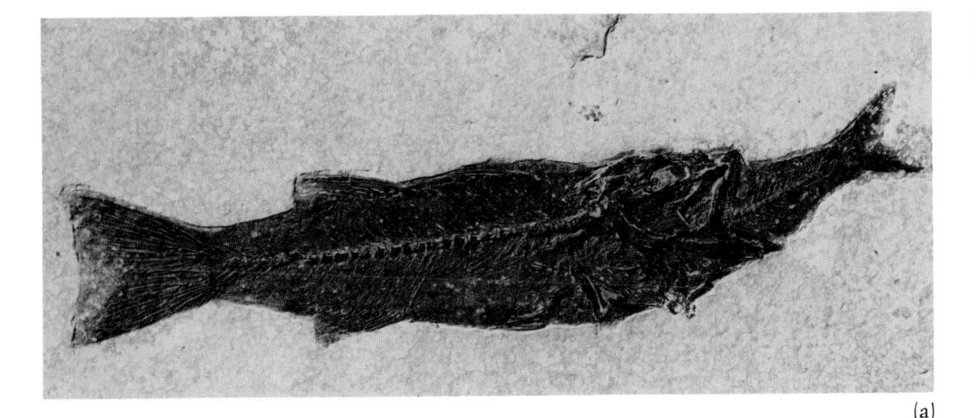

(a)

(b)

(a) *A middle Eocene perch* (Mioplosus) *swallowing the herring* Knightia, *from Wyoming's Green River Formation.*
(b) *A fossil of an extinct species of freshwater fish* Leuciscus miocenicus *closely related to living minnows, this specimen was found in the same Miocene deposit as the plant fossil* (c) *shown on page 15. Fishes dying in their natural environment and soon covered by fine-grained sediment are often preserved as complete articulated skeletons, like this one, and also as in this case some carbonaceous trace of the soft tissues.*

There are some biases that cannot be considered directly from the record. A major example is the fact that in any ancient community there were many species of organisms that did not enter into the fossil record at all. The existence, although as a rule not the closer identification, of such absences can often be inferred on other grounds. For example, wormlike nematodes are among the most abundant of all animals in most living faunas, and it cannot be doubted that they have been so for many millions of years, but they are almost absent from the fossil record.

It has already been mentioned that the preservation of soft tissues in fossils is the rarest sort of paleontological event, and obviously the disappearance of soft parts entails an enormous overall loss of information. Furthermore, the hard parts that are differentially preserved are often broken and scattered by consuming animals or scavengers, as well as by weathering and by stream or ocean currents, before they are buried. Sea shells nevertheless are frequently preserved whole and so, although less frequently, are fishes, but land vertebrates usually are not. The splendid skeletons of reptiles and mammals in museums give a distorted idea of the usual preservation of those groups. Among fossil mammals, particularly, there are thousands of fragmentary specimens for every fairly complete skeleton. Many ancient species of mammals, especially among the smaller ones, are known only from isolated single teeth. In some such instances, it is probable that the animals had been eaten and that what is preserved is only the undigested debris. Yet the whole of the hard parts of animals have been preserved often enough to provide skeletal samples, at least, for most of the main groups that had hard parts. In some vertebrate groups, such as the bony fishes, such fossils are indeed fairly common. As for plants, the preservation of one whole plant from roots to terminal leaves (in those plants that have roots and leaves) is extremely exceptional, and determining the association of such parts that have been separately preserved may be difficult.

From death to burial there are often other factors that cause not so much the loss of information as its confusion. Organisms that did not in fact live together, that were not members of the same local community, are often buried and fossilized together—for example, by stream transport of remains from diverse sources into one sedimentary deposit. In the Geiseltal lignites, previously noted, there are many fossils of aquatic organisms that lived in the swamps and ponds of the middle Eocene; but there are also many fossils of animals that clearly did not live in that environment, although they died there. That is a highly exceptional fossil accumulation in some respects, but the mingling of fossils of different ecological or community origins is quite common.

That brings up another point: that animals frequently die under circumstances and in environments quite different from those in which they lived. Scavenging and decay are often more effective in an animal's usual environment than in uncommon circumstances, where preservation of recognizable parts as fossils may be more likely. Thus some paleontologists have the impression that fossil organisms are more likely to be found where they did not live than where they did. Another spectacular example is the extraordinary concentration of the bones of Pleistocene birds and mammals in the famous tar pits of Rancho La Brea in Los Angeles, California. Although those animals were doubtless living thereabouts at various times up to more than ten thousand years ago, they certainly were not living in the tar pits. They just died there.

Another common sort of confusion of data is also exemplified by the fossils at Rancho La Brea. In any balanced and fairly stable community, there are always many more individuals of herbivorous species than of carnivorous ones. The fossil fauna of Rancho La Brea has so many carnivores in comparison with the herbivores that the ratio cannot be that of a natural and balanced living fauna. It is not difficult to infer the reason for this discrepancy: The herbivores, perhaps in search of water or perhaps just blundering along, were caught in the tar. Once there, they became bait for carnivores, which congregated for the feast and died in the trap.

After preservable parts of organisms are buried, loss of information and biasing of samples are still likely to occur but are usually less than in the earlier phase of taphonomy. The changes that go on during the long presence of organic remains in their tombs in the rocks may be more preservative than destructive. Most of these changes used to be called "petrifaction," which means "converting into rock," and sometimes they still are so called, especially in application to fossil wood. The changes are quite varied, however, and often cannot appropriately be described as the conversion of organic remains to rock. Paleontologists usually speak of these processes simply as fossilization.

Remains of organisms may become fossils, and therefore be fossilized in the literal sense of the word, with little or no change for geologically long periods of

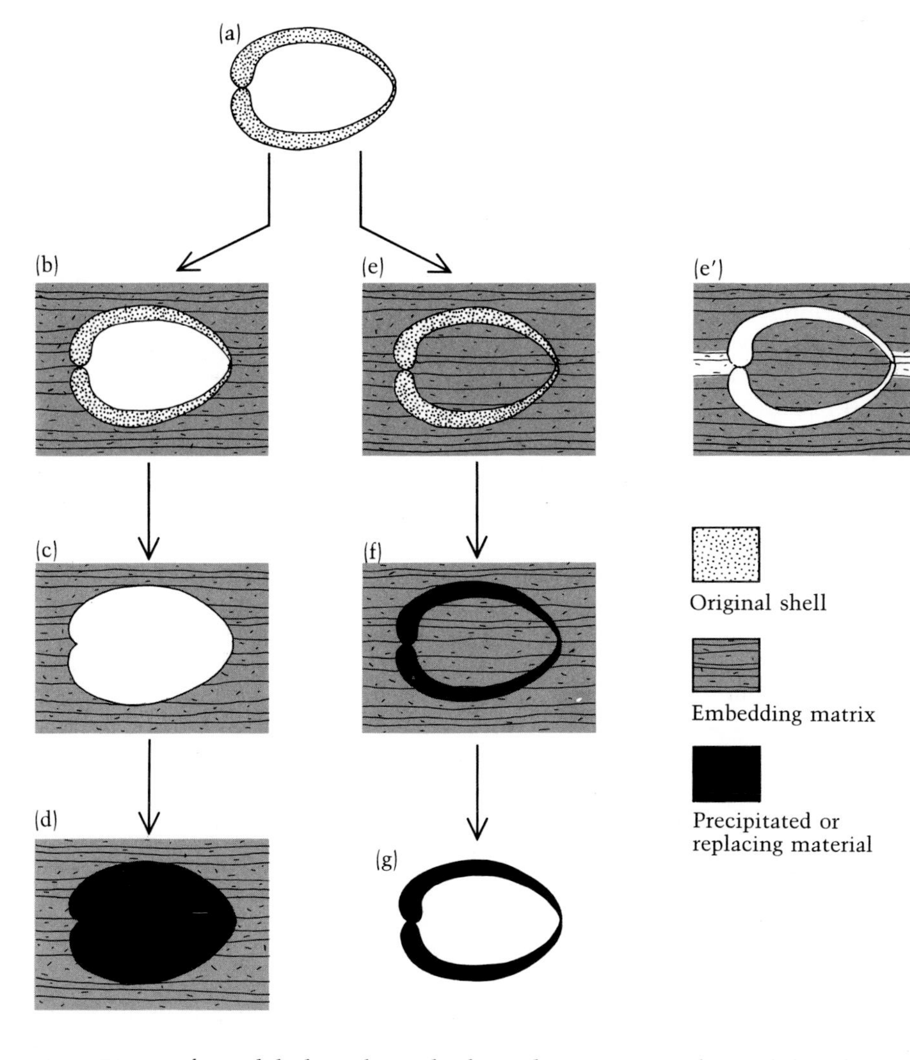

Some processes of taphonomy and fossilization, especially of shells, resulting in fossils as finally studied. (a) *Diagrammatic cross-section of a simple bivalve shell, the two valves still together but the internal space formerly occupied by soft tissues now empty.* (b) *The shell buried without further change. It can be recovered as it was in* (a) *simply by removing the matrix in which it was buried.* (c) *The shell material, more soluble than the matrix, has been dissolved, leaving a vacant space in the matrix that is, in effect, an external mold of the original shell.* (d) *The external mold in* (c) *has been filled by some mineral, often one of the forms of silica, which, with the matrix removed, is a natural cast of the external features of the original shell. (An artificial cast can also be made from* (c) *by filling the cavity with plaster or some other casting material.)* (e) *The shell is buried as in* (b) *but the matrix has also filled the internal cavity.* (e′) *By splitting the matrix and removing the shell material (or if the shell material has been dissolved), an external mold in two pieces and an internal mold in one piece are obtained.* (f) *The shell material has been replaced by some other material, often a form of silica. By using a solvent that dissolves the matrix but not the replaced shell, the original form of the latter can be obtained. For example, silicified fossils in limestone occur rather widely and can be beautifully prepared by immersion in dilute hydrochloric acid, which dissolves limestone ($CaCO_3$) but not silica (SiO_2). There are also several other chemical methods for preparation of delicate fossils and removal of matrix that would be difficult to remove mechanically.* (g) *The result of complete chemical preparation, a replica of the original shell, in this case with a chemical composition unlike that of the original shell. Specimens thus preserved are sometimes called pseudomorphs because the form (morph) is unchanged although the material is different.*

time. Pieces of wood darkened in color but otherwise so unchanged that they can be worked with saw or plane like recent wood are sometimes found in lignite beds tens of millions of years old. Such wood, clearly not petrified, is older than much wood that is petrified in the literal sense of the word. Still more surprising is the fact, discovered as long ago as the 1950s, that a few complex and supposedly very labile organic molecules, such as those of amino acids, may be preserved in fossil shells for as long as 360 million years. It is true that, by that time, such longer molecules as polypeptides and proteins have broken down into simpler or different constituents. Recently, less altered amino acids have been found alone and in combination in younger fossils, aged in tens rather than hundreds of millions of years, and there is some hope for the future that molecular evolution may eventually be studied directly from fossils.

Shells and other hard parts of invertebrate animals are often preserved just so, although there may be a change in the crystal structure or chemical composition. For example aragonite, a form of calcium carbonate ($CaCO_3$) that often makes up the shells of mollusks, may change to calcite, a more stable form of the same composition (also $CaCO_3$). Or the original shell material may be dissolved, leaving only an empty mold in the rock, or it may be replaced by other material. These and some other ways in which shells are preserved as fossils are shown in the drawing on the preceding page.

The mineral matter of bones and teeth is commonly preserved indefinitely with little change in structure or in chemical composition—which is usually a phosphate compound related to, or identical with, minerals in the apatite series. The general chemical formula for this series is $Ca_5(PO_4)_3Z$, in which Z may stand for fluorine (in fluorapatite), chlorine (in chlorapatite), or hydroxyl (OH, in hydroxylapatite). If bones consisting largely of hydroxylapatite are buried for long where the seeping groundwater contains some fluorine, the fluorine slowly replaces some of the hydroxyl. It was this reaction that led to eventual proof that the jaw supposed to belong to "Piltdown man" could not possibly be of the age claimed and must be a hoax—it had not acquired enough fluorine.

Fossil bones and especially the enamel of teeth are also likely to become stained or discolored by chemicals in their burial environments. Beyond that, the usual changes in bones are not changes in their original mineral matter but are by deposition of other minerals, such as calcite or silica (SiO_2), in cavities (microscopic to large) that were empty in the living animals or were occupied by soft tissues that decayed soon after death. Thus, vertebrate fossils become harder and heavier—they are mineralized—but the original bone is not usually petrified as that word is commonly understood.

What is always called petrified wood, even by paleontologists, also often retains its original resistant parts—in this case, the cellulose of its cell walls—and the "petrification" is then again just the filling in of spaces empty or occupied by soft materials that decayed soon after death. The filling may be a form of very fine-grained (crypto-crystalline) quartz (SiO_2) equivalent to agate or chert, as in the popularly known "petrified forests," or it may be likewise very fine-grained calcite ($CaCO_3$), as in coal balls, nodules of mineralized plant remains found in ancient beds of coal. In both cases, the preservation of cell structure may be so perfect that it can be studied under a microscope as well as if the plant were recent. The process of mineralization, especially by silica, may proceed so far, however, that only the gross outer form is preserved and, in a sense, the wood has indeed been petrified.

Among the numerous other phenomena of fossilization, two more deserve passing mention, one because much of our knowledge of fossil insects is based on it and the other because it is unusual to the point of being bizarre. Bits of various organisms and whole small animals, especially insects, are often trapped and embedded in resin oozing from trees. This resin may be buried and may eventually harden into amber, in which the insects and other fossils are preserved. Such fossil-bearing amber is known not only from the Baltic, where it has been collected for jewelry since prehistoric times, but also from Canada, Central America, and other places.

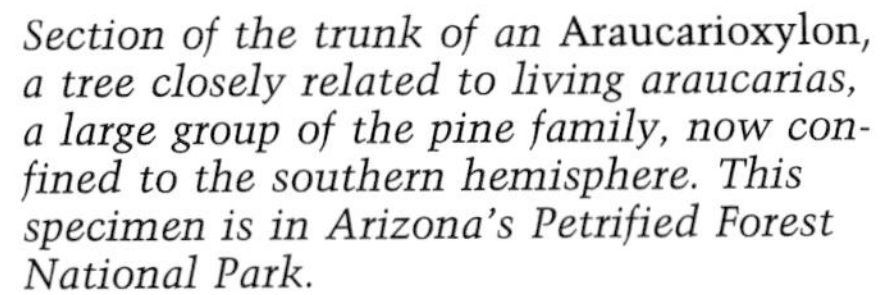

Section of the trunk of an Araucarioxylon, *a tree closely related to living araucarias, a large group of the pine family, now confined to the southern hemisphere. This specimen is in Arizona's Petrified Forest National Park.*

A cross-section of fossilized wood cut with a diamond saw and then polished reveals intricate cellular detail of this specimen. Preservation of such detail usually requires rapid infiltration of the petrifying material. If any of the tissues had already decomposed, mineral matter would have simply filled the hollow spaces left behind, preserving the wood's form but not its cellular structure.

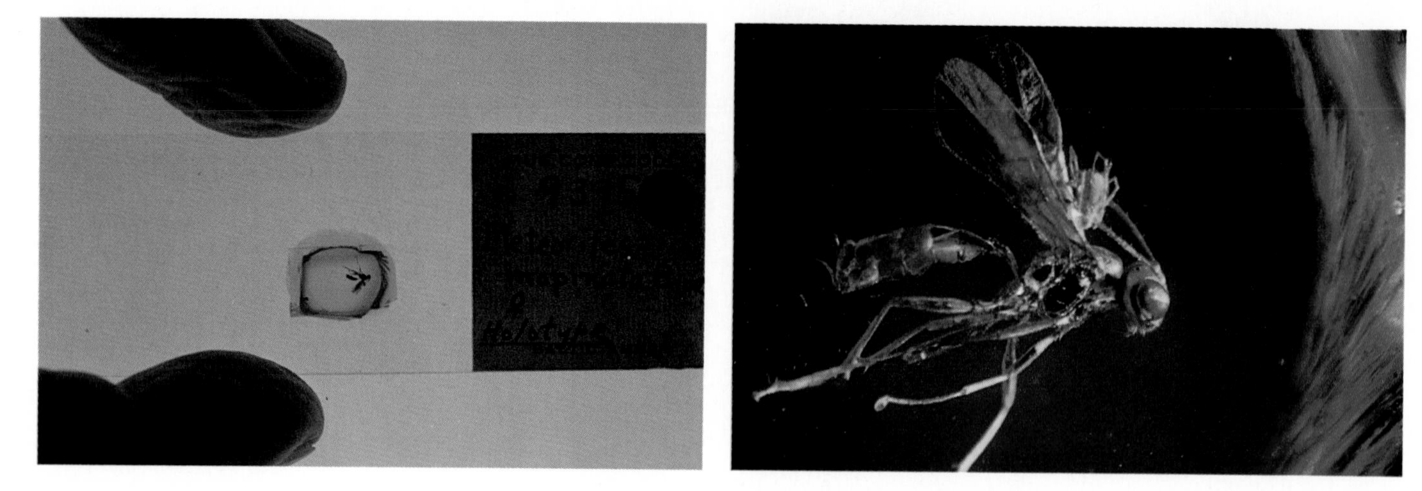

Three different views of a wasp, preserved intact in Oligocene amber from the Baltic Sea in Germany.

The bizarre example involves aquatic reptiles that swam in shallow Cretaceous seas some 80 million years or so ago in what is now Australia. The bones of some of these were buried in sediments at the bottom of the seas, and in a few cases isolated bones and (even more exceptionally) essentially whole skeletons were dissolved, leaving hollow spaces or molds that became filled by precious opal in the original form of the bones. Pound for pound, these are the most costly of all fossils, which accounts for the fact that almost none are to be seen in museums. In terms of scientific knowledge, they are not worth their cash cost.

As time goes on, the sediments in which organic remains are buried may be (and, as they become geologically old, almost surely will be) deeply buried in the crust of the earth. They are likely to become compacted, heated, contorted, changed in various ways. As this happens, the organic remains that might become fossils are often flattened and deformed in other ways. Finally, the rocks are metamorphosed. For example, clays and shales may become slates and schists, and, as they do, the potential fossils in them become harder to identify and eventually are obliterated. The earlier diagenetic ("change-originating") factors in taphonomy lead to fossilization and often to retention of information. In more advanced diagenetic phases, information loss again predominates.

For a fossil to become part of the historical record of life, it must of course be found and studied. With few exceptions, this means that the rocks in which it had become more or less deeply buried must again be exposed at the surface of the earth by erosion, uplift, or frequently both. The most important exceptions are for fossils—almost always microfossils, such as foraminifera or pollen—that are recovered from borings sometimes made for this very purpose and sometimes incidental to exploration for fossil fuels or for other geological resources. Other circumstances under which fossils may be found and collected are highly varied and sometimes odd. In Florida, for example, fairly recent (late Pleistocene) fossil mammals are sometimes collected by diving in deep springs.

In spite of such exceptional examples, the great majority of fossils are found embedded in, or recently eroded from, exposures of sedimentary rocks. (In this connection, all sediments, even when not consolidated or hardened, are rocks to a paleontological geologist.) Yet one could dig at random in exposures of such rocks

for a lifetime without encountering a single fossil. The first discovery of an area or a stratum in which fossils of a given sort are present is often made by chance or serendipitously by someone who was looking for something else—but almost necessarily by someone who knows a fossil when he sees one. More intensive and extensive collecting through the years then follows, often by laborious hands-and-knees examination of rock outcrops. A paleontologist on the prowl for fossils often looks as if he were trying to find a dime that he had accidentally dropped somewhere in a hundred square miles or so of badlands.

The methods of finding and collecting fossils are as varied as the kinds—especially the sizes—of fossils and the way in which they occur. Such variables are much too numerous and complex to discuss singly or in detail here. Examples may be given in general terms and at the extremes of size.

Large fossils—say, the skeleton or even a single bone of one of the biggest dinosaurs—are found because erosion has exposed enough to be visible to the hunter. The finder then digs in to see what is still buried, using pick and shovel, jackhammer, or, if the overlying rock (the overburden) is very thick and hard, perhaps dynamite for a start. When the upper surfaces of the bones present are exposed, they are treated with a preservative, if needed, to keep them solid and together, and then jacketed in plaster-soaked bandages. If necessary, the bones are outlined in separate blocks small enough to be handled at least with block and tackle. Each block is then undercut, carefully turned over, jacketed on the other side, and sent away to the laboratory.

Tiny fossils—for instance, isolated teeth of small mammals or many of the one-celled invertebrate microfossils, such as foraminifera—may also be spotted on the surface if large enough to be seen by the naked eye. It may then be assumed that there is a fair chance that others occur in the same stratum. Or, without actually seeing such a fossil, an experienced collector may recognize a bed likely enough to warrant putting in some exploratory effort. In either case, the procedure is to dig out masses (up to tons at times) of the matrix, the possibly fossiliferous rock. This is then broken up or slaked down by some procedure, of which there are many, and the fossils, if present, are sorted out from the debris by further procedures, again many. The simplest procedure, often adequate for such things

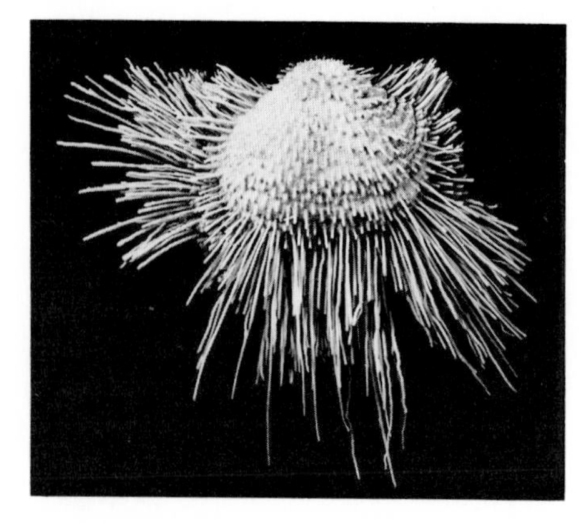

An example of a brachiopod prepared chemically. Waagenoconcha abichi, *an extinct brachiopod, about 250 million years old.*

as tiny teeth in clay or silt, is to slake down the matrix in water and then, or simultaneously, to pass the results through fine-meshed screens. The teeth can then be picked out, preferably under a microscope, from the bits left on the screens.

While on the subject of collecting fossils, one other point must be made: field records are important. Published records of some fossils collected a century or so ago give the provenance as "Tertiary, east of the Rocky Mountains"—that is, geologically somewhere in strata spanning well over 60 million years and geographically somewhere within an area of some two million square miles (well over 500 million hectares). Even from the nineteenth century, most records are better than that, but none made then meet standards acceptable for paleontological research now. For geographic (locality) records, the data now should be accurate within a few yards (roughly meters). For geological (stratigraphic) records, they should be accurate within inches (or better, within centimeters). Adequate fossil collecting requires great skill. Although amateurs sometimes help with fortunate discoveries, they should leave the rest to the professional paleontologist.

The next (and, as I am here broadly defining taphonomy, the last) taphonomic stage is the preparation of fossils for study. Here again the methods and aims are so diverse that they cannot even be enumerated but can only be exemplified. Many, but still by no means all, are discussed in special articles and some books. (One of 852 pages by Kummel and Raup, is cited in the bibliography at the end of this book.) For simple description of external morphology, many fossils come in from the field without need of further preparation. More require at least some fastening together of broken bits and some removal of adhering and obscuring matrix, for which there are various mechanical methods. Matrix can also be removed chemically, most simply, and with most spectacular results, from those fossils that are embedded in limestone (which is soluble in most acids) but are themselves made of silica (which is practically insoluble in most acids). Especially striking has been the discovery that many fossil brachiopods (lamp shells) are thus found to have elaborate projecting spines and other delicate structures unknown until they were prepared by acid. Even fossils that are themselves sensitive to acid and are in recalcitrant matrixes can be freed by preparation using special acids and means of progressive protection as the fossil itself is exposed bit by bit.

Those are among the methods for retrieval of information that was lost (or, at best, not made available) by earlier and simpler ways of laboratory preparation of fossils. Other methods also give information that remains inaccessible without them. Serial sectioning, an old and basic technique in the study of recent organisms, becomes available for the study of fossils by serial grinding. Successive parts of a structure—for example, of a vertebrate skull—are exposed by grinding away one thin layer after another, drawing or photographing the structure at each level or, after light etching in acid, impressing it onto a peel of celluloid or ace-

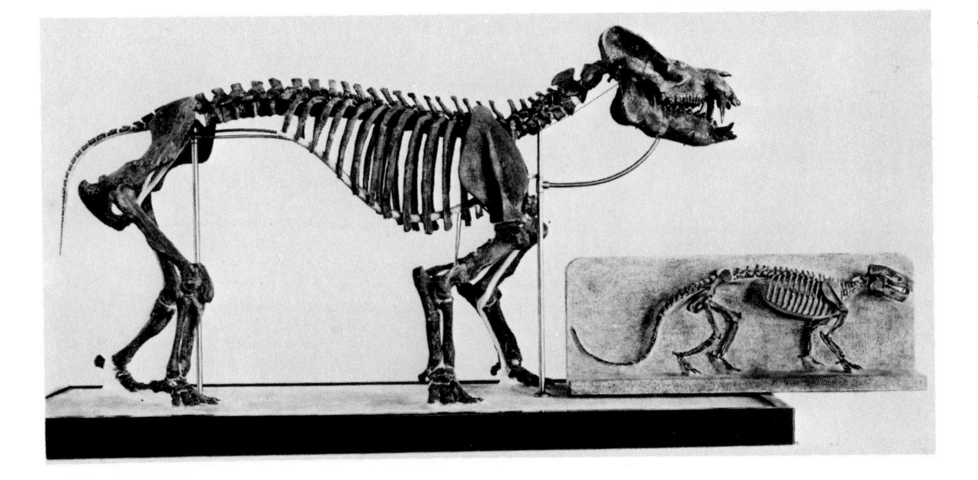

Skeletons freed from the rock and assembled in life pose for study and exhibition. The larger skeleton is Coryphodon, *early Eocene. The smaller skeleton is* Pantolambda, *middle Paleocene, much older but closely related and approximately ancestral to* Coryphodon.

Restorations of Coryphodon *painted by Charles R. Knight, based on the larger skeleton shown above.*

tate, a technique originated by paleobotanists for studying silicified or calcified plant structures.

Internal structures of fossils or specimens that cannot be removed from a covering of matrix without damaging them are now routinely examined by X-rays. Beyond the usual and obvious visual aids, the scanning electron microscope (SEM) applied to special preparations of fossils now reveals much fine detail that was not as accessible, if accessible at all, by older methods. If the fossil itself is not preserved but has left an impression in the rock, features of the fossil can be recovered by making a cast from that natural mold. Or, as an example of one of many neat tricks in this profession, a stereographic pair of photographs may be made and the two prints then reversed so that what was a depression in the mold appears as a projection when viewed stereoscopically.

So the fossils are prepared, each to give up its bits of information to be fitted into the Great History. Study follows, but it does not just begin at this point. It began earlier out in the field, sometimes years earlier, and not just by finding and collecting fossils but also by gathering data and materials for more direct study of the geological aspects of paleontology. At this point, the study centers more on the fossil itself and its biological significance. Some aspects of those studies will be considered in the next chapter.

CHAPTER 2
FOSSILS AS LIVING ORGANISMS

A greatly enlarged drawing of Eoastrion, *a one-celled organism without a nucleus, probably related to the blue-green algae. They are not true algae and more nearly resemble bacteria and are now commonly called cyanobacteria or cyanophytes.* Eoastrion *is from the Gunflint formation in Canada, about two billion (thousand million) years old. Even more primitive organisms well over three billion years old are now known.*

A bone, a tooth, a shell, a leaf preserved as a fossil is not merely an inanimate object, like a crystal, that may be found in similar circumstances. Fossils are what we have (as parts, at least) of once living organisms. The passage of time does not make them any more dead than the animal on a dissecting table, the pinned insect in a research collection, or the leaves of a plant on the sheets of a herbarium. It does, however, make it more difficult, more challenging, and often even more fascinating, to determine their ways of life and their places in nature when they were in fact alive.

Of all fossils, dinosaurs have undoubtedly had the most publicity. They provide interesting examples of the resurrection of animals long extinct and of the accomplishments and shortcomings of those engaged in such endeavors. Although dinosaurs were strange animals and these examples are peculiar to them, the methods involved in their study do exemplify those used in any functional studies of extinct animals.

It is not really known when a fossil relic of a dinosaur was first discovered. It is likely that the year was 1787, when a large "thigh bone" (femur) was found in New Jersey and reported to the American Philosophical Society by members Caspar Wistar and Timothy Matlock. (The Society, which had been founded long before by Benjamin Franklin, is still very active and has its headquarters on Independence Square in Philadelphia.) Of course, Wistar and Matlock could not identify the specimen as the bone of a dinosaur, one of a group of then unknown creatures; and, because the bone itself soon disappeared from record, its identity has not been surely established. (Some fossil bones, probably dinosaurian, had been known even earlier, but they were believed to be human.)

The earliest documented discovery of a fossil that is certainly that of a member of the group later called dinosaurs was made in the region of Tilgate Forest, in England, in 1822. The discoverer, Mrs. Gideon Mantell, the former Mary Ann Woodhouse, was married to a physician who was also a very active amateur geologist and paleontologist. On a roadside, where she was walking while her husband attended a patient, she found a rock in which were embedded strange teeth. The discovery fascinated Mantell, and for several years he devoted all his spare time to collecting further remains in the same region and to consulting the men most learned in such matters both in England and in France. Finally, in 1825, he published a paper on these discoveries. He named the animal *Iguanodon* because of the resemblance of its teeth to those of the iguana, a living lizard. He suggested that the extinct animal was indeed a lizard, enormously larger than an iguana.

In the meantime, remains of another large extinct reptile had been discovered in the vicinity of Stonesfield in Oxfordshire. These came into the hands of Dean William Buckland, an eccentric theologian who was also a pioneering authority on geology and paleontology. Not hesitating as long as Mantell, Buckland published in 1824 the first monograph on what is now known as a dinosaur. Believing it to be a giant lizard, he named it *Megalosaurus,* which means just that.

(a) *A photograph of dinosaur bone fossils at Como Bluff.* (b) *A contemporaneous painting of the collecting of large dinosaurs for Professor Othniel Charles Marsh of Yale University. The late Jurassic Morrison Formation was one of the first and still is one of the richest sources of the bones of dinosaurs and of other animals associated with them. This painting was made in 1879 by Arthur Lakes, a schoolmaster (who was evidently a better teacher than artist). The scene is Como Bluff in Wyoming, where many fossils, most of them now in the Peabody Museum of Natural History at Yale University, were collected. The two men are W. (Bill) Reed, one of the discoverors of this rich deposit in 1877, and E. Kennedy, another bone collector for Marsh in this region. The bones are those of one of the largest dinosaurs, a sauropod, not otherwise clearly identifiable from this picture. A note with the painting, evidently by Reed, says that most of these particular bones were "too rotten to ship," although many like these were shipped. Methods for holding "rotten" or broken bones together and in place were mostly devised later.*

Thereafter, the rate of discovery accelerated, reaching an early high point in the late 1870s. In 1878, a group of complete, articulated skeletons of *Iguanodon* was found in a coal mine at Bernissart, Belgium. From those it was soon seen that the *Iguanodon* did not resemble an iguana but was a monster of unique characteristics. In 1877, dinosaur skeletons were found in the United States at localities in Colorado and Wyoming. These were collected thereafter for the rival paleontologists Edward Drinker Cope, of Philadelphia, and Othniel Charles Marsh, a (nonteaching) professor at Yale University. On the whole, the collectors working for Marsh were more successful than those working for Cope. They collected skeletons of a number of startlingly different dinosaurs, and Marsh's descriptions of them excited widespread interest. Marsh has been called "the man who made 'dinosaur' a household word." The man who, in 1841, coined the word destined for such eventual familiarity was the great British anatomist and paleontologist Richard Owen. He gave it originally in the neo-Latin form *Dinosauria*, derived from the Greek *deinos* ("terrible") and *saura* (literally "lizard" both in modern and in classical Greek, but often taken in the general meaning of "reptile" in scientific use). (The proper Greek word for "reptile" is *herpeton*.)

The discovery of dinosaurs has continued, not only in Europe and North America but also in Asia, Africa, South America, and Australia—in short, on every continent except Antarctica, where it is highly probable that there were also dinosaurs, but they are yet to be discovered. There is always a lapse between discovery and publication. Collecting the bones, clearing them of the rock in which they were encased, and studying them properly are slow and expensive procedures. Nevertheless, the flood of discovery has produced a flood of technical publications on dinosaurs. As almost everyone knows, it has also produced a flood of popular publications, ranging from the merely nontechnical to the sensational and the downright frivolous. There is a whole library of books about dinosaurs ranging in level from preschool to sophisticated adult. Cartoonists, too, have found dinosaurs an inexhaustible subject for fantasy and humor. Paleontologists also enjoy such cartoons, but they are astonished to find that some nonpaleontologists take the cartoonists' frequent association of dinosaurs with cave men as factual. It is really an egregious anachronism: the last dinosaur died some sixty million years before the first nearly human creatures had evolved.

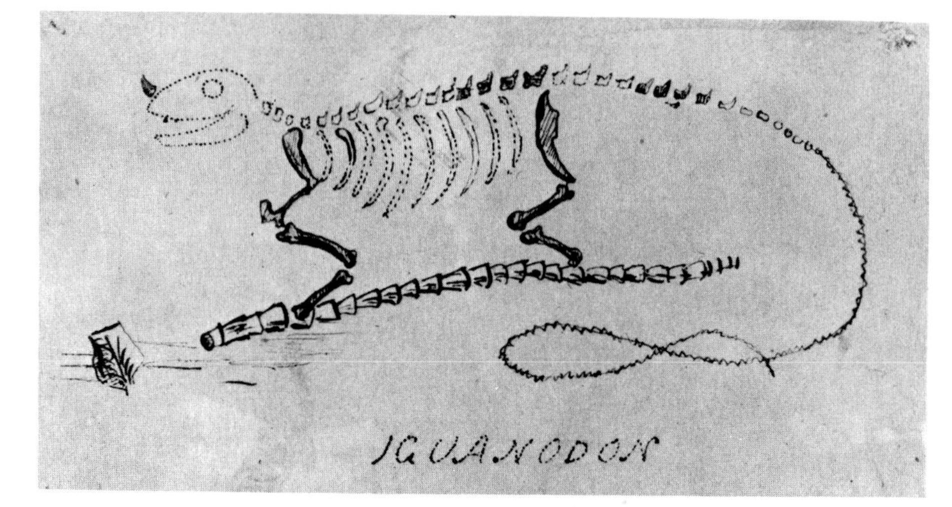

Gideon Mantell's attempt in the 1830s to reconstruct a skeleton of Iguanodon *from the bones then known. Mantell believed the bones to be those of an enormous lizard, and so pictured it. What he interpreted as a horn on the nose was revealed much later to be a spikelike thumb.*

The first thing most people want to know about dinosaurs as living animals is what they looked like in the flesh and skin. Paleontologists share that interest, and with the help of artists, they try to provide such restorations, even though these are of minor importance for technical studies. The first point here is that no extinct vertebrate markedly different from any still alive—and that includes all dinosaurs—can be acceptably shown in a life restoration unless practically all of its skeleton is known. A legend started almost two centuries ago has it that paleontologists reconstruct whole skeletons, and thus can restore whole animals, from a single tooth or bone. The error was already unwittingly illustrated by Gideon Mantell. Although by 1825 he had quite a few bones of *Iguanodon,* he reconstructed the skeleton along the lines of the living iguana lizard. The discovery of articulated bones of animals of the same genus at Bernissart showed that this was radically wrong. *Iguanodon* was, in fact, a bipedal animal with relatively short forelegs and a spikelike "thumb" on each forefoot. (Mantell had one of those spikelike bones, but he showed it as a horn on the nose of his reconstruction. It is an interesting although admittedly frivolous thought that the animal thus thumbed its nose at its first reconstructor.)

Today, many dinosaurs are known by complete skeletons from which competent skeletal reconstructions are available, and reasonable life restorations have in turn been made. Inevitably, some problems have arisen even at this elementary level. The biggest of all dinosaurs, the quadrupedal sauropods with long necks and tails, had comparatively small heads, which tended to separate from the necks in the course of their taphonomy. As a result, an early and famous reconstruction of the skeleton of one of them was fitted out with the wrong head.

It has also rather recently been found that some dinosaur skeletons were reconstructed, and the living animals consequently restored, in unlikely poses—

(a)

(b)

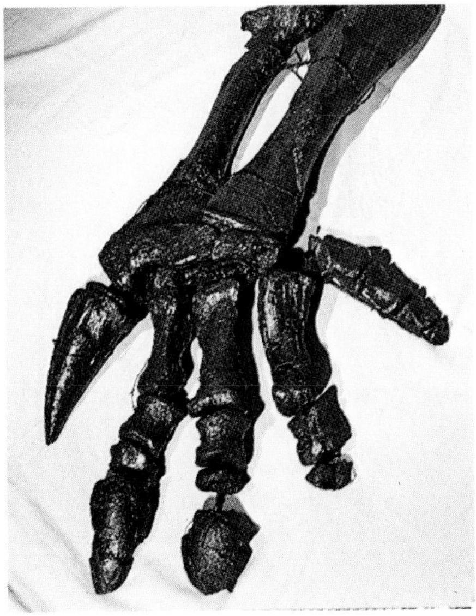

(c)

(a) Iguanodon *skeletons displayed in the Institut Royal des Sciences Naturelles de Belgique. Twenty nine skeletons were found by a miner in 1878 at Bernissart in a layer of clay perforated by a coal pit.* (b) *Skull and cervical vertebrae and* (c) *hand and forearm of the* Iguanodon.

Some of the most distinctive groups of dinosaurs. Each group is represented by a sketch of only one of its members. The whole history of dinosaurs is not yet fully known—to find, collect, prepare, and study even one dinosaur is a long and expensive process. What is known is much more complex than may appear from this simple diagram. The thecodonts were a diverse group that flourished in the Triassic. They are not classified as dinosaurs, but two related thecodonts gave rise separately to the two orders of dinosaurs, Ornithischia and Saurischia. Other thecodonts were ancestral to crocodilians, to the flying reptiles (pterosaurs), and perhaps to birds, although it is more likely that birds evolved from primitive Triassic or earliest Jurassic saurischian dinosaurs that were not yet very different from their thecodont ancestors. The main groups of saurischians are the sauropods and the theropods. Among the sauropods were the largest of all dinosaurs. All were four-footed herbivores with long necks and tails. Theropods ranged in size from not much larger than a healthy chicken to the tremendous Tyrannosaurus. *Some were even larger, but they are less well known. All were bipedal, and most were carnivorous, although some had no teeth and their diet is a matter of conjecture. All ornithischian dinosaurs were herbivorous, but, apart from that, even more striking differences evolved. The four-footed ceratopsians are generally called horned dinosaurs (*ceratops *is from Greek roots meaning "horned face"), and most of them did have horns (one to five in different genera), but the most primitive ceratopsians and a few later ones lacked horns. The ankylosaurs and stegosaurs are four-footed and were at least second cousins. The members of both groups have bony plates. In the ankylosaurs they covered most of the body like armor. In the stegosaurs they formed two lines of erect plates along the back and spikes on the end of the tail. The hadrosaurs, which were bipedal, are often called "duckbill dinosaurs" from the shape of the bones of the anterior ends of the skull and jaws, although, in other respects, the heads had peculiarly varied shapes (see figure on page 38) and, unlike ducks, they had lots of teeth (see figure on page 34). They are usually united with other families, not shown in this diagram, as ornithopods.*

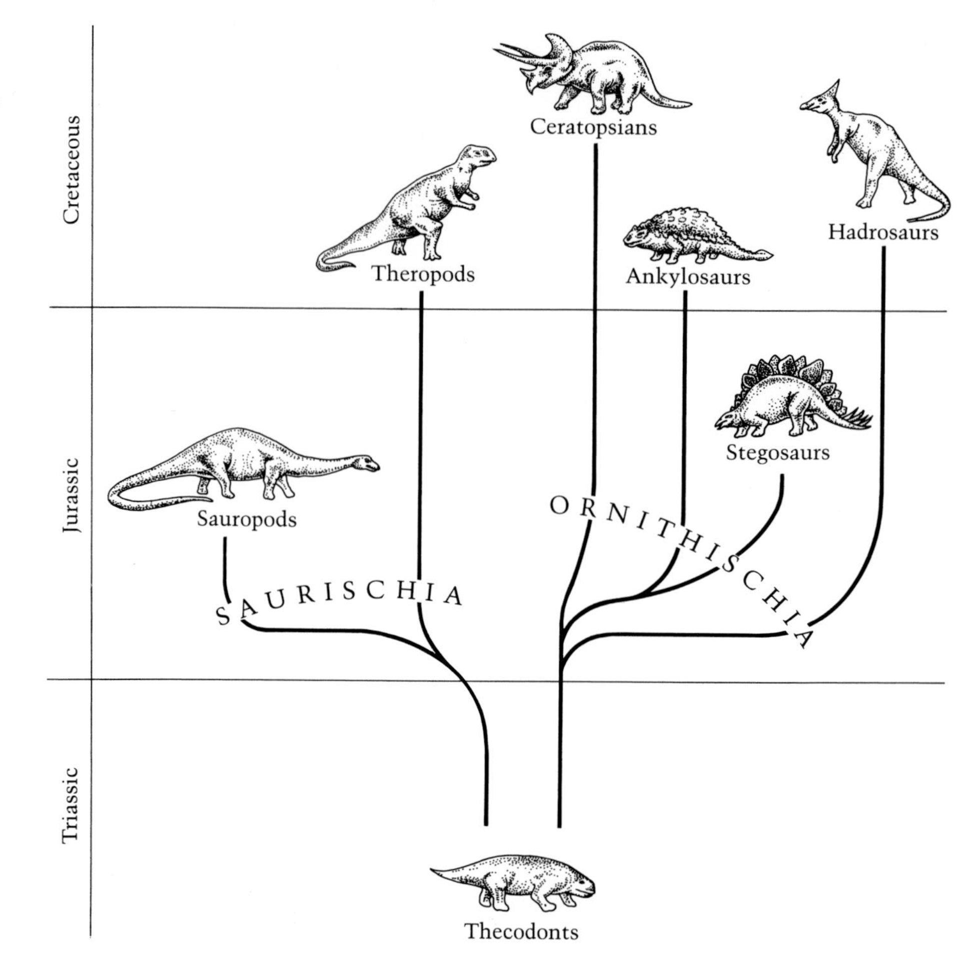

notably, with the forelegs of some quadrupedal species spread akimbo, whereas it is likely that the forelegs were more vertical, with the elbows more nearly under the body. There are several ways to approach such problems of posture and locomotion, points that bear importantly on the habits and ecology of the animals, not only on their appearance. The articulation of the joints can be studied both with the actual bones and with models. It is also possible to model or draw the most important muscles from evidence of their attachments to bones, from associated tendons that are ossified and preserved in some dinosaur skeletons, and from some analogies with the most nearly similar living animals such as some crocodiles and lizards (although none are similar enough for certainty in such comparisons). Furthermore, footprints and trackways made by dinosaurs in mud or other soft surfaces were often preserved after those sediments were consolidated into rock. From such trackways, the stride, the placement of the feet, and other features of pose and locomotion are known for many kinds of dinosaurs.

Given a skeleton in a reasonable pose and a conception of the more relevant muscle masses, the artist usually has only to clothe the bone and flesh in skin to complete a restoration. Skin impressions have actually been preserved with a few skeletons of dinosaurs. The known skins are pebbly, resembling some lizard skins

(a)

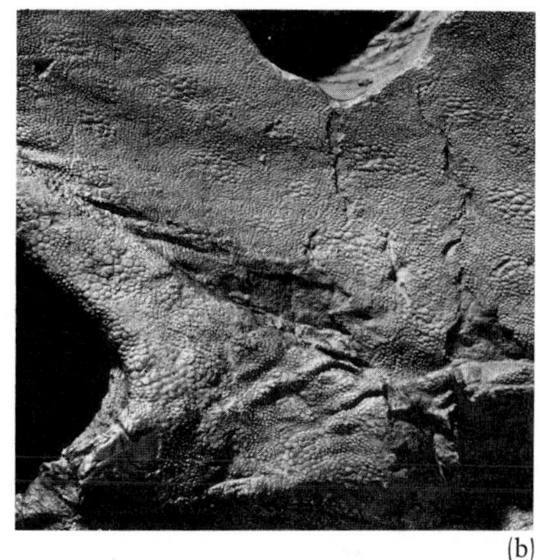

(b)

(a) *A fossil "mummy" of* Anatosaurus. *These animals were air-dried before natural burial and when fossilized there were impressions of the skin in the hardened burial matrix.* (b) *Detail showing the surface pattern of the skin.*

Protoceratops *eggs found by paleontologists working under the direction of Walter Granger. The age is late Cretaceous. The locality was called Shabarakh Usu through a misunderstanding by the Americans, who didn't know Mongolian. The Mongolian guides were just telling them that the water there is muddy: shabarakh, "muddy" and usu, "water." The name of the place is actually Bayn Dzak, which means something like "good forage."*

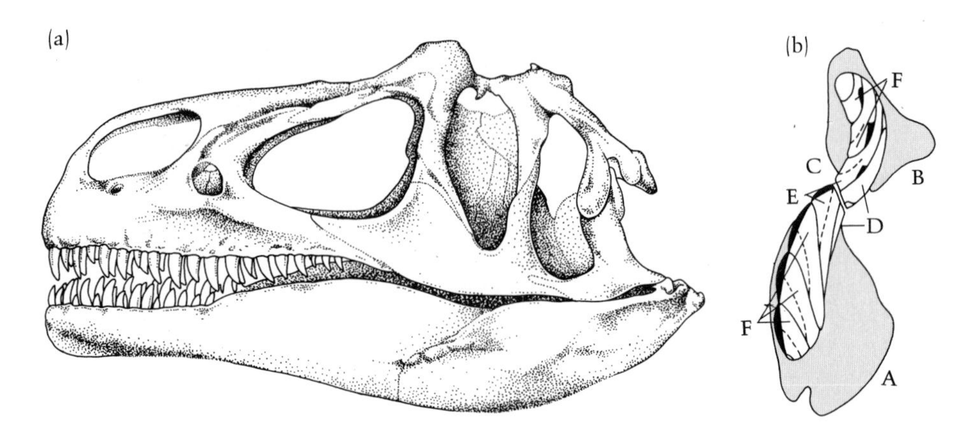

Dinosaur adaptations to foods of different kinds. (a) *The skull of* Allosaurus, *a dominant large Jurassic predatory dinosaur in North America; not only the teeth but also the whole structure of the skull and jaws is adapted to seizing and tearing prey.* (b) *Vertical section through upper and lower jaws of a late Cretaceous hadrosaur. The teeth are stacked in the upper and lower jaws,* F *designating replacement teeth and* D *and* E *those in use. As plant food moves through between upper and lower teeth at* C, *it is chopped by movement of the jaw, and, as this wears down the teeth, they are continuously replaced throughout life. The grey areas are the bones of upper and lower jaws.*

but on a more heroic scale. Some dinosaurs had much of the body covered with bony armor, which makes representation of their external appearance relatively simple. There is no way to learn the colors of dinosaurs, which has given some artists who do restorations in color an opportunity to exercise their imaginations.

It is possible to determine, in a general way, what most dinosaurs ate. The carnivorous dinosaurs were all bipedal (that is, they walked only on their hind legs) and had numerous stabbing or piercing teeth. The largest of them had diminutive forelegs, or arms, with small, grasping hands. Some herbivorous dinosaurs were also bipedal, but they had batteries of cheek teeth kept sharp by shearing against each other. They became ideally adapted for chopping coarse vegetation. Grass did not yet exist in the time of the dinosaurs (all but the earliest part of the Mesozoic era, from about 200 million to about 65 million years ago). There was, however, lots of rough herbage throughout that time. Some of the quadrupedal dinosaurs, especially the ceratopsians (soon to be mentioned again), also had batteries of shearing teeth. The usually enormous quadrupedal sauropods did not have such batteries but had simpler, somewhat peglike teeth. They must have fed on softer, probably mostly aquatic, vegetation. One group of bipedal dinosaurs, technically called ornithomimids ("bird imitators"), although they clearly evolved from toothed carnivores, had no teeth at all. There has been much speculation about what they ate, but it must be remembered that the living toothless birds include diverse species that eat practically anything. One guess about the ornithomimids is that they ate the eggs of other dinosaurs, but that is based in part on the discovery of a single one of them with a nest of eggs of a different dinosaur (the ceratopsian *Protoceratops*). It was therefore named *Oviraptor* ("egg stealer"), but the association was probably pure coincidence.

One considerable group of quadrupedal dinosaurs, Ceratopsia ("horn-faces"), evolved enormous skulls with a bony neck frill. Some had large horns above the eyes, some had also a smaller one on the nose, some had only a nasal horn, and the members of one species had five horns in all, including two small ones on the cheeks. It is not completely clear, but it is a fair speculation that these develop-

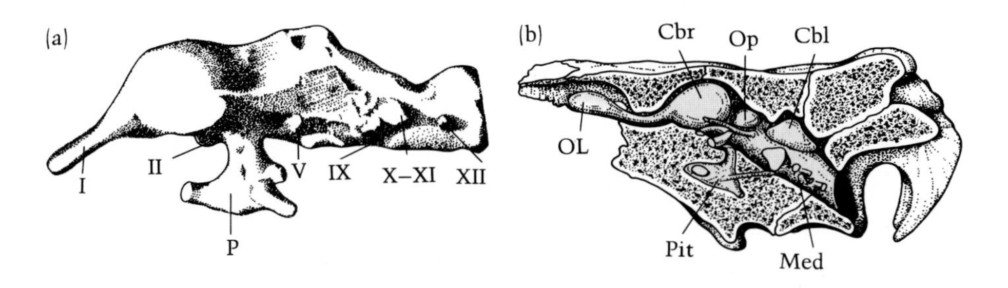

(a) *Internal cast (endocast) of the cranium of* Anatosaurus, *a large Cretaceous hadrosaur. The brain occupied most of this space, but it did not so nearly fill it as do the brains of birds and mammals. The Roman numerals designate the beginnings of the cranial nerves as they leave the brain. The projection marked* P *is the endocast of the pituitary fossa, which contained (but was probably not filled by) the pituitary gland.* (b) *A longitudinal section of the same specimen from which the endocast,* (a), *was made. Here the brain that had been lodged in the skull has been hypothetically restored. This restoration is based on the skull itself, on the endocast, and on comparisons with Recent reptilian brains. The assumption is that the brain almost fills the cranial cavity, which is not always true of reptilian brains and which makes for some, but not really crucial, differences from other hypothetical restorations of the brain of this specimen and of some other dinosaurs. Here* OL *is the olfactory lobe;* Cbr, *the cerebrum;* Op, *the optic lobe;* Cbl, *the cerebellum;* Pit, *the pituitary body; and* Med, *the medulla. Colbert has estimated that, in this dinosaur, the brain weighed about 1/20,000 the weight of the whole body. In the even larger sauropod dinosaur, this figure may have been as small as 1/100,000. We should add, however, that the ratio of adult brain weight to body weight tends to become rapidly smaller with increase in adult body weight of different species and also that, throughout the animal kingdom, the effectiveness of a brain depends more on its structure than on its size. Because a big sauropod was much heavier than* Anatosaurus *and because the external structures of their brains seem to have been about the same, we have little reason to think that* Anatosaurus *had a more effective brain than the largest of the sauropods.*

ments functioned as defensive and offensive armament. They may also have been sported as display or have been a means by which individuals recognized the members of their own species.

The brain of a dinosaur can be reasonably reconstructed from the skull cavity in which it was lodged, even though it did not fill that cavity as nearly completely as the brains of humans and most other mammals do. The brains of dinosaurs were typically reptilian, and, although the brains of the largest dinosaurs seem tiny in comparison with their immense bodies, they were about as large as would be expected—brains similar in function tend to be relatively smaller in larger animals. There is no good reason to think that brain function and related behavior in dinosaurs was any more, or any less, developed than in a modern crocodile. Dinosaurs had an enlargement of the spinal canal in the sacrum, above and between the hips, which has been considered to be a sort of second brain, as in the intentionally facetious doggerel in which it is remarked that a dinosaur:

> . . . had two sets of brains;
> One in his head (the usual place)
> The other at his spinal base.

It is fairly certain that this enlargement was related to secondary control of the massive legs and tail and that normal primary control remained in the true (cranial) brain.

It is also probable that dinosaurs had good vision, although there is no way of telling whether they were able to distinguish colors. Birds, which arose either from very primitive dinosaurs or from their immediate ancestry, now typically have color vision, but they have in other respects become so unlike dinosaurs that they may also differ in this respect. Crocodilians, which arose from the same ancestry as dinosaurs and, among animals still living, most nearly resemble dinosaurs, do not have color vision. The ears of dinosaurs were unlike ours or those of other mammals, but they resembled those of birds and crocodilians alike. The latter living groups both typically have a keen sense of hearing, and dinosaurs probably did too.

Functional characteristics of extinct animals, such as those so far exemplified in the dinosaurs, can be approximately but reasonably inferred in one or both of two ways: by the mechanical relationships of parts preserved, as in the consideration of postures, locomotion, and food habits of many dinosaurs, or by more or

Anatosaurus *from the Upper Cretaceous of North America. The upright skeleton is about seventeen feet tall.*

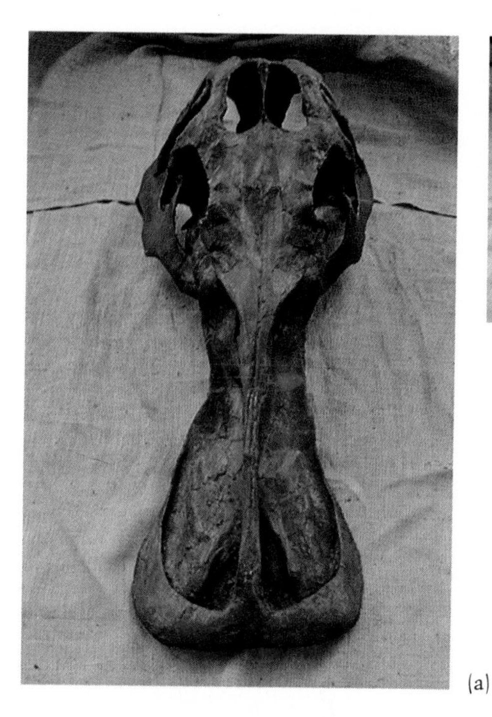

(a)

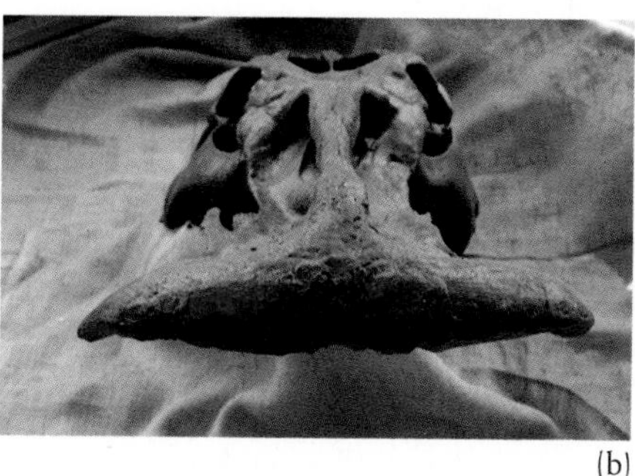

(b)

Two views of the skull structure of anatosaurs. (a) View from above with the "duckbill" below in the picture. (b) A front view of the same skull.

less close analogy with living (and preferably, but not necessarily, related) animals, as in the examples of brain and ear functions in dinosaurs in general or of horn and frill functions in the ceratopsians. In many extinct animals there are, however, observable features that do not lend themselves well to mechanical analysis or to inference from analogies. Then inferences about their functional characteristics are especially difficult to make, and they often lead to conflicting hypotheses or guesses that do not result in a clear consensus. One group of dinosaurs provides a good example of such a situation.

The dinosaurs of the family Hadrosauridae, the hadrosaurs, were herbivorous bipeds with batteries of shearing cheek teeth, as previously noted, but with the front part of the jaws toothless and somewhat expanded and flattened, hence resembling ducks' bills and giving this family the popular name "duck-billed dinosaurs." In some of them, the skulls were otherwise not very different from those of other dinosaurian relatives, such as iguanodons. In one group of hadrosaurs, however, there is a solid bony projection above and behind the eyes, resembling a horn but almost certainly not functioning as such. In other hadrosaurs, there are large bony projections or crests above the skull—or, in the members of one genus, extending far behind it—which are hollow and contain a more or less complex passage.

The possible function of those hollow crests has long been disputed, and it still is. These animals were largely aquatic, and an early hypothesis was that the crest

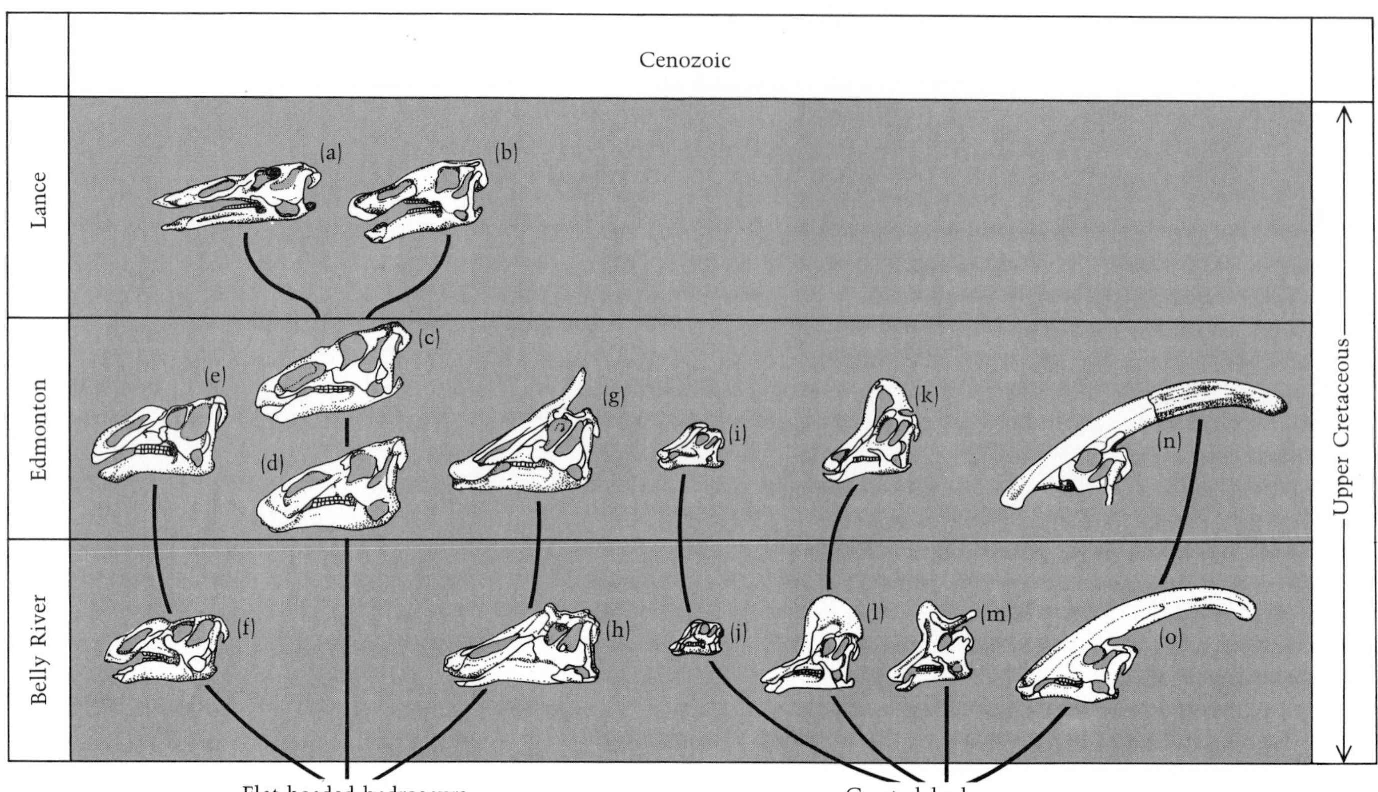

A proposed phylogeny of the various lineages of hadrosaurs, here represented by their skulls, in the late Cretaceous. Other members of the family have been found since 1942, when this figure was first published, but this figure still gives a good idea of the gamut of skull structures in these late dinosaurs. It is evident that the heads alone could have served other dinosaurs for recognizing their own and other species. It is also clear that the complex crests of some of them did not have a function that was adaptive for the family as a whole. Belly River, Edmonton, and Lance are names of geological strata in the sequence of their ages, Belly River oldest and Lance youngest.

was a sort of snorkel, permitting intake of air when the nose was under water. That idea must be abandoned because it has been established that the only usual outside openings to the hollows of the crests were through the nose. Air drawn in through the nostrils went through the passages in the crest and then down to the lungs and was later expelled along the same route. Other hypotheses are:

1. The hollows formed a trap that prevented water (or sand) from being sucked into the lungs. (But that function was much more probably served by closures of the nostrils, analogous to those in living aquatic reptiles.)
2. They held a reserve air supply, making more prolonged submergence possible. (But this is physiologically improbable almost to the point of impossibility.)
3. By prolonging the passage to the lungs, they helped to warm (or cool) and to humidify the air drawn in. (That effect would occur, but, in the inferred habitats and climates of this family, it would probably be of little or no adaptive importance.)
4. The cavities may have been lined with olfactory sensory epithelium, improving the sense of smell. (Possible, but again not of clear adaptive importance, especially inasmuch as otherwise closely similar dinosaurs in the same faunas had no such extension of the epithelium.)
5. The hollows were resonating chambers related to bellowing, such as occurs in crocodiles when they feel sexy. (But the analogy is poor, because crocodiles do not have such resonating chambers.)

6. The crests, including those without chambers or tubes, were species-specific display organs. (They are distinctive in each species, but, if that was their function, why do the air passages go through them in some species and not in others?)
7. Both 5 and 6 are correct. (Perhaps.)

One of the students of this minor but enticing problem evasively concluded that it is nice to leave something to the imagination.

A more broadly significant discussion about the characteristics of dinosaurs began to simmer at least a hundred years ago, came to a boil in the 1970s, and is continuing into the 1980s—rather oddly, because now in the 1980s it is not obvious what new there may be to say. In the popular press, where much publicity has been given to this question, it is usually expressed as an inquiry about whether dinosaurs were cold-blooded or warm-blooded. The question is really meaningless in those terms. The blood of most animals may be either relatively warm or cold at different times, depending on their activities and environments.

In more meaningful terms, several different possibilities and alternatives are involved here. First, and perhaps most important, is discrimination between ectothermy and endothermy. An ectothermic animal has relatively little internal control of its body and core temperature, which is mainly determined by environmental conditions and the animal's reactions to them. In an endothermic animal, such as a human, there are various physiological controls that tend to keep the body within a relatively narrow range of temperatures largely independent of the environment. There are some intermediates, and an animal may even be ectothermic at some times and endothermic at others; but as examples relevant here, almost all birds (and mammals when they are not hibernating) are distinctly endothermic, and, with only a few, usually temporary, exceptions, living reptiles are ectothermic.

The other most crucial pair of alternatives here is between poikilothermy and homeothermy (sometimes spelled and pronounced homoiothermy). A poikilotherm has a distinctly varying core temperature, and a homeotherm generally has a nearly constant core temperature or one that varies only within a narrow range.

Ectotherms are usually poikilothermic in an environment with variable external temperatures, but living ectotherms may be (and often are) nearly homeothermic, despite their poor or lacking strictly physiological controls. Some ectotherms are behavioral homeotherms, keeping core temperatures within a narrow range by orientation to radiation (usually sunlight), by moving between warmer and cooler places, or by exercising or relaxing. Other ectotherms are inertial homeotherms. In them, heat exchange with the environment takes place so slowly that their core temperature varies only within narrow limits. That is more likely to be true of the larger animals, and the large size of most dinosaurs is obviously relevant here. A few dinosaurs were as small as chickens, but the average size of dinosaurs was much greater, and some were the largest land animals that ever lived.

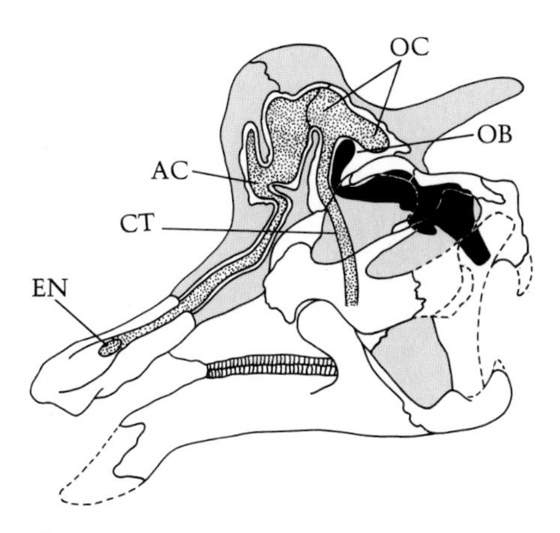

Shape and inferred functional relationship of the passages and spaces involved in the crest of one of the more complexly crested hadrosaurs, Lambeosaurus, *the genus labeled* (m) *in the figure at the top of the preceding page. The left side of the crest has been largely removed to show the course and shapes of passages within it.* EN *is the external naris—that is, the opening to the outer air of one (the left) of the two passages into which air was inhaled. The stippled areas show first one of the paired tubes leading the inhaled air into the crest.* AC *is an anterior chamber of the nasal capsule and* OC *is the region in which (hypothetically) sensor nerves react to the various airborne elements and compounds.* OB *is the inferred olfactory bulb of the brain (restored in black), where the olfactory signals sensed in* OC *are received and passed on to other parts of the brain.*

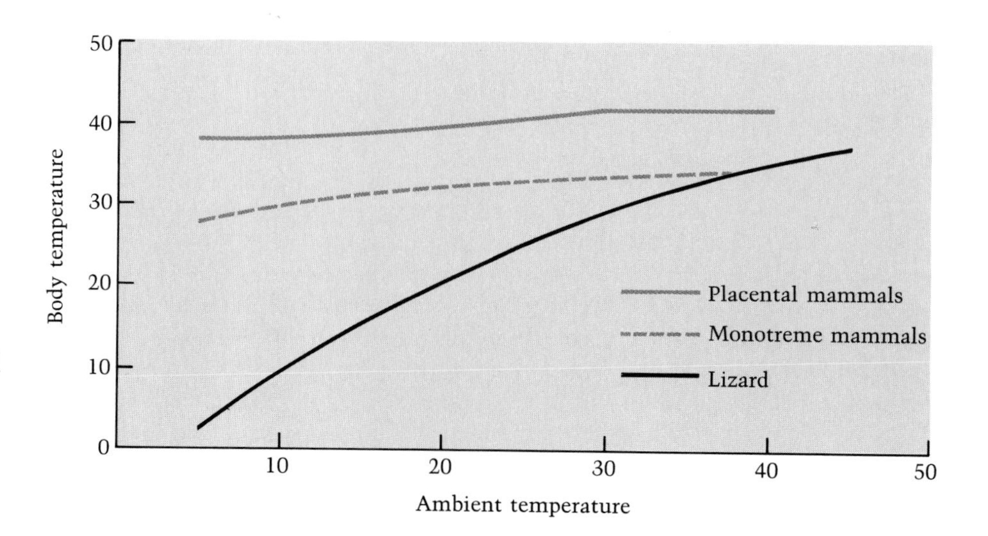

Relationships between body temperatures and ambient temperatures in some living mammals and reptiles. The temperature scales are on the Celsius (or centigrade) scale. The curve for placental mammals is an average for several about the size of a large cat or a small dog. (For comparison, the "normal" human temperature is 37° Celsius, slightly under that of these experimental animals.) Although there is an almost negligible rise in body temperature with rise in ambient temperature, this curve is nearly horizontal and represents effective homeothermy. The data for monotremes is from one specimen each of two of the (three) living genera of egg-laying mammals, Ornithorhynchus *(the platypus) and* Tachyglossus *(the short-nosed echidna). Their average temperature is distinctly below that of the placental mammals here compared and does rise somewhat more with a rise in ambient temperature, but this is still a very flat curve of nearly (but not quite) perfect homeothermy. The curve for a reptile is for a single species of Australian lizard (genus* Cyclodus*, species not stated) of approximately the same bulk as the mammals being compared. Its curve rises rapidly, and its body temperature is nearly the same as the ambient temperature, but it begins to be somewhat lower than ambient temperatures above about 30°C. It represents almost complete poikilothermy. Note that these curves take no account of behavioral or inertial homeothermy.*

The temperature regimes or thermoregulatory systems of animals are among the many things that cannot be directly determined from fossils, either by observation or by experimentation. In such cases, the first and best resort of a paleontologist is to seek some direct parallel, in structure and adaptation, between extinct animals and some still living. Such parallels between the dinosaurs and any animals now extant are so few and so distant that, for purposes of reasonable inference, they hardly exist. The research strategy here must therefore depend almost entirely on detection of some plausible cause-and-effect, but indirect, relationships between the observational data on fossils of dinosaurs and their unobservable thermoregulation. Students of this matter have been extraordinarily ingenious in proposing many different approaches of this sort, but the result has been far from conclusive.

An amusing but also baffling thing about this is that almost every point raised in favor of endothermy versus ectothermy (or of homeothermy versus poikilothermy) in dinosaurs has also been taken as indication of precisely the opposite views. For example, one thing that can really be taken as known about dinosaurs (science fiction to the contrary notwithstanding) is that they all have long been extinct. Years ago, several authorities suggested that dinosaurs became extinct because they were ectothermic, but that was soon countered by the claim that they became extinct because they were endothermic. On the whole, more ectotherms than endotherms have survived up to now, but there is no clear and causal correlation of extinction with either thermal regime.

It would be tedious and unnecessary here to go into all the pros and cons in what has become a very complex and occasionally acrimonious discussion, but mention may be made of some of the points most often brought up. It is now clear that most dinosaurs had an erect posture, with their legs, or the hind legs in the bipedal forms, in a vertical plane. This differs from the posture of the ectothermic living lizards and crocodiles, but it resembles that of the endothermic birds and land mammals. But none of these endotherms are really built like dinosaurs, and the advantage of supporting and moving creatures like dinosaurs on erect legs need not have had any relationship to their thermal regime. In connection with posture, it has been inferred that dinosaurs were highly active and fast-moving animals and that such activity indicates, or requires, endothermy. On the other hand, such analysis as has been made of dinosaur trackways indicates that, when they made the tracks, they were not moving very rapidly. Still they may have moved rapidly and like endotherms on other occasions. And back again in the argument, everyone knows that, on occasion, ectothermic lizards and crocodiles can move very rapidly indeed. Moreover, the shoulder anatomy of quadrupedal dinosaurs is unlike that of any really fast living quadruped.

There is evidence that dinosaurs sometimes went about in rather large groups, and so do many birds and mammals, which are endotherms. But so also do many fish, amphibians, and living reptiles, which are ectotherms. Because endotherms require a higher rate of energy intake than do ectotherms, among living animals the ratio of predators to their prey may be lower in endotherms than in ectotherms. The pro-endotherm researchers find some evidence that the ratios for dinosaurs were more like those of endotherms, but the pro-ectotherm researchers have also found ectothermlike ratios for dinosaurs. Another (one must say better-balanced) group finds that the ratios obtained from the fossil collecting are biased and distorted by so many factors as to be meaningless in this connection.

The histology, or microscopic fine structure, of dinosaur bone is often stressed in discussions of thermoregulation, and again it can be taken as supporting both sides of the argument or neither one. The histology is not just like that of any living animals, but it has some details more common among endotherms and some more common among ectotherms. It is fairly clear that the growth pattern of dinosaurs was more like that of typical, ectothermic reptiles than like that of the endothermic mammals, but that has no evidently conclusive connection with their thermal regime.

It has been argued that dinosaur brains were so small as to indicate ectothermy and also that they were so large as to indicate endothermy. However, it is now reasonably clear that dinosaur brains were much like those of living reptiles in external form and were of the right size for typical reptiles in relation to their body size. Yet there is no clear reason why brain size is necessarily related to thermal regime.

It is sometimes said that dinosaurs have been found in places too frigid for ectotherms, but some ectotherms (lizards) now live as far north as any known dinosaur fossil locality. Moreover, throughout the time of the living dinosaurs, the climates of the earth were more equable and less markedly zonal than they are now, and some of the now northernmost localities were not then so far north.

It is reasonably clear that the known dinosaurs lived in barely seasonal and usually rather warm climates. It is possible to argue that, under those conditions, ectothermy for animals of medium to large size would have an advantage over endothermy because (in the commercial argot now often used in ecology) endothermy would yield too little return to repay its higher costs. As usual, there is a counterargument: The largest animals in warm climates today are endothermic, notably the elephants. It is also argued that there was an ecological relay, the endothermic mammals having replaced the (according to this argument) endothermic dinosaurs. And again a riposte: mammals as a whole group are not ecologically equivalent to dinosaurs as a group, and mammals as large as average dinosaurs now live in climatic regions unlike those known to have been (or likely to have been) dinosaur habitats.

The conclusion of all this is that we do not know (and that we may never find out) what the thermal regime of dinosaurs was. Still it is possible to see at least a slight consensus in the hundreds of pages that have been devoted to this subject. In this, as in their morphological characters, dinosaurs probably were *sui generis*, a world apart, but it is quite likely that the larger of them, at least, were inertially homeothermic ectotherms.

On one point I feel that I can and must go beyond the modestly balanced caution of the preceding discussion. In the belief that dinosaurs were "warm-blooded" and on evidence that they were related or ancestral to birds, some enthusiasts have proposed that birds should be classified as members of the Dinosauria or, at the very broadest, the Archosauria, a group defined as a subclass of Reptilia and including all the dinosaurs and their more or less immediate ancestors. That is utter nonsense, on the grounds both of scientific classification and of common sense. One of the many paleontologists who have both scientific principles and common sense has imagined that, if this idea caught on, the proverb would be "dinosaurs of a feather flock together," and that "the dawn chorus of dinosaurs would awaken us early in the morning." But he adds: "In truth, we need not fear that such absurdities will prevail. Common sense and popular usage are far more powerful influences on language (and on classification, I add as a hope) than is scientific pedantry—especially when the latter is based on such insubstantial grounds."

Is the whole subject nonsensical? Does the inconclusive result demonstrate a waste of paleontological time and talent? Although one may now hope that the turmoil will die down until (or unless) new insight and data appear, the answer to both questions is *no.* Although the basic question about dinosaurs has not been firmly answered and, in my opinion, cannot now be, up to now it has been nevertheless quite heuristic. It has led to some genuinely important studies of thermoregulation in general and also, somewhat serendipitously, into what may prove to be future highways more than byways in the study of fossils as living organisms.

Other recent studies marginal to questions of the function and behavior of dinosaurs have been based on dinosaur eggs, and one of them may be briefly mentioned. Although dinosaur eggs have sometimes been publicized as extraordinary rarities, they are widespread in Europe, Asia, North America, and South America. In France and adjacent parts of Spain and in Mongolia, they are especially numerous and well preserved. The commonest European dinosaur eggs were probably laid by one of the large species of sauropods (*Hypselosaurus priscus*). These eggs are found in strata with an appreciable span in geological time, extending to (or nearly to) the time of final extinction of dinosaurs. A group of German geochemists and paleontologists studied the structure of the eggshells and also analyzed them for isotopes of carbon and oxygen. They found a difference in those isotopes between the earlier and the later eggs, indicating a probable change both in food and in climate, although the exact nature of those changes is somewhat speculative. They also found that, in the latest eggs, most of the shells were pathological in several ways, especially in being abnormally thin. Ultimately, it appears that up to 90 percent of the eggs were abnormal and either were infertile or had embryos that died in an early stage before hatching. The authors ascribe this to the stress of the environmental change and suggest that its effect on reproduction caused the extinction of these dinosaurs.

That is one of the exceptional cases in which definite observational data provide a probable, or at least a plausible, proximate cause for extinction of a given species. In Chapter 5, I will return to extinction as a more general phenomenon in the history of life.

Another aspect of the dinosaurs, here used as examples of the study of fossils as living organisms, is their extraordinary diversity. Although people, including paleontologists, speak of them all under the single broad designation as dinosaurs, they include many different groups—species, genera, families, and still broader categories in classification. In 1887, the British paleontologist Harry Govier Seeley told the British Association for the Advancement of Science that "The Dinosauria has no existence as a natural group of animals but includes two distinct types of structure, which show their descent from a common ancestry rather than their close affinity." Although Seeley was not grammatical ("Dinosauria" is a plural noun) his view was soon adopted, and it is still accepted by practically all paleontologists. The two major groups are ranked as orders in classification and are given Seeley's names, Ornithischia ("bird hips") and Saurischia ("lizard hips"), from the resemblance of their pelves to birds in one group and to reptiles in the other. They also differ in some other basic respects.

Here again the dinosaurs provide an example, and here of a vastly larger project and occupation, that of classifying and naming all known organisms. No one can say with any precision how many kinds—species—of organisms exist on earth today, but the number is certainly in seven digits. When life was just beginning, those billions of years ago, it must have started with just a few kinds, perhaps with only one. Diversification set in early, and by the Cambrian period, some 500 to 570 million years ago (see table on p. 59), although life was still nearly (and perhaps entirely) confined to the waters of the earth, the numbers of

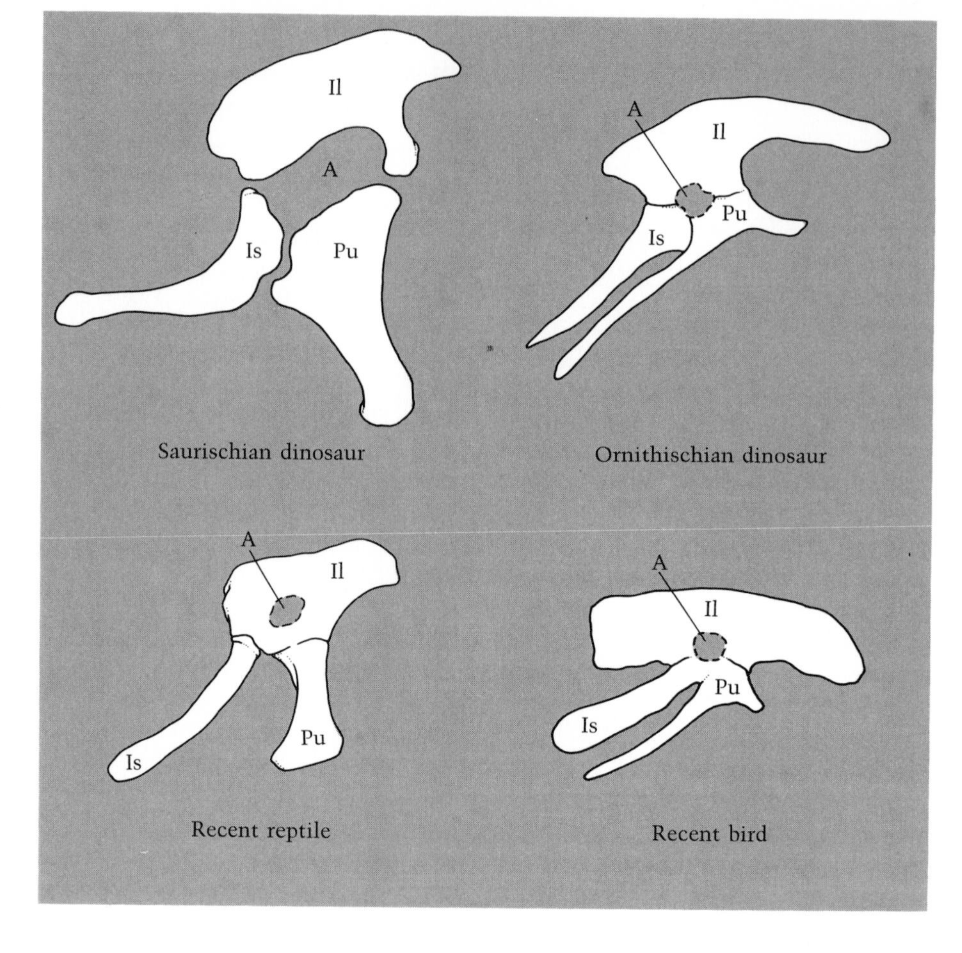

Diagrams of the pelves of the two orders of dinosaurs and of the more typical living members of the class Reptilia and of the living class Aves. These are structural plans and not portraits of particular members of the various groups. In all, the pelvis consists of three bones on each side of the adjacent part of the vertebral column, the sacrum between the hips: the ilium (Il) *above, which articulates with the sacrum; the ischium* (Is), *which extends downward, backward, or both from the posterior part of the ilium; and the pubis* (Pu), *which usually extends from the anterior part of the ilium. These began as separate bones and still occur as such in immature animals, but in adult animals (as in adult humans), they are all fused together. The resemblance of the pelves of the members of one order of dinosaurs with those of most living reptiles suggested the name* saurischia *(= "lizard hip"), and the resemblance of the pelves of the members of the other order to those of many living birds suggested the name* ornithischia *(= "bird hip"). As is shown here, the most obvious difference is in the pubis, which, in saurischians and many other reptiles, is a simple bone at some distance (and quite separate) from the ischium. In the ornithischians and many birds, however, the pubis has a long, rodlike process extending downward and backward near the ischium and sometimes fusing with part of it.* A, *in these drawings, is the acetabulum, where the head of the thigh bone or femur articulates and moves. It is generally open in dinosaurs, but it is a socket with a closed bottom in many other animals (as in humans). Although the peculiarity of the pubis gave origin to the names of the two orders of dinosaurs, they were not—and are not—distinguished solely on that character. Single-character distinctions may be handy in identification, but they are unreliable in ascertaining the true relationships among organisms. It is an odd illustration of the complexities of evolution that birds did not evolve from "bird-hipped" ancestors but from "lizard-hipped" ones or their immediate, also lizard-hipped, ancestry.*

species and larger groups were rapidly increasing. In the following Ordovician period, the number of marine species may have been about as high as it is now, and almost all the nonmarine organisms were yet to come.

One of the findings in the fossil record is that most of the species that have ever existed have no descendants still living. Most of those that do have living descendants were so different from the latter that they cannot reasonably be considered to belong to the same species as their descendants. The total of all the species that have ever existed is so great that their numbers cannot be counted and can hardly even be imagined. The fossil record is only a rather small sampling of the extinct species that actually existed, and we cannot yet even estimate closely how many species may be preserved in that sample. New species of fossils are still being found at a high rate.

To think clearly about the enormously numerous and diverse kinds of organisms, either living or fossil, we need to group and to categorize them in some logical way—in short, to classify them. To label and to talk or write about the various groups in a classification, we must name them. Although classifications can be made in a number of different ways, the system now most used by biologists, including paleontologists, is hierarchic or nesting. Its form is that of a graded series of levels of inclusiveness, similar in concept to a complex of nested boxes. As applied to organisms, this is generally called the Linnaean (or Linnean) hierarchy, from the Latinized form, Linnaeus, of the name of Karl von Linné (1707–1778), a Swede who was primarily a botanist but who undertook to classify all the living organisms known in his time. He regularized (and in a sense froze) a way of classifying or of naming organisms that had been developing for some time in the work of botanists and zoologists but before him in a less uniform and less systematic way. The framework of the hierarchy as now used (modified from the simpler one of Linnaeus himself) is as follows, from higher (or more extensive) to lower (or less extensive) categories:

Kingdom (plural *kingdoms*)
Phylum (plural *phyla*)
Class (plural *classes*)
Order (plural *orders*)
Family (plural *families*)
Genus (plural *genera*)
Species (plural also *species;* the singular is not specie)

The sequence may be, and usually is, more finely divided by inserting categories with the prefixes *super-*, *sub-*, and *infra-*, and sometimes other named categories in the hierarchy. Linnaeus also systematized the forms of names for groups of organisms placed at the various categorical levels, and his system of nomenclature is also still used although with some modifications. This system is called binomial because in it the name of a species, which is considered the basic unit in classification, consists of two words. The first word is the name of a genus and is capitalized; the second word belongs to one species within that genus and is not capitalized. Both words are customarily italicized. Most of us know we all belong to the species *Homo sapiens,* as named by Linnaeus. Names of groups higher than a genus are single words in the plural and are capitalized but not italicized. Names of subfamilies, families, and superfamilies are derived from the names of an included genus with a formal plural ending appended, but the endings for those groups are different for animals and plants—for example, *-idae* is used for families of animals, *-aceae* for families of plants. The human family is Hominidae. Names above the superfamily level are not necessarily derived from those of included genera or families, and they have no overall standard endings beyond the fact that they must be Latinized plurals. We belong to the order Primates, the class Mammalia, the phylum Chordata, and the kingdom Animalia. All names in technical classification are treated as if they were Latin, and many are derived from Latin or Latinized Greek, but their roots may be of any origin or none (that is, they may be simply made up). There are very elaborate, highly legalized codes of nomenclature, different for each kingdom of organisms, but happily we need not go further into them here.

In its modern use, the Linnaean system is just that, a formal system of arranging and naming groups of organisms. How such groups are to be recognized, defined, and placed in the formal system is quite a different and more difficult matter. The category in which a group is placed—that is, its level in the hierarchy—may be (and usually is) defined in other ways; but the group itself, as such, is defined on observed characteristics of its members. For example, although the definition of the species as a category has long been debated, it is generally taken to refer to populations with a limited distribution of more or less variable characteristics and maintaining its unity as such through a considerable number of generations, in sexual (or, more strictly, biparental) organisms maintained by breeding only (or predominantly) within the group. However, as a taxon (plural *taxa*)—that is, as a group of known organisms assigned to a hierarchic category and given a technical (Linnaean) name—a species is always defined in terms of the observed characteristics of a population considered more or less localized in space and, if fossil, also in time. The criterion of interbreeding, for example, is seldom met by direct observation in species of living organisms, and it never can be for fossil animals. It is usually in living organisms and always in fossils inferred from observational data on the characteristics of a sample of a present (or past) population. In this particular respect, the most cogent evidence for assignment to the category of species is evidence that the distribution of variation in some observed characteristics does not overlap that in other known species.

Categories above species in the hierarchy, from genus to kingdom, apply to taxa that are sets of species, usually but not always more than one. Quite a few accepted genera are monotypic—that is, they have only one known included species—and a few recognized families and even higher taxa are also monotypic. (That would probably be even more rarely true if the whole fossil history of the taxon were known.) In practice, it is generally true that the usual categorical ranking of a taxon above the level of species depends on authoritative opinion and evidence about the degree of its distinction from other known taxa—the more the degree of distinction (or less that of resemblance), the higher the category—but this is open to important exceptions and also to current differences of opinion.

I do not propose here to go into all the differences of opinion, some of them mere quibbles but some flatly irreconcilable, or into any of them in depth, but it does seem necessary to mention their existence and extremes. Basically, there are questions about just how one should proceed from observation to classification, and these questions are particularly crucial in paleontology. One extreme view is that classification should be based solely and directly on overall resemblances among taxa, and ingenious (and useful) means of producing a numerical measure of multivariate resemblance have been devised. The most serious objection is that all taxa have had an evolutionary history, a phylogeny, and that this has had biologically important effects on the characteristics of each taxon, the significance of which is lost in a classification based solely on overall resemblance.

Another extreme is that classfication should be based solely on phylogeny, with the further stipulations, in the canonical form of this view, (a) that phylogenies consist solely of bifurcations or dichotomies in lines of descent, (b) that the two lines after a dichotomy always represent two new species distinct from the ancestral species, and (c) that the hierarchical level of any taxon depends entirely on the time when the dichotomy giving rise to its ancestral species occurred—the earlier the time, the higher the category. Among the objections to this system are: that (a) is not true in a practical sense and according to current knowledge of population genetics; that (b) is trivial or untrue in the many, perhaps usual, cases in which, after dichotomy (or multiple fractionation of a lineage), one of the now separate species is indistinguishable from their common ancestor; and that (c) is completely impractical because there is no known way of determining all the dichotomies (or other fractionations) in any phylogeny or their relative dates and, for paleontologists, because this makes the useful classification of fossils both theoretically and practically impossible.

Without spending time on even more esoteric aspects of this subject, I will state briefly what I believe to be both the consensus and the most sensible basic approach to classification. Classification cannot be a complete and detailed expression of phylogeny, but it should be consistent with a reasonable estimate of phylogeny. As will be briefly discussed in Chapter 6, phylogeny cannot be observed and can only be inferred more or less probably from data not directly phylogenetic. In a consistent classification, an inference will be that all the members of a taxon had a common ancestry, although, if the ancestry was a single species (it need not be) or even a single genus or family, that ancestry is not necessarily formally made a member of the descendant taxon. It is also a definitely established factor in phylogeny that some lineages and resulting taxa diverge more widely and evolve more rapidly than others. The degree of difference between taxa in their evolved or derived characters is therefore phylogenetic and is a useful criterion of categorical level. Classifications are artifacts constructed primarily for their usefulness in biological thought and communication. It is therefore desirable to be conservative regarding them and to change a classification radically only when it has in some way come clearly into conflict with the simple criteria stated in this paragraph.

In dealing with nature, either as it is today or as it was through the billions of years of the history of life, we need a classification that conveys some information about the relationships of organisms and a nomenclature that can be used for talking and writing about organisms. Nevertheless simply stating that a species (or some other taxon) exists or has existed at a stated place and time does not give us an adequate idea of life as it was in that place and time. Organisms live and, except perhaps at the very beginning of life, have always lived in communities composed of numerous species that interact with each other and with their environments, including other species and the members of their own species as environmental elements in addition to the physical and chemical aspects of environments.

It follows that, to bring a fossil back to life, you must not only observe its structure, classify and name it, and infer what you can about its functional and adaptive characters, you must also try to place it in a community and to infer as

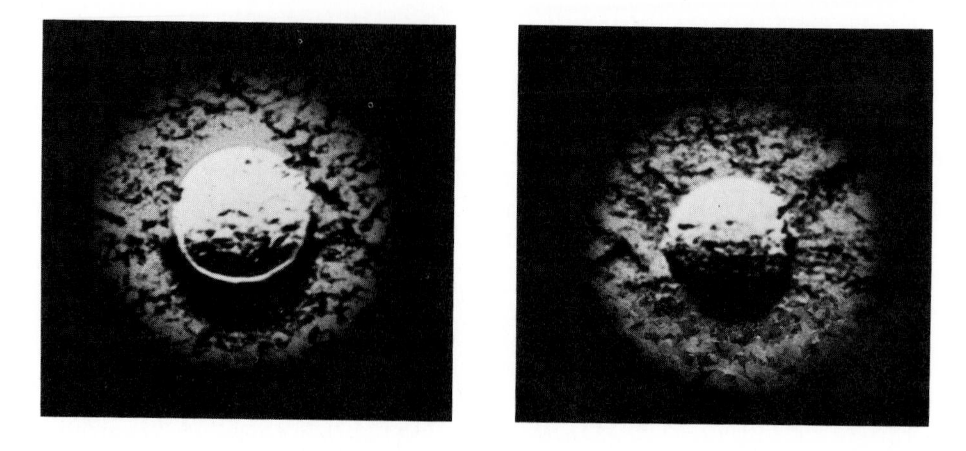

Two cross sections of Eobacterium *are seen in electron micrographs. In the fossil at the left the outer and inner layers of the cell wall are visible. The wall, .015 micron thick, resembles the wall of living bacteria of the bacillus type.*

much as possible about its interaction with other members of the community and with its physical environment. This part of the study of fossils is *paleoecology,* which has become an active specialty in paleontology.

Ecologists often divide their subject into autecology and synecology. *Autecology* is concerned with the relationships of a single species of organisms with its environment. For fossils, that entails largely their functional characteristics as inferred from their structure. That has been exemplified earlier in this chapter by what could have been called the paleoautecology of dinosaurs. *Synecology* is the study of the association and interaction of whole faunas and floras in communities. As applied to fossils, that is the subject of the rest of this chapter, with some examples drawn from other groups, times, and places.

The most obvious interactions in a multispecific community are the flow of nutrients and the flow of energy. In an established, balanced community, the flow of nutrients is typically cyclic, continuing indefinitely to circle through a more or less complex sequence of organisms and, in part, their inorganic environment. The flow of energy, however,typically goes in only one direction. Energy is not annihilated, but, in accordance with the second law of thermodynamics, the usable or free energy is continuously decreased as it activates the population or passes from one organism to another. There must, then, be a continuous input of energy from an outside source.

As is well known, the outside source of energy for almost all recent natural communities is the sun. That energy, incoming as light, enters the combined nutrient and energy flow of communities by photosynthesis in what are usually lumped together as green plants (although, in recent classification, some photosynthetic organisms are not classified as plants but are placed in one or more kingdoms apart from both the classical kingdoms Plantae and Animalia). Photosynthetic organisms thus stand at the beginning of almost all natural energy flows. As those organisms (with quite rare exceptions) derive their nutrients from nonbiotic sources, they are also responsible for the reentry of cycling nutrients into the biotic community.

The simplest possible continuously viable community would be composed of one or more photosynthetic species as composers or transposers of solar energy

Pre-Cambrian seashore area reconstructed from fossils found in South Australia. They are jellyfish-like creatures (a); *the wormlike* Dickinsonia (b); *the segmented worm* Spriggina floundersi (c); Parvancorina (d); Tribrachidium (e); *the sea pens* Rangea *and* Charnia (f); *hypothetical algae and sponges* (g); *and a worm in a sand burrow* (h).

into chemical energy and one or more species as decomposers, expending most or all of the available energy and putting the nutrients back into an inorganic form that is once again available to the photosynthetic species. There is some fossil evidence that extremely ancient communities, from around two and a half to three and a half billion years ago, may have been that simple. They seem to have consisted of photosynthetic composers, forerunners of the so-called blue-green "algae," which have no nuclei and are quite distinct from the true algae, and decomposers, forerunners of the bacteria, the other main group of cellular organisms without nuclei. A speculation made by Darwin (and still considered probable, but without direct evidence) is that the very earliest true cellular organisms were not photosynthetic but derived nutrients and energy from more or less complex molecules that were organic in a chemical sense (which means only that they contained carbon atoms) but not biogenic, not derived from living organisms.

However that may be, there is now considerable fossil evidence that, by about seven hundred million years ago, communities were already quite complex. The Cambrian, about five hundred to five hundred seventy million years ago, is the earliest geological period for which there is abundant fossil evidence, and by then marine communities were almost as complex as most recent marine communities. There were as yet no established land communities.

Those early stages in the evolution of what has ever since been the characteristic overall pattern of the synecology of populations are shown diagrammatically in the following diagram. There is no direct fossil evidence for the two oldest stages shown (to the left), but these are hypotheses based on reasonable indirect evidence from chemical studies of the possible origin of life. The term *prokaryotic* refers to cellular organisms without nuclei, and *eukaryotic* refers to organisms

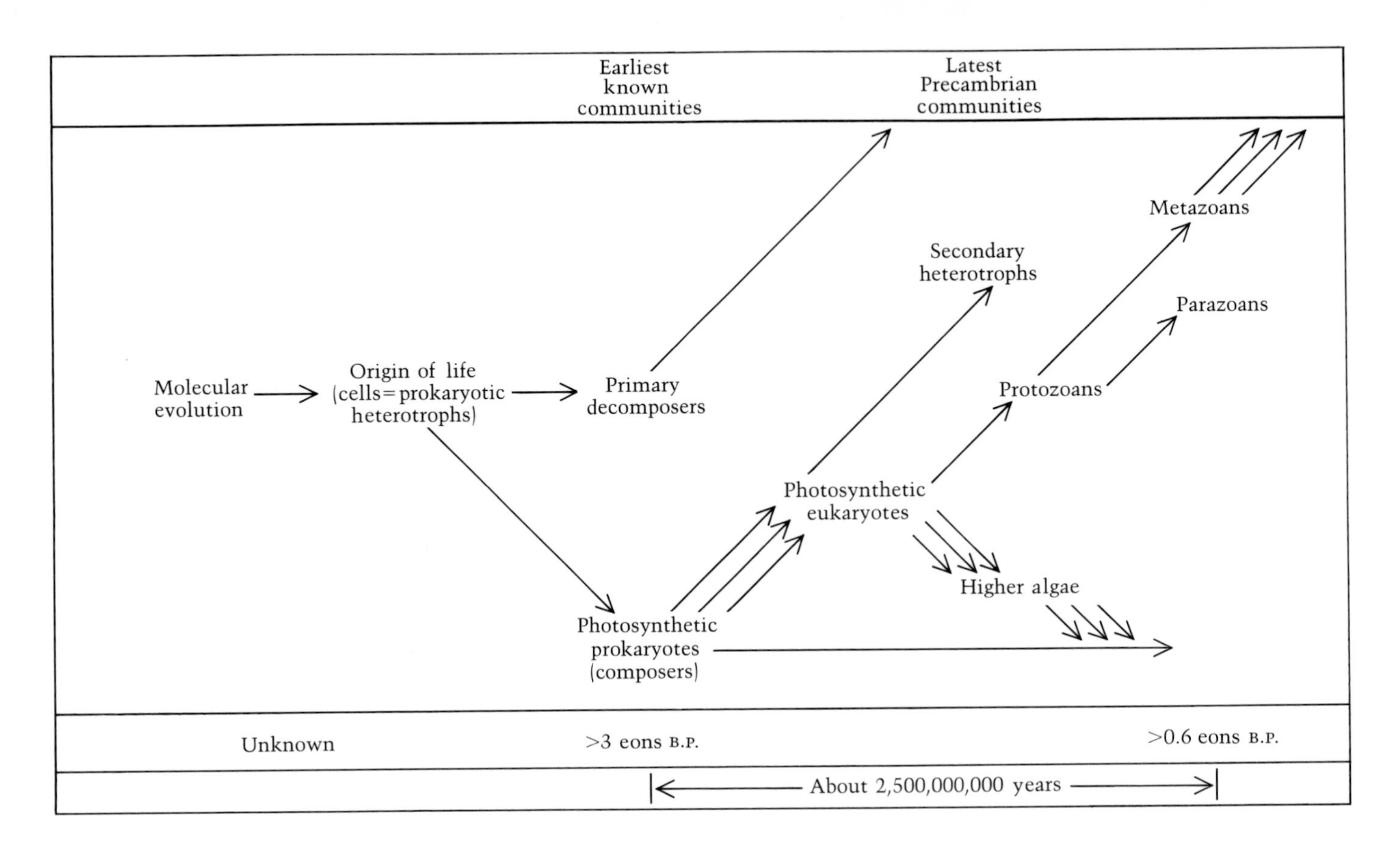

Simplified diagram of the probable succession and relationships of the earliest communities during the long Precambrian. There is definite but not yet fully adequate fossil evidence for this back to about 3.5 eons B.P. *("Eon" is now often used to mean 1,000,000,000 years, and* B.P. *is one of several abbreviations, not yet standardized, for "before the present.") Other terms and the general meaning of the diagram are discussed in the text.*

with nuclei in (most of) their cells. *Heterotrophs* is the term for organisms that cannot synthesize all necessary nutrients and must derive some from photosynthetic organisms. (The latter are known as *autotrophs*). With rare exceptions not important in the present connection, all organisms that are not photosynthetic are heterotrophs. Most or all of the photosynthetic prokaryotes were (and still are) blue-green "algae." The higher or true algae are photosynthetic eukaryotic autotrophs. Protozoans, mostly one-celled eukaryotes, and animals (in the usual zoological sense) are non-photosynthetic eukaryotic heterotrophs. Plants evolved from the higher algae later, after the times shown in this diagram. Parazoans are sponges, multicellular animals that evolved from protozoans independently of other animals. The other multicellular animals, to and including us, are metazoans and are eukaryotic heterotrophs.

In the broadest way, the food and energy flow in any community, since some six or seven hundred million years ago, has consisted of this sequence: (1) *composers* (photosynthetic organisms) → (2) *"herbivores,"* deriving most of their food and energy from the composers, → (3) *"carnivores,"* deriving most of their food and energy from the "herbivores," → (4) *decomposers,* deriving most of their food and energy from members of any of the first three groups and usually not passing these on directly to other organisms. "Herbivores" and "carnivores" are here placed in quotation marks because, in a generalization this broad, these terms do not have just the usual sense. Most "herbivores" do not eat herbage: broadly speaking, mistletoe is a "herbivore." Many "carnivores" do not eat meat: broadly

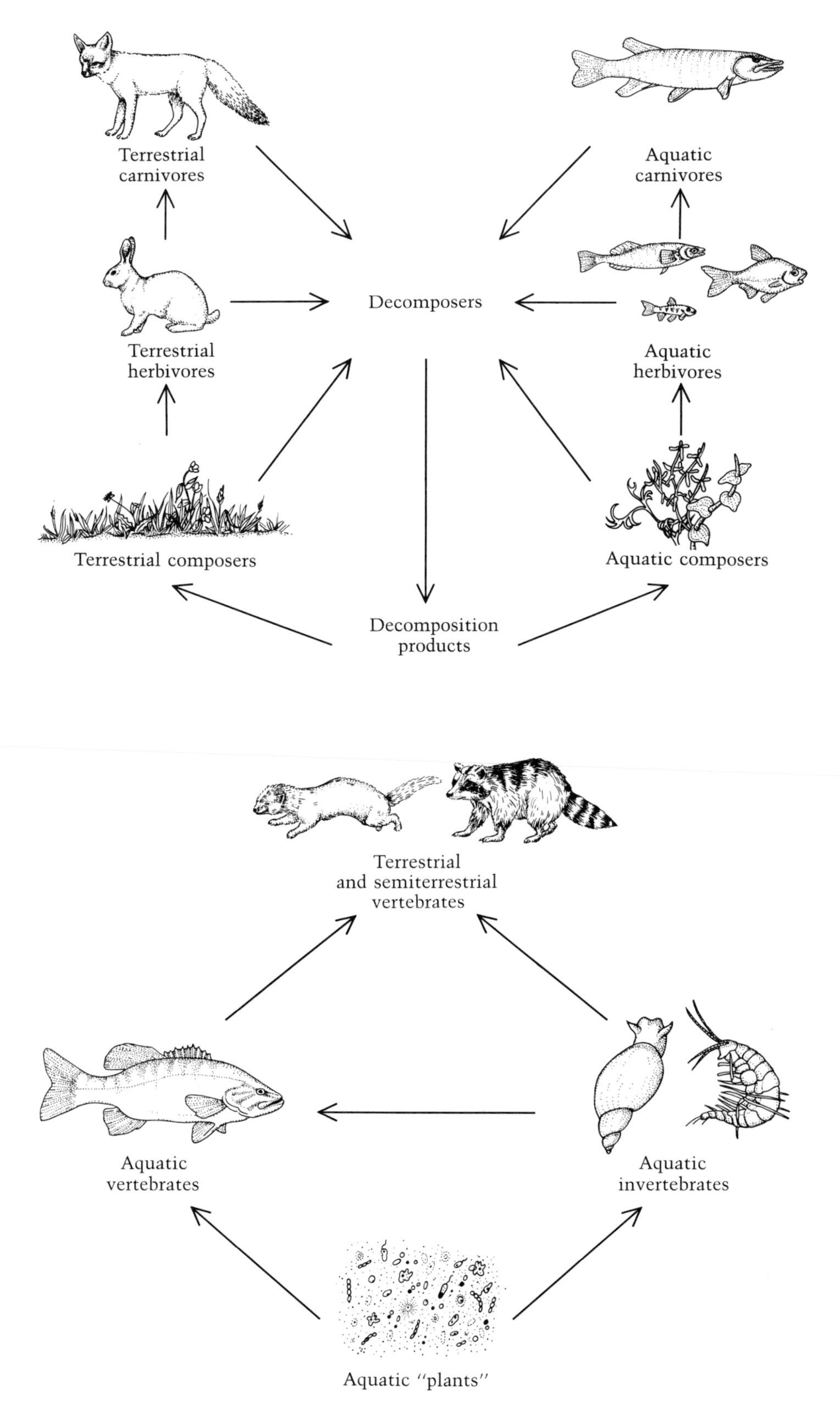

Generalized and highly simplified trophic diagrams for terrestrial (left) *and aquatic* (right) *communities. The "composers" are organisms, mostly green plants, that synthesize organic matter from inorganic sources. The arrows indicate the direction of consumption and acquisition of energy.*

Generalized and highly simplified trophic diagram similar to the one above but for a biocenosis that has interacting terrestrial and aquatic biotas. The word "plants" is put in quotation marks here because it includes all organisms called "composers" in the figure above not all of which are classified technically in the kingdom Plantae. Although I have rearranged it and simplified it still further, this is essentially the main trophic pattern of what Everett Olson has called a "Type I Community." In the figure on the following page, this trophic pattern is exemplified in considerable detail for a fossil community analyzed by Olson.

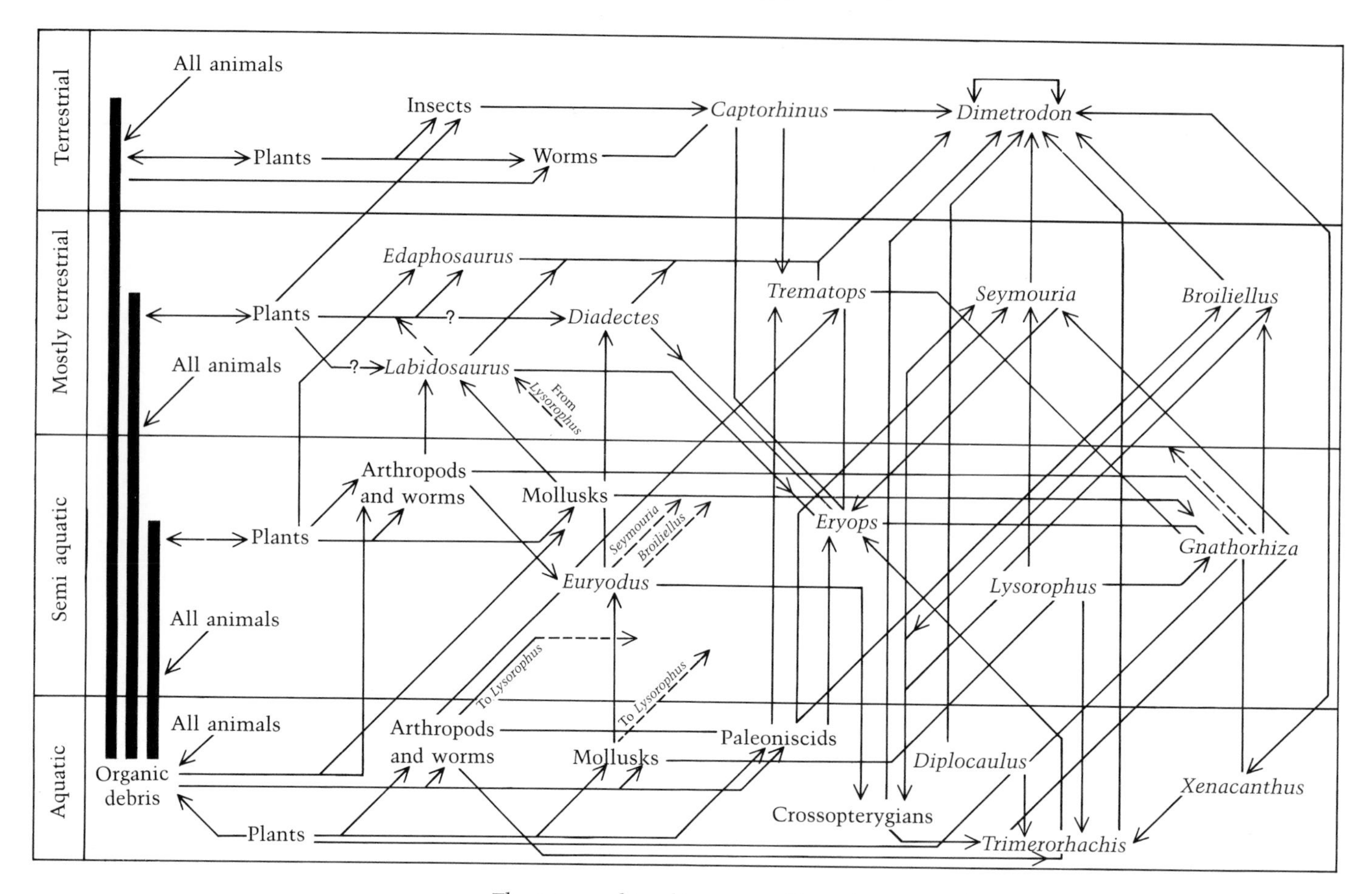

The presumed trophic pattern (flow of food-derived energy) in a complex community known in considerable detail by many fossils collected from a Lower Permian formation in northern Texas. This is a thanatocenosis, an association of remains of organisms by taphonomic processes after their death although they may not all have been parts of a functional community, a biocenosis, while alive. However, the fossils were found in associations such that it was reasonable to conclude that there was trophic interaction between the more terrestrial and the more aquatic organisms. Although they lived in four distinguishable but variable ecological zones, as designated at the left in the diagram, they did all live in one limited area. Those in the same ecology would eat and be eaten by other animals in that zone. Herbivores would generally eat plants in their own zone, but especially for carnivores there was opportunity to eat animals in adjacent zones, as indicated diagrammatically by lines in each zone from or to other zones. Edaphosaurus, Labidosaurus, Dimetrodon, *and* Captorhinus *were terrestrial reptiles.* Lysorophus, Diplocaulus, Trimerorhachis, Euryodus, Eryops, Trematops, Broiliellus, *probably* Seymouria, *and possibly* Diadectes *were amphibians.* Xenacanthus, Gnathorhiza, *and the crossopterygians and paleoniscids were fishes. The other organisms involved are given more easily recognizable, nontechnical names. Olson remarked in the caption that this network "is, of course, overly simple as compared to conditions that must have actually existed."*

speaking, fleas are "carnivores." For such reasons, *parasites* may be inserted into the sequence. *Scavengers* might also be inserted, but, in broad generalization, scavengers may be "herbivores" or (more commonly) "carnivores." If any community is examined in detail, its flow chart for nutrients and energy cannot be put into a sequence of clearly definable levels, much less into linear form. It becomes instead a vastly complicated mesh. Such diagrams are based mainly on the nutrient cycle and are called *trophic,* derived from the Greek word *trophe* ("food").

In applying this most fundamental aspect of synecology to fossil communities, one must first identify the taxa—species, genera, families, and so forth—in the known biota—fauna, or flora, or (preferably but not usually) both. Then one must try to fit each taxon into a reasonable flow chart by inferences about its sources of food and energy and about which taxa obtained food and energy from it. Usually such inferences must be less specific than they are in the study of recent communities. For example, if pandas were known only as fossils, it would probably be inferred that they were herbivorous, even though they would be classified in the order Carnivora, but it surely would not be inferred that they fed almost exclusively on certain species of bamboos.

It has already been stressed that the preservation and collection of fossils result in samples that are always incomplete in several respects. That strongly affects the ecological analysis of fossils. Throughout most of the long history of life, most of the decomposers have probably been bacteria or bacterialike organisms. Some such fossils have been found in exceptional deposits and by exceptional search and study methods, but they are almost completely absent in fossil communities that are quite well known in other respects. There are other strong biases as to what is present in samples from ancient communities and how the fossil remains happen to be where they are found. Thus the ecological interpretation of fossils depends heavily on their taphonomy, and this is a reason for the current heightened interest in that subject, a topic briefly discussed in the previous chapter.

It is a problem for the paleoecologist that he is not dealing with the ensemble of organisms living together, a *biocenosis.* The term is derived from the Greek words *bios* ("life") and *koinos* ("common")—that is, "living together." Similarly fossils found in association constitute a *thanatocenosis*—"united in death"—from the Greek *thanatos* ("death") and *koinos.* Associated fossils are indeed often an incomplete sampling of what was a biocenosis in life; but, as was pointed out in connection with taphonomy, the circumstances of death, transportation, and burial often bring together fossilizable parts of animals and plants that did not live together when they were alive. Thus it cannot be assumed that a thanatocenosis is the fossil representation of a single biocenosis, and this requires careful sorting out by a paleoecologist.

The following table gives the general features of trophic analysis of two ancient marine biotas from the state of New York, one middle Ordovician in age (about 465 million years old) and the other early Devonian (about 390 million

Trophic analysis of two Paleozoic biotas discussed in the text.

	Trophic position in the community				
Inferred biocenosis	Primary producers	Suspension feeders	Herbivores	Carnivores	Scavengers
Intertidal community	Blue-green "algae"	Brachiopods (lamp shells)			Ostracods (small, shelled crustaceans)
Subtidal community	True algae	Corals Brachiopods Bryozoans	Gastropods (sea snails)	Nautiloids (chambered mollusks)	

Fossil Brachiopods Mucrospirifer mucronatus *from the Devonian period.*

years old). Despite the difference in the age of these two biotas, their ecology was much the same, although different taxa had similar roles in the trophic web. As in many marine faunas, it is useful here to distinguish suspension feeders as having a distinct trophic role. The suspension feeders, still abundant in modern seas, are animals that, by filtering or other means, obtain microorganisms or food particles from the surrounding water. The more detailed data, discussed in the book by Laporte cited in the bibliography at the end of the book, show that in these particular thanatocenoses four former biocenoses can be distinguished by their relationship to the sea and coast: supratidal, high intertidal, low intertidal, and subtidal. (For generalization, only intertidal and subtidal are considered here.) Some kinds of organisms occur in several or all of the distinguishable inferred

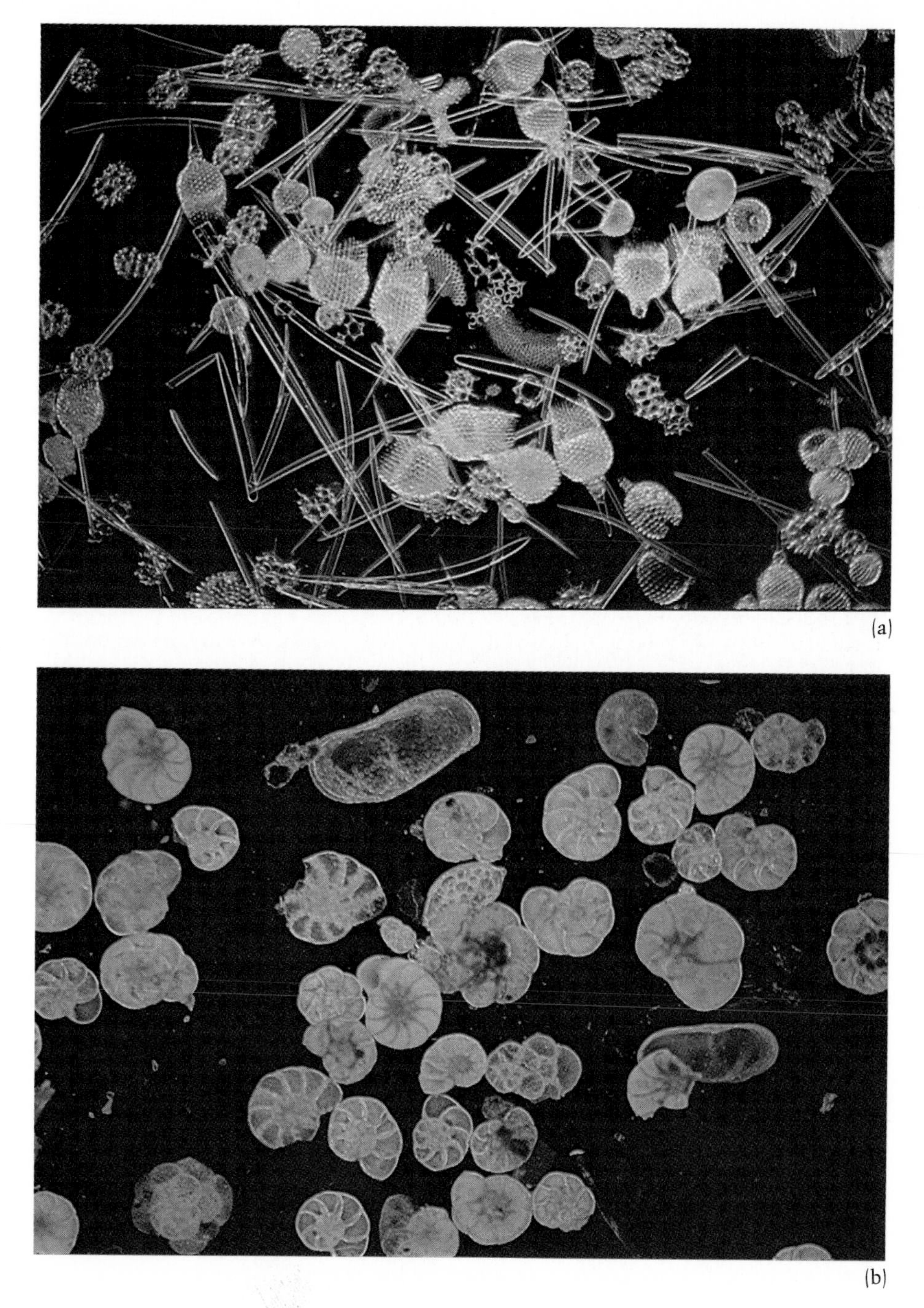
(a)

(b)

A greatly enlarged view of radiolarian skeletons (a) *and foraminiferan skeletons* (b) *viewed under dark field illumination. Large deposits of foraminiferan ooze lie beneath the warmer seas of the world and such sediments have formed significant strata, the White Cliffs of Dover being a well-known example.*

biocenoses, but the genera and species are largely different in different communities of about the same age, and such taxonomic (but not markedly ecological) differences are still greater between the biotas of different ages.

In such studies, distinctions are also made between those organisms that live on the substrate (sea bottom, intertidal rocks, or beaches) and those that burrow within it. A further distinction (autecological for each species but synecological for a community as a whole) distinguishes organisms that are directly attached to a substrate, those that are attached by stems or similar structures, and those that are vagile, moving about more or less freely.

The nature of the physical environment may in part be deduced from the fossil assemblages themselves. For example, it is usually fairly obvious whether a given thanatocenosis represents a marine biota, a fluvial one, a terrestrial one, or a mixture of two or all three. Organisms that were attached to the substrate in life often remain so in death. Ancient reefs are fairly common, were preserved *in situ*, and are readily recognized in thanatocenoses that closely approximate biocenoses. Stalked organisms were more subject to transport and vagile organisms were still more so, but even for them preservation *in situ* is not uncommon.

Almost all fossils were buried in sediments, and in most instances the sediments were laid down in water. Some sediments were originally air-borne—blowing dust and sand or volcanic ash—but even fossils of terrestrial organisms are usually found in water-deposited sedimentary rocks. Much can be learned from those rocks about the physical environment of fossils found *in situ*, and something can be learned from them about the taphonomic effects of transport on fossils not buried *in situ*. In this respect, the energy levels of the depositing agency are important. The simplest point here is that often (not invariably) the energy level was positively correlated with the bulk and weight of transported material. That is, the larger the grains in a sandstone or of pebbles in a conglomerate, the higher the energy level was likely to have been. Taphonomists are also able to calculate the probable energy level indicated for movement of a shell or a bone in terms of equivalent volume of spherical grains or pebbles. In the sea or lakes, energy levels are high in zones with wave action but low in environments below or beyond that action. In streams or floods, the energy level depends on the rate of flow.

CHAPTER 3
FOSSILS AND TIME

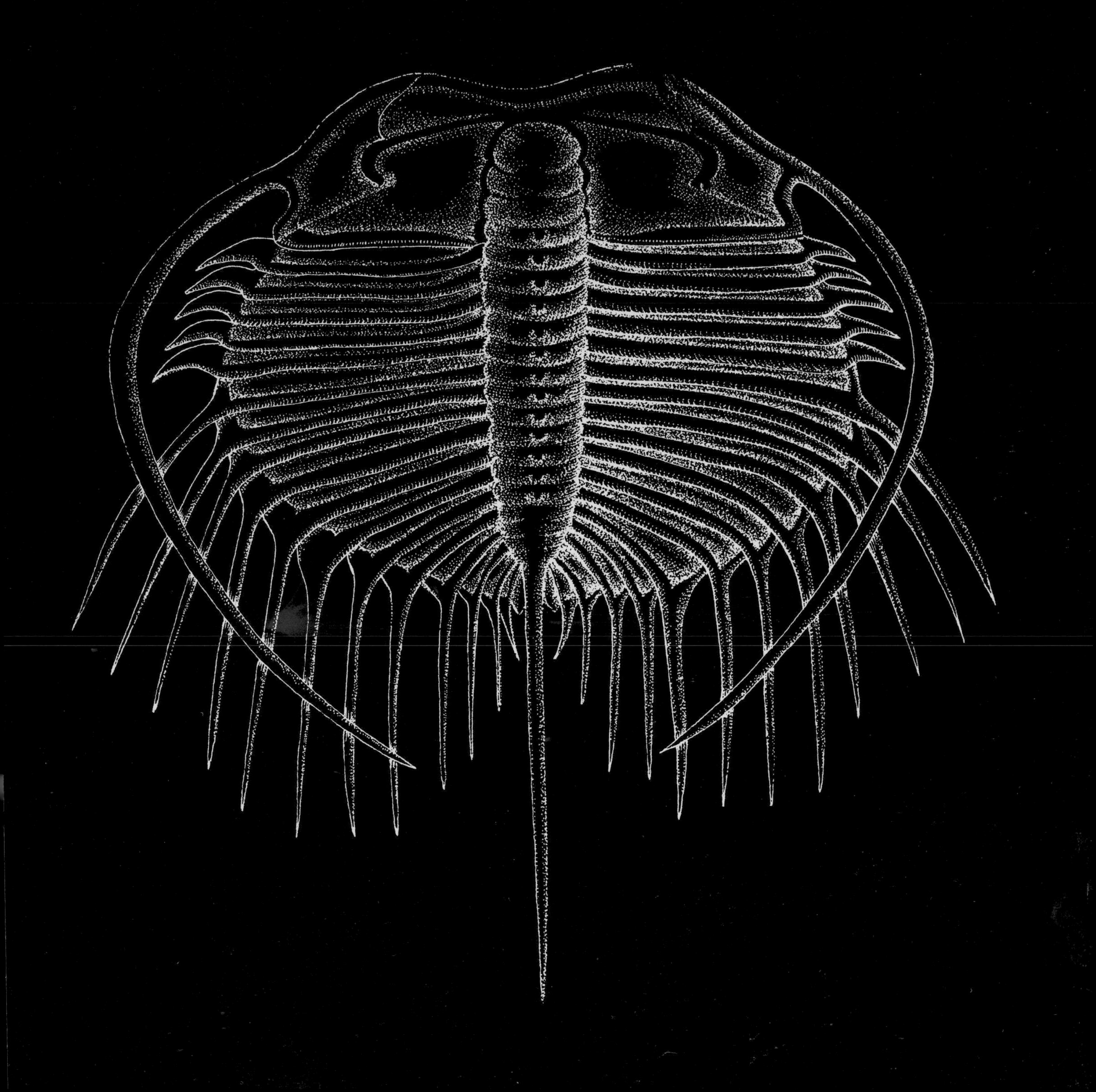

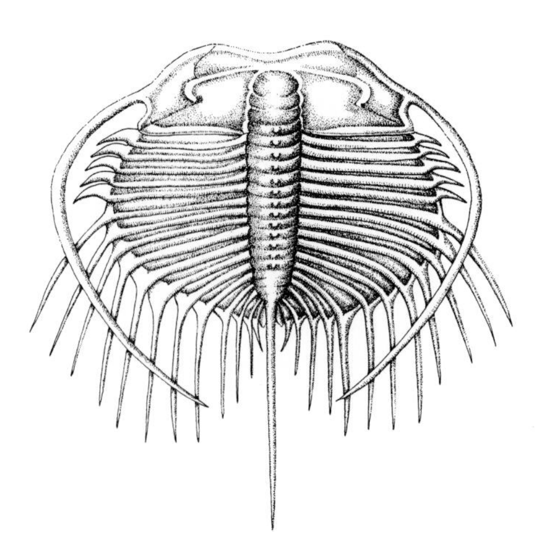

A trilobite, Ctenopyge, *from the late Cambrian, about 520 million years ago. The trilobites, distant relatives of the crustaceans of today, were extremely abundant and varied in the Paleozoic but were extinct thereafter.*

The fundamental reason for studying fossils is that they are a record of the history of life. There are many other aspects, applications, and implications of their study, but the overall significance of fossils is historical. History occurs through the flow of time, and an understanding of fossils requires their placement in that flow.

It was pointed out in Chapter 1 that the establishment of paleontology as a science required recognition both that the rocks containing fossils were deposited in a definite sequence and that the fossils themselves represent a changing sequence in the kinds of organisms found in the sequence of the rocks. That much had been established even before the last overall principle for understanding the sequence of fossils was made clear by Darwin.

As early as 1760, it was recognized by Giovanni Arduino that rocks could be arranged in a sequence as Primary (oldest), Secondary, and Tertiary (youngest). A still younger subdivision, Quaternary, was proposed by J. Desnoyers in 1829. Tertiary and Quaternary are the only terms of that sequence still in use. By the years 1830–1833, when the three volumes of Charles Lyell's great classic *Principles of Geology* were published, the system of sequential or relative dating was well established. Since then, it has continued in use, with considerable expansion and elaboration in detail and some changes in terminology.

Geological time in the sequential system now has generally accepted categories arranged in a hierarchic way, from more to less inclusive, as follows:

Era
  Period
    Epoch
      Age

The successive eras, periods, and epochs have names applicable world wide in principle, and also in practice, for much of the sequence. For the ages there are various different nomenclatures for different regions and purposes. The theoretically worldwide names for all eras and periods and those for the epochs of just the most recent era are given in the table shown on the next page.

Although the Precambrian era includes most of the time during which Earth has been a distinct planet, its earliest part is not known to be represented by rocks now ascertainable in the crust. Various proposals have been made to subdivide such of the Precambrian as is known from rocks, most commonly a division into an earlier Archaeozoic and a later Proterozoic era. Further division into periods and epochs is not yet on a firm or worldwide basis and, in any case, is not necessary for present purposes. Precambrian fossils are still rare, as previously mentioned. They will be somewhat further discussed later in this chapter. Fossils first became abundant in the Cambrian period, beginning about 570,000,000 years ago, and the time since then is sometimes informally lumped together as Phanerozoic, literally the time of "visible animal life," although there are some known animal fossils from still older rocks.

Eras	Periods	(Epochs)	Some major events
	—Dates, years before present—		
		Present	
	Quaternary	(Recent) —10,000— (Pleistocene)	Many extinctions of large mammals Ice Age
		2,500,000	
Cenozoic	Tertiary	(Pliocene) —6,000,000— (Miocene) —26,000,000— (Oligocene) —38,000,000— (Eocene) —55,000,000— (Paleocene)	Early hominids (human family) ↑ Increasing specialization and modernization of mammals │ Great spread of primitive and archaic mammals
		65,000,000	
	Cretaceous		Extinction of dinosaurs; first primates, and many other animals Spread of flowering plants
Mesozoic		135,000,000	
	Jurassic		First birds
		190,000,000	First mammals
	Triassic		First dinosaurs
		225,000,000	
	Permian		Many extinctions of invertebrates
		280,000,000	
	Carboniferous		First reptiles
		345,000,000	
Paleozoic	Devonian		First amphibians; spread of fishes
		395,000,000	First forests
	Silurian		First air-breathing animals
		430,000,000	First land plants
	Ordovician		
		500,000,000	First vertebrates
	Cambrian		Great spread of marine invertebrates
		570,000,000	
Precambrian		700,000,000	First animals
		3,400,000,000	Possible bacteria and blue-green algae; possible first organisms
		4,600,000,000	Origin of earth

The names Paleozoic ("old animal life"), Mesozoic ("middle animal life"), and Cenozoic ("recent animal life"), indicate that these eras have been defined primarily on the basis of their paleozoology. The Paleozoic era was named by a well-known British cleric and geologist, the Reverend Adam Sedgwick, in 1838. The Mesozoic and Cenozoic eras were named by the British paleontologist John Phillips in 1840 first, interestingly enough, in the pages of the *Penny Cyclopaedia*. Phillips was a nephew of an even more famous early British geologist, William Smith, whose importance to the foundation of paleontology as a science was mentioned in Chapter 1.

The names of the periods given in the table above all originated in Europe without any consistent etymological basis. The Cambrian, Ordovician, and

Silurian periods were all named by British geologists working in Wales: Cambrian (Sedgwick, 1835) from *Cambria*, the Roman name for Wales; Ordovician (Lapworth, 1879) from *Ordovices*, a pre-Roman Welsh tribe; Silurian (Murchison, 1835) from *Silures*, also a pre-Roman Welsh tribe that, like the Ordovices, had futilely resisted the Roman invasion. Ordovician was an emendation for what had for 44 years been called by some geologists Lower Silurian and by others Upper Cambrian. In proposing this change, its author, Professor Charles Lapworth (like all those named here, an important figure in the history of paleontology) wrote of his new term that, "like the term Silurian, it is classic in origin but at the same time thoroughly British." (One gathers that the professor was also "thoroughly British.") The Devonian was, of course, named for Devon, an Old English name for the region just across the Bristol Channel from Wales, in an all-star collaboration of the Reverend Adam Sedgwick and Sir Roderick Murchison in 1839. (Sir Roderick was not knighted until 1846, but giving him the title anachronistically seems justified.)

The Carboniferous ("coal-bearing") period was so named in 1822 by William Daniel Conybeare and William Phillips because in Britain rocks of this age include the coal measures on which so much of British commerce has depended. In eastern North America, rocks of this age are also richly coal-bearing, a fact of great significance for study of the world climates and paleontology of that time. In the United States, strata equivalent to those of the Lower Carboniferous of Europe were named Mississippian by Alexander Winchell in 1869, and, in 1891, Henry Shaler Williams applied the name Pennsylvanian to rocks of the upper, coal-bearing part of the Carboniferous system. These names have long been used by American geologists and still are by some, but many American geologists have reverted to the older and more widely used name Carboniferous as the period name for "Mississippian" and "Pennsylvanian" combined.

The Permian was named in 1841 by the indefatigable Sir Roderick Murchison, who, although British (Scottish) himself, based the name on the Province of Perm in what was then eastern Russia.

Triassic is an adjectival form of the Trias of Friedrich von Alberti, a name he gave to this period in 1831 because in Germany, where he studied the relevant rocks, they had been divided into three units—a trias, or triad. That is not true of Triassic rocks elsewhere, but a name does not have to be descriptive in order to be valid. (After all, not all Devonian rocks are in Devonshire!)

There is no doubt that the Jurassic period was named for the Jura Mountains in eastern France and northwestern Switzerland, but there are doubts about when and by whom it can be said to have been named as a geological period. In 1858, the great Alexander von Humboldt claimed paternity because, in 1799, he had referred to the "Jura-Kalkstein" as a distinct rock unit, but that German expression means just a "limestone in the Jura [Mountains]," which hardly merits priority as a name for a geological period. There are other claims, but I would assign the authorship to Alexandre Brongniart (also mentioned in Chapter 1) who, in 1829,

Section of a mural by Jay H. Matternes showing animal and plant life from early in the Oligocene Epoch. This scene is set in the South Dakota-Nebraska region, about 35 million years ago. The large animal depicted at the top center of this mural is Brontotherium, *a titanothere, and to its right is* Subhyracodon, *an early rhinoceros. Below the* Subhyracodon *is* Merycoidodon, *a sheep-like grazing mammal. Directly below the* Merycoidodon *is* Hyaenodon, *an archaic hyenalike mammal, devouring a* Glyptosaurus, *an extinct lizard. The saber-toothed cat is* Hoplophoneus. *At the upper left is* Hyracodon, *a small flat-footed rhinoceros to the right of which is* Protapirus, *an ancestral tapir. The piglike animal below* Hyracodon *is* Archaeotherium *to the right of which is* Proëbrotherium, *the ancestral camel. The horned ruminant below* Archaeotherium *is* Protoceras.

used the term "Terrain Jurassique" for what were essentially the rocks of the Jurassic period of present usage.

Cretaceous means "chalky," and the period was so named in 1822 by J. J. d'Omalius d'Halloy because rocks of this age include the chalk conspicuous both in France and in England. Some chalk in North America (especially in Kansas) is also of this period, but of course many other kinds of sedimentary rocks are likewise Cretaceous in age, as Omalius d'Halloy recognized when he named this period (or "terrain" in the French usage of the time).

I have already noted that the names Tertiary and Quaternary survive from the earliest attempts at a nomenclature of geological ages.

The naming of the epochs of the Cenozoic era with terms ending in *-cene* and beginning with other adaptations of Greek word-roots was begun by Charles Lyell in 1833 but was greatly modified after that by Lyell himself and by others. From an etymological point of view, the result is a nonsensical hodgepodge. The suffix *-cene* means "recent," and it connects these epochs to the Cenozoic era. In succession from oldest to youngest, the literal meanings are: Paleocene, "ancient recent"; Eocene, "dawn of recent"; Oligocene, "few recent"; Miocene, "fewer recent"; Pliocene, "more recent"; and Pleistocene, "most recent." In this book, I have used Recent just so as the name of the present epoch, but Holocene, "entirely recent," is often used with the same meaning. Of course, the names serve to denote those geological epochs in that sequence, and it does not matter that, if taken literally, "fewer" comes between "few" and "more" and "dawn" comes after "ancient," and so on. I will not explain here just how this mixup occurred. (I have done so briefly on pages 79–80 of my 1978 book *Concession to the Improbable.*)

The terms *era, period, epoch,* and *age,* as well as the names applied to particular ones of each, are purely chronological. They denote time not in years or other units of measurement but only as a sequence. That is fairly simple, but the terms and names can be, and have been, applied in different ways. That has led to considerable confusion, which has now been fairly well (but still not entirely) straightened out. For one thing, most stratigraphers and paleontologists now understand that terms and names that in themselves are only chronological, such as "period" or "Cambrian," can be applied to rocks, or to organisms, or to populations of organisms represented by fossils in those rocks. Their application to rocks is termed *chronostratigraphic.* There are special chronostratigraphic terms corresponding with purely chronological terms, as follows:

Chronological	Chronostratigraphic
Era	Erathem
Period	System
Epoch	Series
Age	Stage

That is, the Cambrian system, for example, comprises all the rocks formed or deposited during the Cambrian period; the Eocene series comprises all the rocks formed or deposited during the Eocene epoch; and so on.

There is not in general use a similar corresponding sequence of chronological and paleontological terms. If one wants to refer to all the fossils known from the Cambrian period, they are simply called the Cambrian biota. It may occur to you that things would be simpler if stratigraphers just called all the rocks of Cambrian age the Cambrian rocks. So they do, but they also call them the Cambrian system.

The ordering of rock units in terms of their fossil content is *biostratigraphy.* The basic unit is a *zone,* usually defined as a stratum or a body of strata characterized by certain taxa (named groups of organisms) or assemblages of taxa. This ordering may be done in a number of different ways, the details of which need not be discussed here. In principle, there should be a biochronological system and nomenclature parallel with the biostratigraphic system. A number of proposals of that sort have been made for particular uses or following particular definitions and ideas, but none has yet been standardized, widely accepted, and codified for general use. There are subdivisions of the epochs of the Cenozoic era, sometimes called "ages," and of the periods of the Paleozoic and Mesozoic eras, sometimes treated as epochs but also sometimes defined as ages, that are now more of regional or provincial, rather than of worldwide, usage. For instance, there are such subdivisions for European marine rocks and faunas, and there is another set of them for North American continental (nonmarine) rocks and faunas. Their names are coined by adding an ending, *-an* or *-ian,* to the name of a geographic locality or region where typical rocks and faunas occur. These have been well worked out more or less separately for various areas and kinds of faunas, but there are still some relatively unimportant quibbles about definitions and about the relationships between chronology and stratigraphy involved in these terms.

The ways in which the sequential geological time table has been worked out and the methods of placing particular strata and faunas in that sequence depend on a few general principles that are simple in concept but are sometimes complicated in application. The most basic and important principles and associated methods are those of superposition and correlation.

Sediments are usually deposited in layers, and, if they are preserved along with their fossils, they become incorporated in the rocks in the crust of the earth. They become available for observation, and their fossils become available for collection and study, when they have been exposed at the surface by natural erosion or by human activities (for example, in road cuts or quarries) or when subsurface cores have been obtained for study or for exploration of possible mineral resources. It now seems obvious (although, it has not always seemed so) that, when the strata have not been greatly disturbed, those that lie above others were deposited later and therefore are relatively younger. This, essentially, is the principle of *superposition.* Then the sequence in any one series of local and connected observations is directly determined in the field or in the laboratory from cores—cylinders from a vertical section of rocks below the surfaces of the land or beds of the seas, obtained by drills or specialized instruments.

Difficulties in interpreting local superpositions arise when movements in the earth's crust have obscured or reversed the original sequence of deposition. When the strata have been folded, they may become vertical or even be completely overturned. Then the problem is to find out which way was up when the sediments were deposited. There are many ways of doing that, and modern field stratigraphers are seldom fooled in such cases. A more difficult problem, but one that is less common, arises when one segment of the earth's crust has been thrust over another. Then the rocks below the plane of thrust may be younger than those above it, and the usual sequence of superposition does not apply. The solution involves separate determination of the geological ages of the strata below and above the thrust plane. A few religious fundamentalists have cited such rare occurrences as evidence that the geological time scale is false. That only betrays their ignorance of the literally millions of observations and the centuries of study that have determined, tested, and authenticated that time scale.

There are many places on earth where long stretches of the time scale can be followed by superposition in a single sequence of exposed strata. The Grand Canyon is one of the most spectacular and widely known examples. There the exposed strata extend from far back in Precambrian time and thence upward through the whole Paleozoic era, with some breaks in continuity. Although the sequence in the canyon itself ends in the Permian, the last period of the Paleozoic, it can be followed upward into the Mesozoic era with new continuity by following exposures in tributary canyons, especially that of the Little Colorado River and adjacent areas where the strata are well exposed because of the thinness of plant cover in the surrounding deserts.

That example is almost, but not entirely, unique in its extent. Still neither it nor any other single observed sequence on earth includes strata representing the whole of geological time. The whole time scale has had to be pieced together from

(a)

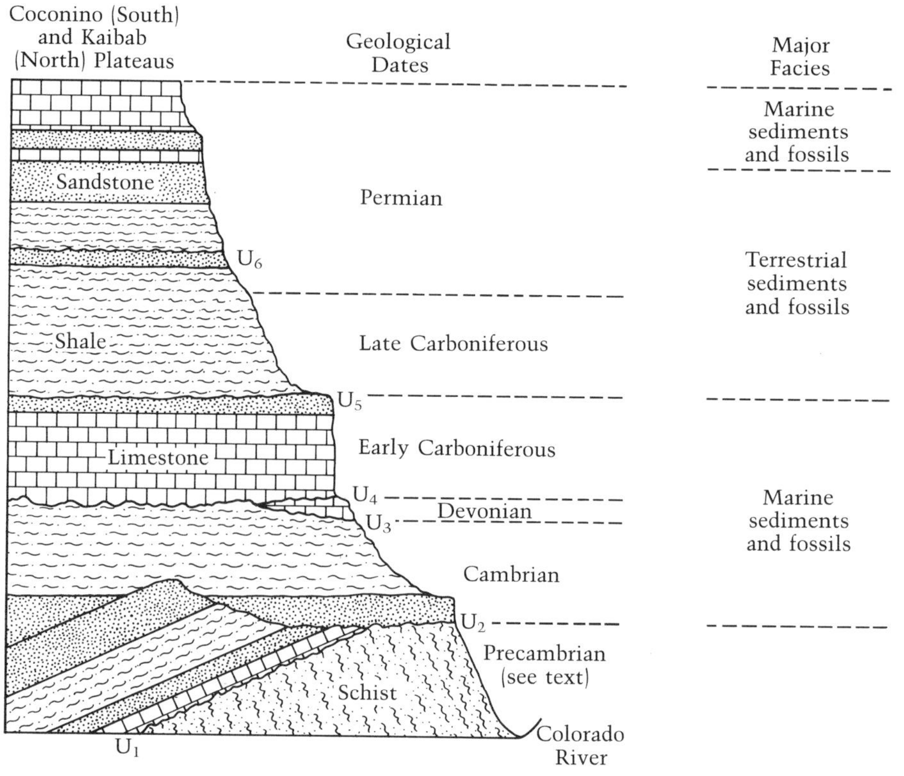

(b)

(a) *View of the north rim of the deepest part of the Grand Canyon.* (b) *Geological analysis of the rocks seen in* (a). *The rocks shown in this diagram are all visible in the photograph of the north rim shown in* (a), *but they are here represented in cross section. The vertical dimensions are drawn to scale over the total of approximately 1,600 vertical meters, but the horizontal distances are not to scale. At the bottom right, the schists are of early Precambrian age. They represent ancient sediments that were metamorphosed by heat and pressure during mountain building. The mountains were then eroded, and a nearly flat surface was formed, on which late Precambrian sediments were deposited horizontally. These were later tilted, as shown at the bottom left, and an irregular new surface with block mountains was formed. Above this, a long succession of strata (all of them still horizontal) was deposited. The wavy lines in the diagram labeled U_1 to U_6 represent ancient erosional surfaces and also lapses of geological time during which no sediments were deposited (or the sediments were later eroded). In geological terms, these are major unconformities, which generally separate strata of distinctly different ages. U_1 is between the early and late Precambrian rocks, U_2 between Precambrian and Cambrian, and U_3 between Cambrian and Devonian. Note that Ordovician and Silurian strata are not present and that the Devonian suffered considerable erosion and is discontinuous. U_4 is between Devonian and early Carboniferous rocks, U_5 between early and late Carboniferous. U_6 is within the Permian, which is here not wholly continuous.*

many different partial sequences of superposition in various regions. Here again the principle is simple, although the practice can be complicated. The principle is that of *correlation,* determination that the age of a given stratum in one region is at least approximately the same as that of a stratum in a different region. In its simplest possible form, this can be exemplified diagrammatically by using letters to represent the ages of strata, from *a,* the oldest, onward, in two short but continuous regional sequences:

First region		Second region
		e
		d
c	← correlation →	*c*
b		
a		

From such a correlation, the geological time sequence from older to younger is clearly given as *a–b–c–d–e.*

It frequently happens that there are breaks, that is, times not represented by strata, in one sequence that can be filled in from another. In simplest diagrammatic form:

First region		Second region
e	←correlation→	*e*
d		
c	←correlation→	*c*
		b
a	←correlation→	*a*

Here, although the sequence *a–b–c–d–e* is not complete in either region, it is determined by correlation between the two, which shows that time *b* is not represented by strata in the first region and time *d* is not represented in the second.

Such piecing together requires some way to determine whether strata in different regions are of the same geological age. That was done classically, and is still done usually, by comparisons of fossils from the two. In the broadest possible way, the more the fossils from one stratum in one area resemble those from a stratum in another area, the more likely it is that the strata in the two areas are of the same age. That follows from the fact that the communities of organisms have changed steadily since a time not long (geologically speaking) after the origin of life. The changes are evident in terms of the taxa of fossils (those groups identified and named) at various times and places. The resemblances and the changes are relative to the taxonomic level—for example, the presence of identical species suggests a closer time relationship than the identity of some families but of no genera or species. The resemblance or difference at any stated taxonomic level can be qualified in various ways—for example, by simple percentages of taxa in common or by such a formula as 100 (C/N_1), in which C is the number of taxa in common and N_1 is the number in the biota with fewer taxa.

A relatively simple and straightforward example of paleontological correlation is provided by land mammals from strata known as the Hiawatha member of the Wasatch formation in northwestern Colorado. The data here used were given, in more detail and in different form, in a monograph by Malcolm C. McKenna. There are 54 definitely distinct species in the collection studied. (The distinction of four more seems uncertain.) Of those, 26 (or 48 percent) were either not precisely identifiable specifically or belonged to species of hitherto unknown age. Twenty-eight (or 52 percent) of the distinct species were identified as previously known in faunas of established age. Most of these previously known species—that is, 25 (or 89 percent)—were known in faunas from a part of the early Eocene epoch designated as the Graybullian subage. A few of those species (seven of the 25) known were also from somewhat earlier and somewhat later parts of the early Eocene. Three species had been known from the late Paleocene epoch but had not previously been known to have survived into the early Eocene. There is no doubt at all that this fauna and the rocks containing it were correctly correlated with those on which the subage and biostratigraphic assemblage zone designated Graybullian were defined. Even the species not previously known in faunas of that subage and zone support the conclusion, because they belong to genera known earlier or later, and they fit into their evolutionary sequences at this stratigraphic level or part of geological time.

A moment's thought brings to mind a problem in the general application of such an apparently simple approach. Obviously, the biocenoses now living in the seas and on the lands are of exactly the same age, but they have almost no taxonomic resemblance. That has been true ever since there have been land plants and animals, some four hundred million years ago. Thus, direct correlation of marine and continental, or nonmarine, strata by their fossils alone is practically impossible. That is why, at the level of relatively small segments of geological time—for example, stages (or zones, in biostratigraphic terms)—different designations are commonly used for marine and nonmarine rock sequences. Still the placing of these in parallel within the broader span of geological time is possible because marine and nonmarine strata are often interbedded or are both present within observed sequences.

Another problem in correlation arises from the familiar fact that biotas in a given sort of environment—say, marine or land animals and plants—differ quite markedly today from one sea or from one continent to another. That has been true in varying degrees throughout geological time. For example, the areas now in North America and those now in Europe had generally similar land mammalian faunas in the early Eocene, and the rocks containing those faunas can thus be rather closely correlated. Later in the Eocene, those faunas became increasingly different, and correlation therefore becomes increasingly complex. The explanation now established is that North America and Europe formed a single land mass in the early Eocene, but they rifted apart at about the end of that time and began to move in opposite directions, a very slow but steady drift still going on today.

The greatest difficulties in paleontological correlation arise when a region has been effectively isolated for long stretches of geological time so that its biotas evolved there in relative, or even in complete, independence from those of any other region. The most striking example known is South America, which was an island continent from some time in the Cretaceous period until some time in the Pliocene epoch. Although two groups of land mammals (rodents and primates) did somehow cross the surrounding marine barriers toward the end of the Eocene, throughout most of the Cenozoic era, the South American land faunas, evolving in almost complete isolation, were so different from those of any other region that direct paleontological correlation of them is almost impossible.

The sequence *within* South America, although still being refined, was fairly well established two generations ago. For correlation throughout that continent, there are now named provincial ages based mainly on the succession of evolving land mammals. Broadly approximate or conventional equivalence with parts of the North American or European sequences could be roughly determined from the fact that, in some places, South American rocks containing land faunas overlie or underlie rocks with marine invertebrate faunas, mostly mollusks. These can be approximately correlated by paleontological resemblances with other parts of the world. Thus a South American land fauna in rocks above, and hence younger than, the marine rocks or in rocks below, and hence older than, the latter could be placed approximately in the worldwide biostratigraphic sequence.

It is always useful and sometimes necessary for increasing accuracy of stratigraphic correlation that paleontological correlation be supplemented by other methods. That is now actively going forward. Geologists, paleontologists, and an interested lay public also want to know what the ages of rocks and fossils are, not only their relative ages (their position relative to other rocks and fossils in a sequence) but also their absolute ages (in terms of numbers of years). During the nineteenth century, attempts to give geological dates in years were merely wild guesses, hardly ever anywhere near the mark. Only early in the twentieth century were methods developed that were sound in principle and promising in prospect. The first such methods were based on phenomena of radioactivity and, with an ever-widening repertory, those are still the methods most used.

The basis of radiometric dating is that some elements, or some isotopes of elements, undergo what is usually called radioactive decay, by which one element or isotope changes into another or into a succession of others. These

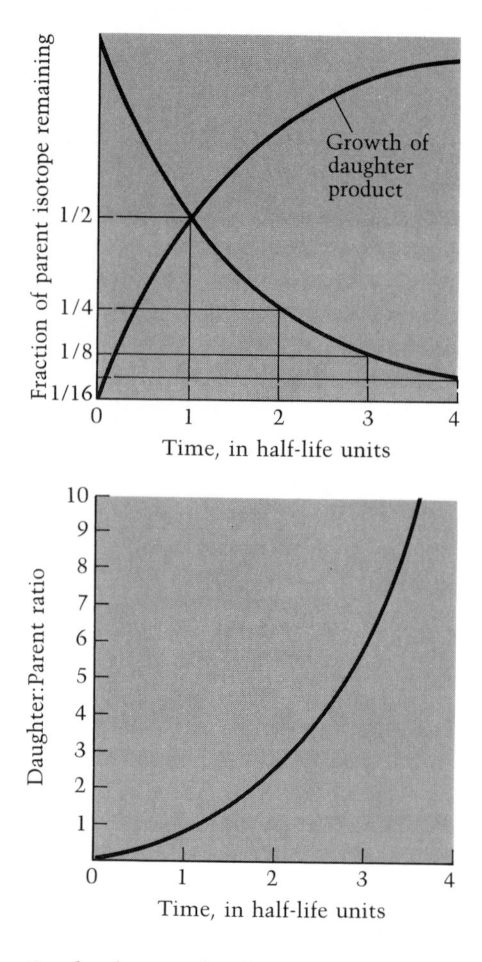

Graphs showing the disintegration of a radioactive element (such as ^{40}K) in a mineral, the growth of a stable "daughter" element (such as ^{40}Ar), and the ratio of daughter to parent.

changes occur at very steady rates, and there is no reason to believe that these rates have changed in the course of geological time. The rates are usually expressed as half-lives, a half-life being the time it takes for one-half of the original element to change into another. When the rate is known and the amounts of the original element and of the result of its decay are measured, it is in principle fairly simple to calculate how long the process has been going on.

The early radiometric dates were usually based on an isotope of uranium, the original element, and an isotope of lead, the result of its radioactive decay. The isotope uranium-235 (or ^{235}U) decays to lead-207 (^{207}Pb) with a half-life of 7.13×10^8, or 713,000,000 years. Uranium-238 (^{238}U) decays to lead-206 (^{206}Pb) with a half-life of 4.51×10^9 or 4,510,000,000 years. Those long half-lives make dating by the uranium–lead method potentially cover even more than the total age of the earth, but several other radiometric methods are now also employed. Of these, the most widely used one at present is based on the isotope potassium-40 (^{40}K), the "parent," which decays to argon-40 (^{40}A), the "daughter," with a half-life of 1.3×10^9 or 1,300,000,000 years. This is also applicable for all of geological time, because radiometric dating can be applied to ages that are multiples of a half-life. Probably the best-known (or at least the most publicized) kind of radiometric dating depends on the decay of carbon-14 (^{14}C). The method is based on principles different from those on which uranium–lead or potassium–argon dating are based but also involving the half-life. Carbon-14 has such a short half-life, less than 6,000 years, that it generally is not useful for dates older than about 60,000 years before the present. It has been a boon for anthropologists and archaeologists, but its scope is too limited to be of much interest to paleontologists.

There are some other methods that produce at least approximate geological dates in years, but these need not all be considered here. I will just mention one more: fission-track dating. Radioactive atoms in crystals, either as constituents of a mineral or as trace elements in one, progressively produce tracks that can be observed and used for dating by a rather elaborate procedure. This sometimes provides dates when no other method is applicable.

The existence of a number of methods by which ages in years (or so-called absolute dates) can be obtained has suggested that any other time scale or method of correlation may not now or eventually be necessary. Nevertheless, geologists and paleontologists continue to use the relative or sequential geological time scale and to rely strongly on paleontological correlation. There are two main reasons for this. First, even with a whole battery of methods for determining so-called absolute ages, there are many rocks to which none of them can be usefully applied. Most igneous rocks can be so dated, but many sedimentary rocks cannot, and with few exceptions fossils are found in the latter. Second, none of the methods of absolute dating is precise. Even with the most favorable circumstances and the best techniques, there is always a margin of possible error, usually estimated statistically and entered as "standard error." Within a given paleoecological province, paleontological or biostratigraphic correlation based on careful

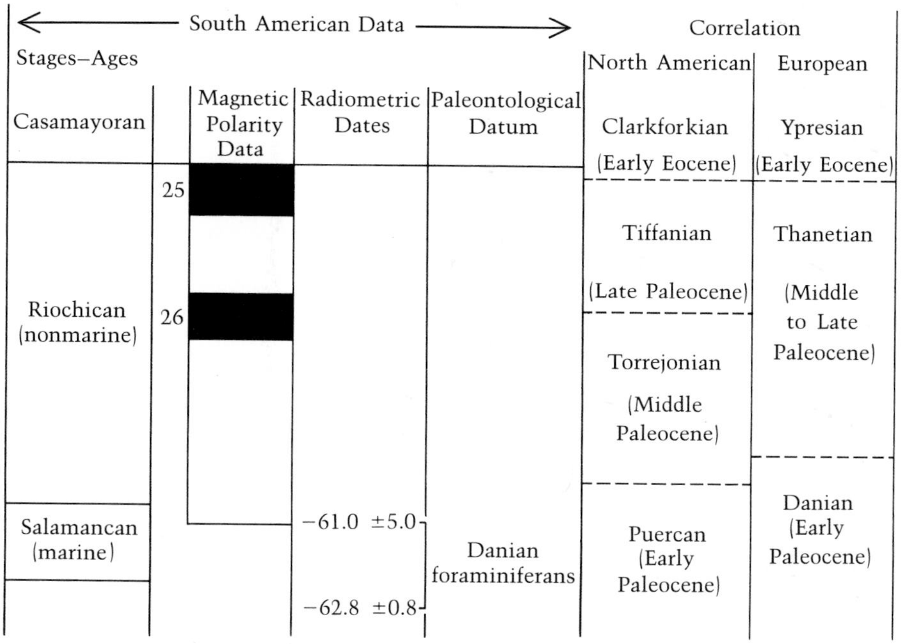

South American Data					Correlation	
Stages–Ages		Magnetic Polarity Data	Radiometric Dates	Paleontological Datum	North American	European
Casamayoran					Clarkforkian (Early Eocene)	Ypresian (Early Eocene)
Riochican (nonmarine)	25				Tiffanian (Late Paleocene)	Thanetian (Middle to Late Paleocene)
	26				Torrejonian (Middle Paleocene)	
Salamancan (marine)			−61.0 ±5.0	Danian foraminiferans	Puercan (Early Paleocene)	Danian (Early Paleocene)
			−62.8 ±0.8			

An intercontinental correlation by the conjunction of three methods. The Riochican stage in Patagonian Argentina is conformable above with Casamayoran and below with Salamancan—that is, these three stratigraphic stages represent essentially continuous sedimentation without significant time gaps. The known fossil fauna of the Riochican is so different from that of any other continent that it cannot be well correlated with faunas in North America or Europe on paleontological grounds alone. Magnetic-polarity determinations have found two anomalies in polarity here represented by the black bars. As isolated events, these could not be correlated with particular anomalies on other continents. However, two radiometric dates (here given in millions of years before the present), one in the upper part of the Salamancan and one just below it, are evidence that the two Riochican anomalies should be the earliest ones after approximately 61 million years before the present. To this evidence is added that of the foraminiferans in the marine Salamancan stage, which are similar to those known in the European marine Danian stage. The combination of these three sorts of data indicates the probability of the correlations shown. This also indicates that the two polarity anomalies are the twenty-fifth and the twenty-sixth before the present in the sequence established in North America and Europe.

field records and adequate fossil sampling usually gives better resolution (that is, resolving power or closeness of estimate or equivalence in time) than can be obtained by any nonpaleontological method. That is often true even between provinces that are somewhat remote from each other.

What the mainly radiometric methods have done and continue to do is to provide a framework of absolute time into which the subdivisions of the sequential geological time scale can be approximately fitted, as has here been done in the table on page 59.

Another promising adjunct for geological dating developed from the fairly recent discovery that the magnetic poles of the earth have repeatedly reversed from time to time. The magnetic pole we call "north," merely by convention, has often been in what we now call the "south" of the earth. Positions of the "north" and "south" magnetic poles in the geological past can often be determined from rocks, both igneous and sedimentary. Many of these rocks contain minerals influenced by magnetism that tended to orient themselves along the earth's magnetic lines of force as they were when the igneous rock solidified or the sediment was deposited. Such rocks may have been affected by later magnetic changes, but there are ways of erasing the effects of these changes and revealing and measuring the original magnetic orientation, now called *remanent* (a word related to, but not the same as, *remnant*). An incidental discovery is that what we call "reversed" magnetism has been more prevalent in geological history than "normal" magnetism, so called because it is the way things are now.

(a) *A greatly enlarged fossil colony of blue-green algae (cyanobacteria) from the Gunflint Chert. The bacteria and cyanobacteria are the oldest known fossils. The age of this specimen is about two billion years.* (b) *Domal, recent stromatolites from the intertidal zone of Hamelin Pool, Shark Bay, Western Australia. These forms and other modern examples are produced by the ability of cyanobacteria to trap, bind, and precipitate sediment.* (c) *Cross section of a domal stromatolite from the Cambrian of South Australia.*

What that has to do with geological dating arises from the acceptable, indeed fairly obvious, postulate that reversals of the magnetic poles affected local magnetic orientations identically and at the same time all over the earth. Thus, in their remanent magnetism, the rocks contain records of events that were simultaneous everywhere. Surely, this should be an aid to correlation, regardless of distance and of ecological and biological disparity—but there is a hitch: the record is simply an on-off binary signal. In itself, a time of "normal" magnetism a hundred years old cannot be distinguished from one a billion years old. Paleomagnetism alone does not measure time. To be useful in correlation, a paleomagnetic record must first be placed at least approximately in the geological time scale by paleontological or radiometric methods—or, ideally, by both. Then it may be possible, by means of the pattern of the paleomagnetic record, to make an exact correlation and to recognize in two or more places the identity of a particular switch from "normal" to "reversed," or vice versa. The application of this both to long-range and to short-range correlation is the aim of much current research. There is one other hitch: there have been geologically long times during which a magnetic polarity switch did not occur. Closer correlation within those spans cannot be obtained by paleomagnetic methods.

Now, having discussed some of the methods and results of the study of geological time, we can turn to a necessarily sketchy review of the history of organisms as seen within this temporal frame.

It is not surprising that the record of fossils in the longest, earliest part of geological time, the Precambrian, is relatively scanty. We would expect the early and primitive forms of life to have been tiny—indeed, individually microscopic—and to have had few or no parts that could have been readily preserved as fossils or that would be recognizable as such. It also militates against the preservation of an extensive early record that the older Precambrian rocks, especially, have been subjected to much pressure, heat, and deformation that would tend to erase most traces of fossils. In spite of those factors, diligent search has produced a considerable array of Precambrian fossils, and their known number is increasing.

Some inferences from the Precambrian record were discussed in Chapter 2 from a paleoecological point of view. The oldest known fossils resemble bacteria and the so-called blue-green algae, or cyanophytes, many of which are not blue-green and all of which are quite distinct from the more advanced, true algae. The bacteria and the cyanophytes have long been considered the most primitive living organisms, and the Precambrian fossil record shows that they were among the oldest, and perhaps indeed the very oldest, of true organisms. The bacterialike fossils and some of the cyanophytelike ones have been preserved in chert, a form of silica (silicon dioxide, $Si0_2$), in several places, notably in Canada, Australia, and South Africa.

The most conspicuous and widespread, but not the oldest, Precambrian fossils are calcareous masses called stromatolites, which were formed by mats or clumps of algae, in the broadest sense of that word. In the Precambrian, the oldest ones were apparently made by cyanophytes, but in the latter part of that long time true

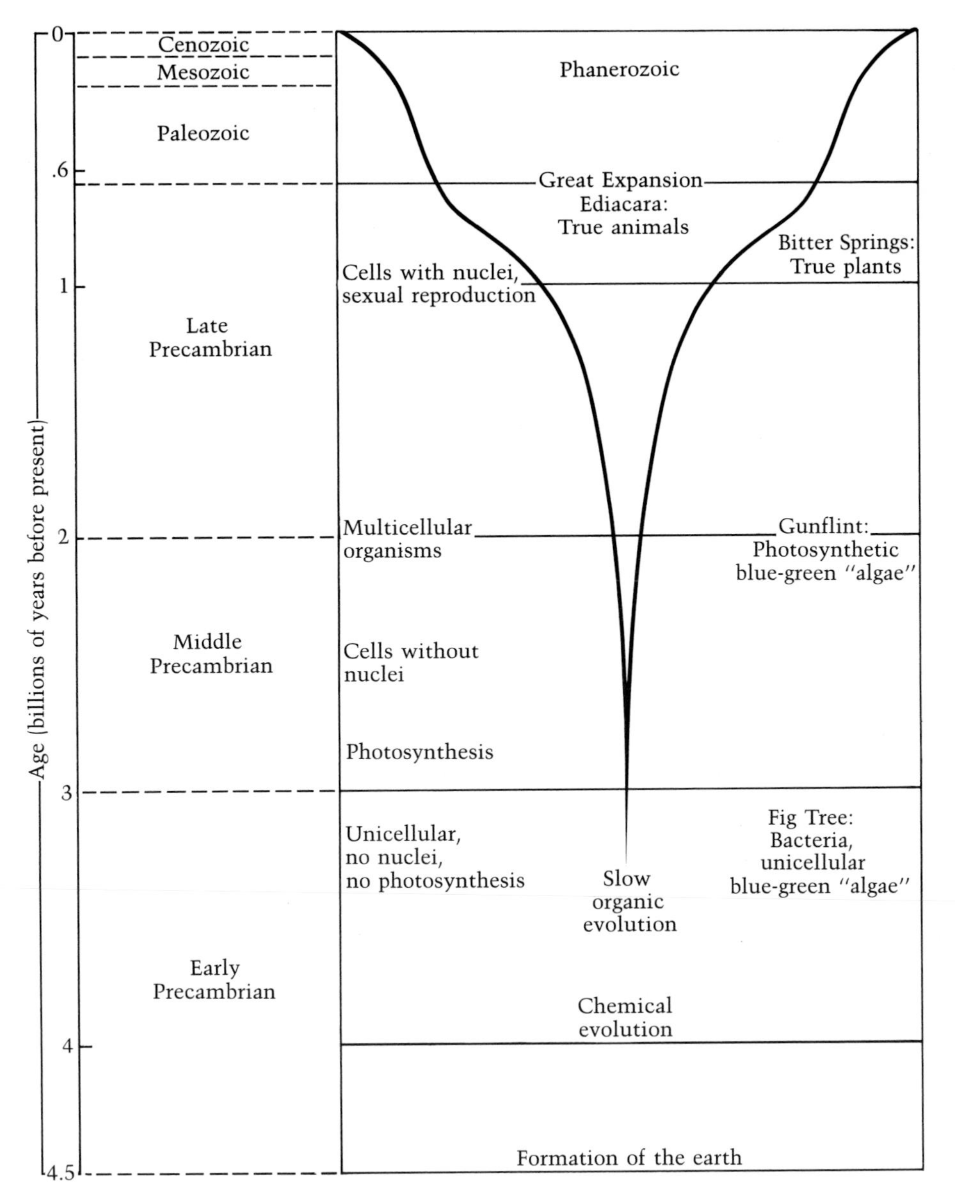

An overview of the history of life. The expanding graph approximates the expansion of organisms as a whole. To the left are approximations of steps in the early expansion, variety, and complication of Precambrian organisms. In the center above and to the right are names of some of the geological formations containing Precambrian fossils and a brief notice of what was new among these fossils. The Ediacara and Bitter Springs formations are in Australia, the Gunflint is in Canada, and the Fig Tree is in South Africa. The word "algae" is in quotes for the organisms usually called blue-green algae because they are more nearly related to bacteria than to true algae. They are sometimes called "cyanobacteria" (blue-green bacteria) or "cyanophytes" (blue-green plants).

algae were also present in the mats that formed stromatolites. The most important difference is that cyanophytes are prokaryotic—that is, their cells do not contain nuclei. In true algae, more evolved plants, one-celled animals (protozoans), and all more evolved animals (metazoans), the cells are eukaryotic—that is, they contain nuclei, which largely control (or affect) their living processes and reproduction. Stromatolites, varying in shape and contents, continued to form in marine environments throughout following geological history, and they are still forming today.

Until little more than thirty years ago, no true many-celled animals, or metazoans, were surely known from the Precambrian. Because they were already abundant and diverse early in the Cambrian period, the apparent absence of metazoans from the Precambrian had long been one of the greatest problems in deciphering the history of life. Then, in 1947, various unquestionable metazoans

(a)

(b)

Two of the oldest known true animals from the Ediacara fauna in Australia: (a) Dickinsonia *and* (b) Spriggina. *All the fossils in this fauna are soft-bodied invertebrates preserved as impressions in what was soft, fine-grained sand when they were buried. Both of those shown here resemble some living segmented wormlike animals, but others in this fauna are more complex, resembling jellyfish and sea pens, and still others are unlike any other known animals.*

(a)

(b)

A richly fossiliferous slab of rock from the late Jurassic of West Germany (a). *The most obvious fossils are two quite different kinds of cephalopod mollusks. The ribbed, tightly coiled shells are ammonoids of the genus* Perisphinctes. *The straight dark objects that look like fountain pens are the hard tips of internal shells of a group of cephalopods that resembled the living squids. Except for fossils of this kind, which as a group are called belemnites, the animals were soft-bodied and are rarely preserved as wholes.* (b) *A slab with* Uintacrinus socialis, *abundant and worldwide late Cretaceous species of stemless crinoids.*

were discovered in the Ediacara Hills (the accent is on the first *a*) in South Australia, some 300 miles (about 485 kilometers) north of Adelaide. Those fossils are of late Precambrian age, on the order of 600,000,000 years before the present. They represent a whole assemblage of animals that lived on mud flats in shallow marine waters. Included are jellyfish, sea pens (relatives of corals), segmented worms (annelids), and some strange forms that are clearly animals but are unlike any of those known in later faunas.

Similar faunas of about the same age have since been discovered at a number of places on other continents, and it seems that the Ediacara faunas, as they are called in a general sense, were worldwide. All the animals were soft-bodied and were preserved in the rocks (as molds and casts) only under somewhat excep-

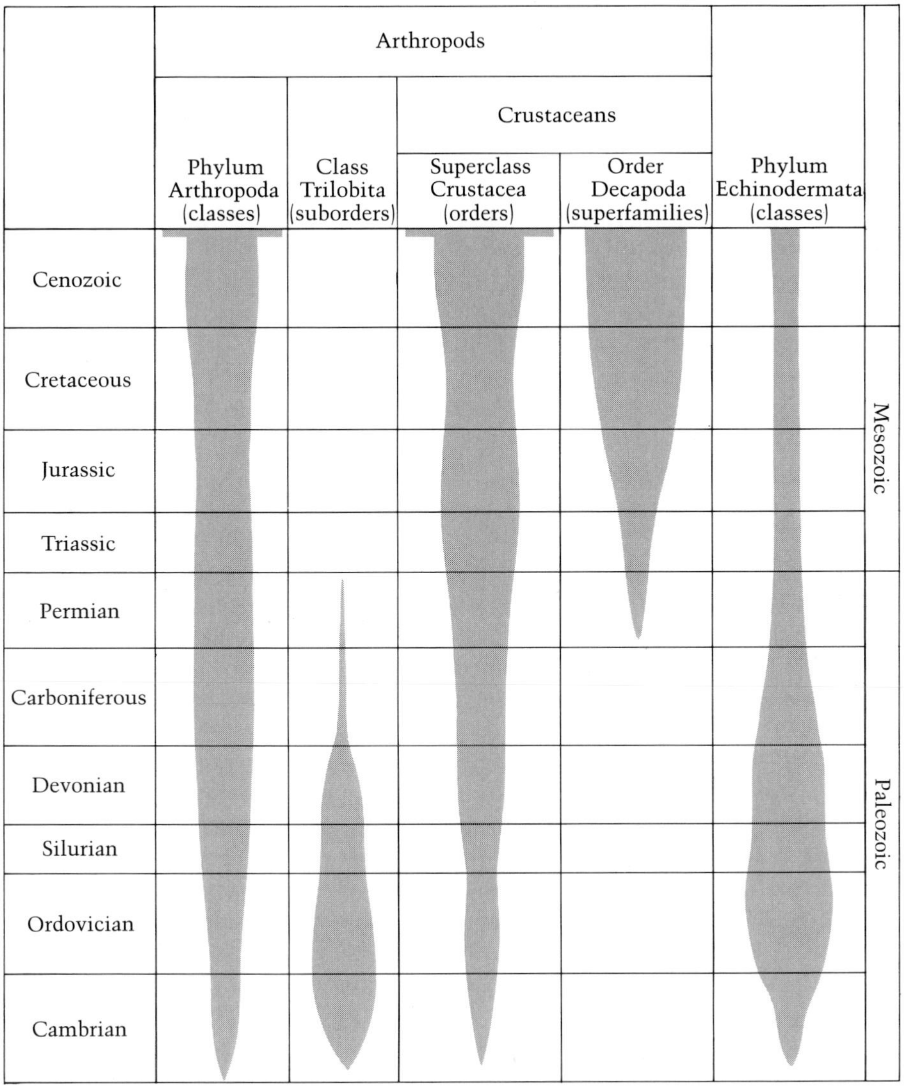

Arthropods
Crustaceans
Phylum Arthropoda (classes)
Class Trilobita (suborders)
Superclass Crustacea (orders)
Order Decapoda (superfamilies)
Phylum Echinodermata (classes)
Cenozoic
Cretaceous
Jurassic
Triassic
Permian
Carboniferous
Devonian
Silurian
Ordovician
Cambrian
Mesozoic
Paleozoic

The diversity through geological time of two of the animal phyla with fossil records that are among the most extensive. The taxa of the phylum Arthropoda have been highly diverse through most of the time from the Cambrian onward. Today they are incomparably the most diverse of all animals. Just one of their classes, Insecta, now probably has more species than all other classes of animals put together. The classification of arthropods here followed has 26 classes in all. Nine of these are not known as fossils: they are shown by the abrupt widening of the top of the leftmost graft. Only four arthropod classes, as here recognized, are extinct. The main expansion in diversity of major taxa occurred in the middle of the Paleozoic. As the graph shows, the suborders of the extinct class Trilobita expanded in number rapidly in the early Paleozoic and then slowly waned to extinction near the end of that era. The number of orders of the superclass Crustacea expanded only slowly during the Paleozoic but steadily on through the Mesozoic and the Cenozoic. Here, as in the graph of Arthropoda as a whole, the abrupt widening at the top of the graph is to indicate the number of taxa not known as fossils—13 orders, in this case. The order Decapoda, which includes shrimp, crayfishes, crabs, and lobsters, is highly diverse today. Only two of the 21 living superfamilies in this order are without known fossils.

The phylum Echinodermata includes five classes with living representatives—Crinoidea (sea lilies), Asteroidea (starfishes), Ophiuroidea (brittle stars), Echinoidea (sea urchins), and Holothuroidea (sea cucumbers)—all of which have known fossil representatives. There are also many extinct classes whose members lived during the Paleozoic, most of them evolving rapidly in the Cambrian and Ordovician. The diversity of the echinoderms declined in the late Paleozoic and remained steady during the Mesozoic and Cenozoic, although of course there were constant changes at lower taxonomic levels throughout those eras.

tional circumstances—that is, when they were buried under fine sand. That goes far toward explaining why Precambrian fossil animals were not sooner found and still do not constitute an extensive record: All soft-bodied animals are rare as fossils throughout geological time. But there is still a mystery to speculate about: Why and how did many animals begin to have hard parts—skeletons of sorts—with apparent suddenness around the beginning of the Cambrian?

There have been other sporadic instances of the local preservation of soft-bodied animals in considerable number and variety—one from the Cambrian was mentioned in Chapter 1. The reasonably continuous fossil record is nevertheless

	Foraminifera (suborders)	Porifera (Sponges) (orders)	Archaeocyatha (orders)	Coelenterata (orders)	Brachiopoda (orders, suborders)
Cenozoic					
Cretaceous					
Jurassic					
Triassic					
Permian					
Carboniferous					
Devonian					
Silurian					
Ordovician					
Cambrian					

The diversity of foraminiferans and of ten groups of invertebrates in terms of the number of their major constituent taxa through geological time. Widths in the graphs are proportional to the diversity of those taxa. The data used are counts of taxa at successive geological times as given in the Treatise on Invertebrate Paleontology. *Such data are not entirely comparable from one group to another, because the authors of the papers on the various groups in the* Treatise *differ from paper to paper, and authors do not invariably have uniform criteria for taxonomic levels. This has to some extent been compensated for by using counts of orders in some cases and of suborders in others. The vertical scale is proportional to time in years.*

Foraminifers are small one-celled organisms, neither plants nor animals, making up the phylum Foraminifera of the kingdom Protista. The sponges, which constitute the phylum Porifera, are often classified as a subkingdom (Parazoa) of the kingdom Animalia; but, because they evidently had quite a different origin from the rest of the kingdom Animalia, some biologists argue that they are better considered as a kingdom by themselves. Ammonoidea (the ammonoids or ammonites) are an order of the class Cephalopoda in the phylum Mollusca. The ammonoids are therefore included in the counts of the orders of Cephalopoda. They are also here graphed by themselves in counts of superfamilies. This shows that their diversity at that level was markedly decreased three times by mass extinctions but soon, geologically speaking, returned by subsequent radiation. Some groups, such as the class Bivalvia (bivalves—clams and other two-shelled mollusks) and the phylum Brachiopoda (lamp shells) have maintained about the same degree of basic diversity since their early radiation. This does not indicate static evolution. Even when the number of supergeneric taxa remained about the same, there was much change in all cases within the taxa and some replacement of taxa at the same level. A few major taxa show an increase in major diversity more or less throughout their known history. In some cases, such as the phylum Coelen-

almost confined to those organisms that are most readily fossilizable, both because of their having characteristic hard parts and because of the favorable impact on them of taphonomic events. Thanks not only to classical paleobotany but also (and especially now) to palynology, there is a fairly good and constantly improving fossil record of the principal groups of vascular plants. Most, but not all, of these are land (or nonaquatic) plants. The essentially one-celled animallike protozoans include many practically nonfossilizable groups, but they also include the eminently fossilizable foraminifers or "forams." Of true (or metazoan) animals, the following major groups, at the level of phyla in the Linnaean system of classifica-

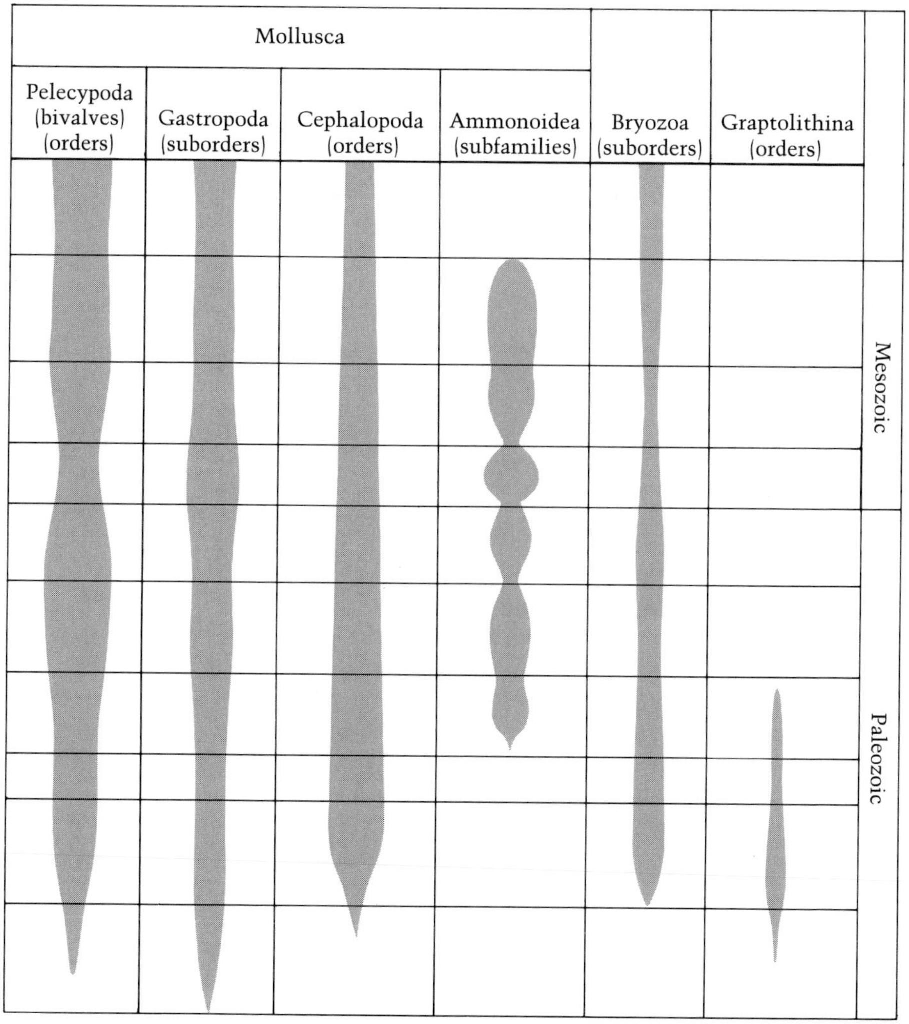

Mollusca
Pelecypoda (bivalves) (orders)
Gastropoda (suborders)
Cephalopoda (orders)
Ammonoidea (subfamilies)
Bryozoa (suborders)
Graptolithina (orders)
Mesozoic
Paleozoic

terata, an apparent sudden increase in the Recent epoch is due to the present existence of softbodied groups that have little or no preserved fossil record. The cephalopods, although still individually abundant (octopuses, squids), have undergone almost steady diminution of major diversity since their initial radiation in the Ordovician. Although they are not separately charted here, the nautiloids were included in that early radiation. They have a rich Paleozoic record, but they are now represented by a single genus (Nautilus) *with only six species.*

The groups selected here and those in the figure on page 73 are among those with exceptionally good fossil records. This is true even for such groups as Archaeocyatha and Graptolithina, whose known fossil records are relatively short.

tion, do include some poorly recorded or unrecorded soft-bodied animals but have fairly good to excellent fossil records:

- Archaeocyatha. This is a peculiar group that look like sponges but that are probably not especially related to them. They appeared at the beginning of the Cambrian and were soon very abundant worldwide, but they became extinct before that period ended.
- Coelenterata. This phylum includes the corals and a wide variety of their relatives. They have been abundant in almost all marine communities from the Cambrian to the present.

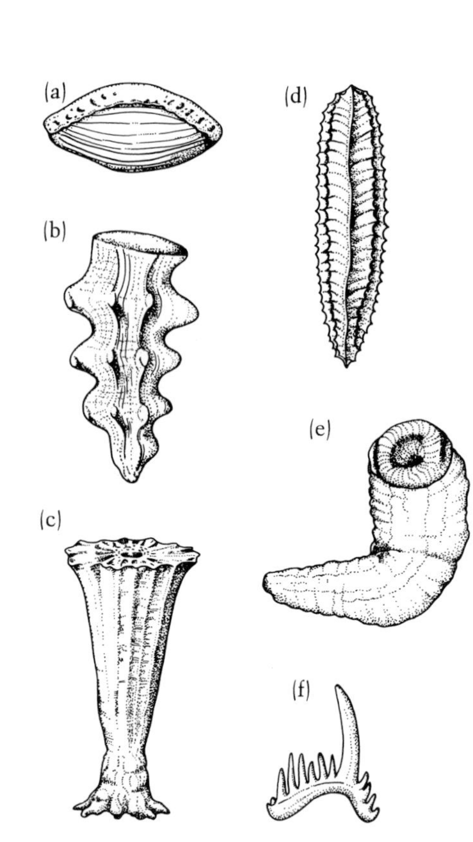

Representatives of some major groups of fossil organisms: (a) A one-celled protistan, the foraminiferan Triticites *from the Pennsylvanian period; about 6.4 millimeters wide. (b) The internal cast of a siliceous sponge,* Hydnoceras *(Porifera); about 20 centimeters high. (c)* Beltanacyathus, *a member of the extinct, entirely Cambrian phylum Archaeocyatha; about 18 centimeters high. (d)* Tetragraptus, *an Ordovician member of the extinct group Graptolithina (graptolites), of uncertain relationships but possibly an offshoot of the earliest chordates and hence of the ancestral prevertebrates; about 7.5 centimeters long. (e) A Carboniferous coral,* Canina; *about 9 centimeters along the curve. (f) A conodont,* Euprioniodina, *from the Devonian period; about 2 millimeters in width. The extinct (Ordovician to Triassic) conodonts are of uncertain relationships, but they were widespread and characteristic in form, and they are of considerable use in the correlation of strata.*

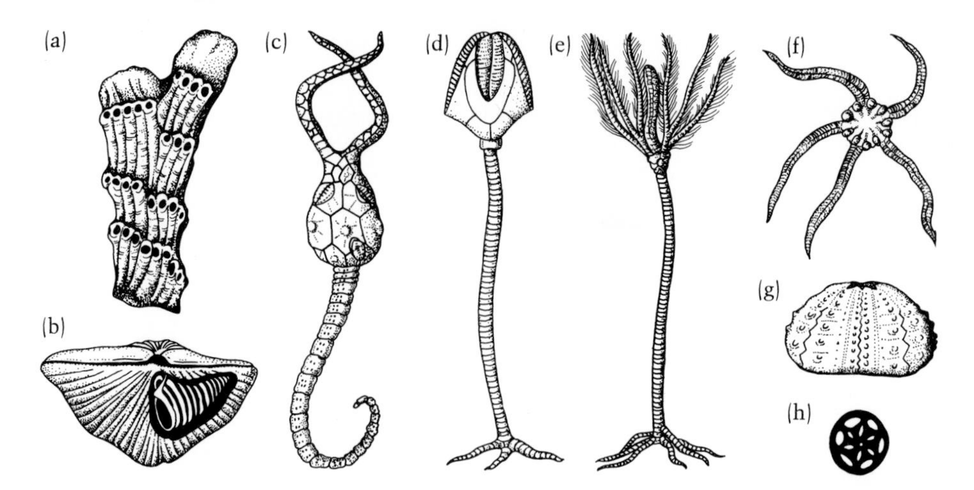

Fossil representation of some still living groups of animals prominent in the fossil record: (a) A Tertiary specimen of Spiropoda, *a bryozoan or "moss animal." This is a fragment, only about 6 millimeters long, of a larger colony. (b) A brachiopod or "lamp shell,"* Spirifer *from the Carboniferous. The shell has been cut open on one side to show the spiral brachidum or arm-bearer, a structure typical of this group and after whose form this genus was named. The width of the specimen is about 6.3 centimeters. (c) A specimen of an Ordovician cystoid,* Pleurocystites, *member of an extinct group of echinoderms, with an unattached stalk and two arms. Width across the body (calyx) is about 20 millimeters. (d) A specimen of* Pentremites, *a Carboniferous blastoid, an extinct group of echinoderms. The body or calyx, borne on a stem, is about 13 millimeters in width. (e) A crinoid or sea lily from the Silurian period,* Botriocrinus, *shown with its stem and "root." The height of the restored specimen is about 18 centimeters. (f) An ophiuroid or brittle star from the Jurassic,* Ophioderma, *a member of another group of echinoderms. The width across the extended arms is about 18 centimeters. (g) Still another echinoderm, an echinoid or sea urchin,* Goniopygus, *from the Cretaceous. The calcareous test or shell is composed of separate but closely interlocking plates, which are only sketchily shown in this diagram. In life, numerous spines projected from the test, but in this specimen, as in most fossil sea urchins, the spines had been lost before fossilization. The width is about 4.5 centimeters. (h) A single plate (or sclerite) from a Carboniferous holothurian, or sea cucumber,* Palaeochiridota. *Unlike other echinoderms, the holothurians do not have tests or external plates, and known fossils of whole bodies are therefore extremely rare. However, the thick skins contain many microscopic calcareous sclerites, which have highly varied and characteristic forms. These are fairly numerous in some marine strata from the Ordovician to the Recent. The diameter of this particular sclerite is only about 0.3 millimeter.*

- Bryozoa. The sea mosses or moss animals, now often considered to constitute two separate phyla, appeared in the Ordovician period and have been abundant in the oceans ever since.
- Brachiopoda. Sometimes called lampshells, brachiopods were abundant in all Paleozoic periods. They were less common thereafter, but they still survive.
- Mollusca. The extremely abundant and diverse mollusks include, among other things, snails (gastropods), bivalves (such as clams and oysters), and the cephalopods (now represented by squids, octopuses, and the chambered nautilus, and including a once extremely abundant but now extinct group, the ammonites).

The top two rows of figures at the right are representatives of some of the groups of mollusks (phylum Mollusca) especially notable in the fossil record: (a) *One of the two shells of a pelecypod (bivalve), the Devonian* Limoptera. *The width of the specimen is about 4.5 centimeters.* (b) Conus, *a gastropod genus abundant and diversified in the Cenozoic. This specimen, from the Tertiary period, is about two centimeters long.* (c) *A Silurian specimen of* Tentaculites; *similar shells range from the Ordovician to the Devonian, but thereafter they become extinct. They are generally considered to be mollusks; but their relationships are uncertain, although they were abundant and their hard structure is well known. The original specimen is nearly 13 millimeters long.* (d) *A nautiloid cephalopod,* Goldringia, *from the Devonian. Many nautiloids, like the sole living genus* Nautilus, *were tightly coiled, but in the Paleozoic some were orthoconic (that is, straight without coiling) and some, like* Goldringia, *were gyroconic (that is, openly coiled). The greatest distance across the specimen shown is about 13 centimeters.* (e) *The Cretaceous ammonite* Baculites. *This is a very young shell, which began as a tight curl and then continued to grow in a straight sequence of chambers. Older specimens generally have lost the initial coil, and some became much larger and longer. This specimen had attained only the length of about 8 millimeters.* (e′) *A segment of a much larger, adult specimen of* Baculites *showing one of the complex suture lines formed by the contact of partitions between the chambers with the outer shell. The width of the part shown is 4.5 centimeters. Throughout the history of the group, most ammonites were tightly coiled, but some (especially in the later Mesozoic) evolved modified forms—some straight (as in* Baculites*) and some odd, even bizarrely twisted.*

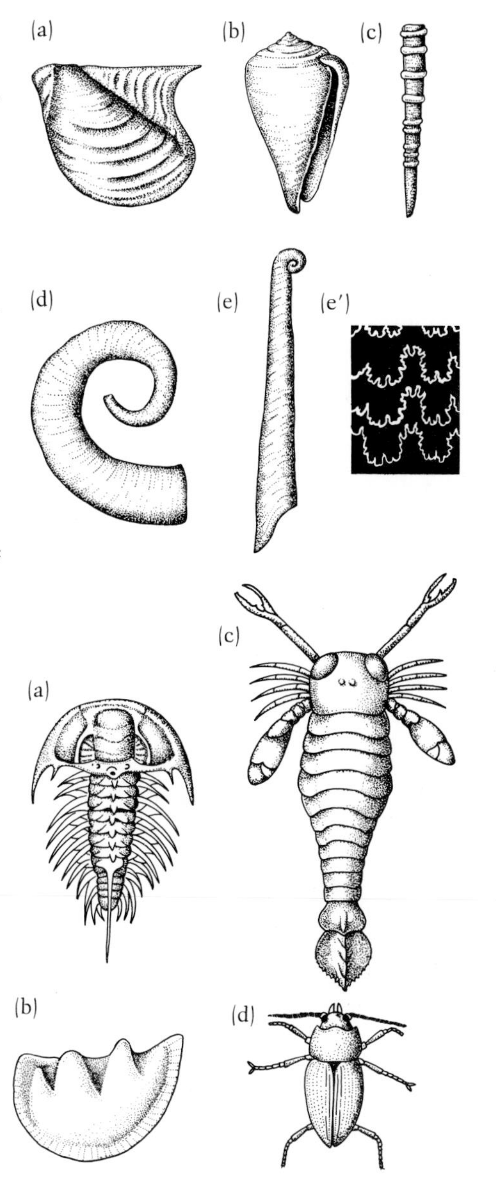

The four figures on the left are representatives of just a few of the very numerous major groups of arthropods (phylum Arthropoda) in the fossil record: (a) *Cambrian* Zacanthoides, *an early but typical trilobite in dorsal view. The total length of the specimen is nearly 4 centimeters.* (b) *A Silurian ostracod,* Kyamodes. *Ostracods, numerous since the Cambrian and still so today, are mostly very small crustaceans that form two shells, which are usually all of them that is found fossilized. The shell here shown is only about 2 millimeters in its greatest dimension.* (c) *A Silurian eurypterid,* Pterygotus. *The eurypterids ranged from the Ordovician to the Permian, and the living horseshoe crabs are their closest surviving relatives (although they are quite different in appearance). Some eurypterids were gigantic as arthropods go. This specimen is about 1.7 meters in length.* (d) *A Jurassic beetle,* Tauredon. *Insects are much the most diverse animals today, and beetles are the most diverse insects. This somewhat run-of-the-mill ancient beetle is about 25 millimeters in body length.*

- Arthropoda. This is now the most diverse and abundant of all animal phyla because it includes the insects (along with other groups of survivors and a number of once abundant groups that are now extinct).
- Echinodermata. The star fishes, the sea urchins, and their many marine relatives, surviving and extinct, have been very abundant in seas from the Ordovician onward.
- Graptolithina. This is an enigmatic group that appeared well along in the Cambrian period and became extinct by the end of the Carboniferous. As noted parenthetically below, the graptolites may or may not have been an offshoot of early chordates.

- Chordata. This is the phylum to which we and other vertebrates belong. The subphylum Vertebrata in general terms consists of the fishes, amphibians, reptiles, birds, and mammals. (The subphyla of living chordates that do not have segmented backbones and thus are not vertebrates are the Hemichordata, which includes the so-called acorn worms and the pterobranchs; the Urochordata or Tunicata, sometimes called the sea squirts; and the Cephalochordata, the lancelets, typified by the animal often called *Amphioxus* although its correct name is *Branchiostoma.* Those three groups must have branched off separately from the ancestry of the vertebrates before the evolution of the latter had reached the vertebrate level. All are soft-bodied, and their entire fossil record consists of a few fossil pterobranchs—unless some authorities are followed in classifying the graptolites as related to the pterobranchs and placing them in the phylum Chordata.)

The spread of marine invertebrates was certainly accelerated around the beginning of the Cambrian, but the rapidity of their major deployment has sometimes been exaggerated. The Cambrian and Ordovician were unusually long periods, the two together spanning some 140,000,000 years. During that time, there was a progressive and great increase in the basic diversity of aquatic animals. By the end of the Ordovician, all the major phyla of the more readily fossilizable animals were definitely present, as were several of the phyla of less fossilizable ones, such as some of the quite diverse groups colloquially lumped as "worms," known from sporadic discoveries with unusual preservation of fossils, such as those from the Cambrian at Mount Burgess in Canada.

It is probable that most of the animal phyla—perhaps all of them—had become differentiated by the end of the Ordovician. Thereafter, there was considerable fluctuation—including, for example, a drop involving unusually widespread extinctions between the Permian and Triassic periods. That episode was the basis for separating the two periods and, with them, the Paleozoic and Mesozoic eras. It is probable that the marine ecological niches, themselves fluctuating in number and kind, remained essentially filled. One striking expansion is evident in the appearance of the most advanced group of bony fishes, those usually classified in an infraclass or superorder called Teleostei (from the Greek *teleos,* meaning "perfect," and *osteon,* "bone"). (Incidentally, the *tele-* in "telephone" and "television" means "far" in Greek but in the Greek alphabet is spelled differently from the *tele-* that means "perfect.") The bony fishes reached this evolutionary level in the Jurassic period and thereafter expanded enormously, becoming amazingly diverse by the beginning of the Cenozoic era. Since then, they have been the dominant fishes both in the seas and in fresh waters.

Some of the most interesting events seen in the fossil record are indicated at their approximate geological ages in the table on page 59. Note that, in such tables, "first" means "oldest now known." It is always possible that further work will turn up records somewhat older. From the Cambrian onward, it is now unlikely that new discoveries will push such appearances back very much. In the Precambrian era, fairly recent studies have pushed back very significantly the earliest known date for organisms, and therefore the latest possible date for the

From the Burgess Shale of British Columbia, a typical annelid, Canadia spinosa, *a polychaete worm of the Cambrian period. Its setae, bundles of fine bristles that functioned as organs of locomotion, are preserved in detail.*

origin of life. It is highly probable that the earliest positively established date for (metazoan) animals will also be pushed back quite significantly, because the Ediacara faunas indicate that, by then animals had been evolving for a geologically appreciable length of time.

Although most or all of the animal phyla existed in the Cambrian and Ordovician and all of those known but two (both of doubtful status) still exist, they have all changed very markedly since their first appearance. These changes have been complex and different in each case, but, in general, they have involved interactions especially of three kinds of evolutionary phenomena. One involves expansion and diversification, which is often manifestly adaptive to different ways of life or to different ecological niches and is therefore usually designated as adaptive radiation. That has occurred at one time or another in almost all the major groups of organisms, and its results at various levels can be seen all around us today. Think, for instance, of the enormous variety of passerine birds, the so-called songbirds or perching birds, all of which have adaptively radiated from a single ancestry in the Cretaceous period.

Another factor in the complex interplay of evolutionary histories is a change in structure within an evolving group. For example, the "perfectly bony" teleost fishes arose more or less gradually from a group of earlier bony fishes known as Holostei. This is one example of evolutionary modifications such as have occurred among most groups of organisms. In them there are marked changes, an extent of anatomical and functional remodeling, between an older group and a younger one derived from (but not necessarily replacing) the older. Such changes produce or define different structural levels, often referred to as "grades" by paleontologists and other students of evolution.

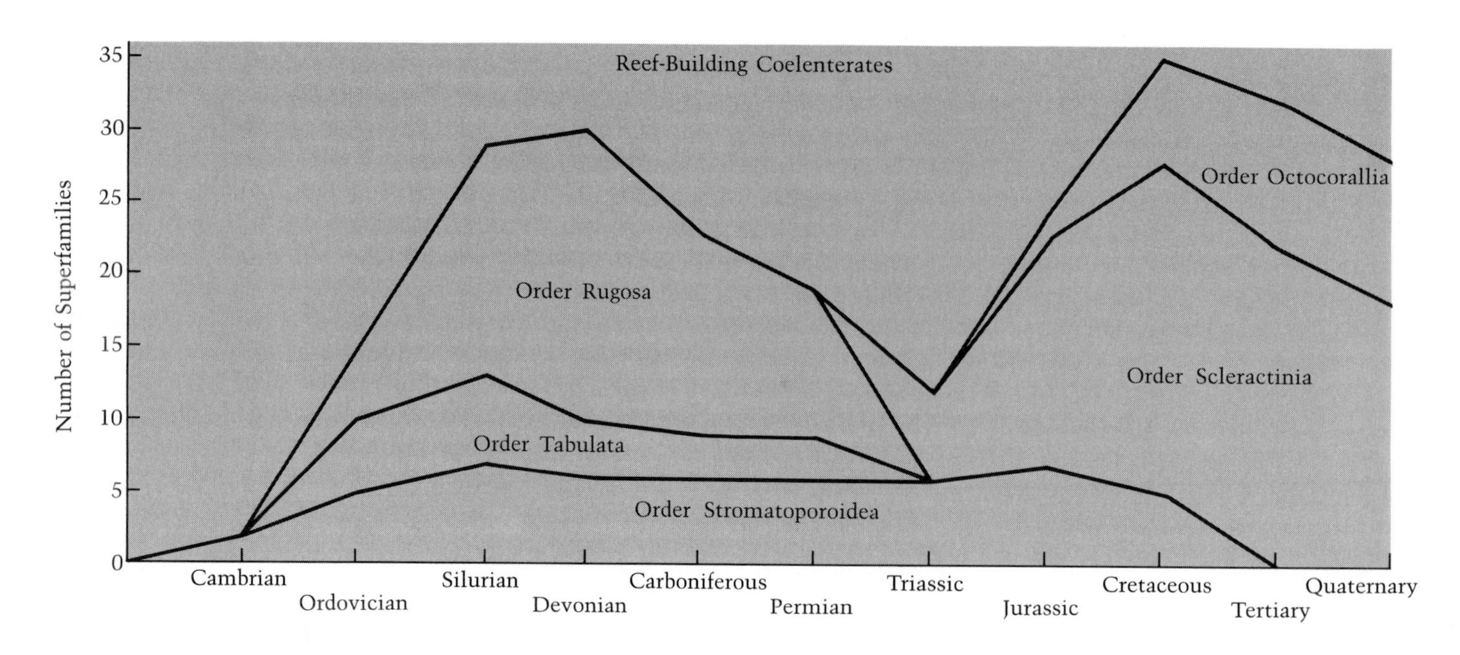

Evolutionary relay or replacement. The Rugosa, Tabulata, Octocorallia, and Scleractinia are different major groups (orders) of reef-building (hermatypic) corals. The Stromatoporoidea were also hermatypic coelenterates, and occurred along with corals, but are classified in the class Hydrozoa, while the corals and their closer allies are put in the class Anthozoa. The vertical scale shows the number of superfamilies. The marks on the horizontal axis (not the spaces between them) show the successive geological periods, and the graph shows the known number of superfamilies in each period as a point above the mark for that period. Thus the graph above the first mark shows that two superfamilies of stromatoporoids are known from the Cambrian but that Rugosa or Tabulata are not surely known before the Ordovician. Distances between the marks that indicate the periods have been made equal (for simplification) but it will be noted from the table on page 59 that the periods were not equal in length. This simplification does not affect the order or extent of the replacements that occurred after extinction of Rugosa and Tabulata in the Permian and of Stromatoporoidea in the Cretaceous.

A third phenomenon also frequently striking in the history of life is that of replacement or relay, in which a group or complex of organisms becomes restricted or dies out and their places are taken by others. One of many examples is provided by the reef-building coelenterates—broadly speaking, the corals known as hermatypic (from the Greek *herma*, "reef," and *typos*, "form"). Reefs, which are produced by complex aggregations of plants and animals, have existed since far back in the Precambrian. From the Ordovician period to the present, the hermatypic coelenterates have been important or dominant in them. In the Paleozoic, these belonged to three distinct groups usually classified as orders: Rugosa, Tabulata, and Stromatoporoidea. (The stromatoporoids are sometimes classified as sponges, but the consensus is that they were coelenterates.) The first two groups became extinct in the Permian and the third in the Cretaceous. In the Mesozoic era they were largely (and in the Cenozoic completely) replaced by two other orders of coralline coelenterates: Octocorallia and Scleractinia. These clearly did not evolve from any of the three known Paleozoic orders. A reasonable hypothesis is that their Paleozoic ancestors were soft-bodied and not preserved in fossil reefs, that in the early Mesozoic they began to secrete heavy skeletons, and that this moved them into the adaptive zone, or complex of ecological niches, left empty by the extinction of the orders Rugosa and Tabulata.

There is no evidence that there was land life in the Precambrian and the earliest part of the Paleozoic, and the probability is that there was none. The emergence of plants and animals from the waters brought them into a great series of new and empty environments, which, bit by bit and step after step, were occupied

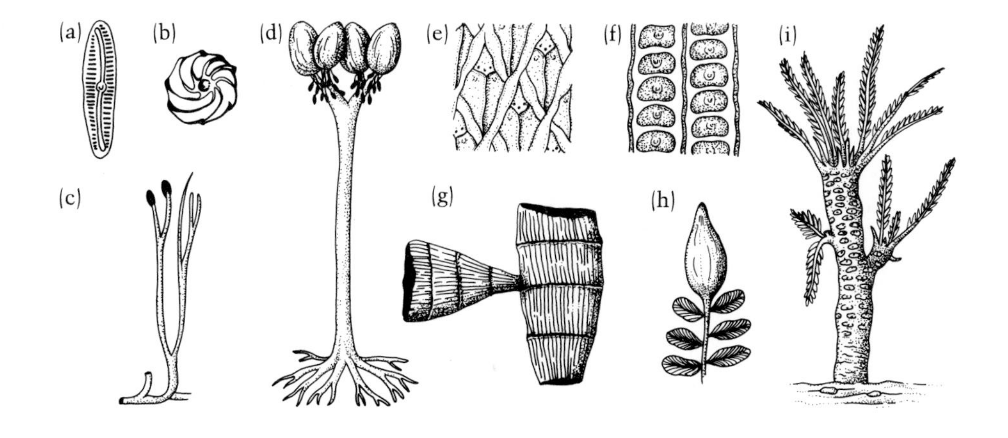

Fossil representatives of some relatively primitive plants and plantlike organisms: (a) *The siliceous skeleton of a diatom, one-celled photosynthetic organisms sometimes classified as protistans and sometimes as algae. They are on the evolutionary level of Precambrian ancestors of plants, but they did not begin to secrete the highly varied siliceous parts until the Cretaceous. Marine at first, they are now present in almost all persistent bodies of salt or fresh water, and the siliceous parts in places have formed enormous deposits of diatomite. This is a microscopic Tertiary specimen, greatly enlarged, of a genus that is also common today.* (b) *The reproductive organ of one of the one-celled algae,* Trochiliscus, *known as charophytes. These organs are often preserved as fossils when calcified, and they occur in marine sediments from the late Silurian to the Recent. This one is only about 0.8 millimeter in diameter.* (c) *A reconstruction of one of the earliest vascular land (or land and freshwater) plants,* Rhynia, *which lived during the Devonian. Close relatives are known from the late Silurian and perhaps the early Carboniferous. Some simple living plants have been considered survivors of the group, but this is no longer generally accepted. This reconstruction is about 12.5 centimeters high.* (d) *A reconstruction of the whole adult plant of a lycopsid,* Sigillaria, *from the Devonian and the Carboniferous. These were among the earliest large trees, this one more than 9 meters high. It is one of the lycopods, which, as shown in the figure on page 82, flourished in the late Paleozoic and are scantily represented by small shrubs today.* (e) *Characteristic bark, with leaf scars, of a related Carboniferous lycopod,* Lepidodendron. (f) *Characteristic bark, with leaf scars, of* Sigillaria. (g) *Internal cast of the pith cavity in a segment of the trunk and the beginning of a branch of a Carboniferous specimen of* Calamites, *a sphenopsid. This group flourished in the late Paleozoic and survives in the smaller horsetails or scouring rushes of the present time. The diameter of the trunk or main stem of this fossil specimen is about 3.8 centimeters.* (h) *Reconstruction of a ripe seed and part of the adjacent foliage of a Carboniferous pteridosperm or seed fern,* Neuropteris. *These were among the most abundant plants in the Carboniferous and Permian, and, because their foliage (the part most commonly fossilized) is so like that of ferns, the late Paleozoic used to be called the Age of Ferns. However, the so-called seed ferns are not ancestral (or even closely related) to true ferns. They became extinct in the Triassic. The length of the seed in this reconstruction is about 4.75 centimeters.* (i) *Reconstruction of the whole plant of a Jurassic cycadeoid,* Williamsonia sewardiana. *Known only from the Triassic through the Cretaceous, the cycadeoids were not ancestral to the true cycads, ten genera of which still survive, but the two groups probably arose from the same group of ancestral plants. This reconstructed tree was nearly 2 meters high.*

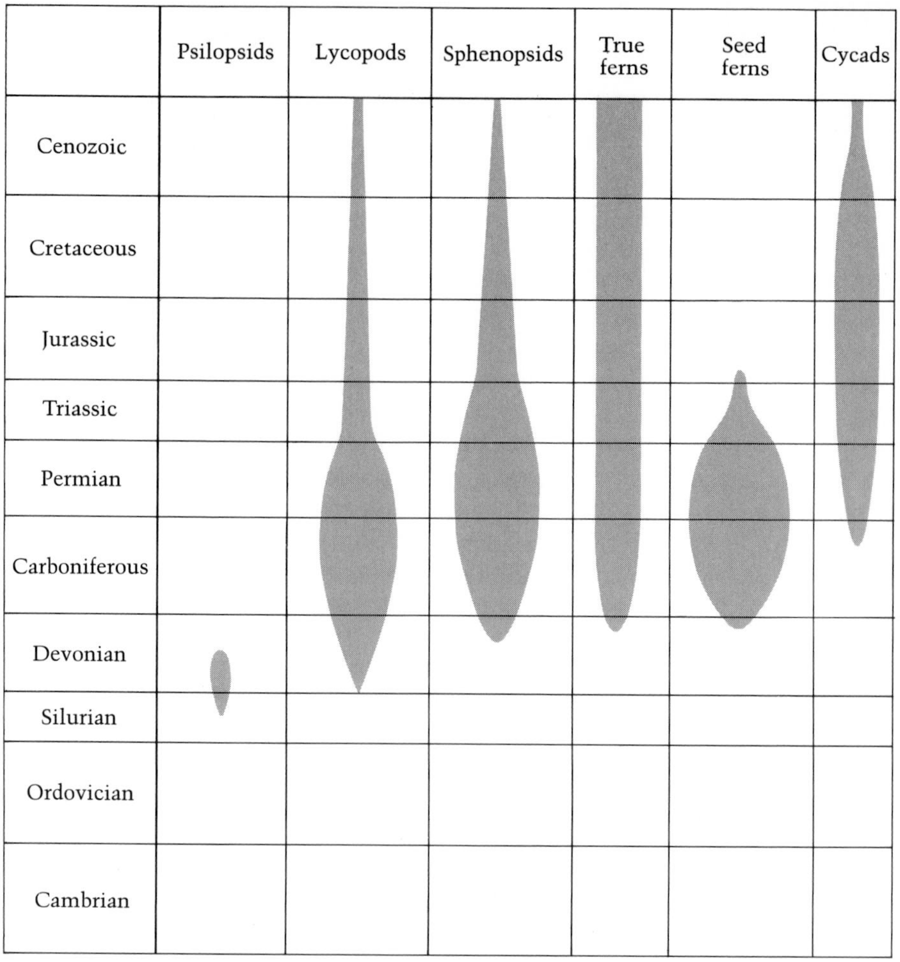

Psilopsids
Lycopods
Sphenopsids
True ferns
Seed ferns
Cycads
Cenozoic
Cretaceous
Jurassic
Triassic
Permian
Carboniferous
Devonian
Silurian
Ordovician
Cambrian

The distribution of major groups of vascular plants. The widths of the graphs for those groups are approximate and somewhat subjective estimates of relative known abundance and diversity in geological time. The origin of vascular plants is not yet pinpointed, but it probably occurred in the Silurian. Successive dominance of different major groups is evident. In the late Paleozoic, the dominant plants were: lycopods, which survive in the clubmosses of today, the living plants with the longest known history; the sphenopsids, which also slenderly survive in the horsetails or scouring rushes of today; the seed ferns, long extinct; and the cordaites, also long extinct. The Mesozoic was dominated by: the extinct cycadeoids, whose closest living relations are the cycads; the ginkgos, now with only one living species; the conifers, which have undergone some diminution but still survive richly; and finally the angiosperms or flowering plants. The origin of the latter is not yet clear, but in the early Cretaceous they expanded rapidly, and they are today by far the most widespread and abundant vascular plants.

and ecologically saturated with new and continuously changed floras and faunas. Until recently, the oldest surely known land plants were from the Silurian period, but now there is micropaleontological (palynological) evidence that some even more primitive land plants, perhaps not yet fully adapted to nonaquatic life, occurred as early as the middle Ordovician. In the Devonian, many plants were fully adapted to land, and large, relatively primitive nonflowering trees formed whole forests. Those continued in the great and almost worldwide coal forests of the late Paleozoic. It is hard to place closely the time of the origin of flowering plants, but it was probably early in the Mesozoic. By early in the Cretaceous period, flowering plants—most of them trees—were dominant in many regions, as they are even more today (with partial exceptions, especially in polar or alpine environments).

The first records of land-living, air-breathing animals are of scorpions from the Silurian period. Thereafter, scorpions—and, from the Carboniferous onward, spiders, which are relatives of the scorpions—have an almost continuous partial fossil record. These are members of the phylum Arthropoda, which was already exuberantly represented in the Cambrian, as today, by marine members—in the

Cycadeoids
Ginkgos
Cordaites
Progymnosperms
Conifers
Angiosperms (flowering plants)
Mesozoic
Paleozoic

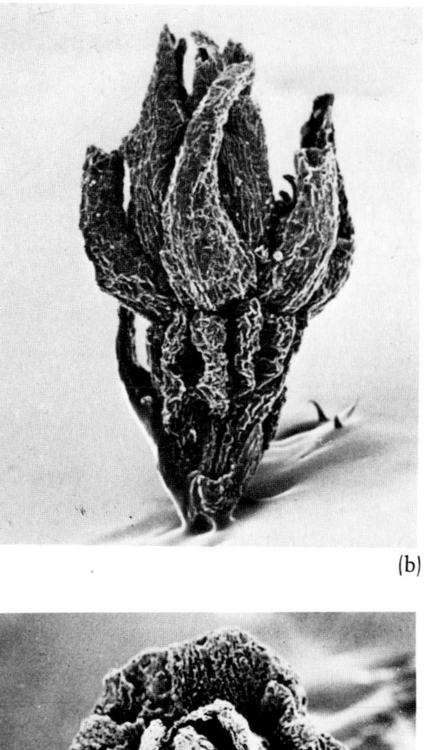

(b)

(c)

(a)

(a) *The surface of a trunk of a common Carboniferous treelike lycopod,* Lepidodendron, *with its typical pattern of leaf scars.* (b) *A flower of the species* Scandianthius costatus. (c) *An apical view of a flower of the genus* Hypogynorus. *Both fossil flowers are from the Upper Cretaceous of Sweden. These specimens are among the best preserved fossil flowers available.*

(a)

(b)

(a) *A well preserved spider* Trigonomartus pustulatus *from the Middle Pennsylvanian period preserved in a siderite concretion. Mazon Creek–Braidwood Fauna, Kankakee County, Illinois.* (b) *A fossil scorpion from the Green River formation. This formation consists of sediments laid down in a large inland freshwater lake during the early Eocene, some 50 million years ago. It contains thousands of well-preserved fossils, including the oldest known bat, innumerable fishes, hundreds of insects, and some arachnoids, the invertebrate class to which spiders and scorpions belong. Fossils resembling scorpions, such as* Palaeophonus, *are known from the Silurian period, at least 400 million years ago. As Recent scorpions are air-breathing land dwellers, these Silurian forms may have been the first animals to come out of the waters onto the lands. That is still uncertain, however, as they had close relatives that were fully aquatic.*

Paleozoic, especially by trilobites, which became extinct in the Permian. By far the most successful group (class) of arthropods are the insects, which are almost exclusively nonaquatic as adults (imagos), but many of which have fresh-water larvae. Insects enter the fossil record in the Carboniferous. Since then, they have increased quite steadily until today they are both the most diverse and the most abundant animals.

Many other groups of animals have left the water, especially land snails, which have a fair fossil record, and several kinds of worms, which do not. Of primary interest to most of us, who are adaptively also completely nonaquatic in spite of sailors and scuba divers, are the vertebrates that became nonaquatic. The earliest known vertebrates were aquatic and were fishes in the usual sense of the term, although, as they had not yet evolved jaws, they are technically placed in a different class from true fishes, Agnatha (from the Greek *a,* "without," and *gnathos,* "jaw"). They definitely appear in the record in the early Ordovician and (as yet) doubtfully in the late Cambrian. The agnathans were abundant in the Devonian, but most of them became extinct by the end of that period. Thereafter, they are rare fossils, but they do still barely survive as cyclostomes, the lampreys (which, despite crossword puzzles, are not eels) and the hagfishes.

In the Devonian, the agnathans shared dominance with the extinct group of armored jawed fishes called Placodermi. Thereafter, the cartilaginous fishes (Chondrichthyes, from the Greek *chondros,* "cartilage," and *ichthys,* "fish"), sharks and their many allies, and the bony fishes (Osteichthyes, from the Greek *osteon,* "bone," and *ichthys*), a relatively few of which are cartilaginous despite

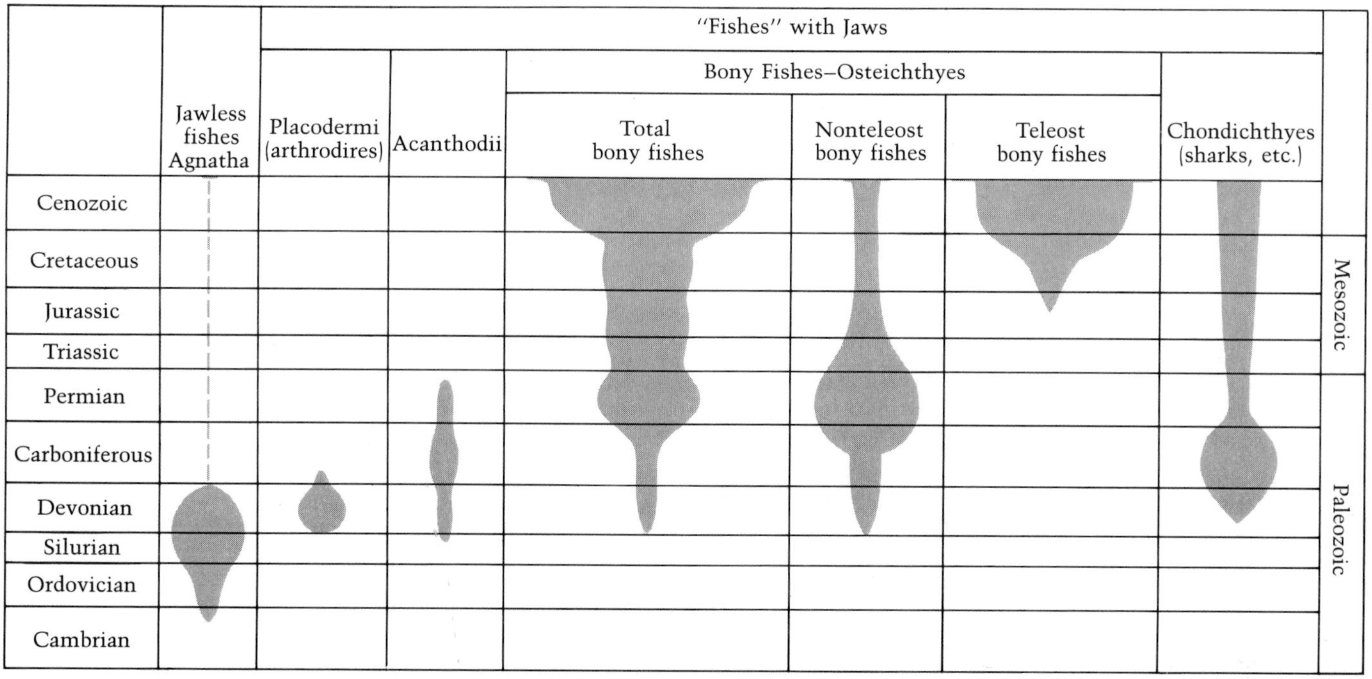

	Jawless fishes Agnatha	"Fishes" with Jaws						
		Placodermi (arthrodires)	Acanthodii	Bony Fishes–Osteichthyes			Chondichthyes (sharks, etc.)	
				Total bony fishes	Nonteleost bony fishes	Teleost bony fishes		
Cenozoic								
Cretaceous								Mesozoic
Jurassic								
Triassic								
Permian								Paleozoic
Carboniferous								
Devonian								
Silurian								
Ordovician								
Cambrian								

The distribution and diversity of known fossils of fishlike vertebrates through geological time. The vertical scale represents time and the horizontal scale represents relative numbers of major taxa within each labeled still larger taxon, in this case scaled as numbers of orders in each class and two selected subclasses of the Linnaean hierarchy. These groups are generally called "fishes," but they are so basically and anciently distinct that they are no longer accepted as constituting a single class, Pisces, in the subphylum Vertebrata. The classification here used has five separate classes, following a conservative arrangement—as, for example, in Romer's Vertebrate Paleontology *(last revised in 1966), except that Romer questionably made the Acanthodii a subclass of Osteichthyes. Within the classes, I have counted orders—not from Romer but by compilation from numerous paleontologists less conservative in recognizing larger numbers of orders.*

Agnatha (from Greek roots for "without jaws") is the oldest known group of fishes, the first of which were near or in the ancestry of all later vertebrates. Until the end of the Devonian, agnathans were heavily armored; hence they were well preservable as fossils and are now well known. There is a tremendous gap in the fossil record, from the Devonian to the Recent, without known agnathans, but two orders, lampreys and hagfishes, are living now. These are without easily fossilizable hard parts, which probably explains the gap in the fossil record. Among the jawed fishes, the arthrodires (class Placodermi) appear to be a rapidly specialized and soon extinct side line. The acanthodians were more fishlike and less obviously specialized. They are extinct as such, but may have been ancestral (although this is a matter of considerable controversy) to one or the other (or perhaps both) of the other two classes recognized here.

The name Osteichthyes means "bony fishes," and most of this class, living and fossil, have extensive bony skeletons, although these are reduced in a few. Some students separate the bony fishes into three distinct classes: Crossopterygii (lobe-finned fishes), Dipnoi (lung fishes), and Actinopterygii (all other bony fishes). This is not a serious matter of disagreement but rather of judgment about when and how much they became differentiated. The Crossopterygii and Dipnoi probably had a common ancestor, and that ancestor probably had a common ancestry with the Actinopterygii. The bony fishes—Osteichthyes—are here charted first as a whole and then separately within nonteleost and teleost subclass, the latter having evolved from the former in the early Mesozoic.

The class Chondrichthyes is so called because living representatives have skeletons of cartilage and no bones, although some early ones did have true bones. The living ones include sharks, rays, and their relatives. The chimaeras or ratfishes, with two living orders and a somewhat dubious fossil record from the Devonian onward, are here included in the Chondrichthyes as a subclass, but are sometimes considered a separate class. Some students believe them to have evolved from early Devonian arthrodires. If this is confirmed, they should probably be considered a subclass of Placodermi.

This figure clearly shows the great changes of dominance in the composition of faunas of primarily aquatic vertebrates in terms of diversity. In those terms, the Devonian (sometimes called the Age of Fishes) was dominated by agnathans and placoderms. Both those groups disappear from the fossil record in the Carboniferous, when the sharks and their relatives were somewhat more basically diverse than other fishes. In the Permian and ever since then, the class Osteichthyes has been dominant in this sense; but in the Permian and early Mesozoic, nonteleosts were the dominant representatives of the class. In the later Mesozoic, and overwhelmingly in the Cenozoic, teleosts were dominant, as are today.

the name, shared dominance in the seas, and the latter were solely dominant in fresh waters.

Among the bony fishes, from the Devonian onward, were lungfishes, three of which survive as relics in Australia, South America, and Africa, and the related crossopterygians or fringe-fins (from the Greek *krossoi,* "fringe," and *pterygion,* "fin"), one of which, *Latimeria,* survives in deep waters of the Indian Ocean off Africa as an extraordinary relic. We ourselves are (in a sense) survivors of the crossopterygians, for it was from an earlier Devonian member of the latter group that the oldest (late Devonian) amphibians, notably *Ichthyostega,* found in Greenland, evolved. This and numerous other transitional forms in the known fossil record give the lie to the "fundamentalist" claims, or mistaken literalist interpretation of the Bible, that no intermediates, or "missing links," between major groups have been found as fossils.

Archaic amphibians, some of great size, radiated through the late Paleozoic and were still numerous in the following Triassic period. Thereafter, all the numerous and sometimes bizarre archaic amphibians were extinct, and only three groups, evolved from obscure or unknown Triassic or earlier ancestors, survived through the rest of the Mesozoic to the present. The frogs and toads—order Anura ("tailless"), radiated abundantly and are still represented worldwide by many families and lesser taxa, all of them, however, rather stereotyped in structure. They have a somewhat spotty (but fairly good) fossil record from the Jurassic onward. The salamanders and their kin, order Urodela ("visible tail," from the Greek *oura,* "tail," and *delos,* "visible"), are not yet surely known before the Cretaceous. They have an inadequate but nearly continuous record through the Cenozoic. They are now widespread and commonly known under many vernacular names, but they are often mistaken for lizards by nonzoologists. The other surviving group is the Apoda ("footless"). This order consists of only a few living genera of elongated legless amphibians. They are sometimes mistaken for earthworms, but few people have ever seen one of them because they do burrow like worms and are mostly confined to the tropics. There is virtually no fossil record for them.

Amphibians can walk on land (or burrow in it) as adults, but with relatively few exceptions they must lay their eggs in water and go through an early phase there. Full adaptation of vertebrates to land life depended upon the evolution of eggs that could be exposed to air and the elimination of the fishlike larval or tadpole stage after hatching. Those developments occurred early in the Carboniferous period, when the first reptiles evolved from ancestral amphibians. The abandonment of the fresh waters may not have been absolute for the earliest reptiles—and for some of them it turned out to be only temporary, geologically speaking—but it surely was well established by the Permian: a fossilized typical reptilian egg of that age has actually been found. (In most of the fossil record, eggs are quite rare, although, as has been mentioned, dinosaur eggs of Cretaceous age are abundant at a number of localities.)

A tremendous radiation of reptiles was under way in the Permian, and reptiles were then already the dominant nonmarine vertebrates. The Permian could well

A complete skeleton of a large plesiosaur, Plesiosaurus dolichodeirus, *from the early Jurassic of West Germany preserved in shale matrix. Some plesiosaurs had long, snakelike necks as can be seen from this specimen.*

Reconstructed skeleton of a large archaic labyrinthodont amphibian, Eryops, *from the early Permian of Texas. These early amphibians, with their large heads, short, squat legs, and fairly long tails, were obviously quite unlike any amphibians now surviving.*

be included in an Age of Reptiles, although that term is almost always limited to the Mesozoic era. That radiation led to a large number of decidedly different major groups, notably at the rank of orders. A widely accepted classification (by the late A. S. Romer) recognizes seventeen orders of reptiles, of which thirteen are extinct and only four are still living—one of those only barely, being represented by a single endangered species.

In the Mesozoic, the adaptive radiation of reptiles had taken them into practically every environment then possible for them, notably including life in the sea and in the air. Some reptiles left the land and reverted to the seas, becoming completely aquatic, living their whole lives and breeding in the sea. This required that their young be born alive and with most of the capacities of adults. That surely is known to have been true of the ichthyosaurs, because an unfortunate mother was buried and fossilized in the act of childbirth. It may also have been true of the plesiosaurs; but, because they had somewhat turtlelike paddles, they may have made their clumsy way far enough up on a beach to lay their eggs on land, as present-day turtles do. (The living sea snakes never come ashore. They are ovoviviparous, the eggs are retained and hatch within the body of the mother.)

There are now no completely aerial vertebrates or other organisms that pass their whole lives and reproduce while airborne. Probably there never have been,

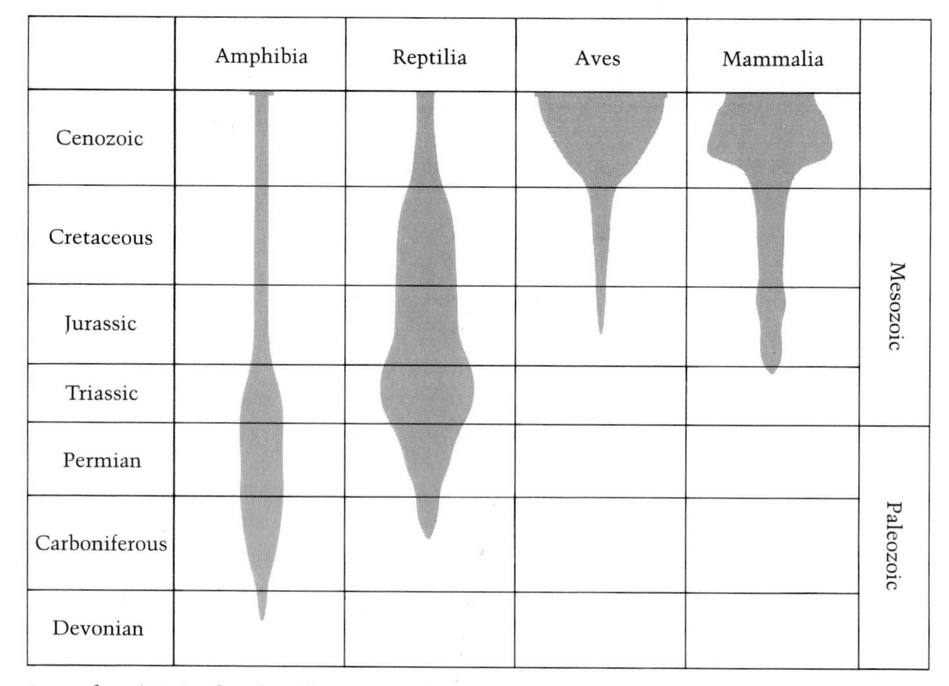

The diversity of tetrapod vertebrates through geological time. Scaled as in the figure on page 85, but here entirely by number of orders. These four classes of vertebrates are commonly grouped in the superclass Tetrapoda, "four-footed," because their earliest representatives (and most of their latest) were in fact four-footed, although many reptiles, all birds, and some mammals became two-footed, and some reptiles and mammals eventually had no functional feet. Some amphibians and most reptiles, birds, and mammals have been essentially terrestrial, but most amphibians have been at least partially aquatic. Some reptiles, birds, and mammals became partially aquatic and some reptiles and mammals became wholly so. The Carboniferous and Permian are sometimes called the Age of Amphibians. By the Permian, however, the number of orders of reptiles already exceeded the number of orders of amphibians. There was a remarkable, complete turnover of orders of amphibians between the Triassic and the Jurassic. The whole Mesozoic (Triassic, Jurassic, and Cretaceous) is commonly called the Age of Reptiles. In terms of orders, the greatest diversification of the reptiles occurred in the Triassic, and it is well known (and discussed elsewhere in this book) that the most marked reduction in the reptiles came toward the end of the Cretaceous.

The birds were expanding in the latter part of the Cretaceous. The record as now known shows quite regular expansion of the number of orders of birds during the Cenozoic, but the record of early birds is still incomplete, and it is probable that most orders already had become differentiated in the middle Cenozoic or even earlier. This graph, being based on numbers of orders, does not reveal some radical changes at lower hierarchical levels, notably a remarkable relay between late Mesozoic and early Cenozoic birds and, during the Cenozoic, a virtual explosion within a single order, Passeriformes (the perching birds), which now includes more genera and species than all the other living orders (25, in the classification used here) put together.

The known record for early mammals is still quite incomplete for some places and times, but it is steadily being improved. There was a marked turnover or relay by extinction of some early orders during the Cretaceous, followed by an expansion of orders of placental mammals beginning near the end of the Cretaceous and becoming a figuratively explosive radiation during the early Cenozoic. The basic diversity of mammals was greatest fairly early in the Cenozoic (in the Eocene epoch) and has declined almost steadily since then. The classification here used has 18 living orders, 17 of which were already in the fossil record in the Eocene. The change at the ordinal level thus was due almost completely to extinctions going on during the middle and late Cenozoic. The one living order not known from the Eocene is Hyracoidea—the hyraxes, damans, or conies. It is probable that they had evolved in the Eocene, but their fossils have not yet been found there. Eleven orders known from the Eocene have become extinct, but only three of those extinctions occurred in the Pleistocene or early Recent. This has an important bearing on the problem of extinction discussed elsewhere in the text. As with the birds, it is also useful here to note that the coarser pattern produced by the tabulation of orders obscures some important features of finer patterns. Among the mammals, just two orders—Rodentia (rodents) and Chiroptera (bats) have far more genera and species than any other orders, although in this case not more than all the other orders together. At the family level, the Recent rodents comprise about a quarter of the living families, the Chiroptera about a seventh, and the two together about two-fifths.

but many groups have been airborne to the extent of being free-flying. One group of Mesozoic reptiles evolved into numerous flying forms, the pterosaurs ("winged reptiles," from the Greek *pteron*, "wing," and *sauros*, "lizard"). The pterosaurs had no feathers. They flew by means of membranes of skin attached to their fingers, as bats do. As flyers, they probably were not as agile and steady as either bats or birds, and the radiative evolution of Cretaceous birds may have had something to do with the extinction of pterosaurs in that period.

It is widely known that both of the two orders of dinosaurs became extinct at or about the end of the Cretaceous. By the close of that period, most of the orders

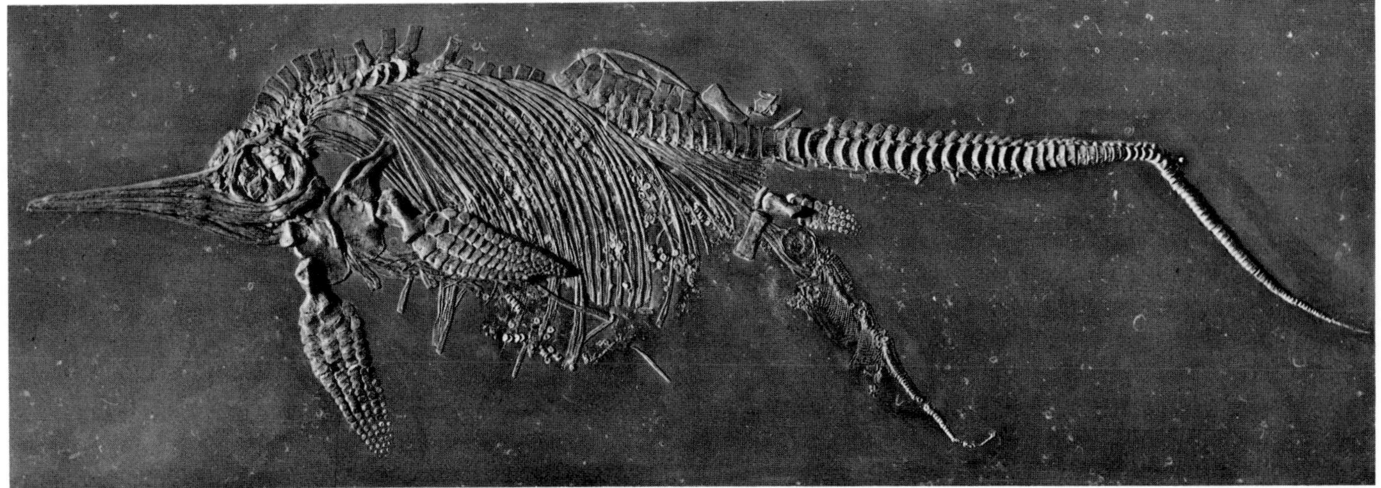
(a)

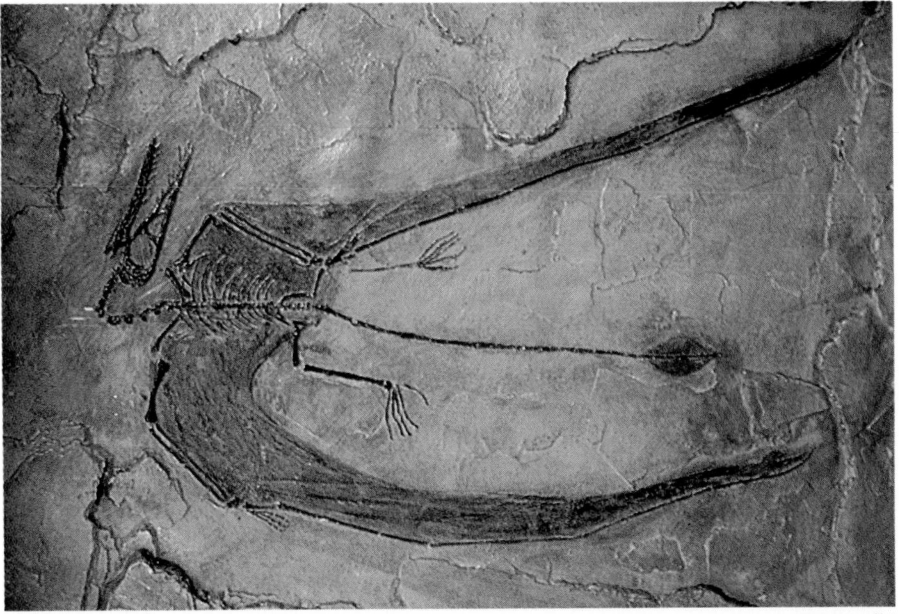
(b)

A fossilized ichthyosaur from Holzmaden, West Germany (a). *Ichthyosaurs were strictly marine, dolphinlike reptiles, that were widespread from the middle Triassic to the late Cretaceous. Those from Holzmaden were early Jurassic in age. There is a relatively tiny ichthyosaur extending down to the right from behind the rear paddle of the big specimen. This has been found in several Holzmaden ichthyosaurs, one of them in the American Museum of Natural History in New York. There is a difference of opinion whether these are young ichthyosaurs extruded from their mother or young ones that had been eaten whole by the big one.* (b) *A flying reptile, one of the pterodactyls abundant in the Jurassic and Cretaceous. This particular one,* Rhamphorhynchus, *is from the Jurassic lithographic limestone at Solnhofen, West Germany. It is unusually complete and well preserved, with its leathery wings suspended on a tremendously elongated finger and the steering fin at the end of its long, thin tail. Note that, in death and under pressure of sediment, the head was so doubled back on the flexible neck that it appears upside down.*

and lesser groups of reptiles were extinct, but that had been occurring gradually over a geologically long time. Of the four orders that survive today, three have long Mesozoic and Cenozoic fossil records and are well known: Chelonia (from the Greek *chelone,* "tortoise"), consisting of the tortoises, turtles, and their relatives; Squamata (from the Latin *squama,* "scale"), the lizards and snakes, the two so closely related as to be classified in the same order (snakes evolved from

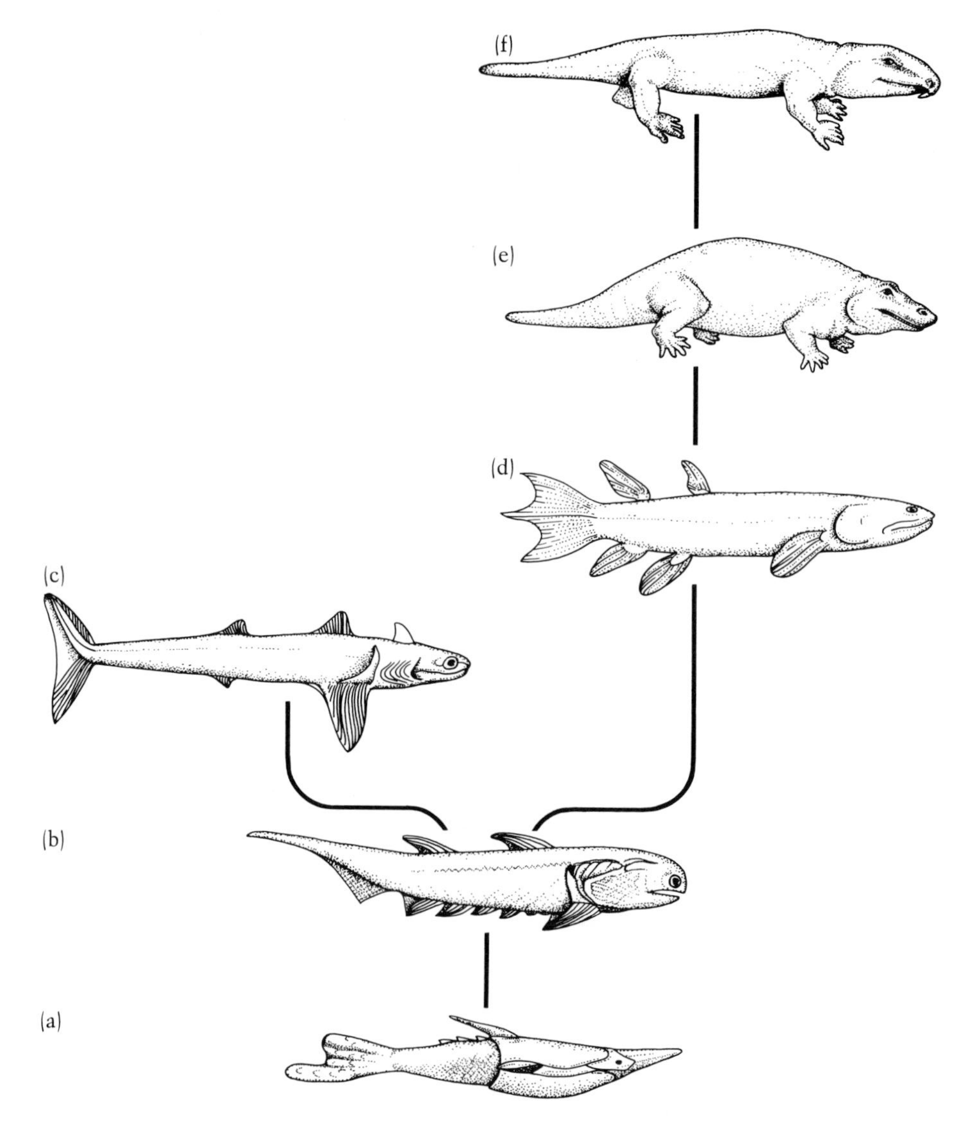

Restorations of some fossil vertebrates: (a) Pteraspis, *a Devonian agnathan, or jawless fish; length about 23 centimeters.* (b) Climatius, *a Devonian acanthodian; length about 7.5 centimeters.* (c) Cladoselache, *a Carboniferous shark; length about 91.5 centimeters.* (d) Eusthenopteron, *a Devonian crossopterygian; length about 76 centimeters.* (e) Eryops, *a Permian amphibian (labyrinthodont); length about 1.5 meters.* (f) Labidosaurus, *a Permian reptile (cotylosaur); length about 61 centimeters. The lines indicate descent of the major taxa (classes) exemplified, not direct ancestor-descendant lines of the genera shown. In each case, with the probable exception of* Eusthenopteron, *the actual ancestor was more primitive than the example given. It is still dubious whether the Acanthodii, here exemplified by* Climatius, *included the ancestors of the cartilaginous fishes, or the bony fishes, or both, or neither.*

limbless lizards); and Crocodilia (from *crocodilus,* a Latin adaptation of the Greek *krokodeilos*), the crocodiles, alligators, gavials, and their relatives.

The less familiar order of surviving reptiles is Rhynchocephalia (from the Greek *rhygchos,* "snout," and *kephale,* "head"—gamma before chi is pronounced and latinized as *n*). The last survivor of this group is the species *Sphenodon punctatus,* now usually called "tuatara" in English, adopted from one of its names in Maori, the language of New Zealand natives. It abounded on the main islands of New Zealand, but now only a few individuals, on islets off the coast, live outside of captivity. The tuatara has hardly changed in the 140,000,000 years since the late Jurassic, and it is an outstanding example of what were called "living fossils." In the Triassic, there were numerous rhynchocephalians, some of them much larger than *Sphenodon,* which looks like, but is not, a lizard. The Triassic rhynchocephalians had larger beaked snouts, which give the order its name.

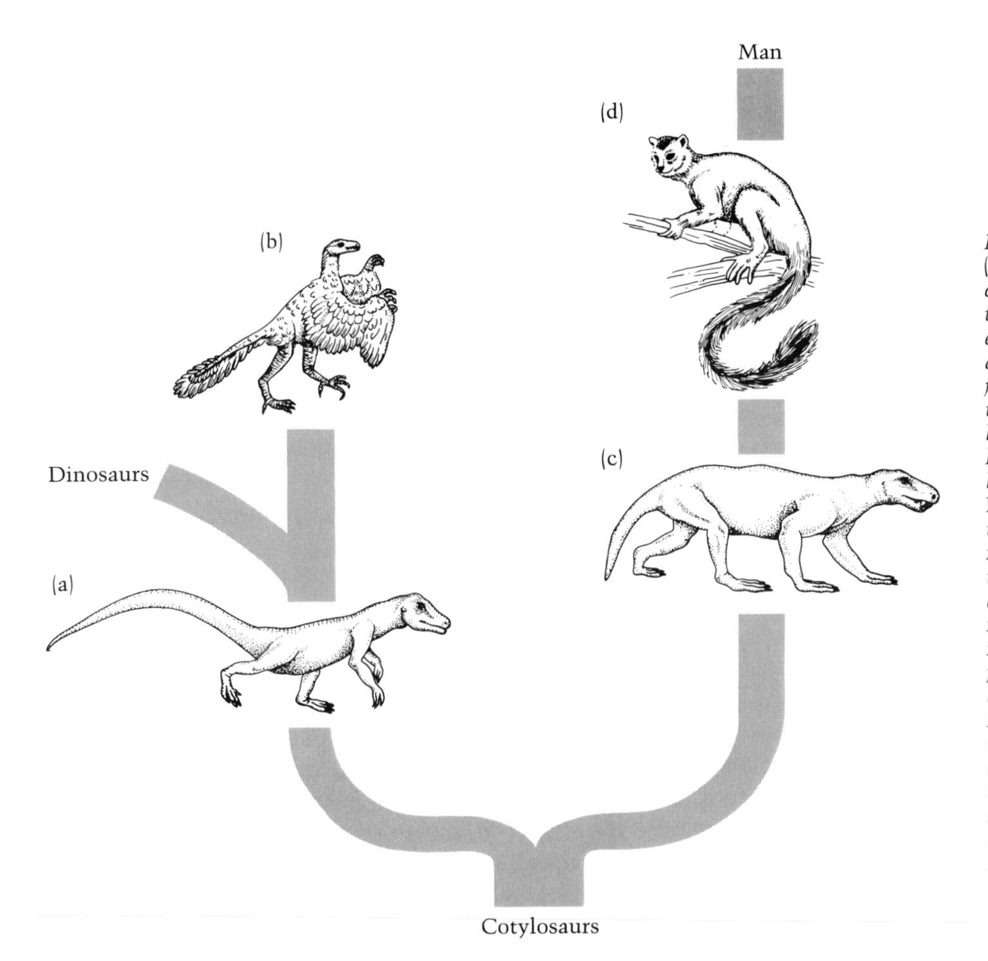

Restorations of some fossil vertebrates: (a) Ornithosuchus, *a late Triassic thecodont, exemplifying the group from which the dinosaurs, other archaeosaurs, and eventually the birds evolved; length about 91 centimeters. These reptiles could facultatively walk on four feet or run on two.* (b) Archaeopteryx, *a middle Jurassic bird, the oldest and most primitive bird known and near or in the ancestry of all birds, length about 46 centimeters.* (c) Lycaenops, *a Permian mammal-like reptile (therapsid) exemplifying the group of reptiles from which mammals evolved toward the end of the Triassic. Length about 1.25 meters.* (d) Notharctus, *a primitive Eocene primate (lemuroid), exemplifying the broader group of early primates from which monkeys, apes, and eventually man evolved. There is doubt about how close this particular genus was to the ancestry of later primates. The length of head is about 7.5 centimeters. As in the preceding figure the gray pathways indicate relationships of the broad groups (orders or suborders) exemplified, and not necessarily direct lines of descent.*

Among the swarms of reptiles, some groups that became differentiated early in the history of the class Reptilia are especially significant for the outcome of their further evolution. One of these taxa, the order Thecodontia (from the Greek *theke,* "case" or "socket," and *odon* "tooth") gave rise through three different lines to the Crocodilia and to the two orders of dinosaurs. The birds later arose either from the line that also gave rise to the dinosaurian order Saurischia or from an early offshoot of that order.

The other very early group of reptiles with subsequent and up to now permanent historical importance was Pelycosauria (from the Greek *pelike,* "basin," and *sauros,* "lizard," from the reptilian structure of the pelvis). The pelycosaurs arose in the late Carboniferous, flourished in the Permian, and became extinct as such early in the Triassic. In the meantime, they had given rise to the descendant order Therapsida (from the Greek *ther,* "beast" or "mammal," and *apsis,* "arch" or "vault," from the mammallike structure of the sides of the cranium; the origin is sometimes incorrectly and nonsensically given as from the Greek *theraps,* "an attendant"). The therapsids arose in the middle of the Permian period, radiated greatly in the later Permian and in the Triassic, and had one known last survivor in the middle Jurassic.

(Here it may be remarked parenthetically that John C. McLoughlin, a zoological artist turned paleontologist, has proposed to put the mammals and therapsids, but not the pelycosaurs, into a single class Therapsida and to put the birds, all dinosaurs, and the thecodonts into a single class Archosauria, to which he also adds the pterosaurs because, like the birds, they are a supposed offshoot of the dinosaurs. The principal argument for this is that the therapsids are supposed to have been endothermic like the mammals, and the thecodonts, pterosaurs, and dinosaurs are supposed to have been endothermic like the birds. In Chapter 2, I discussed this point about the dinosaurs and expressed the opinion that there is not sufficient real evidence that they were endothermic. The same can be said about the thecodonts and the therapsids. In any case, this proposed reclassification does not more clearly express relationship of ancestry and descent than had already been done. Furthermore, even if we really knew whether the therapsids, thecodonts, and dinosaurs were endothermic—which we don't—this would neither require nor justify so radical a rearrangement of classification and such contradictory redefining of hitherto well-defined names for higher taxa.)

The earliest mammals, clearly and generally accepted as such by students of them, occur in the late Triassic and the immediately following early Jurassic, a transition called the Rhaeto-Lias in Europe. They underwent a limited or somewhat subdued radiation in the Jurassic. Then, in the Cretaceous, a single group from that first radiation began to radiate anew, first in a limited way and then much accelerated in rate and in scope. Eventually, with the usual changes and replacements, almost all the mammals now living, both marsupials and placentals, came out of this major late Mesozoic and Cenozoic radiation, or sequences of radiations. Only the egg-laying monotremes (the platypus and the echidna) of the Australian Region (which includes New Guinea) were exceptions to that sweeping generalization. Their history is not really known from fossils, but they must have originated early in the Mesozoic and have been quite separate from all other mammals ever since then.

As the placental radiation (or subradiation) was occurring, in the very late Cretaceous, the first known members of the order Primates appeared. Thereafter, the primates, too, had a rather complex series of radiations, progressional changes, and replacements. Among these many strands was the lineage that led to us, *Homo sapiens.* Just when this ancestral group (itself splitting somewhat into more than one precise lineage) split off from the ancestry of the apes most nearly related to us (gorillas and chimpanzees) is not exactly determined and is in part a matter of nomenclature. It is probable that the human family, Hominidae, was distinct by the late Miocene and sure that it was so well back in the Pliocene. Just when our genus, *Homo,* appeared as such has become almost entirely a matter of definition and is not really worth arguing much about at present. *Homo* certainly existed fairly early in the Pleistocene and *Homo sapiens* by (or shortly after) the middle of the Pleistocene. So here we are.

CHAPTER 4
FOSSILS AND GEOGRAPHY

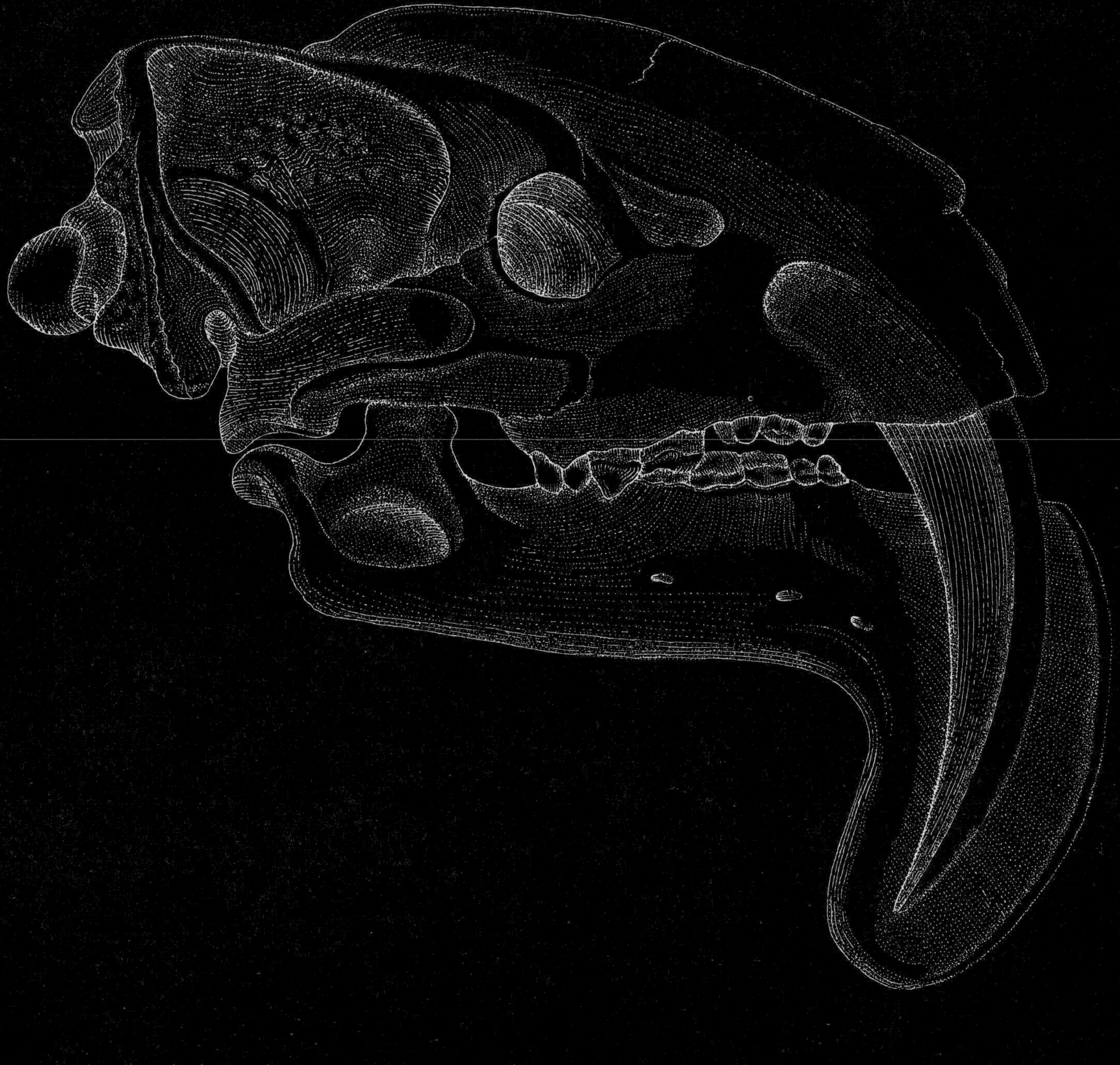

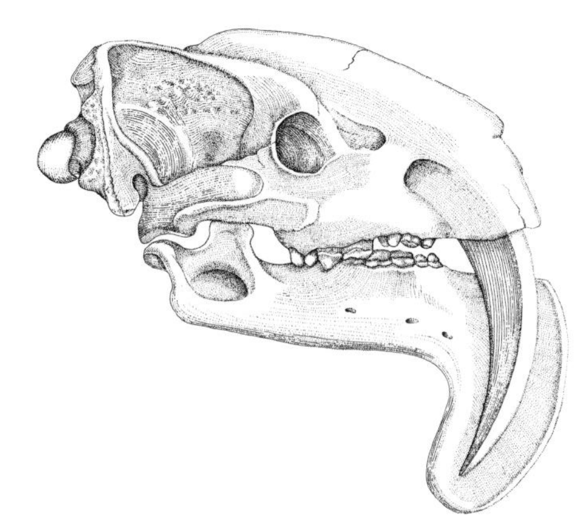

Skull and jaw of the marsupial sabertooth Thylacosmilus atrox *from the early Pliocene of Argentina, about five million years ago. This is a remarkable example of convergence with the separately evolved placental sabertooths such as the genus* Smilodon, *which later invaded South America from North America and then became extinct on both continents.*

Biogeography is the study of the distribution of organisms on the planet Earth. Data for such study start, but do not end, with observations of the times and places in which particular species or other taxa of organisms have occurred (or occur now). Beyond that, biogeography has many facets, branches, or methods of approach. What must have been the oldest such approach surely occurred among the earliest humans, and, although long prescientific, it was what is now called ecological. The kinds of organisms present in a given locality or region depend on environmental factors. The plants and animals present are different, for example, in forests and on open plains. Before the effective interference of humans, the presence of forests or plains depended on local climates and soils almost entirely—and it still does, to a considerable degree. In the seas, the ecological determinations are different but equally strong and perhaps even more varied: the nature of the bottom or substrate; the temperature and the chemistry of the waters; the presence and extent of a tidal zone; the depth at which organisms live; the penetration of light; and still other factors.

Biogeography from that point of view requires data not only on the organisms themselves but also on their environments. It must further be noted that the environments of organisms are not only physical and chemical but also biological. For a species, the environment of each individual includes the other members of its own species and also those of all the other species in its community or biocenosis. There is no clear, acceptable boundary between ecological biogeography and ecology. Some of the more strictly ecological aspects of both living and fossil biotas were briefly discussed in Chapter 2. Their more strictly geographical bearing is relevant in the present chapter.

Extensive areas with characteristic and more or less uniform biotas are called biomes by biogeographers. These may be variously subdivided into distinguishable communities, which are more local geographically, but biomes are usually fairly large. In the whole of North America, for instance, some twelve or fifteen land biomes are commonly recognized. These may be designated by the vernacular names of one or more plants and at least one animal—in this example, usually a land mammal. Thus a so-called spruce–caribou biome covers most of Canada, much of Alaska, and some parts of Montana, although caribou do not in fact occur in much of the biome so designated. The high plains of the central United States, as another example, have been called the needlegrass–antelope biome (which extends also into southern Canada), although the erroneously named antelopes, properly pronghorns, have not occupied the whole biome since early prehistoric times, if ever. Alternatively, such biomes may also be given general names based on vegetation alone or on vegetation and climate. The spruce–caribou biome is also called, or included in, the North American coniferous forest biome, and the needlegrass–antelope biome is also called the North American temperate grassland biome. Such terms refer to conditions more or less as they were found by the first European occupants, not as they are today.

The term *biome* is also applied in a different way to areas throughout the world that have similar climates and are characterized by plants (and, to some extent, animals) that are similar in form or habit within the different regions but not necessarily related to each other. For example, there is a major terrestrial biome (in this sense of the word) defined as "temperate grassland." It occurs in North America, where it is essentially the same as the so-called needlegrass–antelope biome. It also covers a vast extent through (mainly) central Asia and lesser but still considerable areas in South America (the pampas of Argentina) and in Australia (most of a ring around a central desert region). In all four continents, this biome has—or had, in earlier but geologically Recent times—grasses, shrubs, and some trees (mainly in galleries along streambanks). On each continent, it also had multitudes of grazing and some browsing animals and various carnivores preying on the herbivores. From a purely ecological point of view, these biotas were—and, to the extent that they survive, still are—well comparable. Nevertheless, from a taxonomic point of view, they were—and, to the same extent, still are—remarkably different. There is some limited botanical resemblance between the temperate grasslands in North America and Asia, on one hand, and in North America and South America, on the other hand, but there is very little such resemblance between any of those continents and Australia. Among the land mammals, the most numerous grazers in the four continents in recent times were radically different taxonomically: especially bison and pronghorns in North America, wild horses and wild asses (onagers) in Asia, rodents in South America, and kangaroos in Australia.

The main point here is that differences among biomes and lesser biotic subdivisions within a single continent can be largely explained in terms of climate and other existing ecological factors, but taxonomic differences between biotas in ecologically similar but widely separate regions cannot be so explained. As will become apparent, the explanation is not ecological but historical.

When biogeography was developing as a distinct branch of science in the nineteenth century, attention was focused mainly on mapping and characterizing the major regions of the lands of the earth in terms of their faunas. Thanks primarily to two British zoologists, Philip Lutley Sclater and William Lutley Sclater, father and son, the living faunas of land mammals were ascribed to six regions:

- Palaearctic (or, in American usage, Palearctic): Europe, Asia north of the Himalayas and excluding the Arabian Peninsula, but including Africa north of the Sahara Desert, Iceland, and Japan.
- Nearctic: nontropical North America.
- Neotropical: South America, tropical North (or Central) America, and the West Indies.
- Ethiopian: Africa south of the Sahara, the Arabian Peninsula, and Madagascar.
- Oriental: southern Asia and the East Indies (including the Philippines but excluding New Guinea).
- Australian: Australia, New Guinea, New Zealand, and adjacent smaller islands.

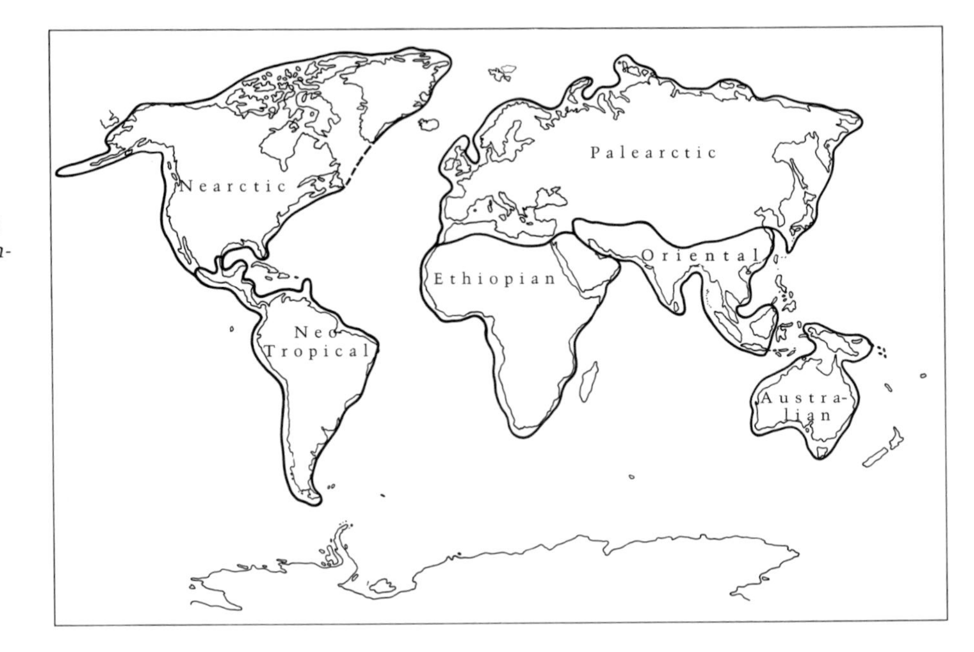

A new version of the Sclaters' biogeographical regions. These regions were based on extensive characteristics of land faunas, especially those of birds and mammals. This form of the map recognizes the Sclaters' six original regions, but it redefines them and restricts them more than the Sclaters or most later biogeographers have done. The principal difference is that I do not consider it either practical or useful to include in those classical major regions islands that do not have continental faunas. Islands with continental faunas—for example, the East Indies (as far as Bali), New Guinea, Japan, Great Britain, or Ceylon—are still included in the regions to which they have been classically assigned. However, islands with faunas distinctly different from those of continents—notably the East Indies between Bali and New Guinea, almost all oceanic islands in the Pacific and Atlantic, Madagascar, and New Zealand—are not included in the classical regions. These might be (and sometimes have been) specified as regions distinct from those of the continents, but it is more accurate as well as more instructive to treat them as what in fact they are: biogeographically distinct islands or archipelagos. This is discussed further on pages 100–102.

In its essentials, this arrangement is in general use now for land animals as a whole—and sometimes also for plants, although their biogeography tends to follow somewhat different lines. The Nearctic and Palearctic regions, which resemble each other more than do any two of the Sclaters' other regions, are now often considered subregions of a single Holarctic region. Most (or sometimes all) of the Arabian Peninsula is now often mapped as part of the Palearctic rather than of the Ethiopian region. Madagascar and New Zealand are now often considered separate subregions (or even separate regions), but New Guinea is not separated from the Australian region by zoologists. Islands such as the East Indies between Bali and New Guinea, most of the Antilles, and most of the smaller islands far out in the oceans have land faunas not really comparable with those of the continents or with the large islands near continents (such as Great Britain, Sumatra, Borneo, and others). It has therefore been questioned (by me, among others) whether they really fit into the Sclaters' system of regions, which is based essentially on continental faunas. Be that as it may, the Sclaters' regions on the whole are real large-scale zoogeographic units, each with a distinctive kind of taxonomic mix.

As taxonomic distinctions like those seen in the zoogeographic regions cannot be explained simply on an ecological basis, how are they to be explained? As with so many things, Charles Darwin was virtually the first to see this problem and to see where its solution must be sought. While in South America during the 1830s on the voyage of the *Beagle* he observed, as travelers had before him, that many South American animals are strangely—even bizarrely—unlike those of other continents. He also observed, as his predecessors had not so clearly, if at all, that this was true even when their "climate or condition"—as we would now say, their ecology—did not differ from that on other continents. He then added the observation that some fossils, including those found by him, were antecedent to, and related to, those still living and peculiar to South America. He later remarked that this was one of the main clues that set him on the way to knowledge of evolution. The overall importance and outcome was that Darwin showed that a causal understanding of biogeography must necessarily be historical.

In *The Origin of Species,* Darwin included two chapters entitled "Geographical Distribution," and these may be taken as the foundation of historical biogeography. The most directly historical evidence in this approach to biogeography is provided by fossils. Darwin did use some evidence from fossils in his groundbreaking discussion of this subject. The data on the distribution of organisms through geological time were then so few, however, that Darwin had to treat this subject mostly by deduction from observations of recent organisms. It is still true that historical biogeography is based on the distribution of organisms in the Recent epoch as well as in all the past geological epochs since life began. By the end of the nineteenth century, there was already enough fossil evidence, especially of land mammals, that a volume explicitly devoted to historical biogeography appeared. This volume, entitled *A Geographical History of Mammals,* was published in 1896 by Richard Lydekker, a great English naturalist who was also among the vertebrate paleontologists most important in the history of their special science.

Lydekker demonstrated that the regional differences in mammalian faunas do have a causal history and that this may be elucidated in considerable part by the evidence of fossils. It was already clear that there have been great changes in regional faunas through geological time that can be attributed in part to more or less constant evolutionary modifications in the lines of descent (or phylogenies) of organisms, in part to the occasional spread of various groups from one region to another, and in part to the also occasional but frequent local or universal extinctions of many groups. In Lydekker's day, the horses already provided excellent examples of all three of those factors, as they still do now in greater and more secure detail.

In North America, which was the center of evolution of the horse family (Equidae) from the middle Eocene into the Pleistocene, there was almost constant change in the characteristics of horses and also considerable expansion in the kinds and numbers of separate lines of descent. These changes were largely ecological, correlated with changes in environments and in the trophic roles of the various horses. The composition of Asiatic, European, and eventually African faunas was also changed markedly by the repeated spread of waves of horses of various kinds from North America to Asia and thence on to Europe and to Africa. In South America, too, the faunas were eventually much changed by the spread of horses, among other animals, from North America. There were also extinctions throughout most of the history of the horses, and finally on a large scale: at first, all the browsing horses throughout the world became extinct, then all the grazing horses in North America and South America. Grazing horses (in the broad sense,

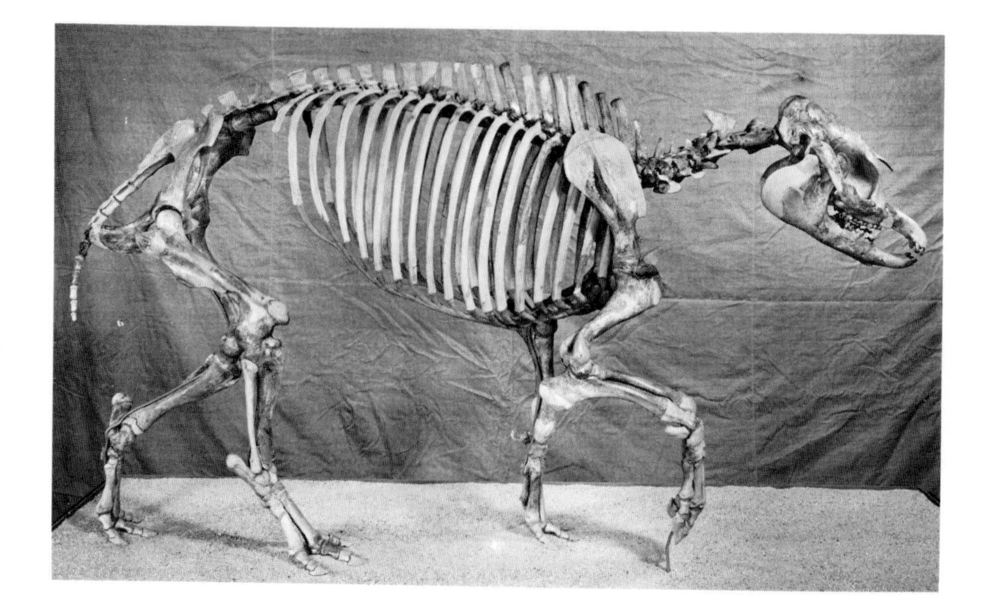

The skeleton of an extinct Pleistocene species of tapirs, Tapirus excelsus, *from Missouri. The tapir family, Tapiridae, originated in North America and spread widely there and also into Asia. In the Pleistocene they also spread to South America. They are now extinct in North America and in Asia north of the tropics but have survived in the tropics of South America and Asia. The historical connection between their now isolated areas was across the Bering land bridge.*

these include the several species of asses and zebras) survive in Asia and Africa, but they are now recently extinct as wild animals in Europe.

Horses and other land animals repeatedly spread from North America to Asia across what is now a broad sea barrier. There was also a spread of some land animals from Asia to North America. This indicated to biogeographers of Lydekker's generation (and still does to those of ours) that there was a land connection at various times in the geological past where a sea barrier now exists. There followed, roughly from 1895 to 1915, what might be called a land-bridge rush. Every notice of the distribution of related plants and animals in areas separated by marine barriers was the occasion for some biogeographer to make a hypothetical direct connection by a land bridge between those areas. Tapirs live in southeastern Asia and in South America, so draw a land bridge (or even a whole, now sunken continent) across the South Pacific. A fossil horse called *Hipparion* has been found in France and in Florida, so get it across the North Atlantic on its personal bridge in a convenient straight line. At the height of this sort of thing, in 1907, a German biogeographer named Theodor Arldt published a book with maps showing all the transoceanic land bridges that had then been proposed on such evidence. They crisscrossed all the oceans and effectively dried them up.

The need for such imaginative extremes was controverted in a now classical study by the vertebrate paleontologist William Diller Matthew, Canadian by birth but a resident of the United States throughout his adult life. In this work, published in 1915, he showed that most of the hypothetical bridges were unnecessary to explain the observed facts. For example, fossils show that tapirs were formerly widespread in North America and in Asia. Their present distribution is more simply (and much more probably) explicable by spread between those continents and southward from them into Malaysia on one side and into Central and

South America on the other. The only past land connection required was across what is now the Bering Sea between Alaska and northern Asia, and for that connection there is incontrovertible evidence. Thus three or four land connections in the past might explain the known instances of intercontinental spread of land mammals—and perhaps of all land animals.

Another point made by Matthew was that most dominant land mammals, and perhaps various other groups of organisms, evolved on the northern continents, whence some of them spread to the three southern continents (Australia being excluded from consideration). He suggested that this was influenced by differences in climate, hence the somewhat misleading (or at best inadequate) name of this one of his works: *Climate and Evolution.* Later study has shown that this particular thesis was simplistic. It is indeed now clear that more groups of mammals and of some other animals spread from the northern to the southern continents than in the opposite direction. Still, each of the three southern continents was itself a major center of the evolution of mammals and of a number of other groups. Matthew was aware of that, too, but he saw it in a somewhat different light.

The examples most relevant at this point and now best understood, although still not completely, are provided by the fossil and living mammals of South America and North America. Recent analysis (by me, among others) shows that, in South America early in the Pliocene epoch, only a single mammalian family (Procyonidae, the raccoon family), only 4 percent of the known families of South American land mammals at that time, was of immediate North American origin. All the others, 96 percent, had evolved in South America itself, 37 percent from ancestors that reached that continent in the late Eocene or early Oligocene and the remaining 59 percent from ancestors that had been there since the end of the Cretaceous period. Among the now living land mammal families of South America, 44 percent are of North American and 56 percent of South American origin.

In Australia, there is still almost no knowledge of fossil mammals older than the Miocene, but it will surprise no one that all the known Australian marsupial families from Miocene to Recent are known only in the Australian region and almost certainly originated there. Contrary to what seemed logically most likely in Matthew's day, the earliest ancestral marsupials, if they were not already Australian, are much more likely to have come to Australia from the south than from Asia. The living mammalian fauna of Australia does include many placental (hence nonmarsupial) mammals in addition to man and his importations. The ancestors of these, rats (family Muridae) and bats (seven families), quite surely did come from Asia in the late Cenozoic. The fossil record of these groups in Australia is almost nil at present, but the families are well known as fossils in Eurasia. I will return to these points later.

It is now fairly evident that Australia and New Guinea have not been directly attached to the continent of Asia for many millions of years—and perhaps they never were. A question therefore arises: How could any of Australia's animals

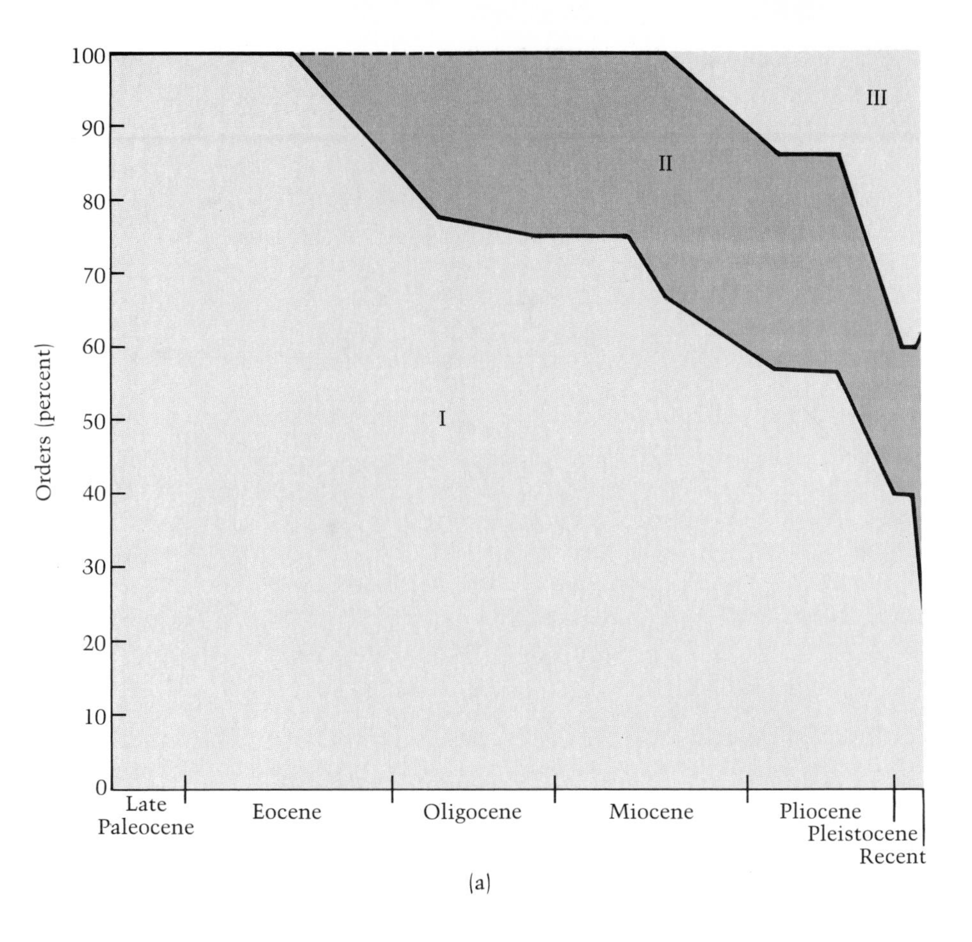

A graph of the broadest outlines of change within the mammalian fauna of South America during most of the Cenozoic. From the late Paleocene (left) *to the Recent* (right), *the epochs are shown approximately in scale with geological time. The vertical scale shows percentages of orders in* (a) *and percentages of families in* (b) *in the known faunal groups in the various epochs and ages. The taxa are divided into faunal groups according to when they appeared in South America. In* (a), *group I comprises the orders already present in the late Paleocene; in* (b) *it comprises the families of those orders that were present then and other families of those orders that arose thereafter. The percentage of the total accounted for by group I declined markedly with the appearance of new orders and families in the early Oligocene. The time was probably somewhat earlier (in the late Eocene), but the known fossil record is still inadequate there. A more marked decline in group I orders and families (and, to lesser extent, of group II orders and families) began in the early Pliocene with the appearance in the known record of the first late migrants from North America. That was accentuated in the late Pliocene and through the Pleistocene into the Recent.*

The geographical origins of the orders in group I are not yet clearly known. Those in group II came by waif dispersal either from North America or from Africa, but whether from one or the other (or one each from both) is not yet firmly decided. All the mammals in group III unquestionably came from North America, but not all at once: some of them had still more distant origins in the Old World but spread to South America by way of North America.

have been derived from Asiatic ancestors? That brings up the biogeography of islands, a subject that early fascinated biogeographers and still does. Both geologists and biogeographers have long recognized a distinction between continental and oceanic islands, although they do not always define them in exactly the same way. To a geologist, a continental island is one with structures and rocks, such as granite, of the sort usually found in continental contexts. To a biogeographer, a continental island is one whose biota is generally similar to—and may be considered as an extension of, or a fairly unbiased sampling from—that of a more or less adjacent continent. Great Britain and Ireland are continental by both definitions. The Seychelles may be considered continental by geologists, but are definitely not so considered by biogeographers.

The distinction is not always clear. The island of Madagascar, for instance, is decidedly continental geologically. It has a rich biota mostly derived from African sources, but this biota is nevertheless quite different from the present African one, and it cannot reasonably be considered to be either an extension of, or an unbiased sampling from, the latter. Thus, it is considered oceanic by many biogeographers. There was long an almost acrimonious division of opinion among biogeographers about whether the West Indies (except those, such as Trinidad, that have clearly South American biotas) should be considered continental or

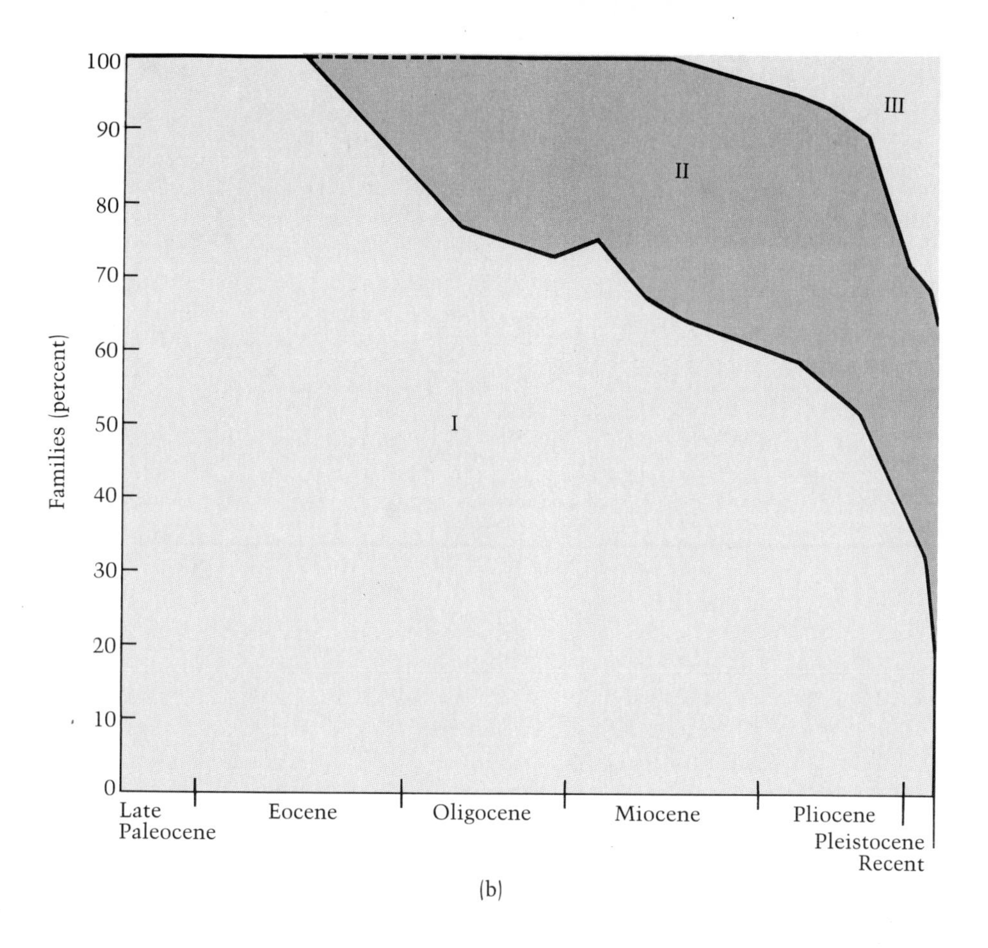

(b)

oceanic. The consensus, still sometimes disputed, is that these islands are biogeographically oceanic. A point that arises in such cases is whether the islands in question have been connected parts of adjacent continents. It is probable that Madagascar was once continuous with Africa, but so long ago that its present biota is markedly distinct. It was just this point that was so controversial with respect to the Antilles: with some dissent, the consensus is that they never were connected parts of North America. On the other hand, it is now definitely established that Great Britain, at one end, and Sumatra, Java, and Borneo, at the other end, were connected parts of Europe and Asia, respectively, at times up to only a few thousand years ago, and they are biogeographically still continental.

No matter how far they may be from other land, oceanic islands of some size and duration usually have some native plants and often some animals, too. The question then is: How did they get there? Darwin discussed this in his Chapter XI (in the first edition; eventually Chapter XII) of *The Origin of Species* (1859). He proposed that plants got there by what he called "accidental means." He described experiments by himself and others to determine how long seeds could float in sea water and still germinate, and decided that some could be "floated across a space of sea 900 miles in width, and would then germinate." He noted that seeds could also be transported by drift timber and in various ways by birds.

In the work previously mentioned, Matthew discussed the probability of "over-sea migration" by animals, including land mammals, on "natural rafts." He suggested that this explained the faunas of oceanic islands, in which category he included Madagascar, New Zealand, and the Greater Antilles. Since then, there have been many other discussions of the colonization of oceanic islands, and other means of producing this have been suggested and in some instances exemplified. An interesting example is that Pleistocene fossils of relatively small, now extinct proboscideans (relatives of elephants) have been found on several islands of the Malay Archipelago (in Indonesia) that almost certainly had no connections with other islands or with Asia at the time. Those somewhat bulky creatures must have swum across the not very wide straits between the islands.

Such colonizations have been called "waif dispersals." I have called them "sweepstakes dispersals" because, as in a sweepstakes, the probabilities of success are small, but, in the course of enough chances—in enough years of geological time—there are some winners. What especially distinguishes such dispersals is not only that the probabilities are small but that the outcome for a particular species must be all or nothing. What is involved is the successful crossing, by a species of plant (usually as a seed) or animal, of a barrier in which the seed could not grow or in which the animal could not long survive or ever be a successful colonist. In the case of the oceanic islands and terrestrial species, such a barrier is a strait or sea. Similarly barely permeable barriers may, however, also exist on land—for example, a mountain range or desert in which a lowland animal or a forest animal could not tarry long and survive. They may also exist in oceans—for example, a current or zone of especially cold or warm water in which animals with a narrow and different temperature tolerance could not long survive. Both on land and at sea there may thus be what Robert H. MacArthur and Edward O. Wilson called "habitat islands" (in an innovative book that has stimulated much discussion, and is cited in the bibliography at the end of this book).

The chances of waif or sweepstakes dispersal over considerable distances are evidently improved by what I have called "island hopping" (what MacArthur and Wilson call "stepping-stone dispersal"). This has occurred when dispersal has involved step-by-step progression along a chain or sequence of islands. There can be little doubt that, in some important instances, this has been an essential factor in historical biogeography or paleobiogeography. One of the most important examples, albeit an inference and not an observation, is the movement of placental mammals from mainland Asia to Australia. They must have island-hopped down the chain of Sunda Islands to New Guinea and thence to Australia. (They may not have had to make that last hop because Torres Strait may not have been there at the time.) It is now fairly certain that marsupials did not take this route. Their likely route (and again that of the placental mammals) will be mentioned later.

When two separate land areas earlier separated by a marine barrier became united by land, which has demonstrably happened repeatedly in the course of geological history, there has almost always been some spread of terrestrial plants

A female and its young of the living species Bradypus tridactylus. *These belong to the family Bradypodidae. This group evolved in South America as a distinct family believed to have had the same remote origin as the family Megatheriidae, which evolved independently into immense extinct ground sloths such as* Megatherium.

and animals from one to the other. Usually, the spread or migration has occurred in both directions. If interchange involves a considerable number of taxa spreading in both directions, it may be inferred that indeed there was a land connection. If, however, relatively few taxa are involved at any one time (geologically speaking), and especially if the spread seems to have been in one direction only, the most probable inference is that the spread was by sweepstakes dispersal across a strong barrier.

As previously mentioned, a member of a single family of land mammals of North American origin (Procyonidae, raccoons) suddenly appeared in the early Pliocene fossil record of South America. At about the same time, the first family of land mammals of South American origin (Megalonychidae, one of several families of ground sloths) suddenly appeared in the North American fossil record. There was thus a two-way spread, but on so limited a scale that it was almost certainly by sweepstakes dispersal without benefit of a land connection. That is the more likely because the animals in both groups concerned were especially fit for island hopping—in a sense, they held more tickets in the sweepstakes than most mammals do. Most procyonids are at least semiarboreal, and many of the megalonychids, despite their designation as "ground" sloths, were also at least semiarboreal. Trees floating out to sea with some animals in them are an established means of waif dispersal or island hopping.

By the early Pleistocene, twelve families of land mammals of North American origin were widespread in South America. Central America, or what is now best designated as tropical North America, had (as far as is known) an entirely North American mammalian fauna before the Pliocene. By the early Pleistocene, however, it had at least fifteen families of land mammals of South American origin, all but five of which still survive there in communities that have an approximately equal number of older North American inhabitants. Of the originally

Glyptodonts, heavily armored distant relatives of armadillos, are known from the middle Eocene but must have originated in South America at an earlier date. From the Miocene onward they were highly varied and abundant all over South America. In the Pleistocene they spread to North America where they were also abundant, mostly in our southern states, although less varied than in South America. Around the end of the Pleistocene they became extinct on both continents. This particular specimen is from the Pleistocene of South America and is of the typical genus Glyptodon.

South American families, seven spread widely into nontropical North America, and only three of those are still present in that region, each with only a single species there (our opossum, porcupine, and armadillo).

From these observations, it is a reasonable inference that, from a time not long (geologically speaking) before the early Pleistocene, there was a land connection between North America and South America. That led to an extensive intermingling of the two continental faunas in nontropical North America and over most of South America, but this was less extensive in nontropical North America. Geographically, the way was open; but ecologically (or, in the main, climatically) it was quite selective.

That land bridge still standing is objective proof that land bridges can indeed exist as such, being formed by geological forces. This one was a sort of filter in its effect on the animals that spread or migrated across it. The whole now tropical North American (or Central American) zone had a filtering effect, but this culminated approximately where the tropical lowlands met (and still meet) the warm-temperate regions in Mexico. None of the native South American ungulates or primates,and very few of its native marsupials, rodents, and edentates, got beyond the filter zone on their spread toward North America. From North America, it is rather curious (but again ecologically explicable) that the browsing mastodonts got through to South America, while their relatives the grazing elephants ("mammoths" is just a name used for extinct species of elephants) did not. Somewhat harder (but not impossible) to explain ecologically is the fact that horses got through from North America to South America, while the bison and pronghorns, grazing ungulates like the horses, did not.

Another example of the effect of a land connection forming from geological causes between two land regions previously separated by a strong barrier is provided by the Cenozoic history of Europe and Asia as it influenced the biogeography of ancient and recent land mammals. On a geographic map of the present Earth, Europe and Asia look as if they were a single continent, Eurasia, separated only by human history and not by nature. They have not always been so. For long stretches of time, lands of most of present Europe and most of present Asia were separated by an epicontinental sea—that is, a relatively shallow sea over what is

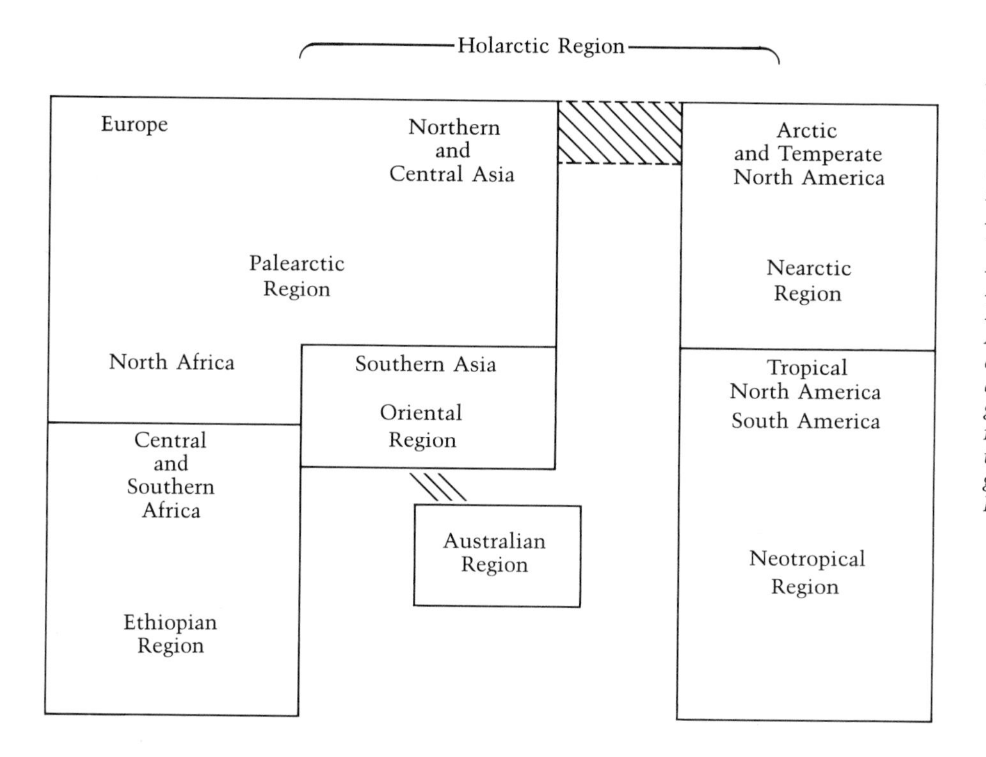

Schematic representation of continental faunal biogeography in the Recent epoch, a still further modification of the classical Sclater regions. Areas separated only by solid lines are now (or have recently been) connected lands. The Australian region has never been connected with Asia, but it has had some interaction with the Oriental region by means of island hopping through the East Indies. Northern North America (the Sclaters' Nearctica) is not now connected with Asia, but it was so periodically up to about 10,000 years ago by a land bridge across what is now the Bering Strait. Migration both ways resulted in more faunal resemblance, and it underlies the use of the term and concept Holarctica as a region (or superregion) including both Palearctica and Nearctica.

essentially a broadly downwarped area of continental crustal rocks. (The Baltic Sea and Hudson Bay are present-day examples of epicontinental seas.)

The former presence of that barrier sea between early Cenozoic Europe and Asia is revealed by stratigraphy and invertebrate paleontology and is reflected by the paleobiogeography of land mammals. Early Paleocene mammals bearing on this point are not yet well known, but middle to late Paleocene and early Eocene land mammals are fairly well known in western Europe and in central and eastern Asia, and they are becoming better known each year now. At those times, the faunas of Asia and Europe were quite radically different, indicating the presence of a strong barrier between them—doubtless the epicontinental sea known also from other evidence. Thereafter, there was some fluctuation in faunal resemblance, but, by the Pleistocene, the once separate regions were as fully connected as they are today. In the land faunas, there were, of course, still some differences in local faunas due more to climatic and other ecological factors than to more strictly historical causes. Nevertheless, the broad and not particularly selective continuity of land from western Europe to eastern Asia had led to an essential similarity of land floras and faunas throughout. Such a land connection—which, after its topographic formation, offers no significant barrier to the spread of terrestrial biotas—has been called a corridor because of the freedom of passage that it affords.

The Eurasian example of a corridor arising across what had been a strong barrier is unusual but not unique. As another example, during much of the Cretaceous there was another such barrier, also a north–south epicontinental sea, that divided North America into eastern and western parts. In this case, however, its biogeographical effect is not quite clear because the paleontology of land animals in the region east of the sea barrier is not well documented.

A hypothesis once commonly accepted was that there had been a more or less mid-Cenozoic east–west epicontinental sea dividing South America into northern and southern parts. In this case, the fossil documentation does settle the matter, showing that the hypothesis was false. Land faunas from north of the supposed barrier have some local peculiarities, as is to be expected, but they are essentially like those from the far south. There was a corridor, not a barrier, between them.

Thus, in consideration of the spread or (in that sense) migration of land biotas, we have waif dispersal, filter dispersal, and corridor dispersal. Between waif dispersal and the others, the difference is practically absolute. Waif dispersal is an all-or-none matter, largely stochastic, or apparently governed by chance, in that the most nearly determinate element is statistical: The probability of waif dispersal is different for different taxa. Filters and corridors act more definitely in a determinate way. The determining factors are mainly ecological. They depend on what elements of floras and faunas can live and propagate in an area between two regions. If the requirements are relatively rigid, met by a small proportion of the biotas involved, there is a biogeographic filter. If much or most of the biotas can live and propagate in the connecting land area and hence spread over it with little hindrance, there is a corridor. The difference between filter and corridor is clearly relative, not absolute.

Up to this point, the discussion of biogeography has been centered mainly on terrestrial biotas, with land mammals as good examples. That is not only because I am most familiar with these aspects but also because, from Darwin onward, such biotas have been most involved in the development of biogeography as a science. Nevertheless, the aquatic (or more particularly the marine) faunas, mostly of invertebrates, have been increasingly studied from all three biogeographic approaches: descriptively geographical, ecological, and historical. The principles involved are much the same as for terrestrial faunas, but the nature of oceanic environments makes the application of those principles frequently different.

The geographic study of marine invertebrates involves the recognition of regions or provinces with characteristic faunas. This has not yet resulted in a scheme so simple and generally accepted as that of the geologically Recent nonmarine vertebrate faunal regions discussed early in this chapter. The boundaries of marine biogeographic regions are not nearly so clearcut. Recent oceans are all continuous among themselves, so that the distribution of marine faunas depends more on ecological factors than on geography per se. That has also been usually

(a)

(b)

(but not always) completely true in the geological past. The fact that many marine invertebrates have juvenile or larval dispersal phases also promotes their being less dependent on strictly geographic configurations. Thus, in ecologically similar conditions, marine faunas or particular marine taxa tend to be more widespread and their boundaries to be less fixed than those of land faunas and taxa. That is why, as has been mentioned, marine invertebrate fossils are often more useful or reliable than terrestrial vertebrate fossils for long-distance stratigraphic correlation.

There are few, if any, marine barriers that cannot be crossed by some strictly nonmarine plants and animals. The Hawaiian Islands, for example, are about as isolated from any other land as is possible, and they almost certainly have been so throughout their existence. Nevertheless, before the catastrophic results of human occupation and the introduction of so many exotic plants and animals, they had a rich biota of truly native plants and animals, the ancestors of which reached them by sweepstakes dispersal over formidable oceanic expanses. For strictly marine taxa, however, land is an almost absolute barrier.

A particularly interesting example that has been analyzed by an invertebrate paleontologist (Wendell P. Woodring) is provided by the Isthmus of Panama. Sequences of Cenozoic marine molluscan faunas from Paleocene to Recent are known on both sides of the isthmus. Into the Miocene, the faunas on the Pacific side and those on the Caribbean side were almost identical. During that time, there evidently was no important barrier between them. In the Pliocene, the resemblance decreased somewhat, and since the end of the Pliocene, some two million years ago, the faunas on the two sides of the present isthmus have been evolving independently. This clearly fits in with the independent evidence from the land mammals (previously noted in this chapter) that sweepstakes dispersal of mammals began in the early Pliocene—probably by way of intervening islands, for which there is also some geological evidence— and that a complete isthmian land connection was present by the end of that epoch.

Before human occupation, the Hawaiian Islands had a rich biota of truly native plants and animals. Shown above are examples of Hawaii's extinct flightless birds. The restorations shown here were made from the bones of birds extinct before the Hawaiian Islands were discovered by non-Polynesians. Hence the colors are due to the artist's imagination.
(a) *The bird to the right is an ibis* Apteribis glenos, *a member of the ibis family,* Threskiornithidae. *The two smaller birds in the picture are flightless rails, also extinct, and have yet to be named. (It should be noted that no living ibises have ever been reported from the Hawaiian Islands.)* (b) *An extinct goose* Thambetochen chauliodous *very much like the living but threatened nēnē.*

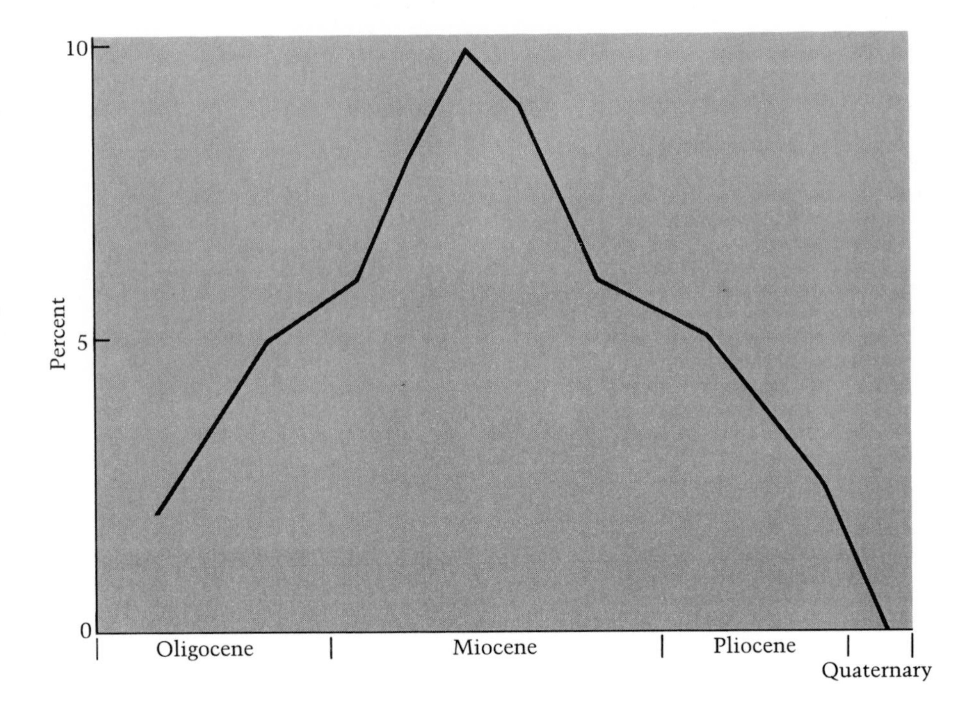

A zoogeographic effect of the rise of the Isthmus of Panama. The graph shows the approximate percentage of genera and species of fossil marine mollusks formerly living in the western Atlantic part of the Caribbean faunal province that are now extinct there but survive in the eastern Pacific Panamic province. The faunas range from early Oligocene to Recent, as shown along the horizontal axis. The peak in the middle Miocene coincides in time with almost complete identity of the faunas of the Tertiary Caribbean province, which then occurred on both sides of what is now the Isthmus of Panama. The decline of the graph to zero at present indicates increasing difference between the faunas on the Atlantic and the Pacific sides as taxa formerly occurring on both sides became extinct in the Atlantic. There was also increasing divergence among species of those genera that continued to occur on both sides.

That sequence also exemplifies some other kinds of biogeographical events and inferences. For one thing, during most of the Cenozoic there was a single province of marine invertebrates, called "Tertiary Caribbean" by Woodring. It included most of the Caribbean and a small part of the western Atlantic as well as the part of the eastern Pacific now adjacent to the isthmus and to northwestern South America. Now there are two faunal provinces in these regions, one on the Pacific side, sometimes called the American Pacific warm-water region (or province), and the Caribbean province on the other side. A different sort of switch in land faunas had the same paleogeographic cause: The rise of the Isthmus of Panama caused the transition of what is now tropical North America from the Nearctic region to the Neotropical region.

Another effect was that closing of the oceanic connection across what became the Isthmus of Panama necessarily had an important effect on ocean currents. Until that closure, much of the westward flowing current from equatorial Africa must have continued between the Americas into the north equatorial current of the Pacific. Since the closure, the current into the Caribbean has in part eddied into the Gulf of Mexico and in part circled into the Florida current and the Gulf stream. Currents strongly affect both the dispersal of marine animals and the regional environmental conditions. This change has not only stopped dispersal of

Atlantic warm-water marine organisms into the Pacific but also changed the ecology of those organisms in the Caribbean.

Changes in ocean currents have occurred periodically from the Cambrian period onward. (Data for the Precambrian are still inadequate.) The number, positions, and characteristics of marine faunal provinces have changed along with the currents. For example, it has been estimated, on this basis, that there were approximately thirteen marine biogeographical provinces in the Silurian, fourteen in the early Permian, and eight in the latest Permian, when there was a change in sea level. By similar criteria, about eighteen marine faunal provinces may be recognized today.

Both in the sea and on land, there have been numerous changes in the numbers, boundaries, and compositions of biogeographic entities in terms of realms, regions, provinces, biomes, and other more or less localized floras, faunas, or both (biotas). Examples have been given, and there are many others in the literature of paleobiogeography. It may be said, however, that studies of this more complex sort have not yet been so numerous, nor have they progressed so far, as the relatively simple presentation of data on the past and present geographic distributions of particular taxa, ranging in taxonomic level from species to classes. Of the two large data-centered books cited at the end of this book, the one edited by A. Hallam is almost entirely devoted to the distribution of particular taxa. The other, edited by Jane Gray and Arthur J. Boucot, is largely so, but it also includes some discussion of geographically definable biotas as such. The distinction between the two sorts of studies is real but not always clear. For example, students of ammonites, extinct relatives of the living chambered nautilus, discuss paleobiogeographic realms and provinces, but they define them entirely in terms of ammonites alone. That has also been done for many other groups of marine invertebrates that are common as fossils, notably corals, brachiopods (lamp shells), and bivalves (clams and their innumerable and highly diverse relatives), as well as the one-celled (protozoan) foraminifers (or "forams") of economic paleontology.

The most obvious differences in environments and in geography are those between land and sea, with nonmarine waters as a third basically distinct environment. Through geological time, these can often be distinguished by the kinds of sedimentary rocks deposited in them. The commonest of such rocks, mostly shales, sandstones, and limestones, may have been deposited in any of the three major environments, but limestones only very exceptionally on dry land. The structures, grain sizes, and chemistry of the rocks often give special clues to their origins. For example, sandstones consolidated from dunes (wind deposition on dry land), deltas (river deposition at the mouths of streams, in lakes, or in the sea), or sand bars (formed in seas by wave and current action, usually near shore) generally have structural differences in their bedding that reveal their origin. Chemical deposits, such as gypsum (a hydrous calcium sulphate, $CaSO_4 \cdot 2H_2O$) or halite (the mineral name for common salt, sodium chloride, NaCl), are known geologically as evaporites. They were formed by evaporation of water saturated with those or similar salts. The water may originally have been either sea water or river water flowing into a lake without an outlet.

Fossils usually reveal the original environment more readily than do the physical and chemical nature of the rocks in which they occur. There are many major groups of animals, especially invertebrates, that live predominantly or only in the seas and always have. A fossil coral reef was certainly formed in a sea, and so was any fossil community including sea urchins and "moss animals" (bryozoans). Bivalves live in both salt and fresh water, but they are much more numerous and varied in seas, and the marine and freshwater taxa are easily distinguished. Among the vertebrates, fishes are of course aquatic, although a very few do come out temporarily on land, not merely into fresh water. It is often (but not always) possible to determine whether a fossil fish fauna was living in the sea or in fresh water. There has been much debate (and there is still some doubt) about whether the first vertebrates, which were jawless fishes of the class Agnatha, were saltwater or freshwater inhabitants. (Saltwater seems more likely.)

Amphibians are freshwater and land animals, none now and probably none ever marine. Most reptiles now necessarily breed on land. The only present exceptions are the ovoviviparous sea snakes. In the geological past, however, there were many reptiles that were completely aquatic and mostly marine. These include the extinct ichthyosaurs, plesiosaurs, and mosasaurs, and a few more obscure groups, all readily recognized as aquatic. As everyone knows, turtles lay eggs on land, but most of them are otherwise aquatic. Most mammals are completely terrestrial, but the completely aquatic whales and their kin (of the order Cetacea) are readily recognized as such, both as fossils and as living animals. The only other completely aquatic mammals are the sea cows (order Sirenia). Fossil and recent seals are also readily recognized, and they indicate the proximity, at least, of marine waters.

Taphonomic study has shown that the fossil remains of completely terrestrial vertebrates are usually found in rocks that were water-laid. Nevertheless, they indicate that there was land nearby even when their remains were buried in water-borne sediment, and that the presence of water at that time and place was superficial and generally temporary. It is true that the fossil of a terrestrial dinosaur was once found in definitely marine rocks. The animal, alive or after death, must have been carried by currents far out to sea, but such an occurrence is almost unique.

For the present continents and the continental islands associated with them, it has been possible to map which areas were land and which were seas at various times in the past. Each of the now existing continental land areas has been partly under seas in various parts, not only once but repeatedly through geological time. It is thus possible to superimpose upon maps of these continental areas a pattern of sea and land at many (not all) stated past geological times. That sort of paleoge-

The plesiosaur Kronosaurus, *a Cretaceous marine reptile, is the largest known plesiosaur with an enormous head, about 2¾ meters in length, and a total length of almost 13 meters. It is known only from Queensland, Australia.*

The mosasaur, Clidastes propython, *was a voracious predator of the Cretaceous. The jaws of this marine reptile were lined with pointed teeth so that large prey could be dismembered and swallowed. Mosasaurs were very large marine reptiles that evolved from earlier nonmarine lizards. All known mosasaurs were of late Cretaceous age, this branch of the lizard superfamily becoming extinct at the end of the Cretaceous. This particular specimen is a composite of at least two partial skeletons from Logan County, Kansas.*

ography has long occupied historical geologists and paleontologists with increasing detail and probability as knowledge has progressed. Until relatively recently, however, attempts to make paleogeographic maps for the whole world and for fairly remote geological times were based on what now appears, beyond a reasonable doubt, to have been a mistake. On the evidence earlier known and on principles that then seemed probable, the consensus was that the present continents, although changing in form and extent, remained relatively stable in position on the globe. The discovery that this is not true has resulted in a veritable revolution in some aspects of paleogeography and hence also in paleobiogeography.

That the continents have indeed drifted over the earth was suggested long ago, but it was then merely an unsupported guess or, at best, an inadequately tested hypothesis. Early in the twentieth century, this idea was more clearly stated, and it began to be backed by more definite geological evidence. Serious attention to this hypothesis can be dated from 1915, when Alfred Wegener, a German meteorologist who had broadened his scope into geophysics, published a small book entitled *Die Entstehung der Kontinente und Ozeane*—"The Origin of Continents

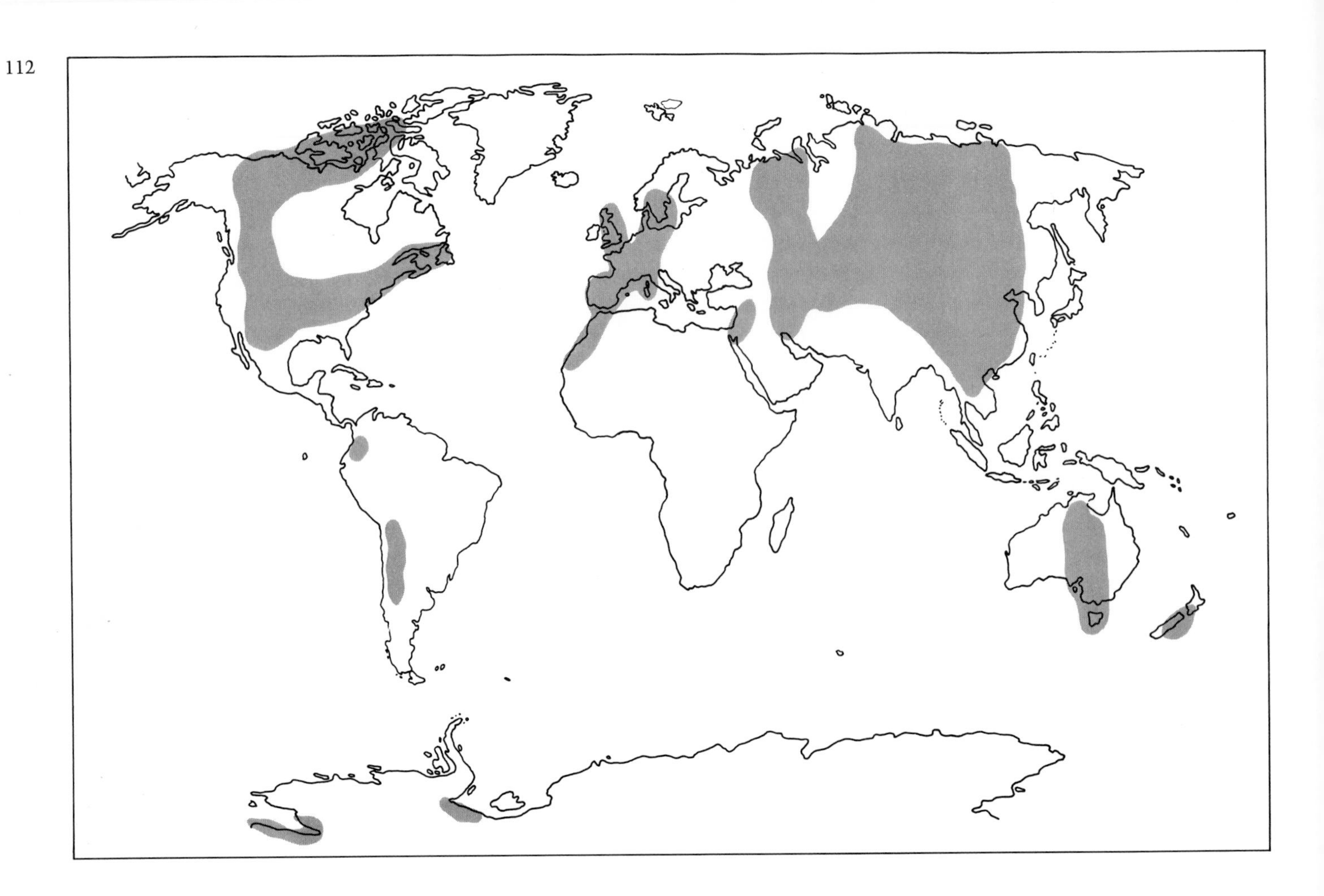

Approximate extent of known Cambrian seas superimposed on a map of present land areas. This is based on the presence of known marine fossils in accessible present rock exposures of Cambrian age. The conformation of land and sea was certainly very different in the Cambrian. The information on a map like this is incomplete in several respects: It includes information about places now land that certainly (or probably) were under Cambrian seas, but it includes no indication of where these places were on the globe during the Cambrian. It includes only indirect information about the places on present land areas where there were no Cambrian seas, and it includes almost no information about the presence of marine Cambrian rocks under Recent seas. (No Cambrian sediments are known to be present in oceans beyond the continental shelf.) For a tentative approximation of the real configuration of lands and seas in the Cambrian, see figure on page 114.

and Oceans." During Wegener's lifetime and for some years thereafter, this hypothesis remained highly controversial. Wegener died in 1930, at the age of 50, while exploring on the Greenland icecap. By that time, some geologists were strongly supporting his views, but many more were just as strongly rejecting them.

Paleontologists were then (and remained for years thereafter) almost unanimous in opposing, or at most not supporting, these revolutionary ideas. That was not, as might be supposed, because paleontologists are particularly conservative. They found that the history of life, so far as it was then known to them, could be explained just as well (and some points in it could be explained better) by stable continents than by continents that drifted as Wegener and some other supporters of continental drift mapped the supposed past geography of the earth. They also found that the supposed paleontological support for continental drift specified by Wegener and some other nonpaleontologists was misinterpreted or downright wrong.

The general acceptance of continental drift has come mainly since about 1960 as a result of evidence either only dimly glimpsed and not yet really understood or not known at all much earlier than that date. This evidence came especially from two lines of research: paleomagnetism and ocean-floor spreading. From those and

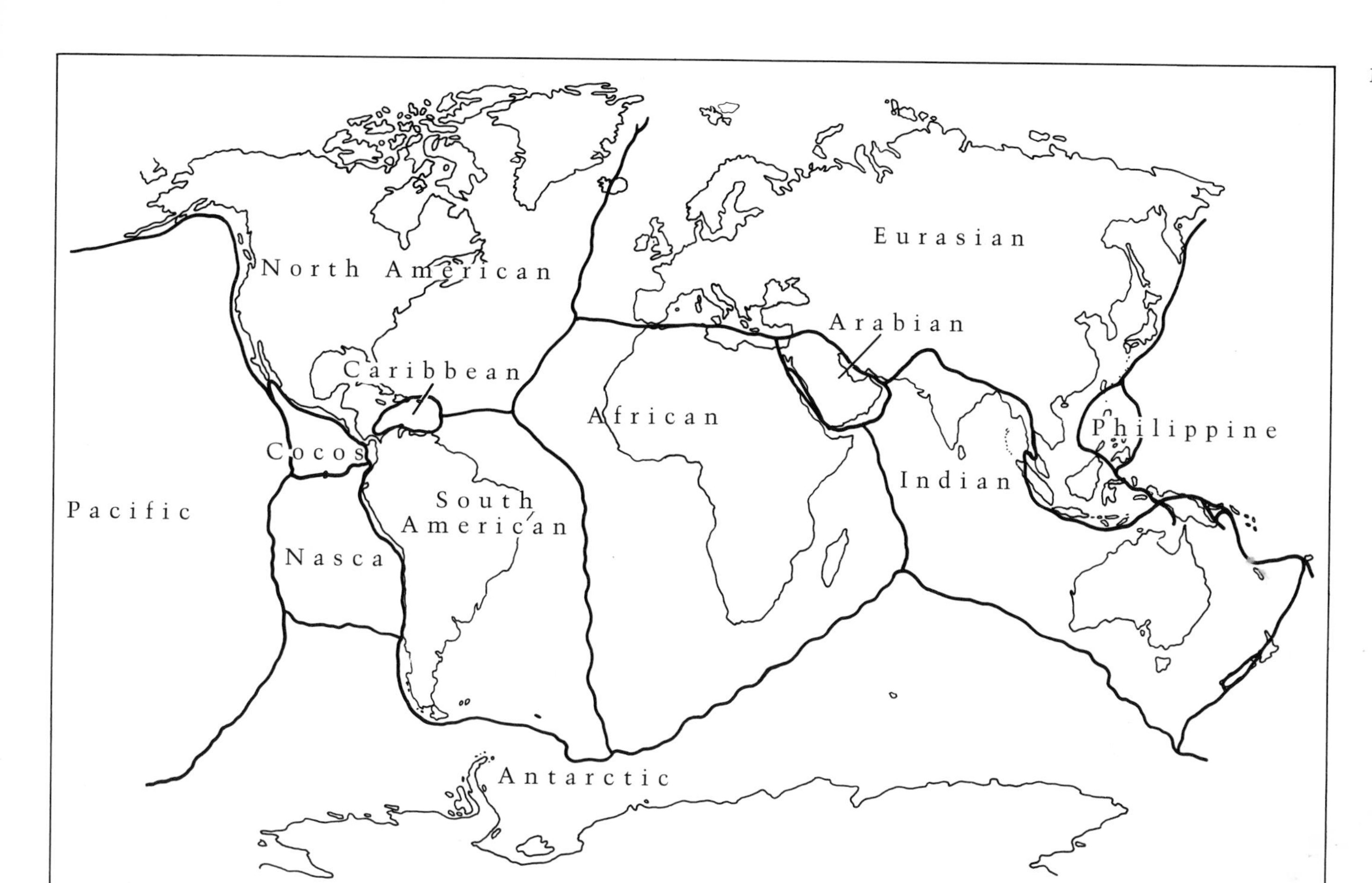

The main tectonic plates at the present time. Note that most of these plates have continents or other lands that are riding on them, so to speak, but that they also include present oceanic areas.

allied studies was developed a more inclusive historical theory of global geography: the theory of plate tectonics. The gist of this theory is that the crust of the earth is a mosaic of fairly rigid plates that may—and sometimes, but not always, do—move with respect to each other. The continents, as wholes or parts, ride on such plates and can thus be united or separated as the plates move.

That the motion has in fact occurred and is still going on is indicated in part by paleomagnetism, the remanent earth magnetism that was mentioned in another connection in Chapter 3. As discussed there, the occasional reversals of this magnetism help in correlation. Remanent magnetism also indicates the direction of the magnetic poles at the time when the rock solidified (if it is igneous) or was deposited (if it is sedimentary). On the postulate that the magnetic poles have always approximated the poles of rotation, the direction of the latter poles is indicated at the place and time of a paleomagnetic determination. Repeated determinations have shown that the direction of the poles differs quite markedly at different geologic times for essentially the same geographical positions. This has been called polar wandering, but it is much more probable (and is generally agreed) that it was the plates and the continents on them that were doing the wandering. The polar orientations also show that the positions of the plates and

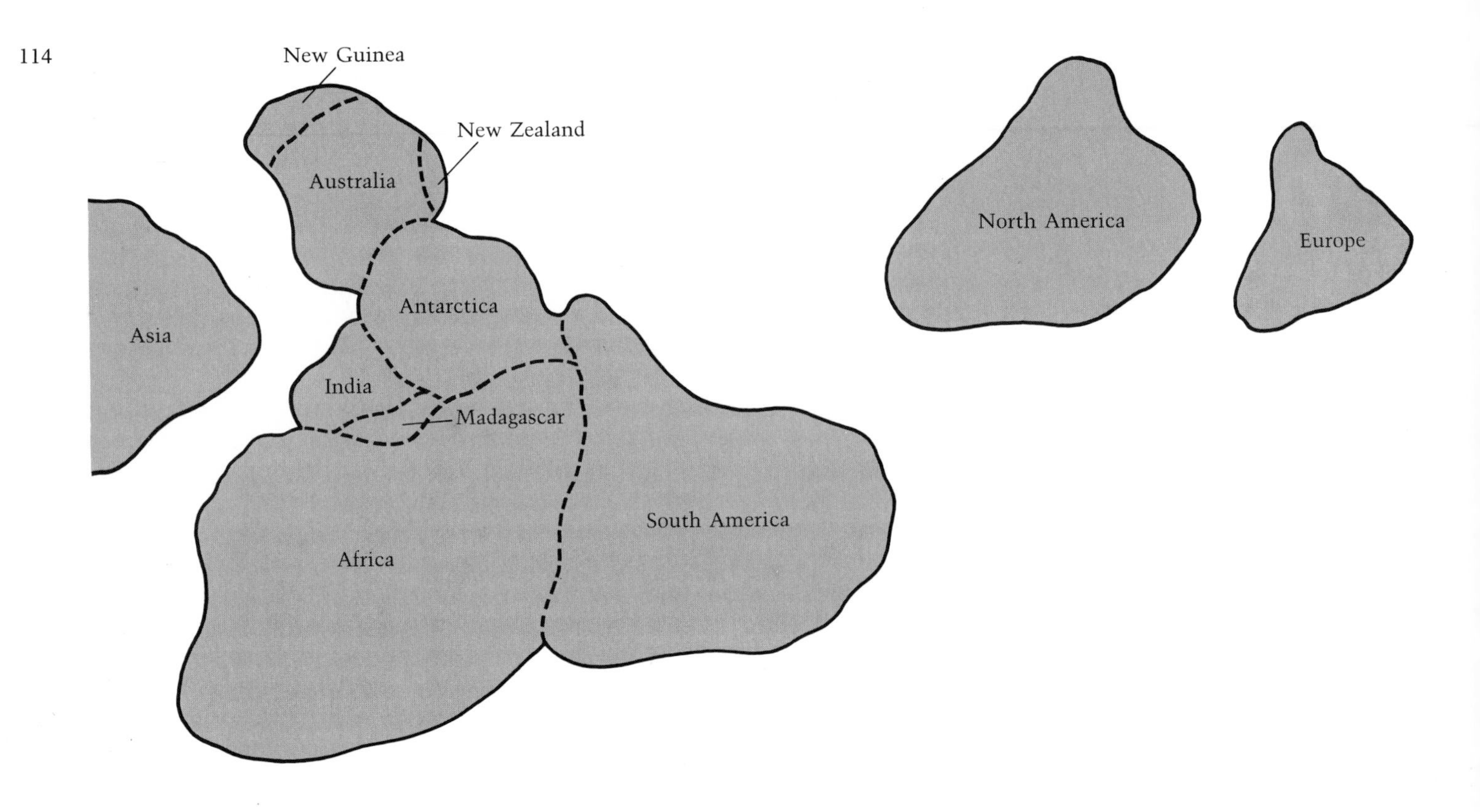

A highly simplified and stylized schema of one of several possible configurations of lands during the Cambrian period. These lands may be considered as (in a sense) ancestral to present continents and some large islands. The dashed lines indicate later subdivisions of what, in this interpretation, are considered to have been connected lands in the Cambrian. The main land mass (to the left of center) is an ancestral form of Gondwanaland. Its present subdivisions and the separate ancestral continents are labeled with their modern names.

present continents have changed not only with respect to the poles but also with respect to each other.

The other main line of evidence has come from detailed study of the ocean floors. It has been found that ridges in those floors, long known in less detail, are lines along which previously molten rock from deeper in the earth's crust is welling up. As it does so, it solidifies and pushes away the previously formed igneous rock on each side of the ridge. This line marks the edge between two crustal plates, and the plates, along with any land on them, are thus moved—slowly, even by geological standards. Where two moving plates meet, or collide, one may move horizontally along the edge of the other. That is happening along part of the west coast of North America, where the Pacific plate is moving north along the North American plate. Or one plate may be forced down (subducted) under the other. That is happening to another plate under the Pacific Ocean, the Nasca plate, as it meets the western side of the South American plate.

(This change in paradigms and principles brought about by the acceptance of continental drift is of unusual interest for the psychology and history of science. It is well treated in the book by Ursula Marvin cited in the bibliography at the end of this book.)

Biogeography in general, and paleobiogeography in particular, must now be seen historically against a dynamic background in which the conditioning physical geography has undergone dramatic changes. Just what those changes were has been worked out, in some respects, for the last two hundred million years or so of the earth's history, but there are still many points of detail and some of more general importance that are undecided and unknown. The biogeography of that span of time, approximately the Mesozoic and Cenozoic eras, must be placed within the geography indicated by geophysical evidence.

It now appears probable that at or shortly before the beginning of the Mesozoic era (thus toward the end of the Paleozoic), there was essentially a single great land mass comprising crustal plates that would later become our more or less separate continents. That is the concept called Pangaea, from the Greek *pan* ("all") and *gaia* ("land").

The rest of the earth's surface must then be visualized as a single ocean, Panthalassa, from the Greek *pan* ("all") and *thalassa* ("sea"). Later, throughout the Mesozoic, Pangaea was breaking up, at first, probably, by the separation of its northern and southern parts by a seaway. The northern part, including what would become North America and Eurasia (except India), is called Laurasia, a term concocted from Laurentia (a name for a part of Canada constituting its geologically ancient core) and Eurasia. The southern part, destined to become South America, Antarctica, Africa, India, and Australia, is called Gondwana or Gondwanaland, a name vastly expanded from that of a relatively small region in India inhabited by people called Gonds.

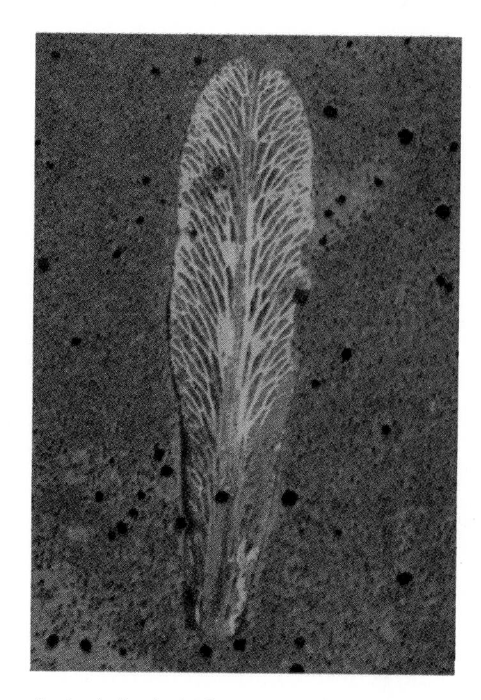

A single leaf of Glossopteris *from New South Wales in southeastern Australia. Leaves of* Glossopteris *range in length from an inch or two to twenty inches or more.*

The name of Gondwanaland was proposed by the Austrian geologist Eduard Suess in 1885, thus far antedating its present usage. It was long used as a term for a supposed continent including South America, Antarctica, Africa, India, and Australia *in their present positions* but connected by land in place of all the now intervening seas, including the whole of the south Atlantic and Indian oceans. The present view is that no such continent ever existed and that the components believed to have formed parts of what is still called Gondwanaland drifted apart on plates as ancient Gondwanaland broke up.

The concept of Gondwanaland was (and still is) supported in considerable part by paleontological evidence, especially that of the peculiar late Paleozoic *Glossopteris* flora, named after a genus of plants with fernlike fronds, fossils of which had early been found in all the major regions included in Gondwanaland. Much later (1970), there was discovered in Antarctica a fauna characterized by the Triassic reptile *Lystrosaurus,* previously known from Africa and India. This was at once hailed as further evidence for Gondwanaland as a unit and for continental drift. The find rightly received much publicity in the popular and the technical press. There are, however, hints that the situation may not have been as simple as it seems at first sight. *Lystrosaurus* is not known from either South America or Australia, both generally believed to have been parts of a unified Gondwanaland when that reptile lived. Moreover, both the plant *Glossopteris* and the reptile *Lystrosaurus* are known from parts of Asia well north of India in regions generally believed to have been parts of Laurasia, not of Gondwanaland, when those organisms lived.

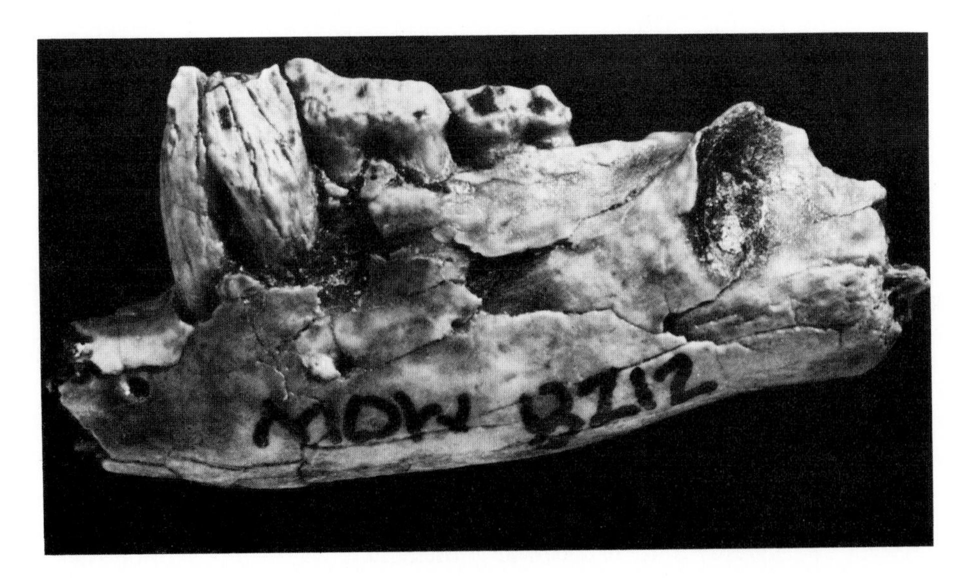

Most of the left lower jaw of the first fossil land mammal known from the Antarctic region. It was found in 1982 on Seymour Island (also known as Vicecomodoro Marambio) near the northern end of the Antarctic Peninsula. It belongs to the long extinct marsupial family Polydolopidae, otherwise known only from South America. Its probable age is late Eocene, hence at least 40 million years ago. The Polydolopidae are not closely related to and could not be ancestors of any known Australian marsupials, but this discovery shows that some dispersal of marsupials, in one direction or the other, did early occur between South America and Antarctica. This adds objective evidence to the view that dispersal in either direction between those continents at a still earlier date could have occurred by way of Antarctica. Australia was near Antarctica until about 45 million years ago, when its long drift to its present position began.

On an earth with geographically shifting continents and oceans, paleobiogeography not only is coordinated with paleogeography but also supplements the geophysical evidence for it. Three examples will illustrate and clarify this relationship.

The first example involves the past and present distribution of marsupial mammals. Their geographic history was long discussed as a puzzle without a clear answer. There is now an answer that is probably correct in the essentials if not yet in all the details. Marsupials are now most characteristic of Australia and South America. It seemed nearly certain that this had been true for both continents ever since some time in the late Cretaceous, and this has now been objectively confirmed for South America. Therefore, the spread of marsupials over the two continents by that time must have involved a connection or some sort of negotiable route between them.

It used to be possible to think of a land bridge for the marsupials right across the Pacific, and some daring biogeographers did think (or perhaps one should say *dream*) of that. It was much more plausible, however, to hypothesize that marsupials, definitely known to have been present in North America in the late Cretaceous, spread from there to South America, on the one hand, and to Asia and thence to Australia, on the other. That was Matthew's view, and it was the most reasonable at the time. With the subsequent great increase in knowledge, it is not now reasonable. There is now evidence that Australia was in the vicinity of eastern Antarctica until some time in the early Cenozoic, probably the Eocene, and far from any possible route from Asia. South America was then also in the vicin-

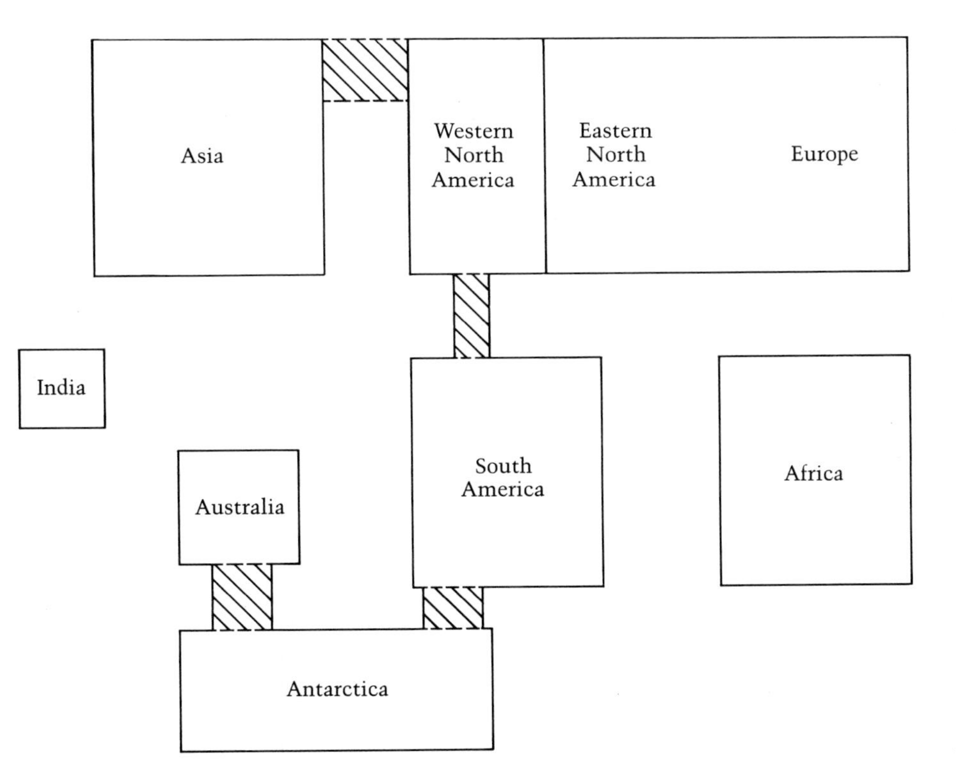

Paleobiogeography of the land faunas of latest Cretaceous to earliest Tertiary times. This is a schematic rendering comparable to that for the Recent in the figure on page 105. It also illustrates, as does the figure on page 112 for a much earlier time, how the configurations of land and sea have changed through geological time. The line between eastern and western North America indicates some differentiation between the faunas of this continent in areas that were separated at first by an inland sea and later (in the Paleocene and Eocene) by other ecological factors. It is unlikely that there were continuous land connections at these times between North America, South America, Antarctica, and Australia, but, in the latest Cretaceous and into the Paleocene or early Eocene, there were probably routes of waif or sweepstakes dispersal, here indicated by the crosshatched connections. That explains the early spread of marsupials. It is still uncertain where the marsupials originated, but it was in one of these four continents. South America, Antarctica, and Australia then became isolated island continents on which further marsupial evolution went on independently. In the Miocene, marsupials became extinct in North America, and they also became extinct at an unknown time in Antarctica. Antarctica is not taken into account in the Sclaterian regional biogeography of Recent land faunas because Antarctica has hardly any animals that are entirely nonmarine in a strict sense. At the time indicated here, India was a large island drifting from Africa to its union with Asia, where it became a part of the Recent Oriental Region.

ity of, but perhaps not so close to, western Antarctica. The late Cretaceous and early Cenozoic mammals of Asia are now also fairly well known,and there were no marsupials among them. Thus the only really likely hypothesis at present is that marsupials spread between Australia and South America, in one direction or the other, by way of Antarctica. As far as is known or can be inferred, only marsupials—and of them probably only one primitive family—spread in this way. It is therefore improbable that the connection was by way of continuous habitable land, and it is more likely that it was by means of sweepstakes dispersal or island-hopping.

The drift of Australia has another interesting bearing on paleozoogeography. The Australian tectonic plate did break away from Antarctica in the early Cenozoic—it was probably the last piece of Gondwanaland to do so. Thereafter, it drifted steadily northward until, at some time in the Miocene, in approaching its present position, it drew close to a chain of islands extending outward from the mainland of Asia. There is fossil evidence that the rat family (Muridae) evolved in Asia, probably in the early Miocene, from still earlier members of the field-mouse family (Cricetidae). Not long thereafter, rats must have island-hopped from the mainland to New Guinea and Australia, where they underwent a remarkable adaptive radiation on those isolated lands.

Another informative example of the interplay of plate tectonics and biogeography is provided by the history of European and North American terrestrial biotas in the Mesozoic and Cenozoic. Geological evidence indicates that, during most of the Mesozoic, what are now the two continental plates were fully connected. Although there are local (mainly ecological) differences in the regional biotas, the fossil evidence is in general agreement with that notion, for the land mammals especially in the Jurassic. In the late Paleocoene and early Eocene, the terrestrial vertebrate faunas of Europe and North America were so similar that the land connection must have been a broad corridor. That close resemblance ended abruptly (geologically speaking) at the end of the early Eocene. This evidence from the fossils dates the final break of a North American plate from the rest of Laurasia with even more precision than do the geophysical data. Thereafter, the biotas of the two now distinct continents evolved independently, except when there was some periodic interchange through Asia. The remaining Eurasian part of Laurasia apparently did not break into separate major tectonic plates, although (as previously noted) an epicontinental sea did for some time act as a biotic barrier between the western (European) and eastern (Asiatic) continental land areas.

The third example to be given here is instructive in a different way: it indicates that the make-and-break of drifting continents does not, after all, account for all the intercontinental relationships of faunas and floras. Land bridges, even more restricted than Matthew correctively concluded, are after all part of the history. There is fossil evidence, from the late Mesozoic and the early Cenozoic, of some fairly selective interchange of animals and plants between Asia and North America. Thereafter, there were periodic interchanges, at times more expansive and at other times less expansive. An irregular alteration continued down to the Recent epoch, when natural interchange is effectively (but perhaps temporarily) stopped. This is explicable not by the make-and-break of the two tectonic plates but by the rise and fall of a land bridge with a variable amount of filtering. Its base is still there under the Bering Sea, which now is serving as a sort of aquatic filter bridge between the Arctic and the North Pacific oceans.

Malcolm McKenna has pointed out that plate tectonics adds two more possibilities to the interpretation of changing resemblances among biotas that involve corridors, filter bridges, and sweepstakes dispersal. One possibility, called "Noah's Ark dispersal," is that part of one land mass might break away and drift to contact with another land. There is a consensus that what is now India broke away from its connection with Africa in Gondwanaland and drifted to final collision with Asia, ferrying plants and animals all the while. Thus a movement of those organisms from Africa to India would be strictly one-way, which is highly unlikely for a bridge or any land connection with both ends connected at the same time. That is a distinct possiblity under plate-tectonics theory, but there is no clear evidence for its occurrence. McKenna's other suggestion, called a "Viking

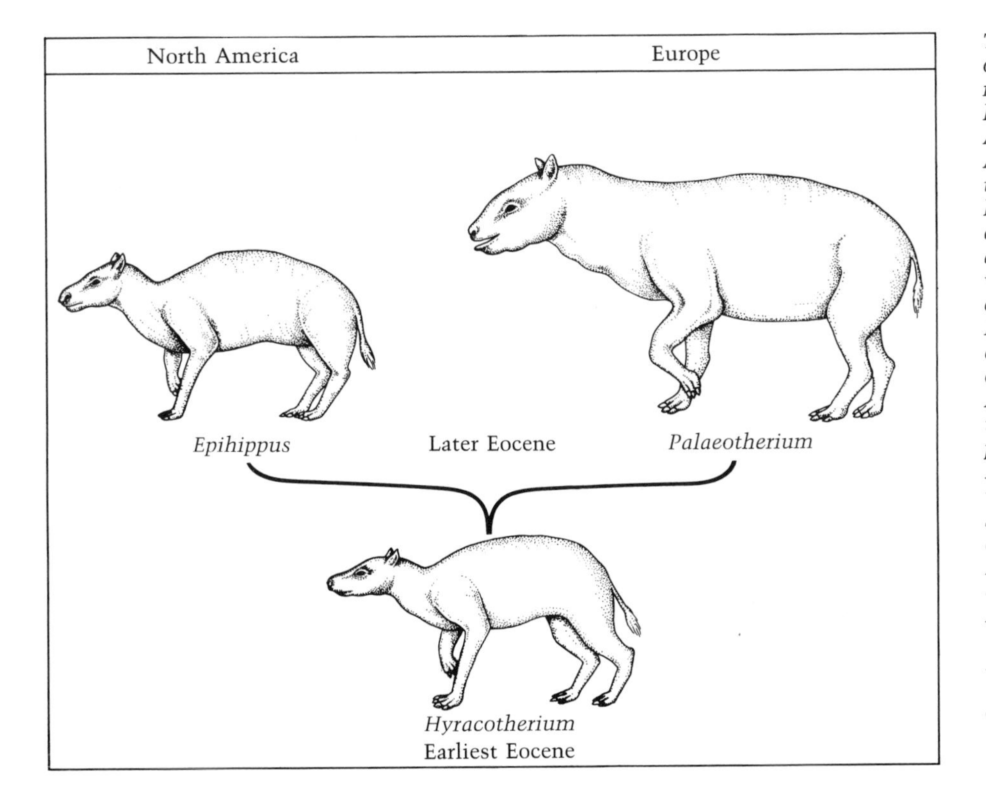

*The evolutionary results of the separation of North America and Europe by continental drift. In the early Eocene, the lands now constituting parts of North America and Europe were continuous. Among the animals ranging freely over these lands were the ancestral horses known as eohippus (*Hyracotherium*, in correct taxonomic language). Fossils of eohippus are virtually indistinguishable whether found in Wyoming, in England, or elsewhere in what was then a united land mass. Near the end of the early Eocene, the North Atlantic Ocean began to open, becoming a barrier between North America and Europe. Thereafter through the Eocene, land animals evolved independently on the two continents. In North America, later Eocene horses, up to the late Eocene* Epihippus, *changed little superficially, although some details, especially in their teeth, did evolve. In Europe, more rapid (or at least more obvious) evolution produced the palaeotheres, including* Palaeotherium. *These were quite different from contemporaneous North American descendants of eohippus. For example,* Epihippus *still had four toes on the front feet, but the front toes of the palaeotheres had been reduced to three—a change that occurred later (in the Oligocene) among North American horses.*

funeral ship," is that a plate drifting from one continent to another, like the Indian plate from Africa to Asia, might have had fossils already in its rocks when it broke away. After its arrival, the fossils could be taken as having existed as living organisms in the terminal continent—Asia, in this example—whereas they really lived in the continent of origin—Africa, in this case. This, too, is quite possible under plate-tectonic theory, but again there seems as yet to be no clear evidence that it did occur.

What has been said so far about biogeography and plate tectonics relates, as stated, to the two hundred million years or so since the late Paleozoic, less than five percent of the age of the earth. It is nevertheless the most interesting part for most of us because it has the best historical record, both physical and biological, and because it has had the most determinative influence on what we now see around us. The analysis and the mapping can doubtless be carried back still further in time, but it becomes more hopelessly fragmentary and dubious as we try to take it back through the Paleozoic. A possibly insuperable difficulty on the physical side is that much (if not all) of the original floors of the oceans, or of Panthalassa, has been long since subducted and fused in the layers below the crustal plates. Still, the rocks preserved on the present continents and islands do preserve some paleomagnetic data and some rock and fossil records of local lands and mostly epicontinental seas. A sort of paleogeographic mapping has been done on the basis of Paleozoic faunal regions, but such maps are still incomplete and sometimes conjectural. Most of the paleobiogeographic data now available are entered on maps of the continents as they now are. In this, as indeed in all branches of science, it is encouraging for scientists, students, and all interested others to know that much that is knowable is not yet known.

As the study of biogeography (both paleo- and neo-) has become more intensive and more complex, it has inevitably developed a number of different theoretical approaches, sometimes designated as "models" (erroneously), as "hypotheses," or (also erroneously) as "philosophies." A recent program for a symposium on this subject speaks of these as the "dispersal," "vicariance," and "ecological determinism" models. The implication seems to be that these are competing and mutually exclusive. In the dispersal model, the premise is taken to be that present distributions, or those of any one time, are the results of long-distance dispersal among separate localities. Vicariance, as expounded in some quarters, is quite complex, but it includes the idea that the presence of related organisms in different regions results from fragmentation of populations from an earlier single and common ancestry that occupied all those regions. Ecological determinism is defined as the view that present distributions, or (presumably again) those at any particular time, result primarily (if not wholly) from existing ecological conditions rather than from historical factors.

The fault of those alternatives is that each of them is wrong if taken alone because all of them are right if taken together. It has been known from the very start of biogeography as a science (certainly it was clear to Darwin) that any fauna or flora is a result of all three of those processes. An adequate explanation of the biogeography of any biota must take all into account and use all as approaches to a causal interpretation of biogeography. The fossil record is crucial in this respect, and that is one of the great values of the study of fossils. Its historical record shows clearly that history itself is an important factor, but not the only causal factor, that must be understood for competent biogeography. The different approaches seem competitive only to the specialist who feels that he is in possession of the whole and single truth.

CHAPTER 5

EXTINCTION, ORIGINATION, AND REPLACEMENT

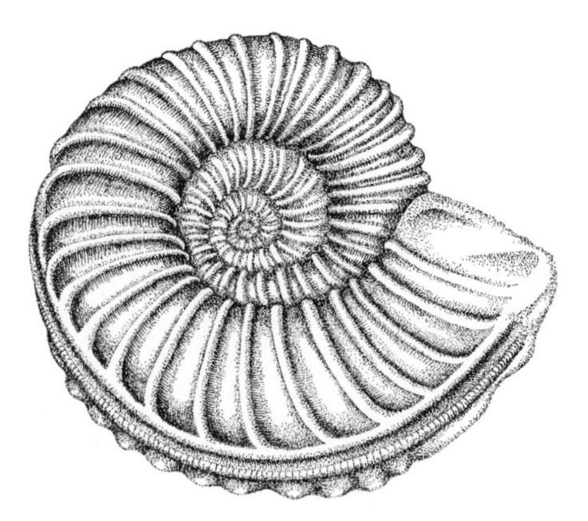

An ammonoid Asteroceras *from the Jurassic period. Ammonoids were relatives of the nautiloids, tentacled mollusks that were abundant for hundreds of millions of years but now survive only in a single living species, the chambered or pearly nautilus.*

All organisms are subject to change through time. Most individuals change in the course of their lifetimes. Such changes are preprogrammed in seeds, zygotes, or other propagative cells and may follow a fairly straightforward course (as in most trees and most mammals) or involve extraordinary remodeling (as from a tadpole to a frog or, still more extreme, from a caterpillar to a butterfly). Changes also occur in individuals according to their own actions, their personal histories, their surroundings, and a multitude of experiences. These changes are not hereditary, but they can occur only within the scope or reaction ranges delimited by individual heredity and by the genetic range of the species as a whole.

Individual changes, however caused, do not constitute evolution. Evolution, as that term is now defined and understood, occurs not in individuals but only in populations and through a succession of generations. Evolutionary change may vary greatly in its rate—a matter for later consideration—but it is usually slow in terms of human experience or recorded history. It can be readily simulated in experiments, and it has been observed in a number of natural populations, but always on a scale almost infinitesimal in comparison both with the billions of years in the history of life and with the extremes of diversity that evolution has produced among millions of organisms.

When there was still legitimate debate about the reality of evolution, one of the arguments against it was that no difference was found between animals (especially ibises) mummified by the Egyptians a few thousands of years ago and the same species living in the nineteenth century A.D. We now know that there were two fallacies in that argument. One is that the time scale was wrong. Only in exceptional circumstances would evolutionary change be evident after so trivial a segment of cosmic time. The other is that evolution itself commonly produces a state of equilibrium or stasis in which change occurs very slowly (if at all) over considerable lengths of time. Such periods of stasis are not indefinitely long on the relevant time scale. Eventually, either the effects of slow change build up or extinction intervenes.

The significance of fossils for the study of evolution thus becomes obvious. They are the only direct record of what has in fact occurred in sequences of reproducing populations and in the course of time on an evolutionary scale.

That was evident to Darwin, who was known as an eminent geologist and paleontologist before he was known to be also an evolutionary biologist. It has been mentioned that one of the first of the clues that led Darwin to evolution was provided by South American fossils. When he came, years later, to the writing of *The Origin of Species,* he was nevertheless bothered by the fact that the fossil record, as known to him in the 1850s, was almost completely lacking in what he called "intermediate varieties"—that is, fossils intermediate in character between earlier and later known fossils. He devoted one chapter, "On the Imperfection of the Geological Record" (Chapter IX in the first edition, eventually Chapter X), to this problem. He there demonstrated that the geological record, and therefore the fossil record, is indeed incomplete.

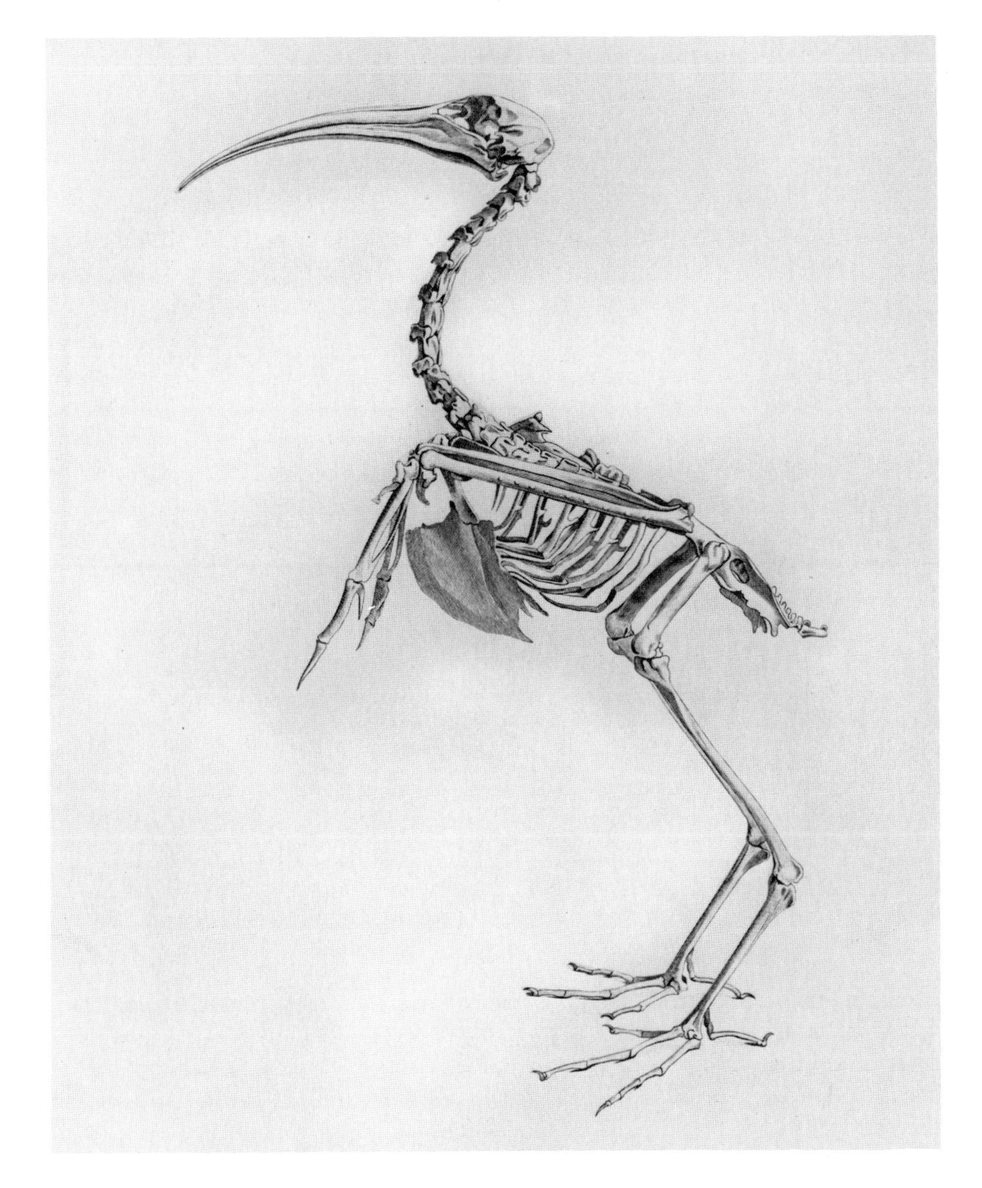

Skeleton of a mummified sacred ibis from Thebes, Egypt, from a figure in Cuvier's Discours sur les révolutions de la surface du globe *("Treatise on the Revolutions of the Surface of the Earth"), 1825. In an appendix to this great work, Cuvier carefully compared the still living species with the remains of ibises found buried in ancient Egyptian tombs. He concluded about this species: "I have shown that it is still now the same as in the time of the Pharaohs. I am well aware that I am referring only to individuals two or three thousand years old, but nevertheless this goes back as far as possible." This was taken by Cuvier (and by some early eighteenth-century naturalists following him) as evidence that species do not change in the course of time.*

We can now reaffirm that the available record is in fact extremely far from including sedimentary rocks of all ages and in all parts of the earth. It does follow that a really complete fossil record simply does not exist. We now have evidence for generalities as to the course of evolution, and we can fill in many details, but many details will never be known in full. As to the basic question, whether evolution is a fact, even in Darwin's day the fossil record already gave an answer. *The Origin of Species* went into this in a chapter entitled "On the Geological Succession of Organic Beings" (Chapter X in the first edition, later Chapter XI).

It is still worthwhile to consider some of Darwin's statements on this subject:

The change in faunas over geologic time has, in general, been gradual. As witness to this, Darwin noted that Lyell had shown that the percentage of living species increased gradually throughout the Cenozoic. In the previous chapter, he

An Early Silurian specimen of Lingula cuneata *which, although superficially similar to the present-day* Lingula, *is approximately 430 million years old. This specimen comes from the Grimsby Sandstone, Lockport, New York.*

had noted that new species usually seem to appear instantaneously, geologically speaking, but he ascribed this to the incompleteness of the record—another point for later discussion here. Note, however, that Darwin was here following Lyell in discussion of constant change in faunas as a whole, and not particularly within the lineages of species. The change in whole faunas (or floras) was, even then, evident from the fossil record, most clearly and conclusively in terms of changes in groups higher than species, such as genera, families, orders, and even higher taxa. The much greater knowledge of the fossil record since Darwin has conclusively supported that view. Despite evident gaps in the record, it has also produced conclusive evidence of evolution within species and not only within faunas and floras as a whole.

Next Darwin noted that taxa ("species of different genera and classes," as then ranked) "have not changed at the same rate, or in the same degree." An example still valid is that a tongue shell, *Lingula,* has changed only specifically from the Paleozoic until now while practically all its Paleozoic contemporaries were quite unlike anything now living.

"Species once lost do not reappear." That is true at the specific level, except for an instance or two in which an organism believed to be *recently* extinct was later found living. The discovery of the living fish *Latimeria,* belonging to a group (the

Coelacanthini) that had been believed extinct for more than sixty million years, is not an exception. At the specific, generic, and family levels, it is quite different from any of its known Paleozoic and Mesozoic relatives. Therefore, this was not the reappearance of a "lost" species, genus, or family. Incidentally, this is a splendid example of the incompleteness of the fossil record. We now *know* that there were coelacanths living all through the Cenozoic, but the thousands of fossil Cenozoic fishes in collections do not include a single specimen of that group.

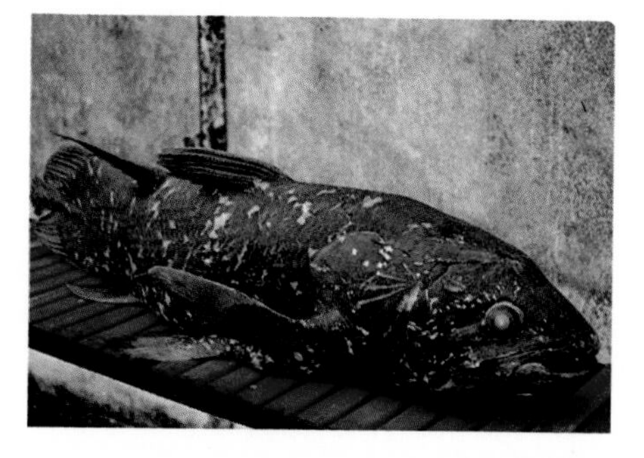

The living fish Latimeria, *which belongs to the group Coelacanthini that had been believed extinct for more than sixty million years. A living* Latimeria *was discovered in 1938 and a second was caught off the coast of Madagascar in 1952.*

After some remarks on extinction, Darwin went on to note that, with the interplay of disappearance of various groups from the fossil record and the appearance of others, the populations at any one time were broadly similar, although not exactly the same, in many parts of the earth. As he correctly remarked, that is more generally true of marine than of nonmarine faunas. He added that groups (higher taxa) now sharply distinct were often less distinct, or were accompanied by groups more or less intermediate, as one followed them back to earlier times in the fossil record. Other telling points were that the fossils of any one geological age were generally more or less intermediate between those just before or just after them, that similarities of fossil faunas became less the greater the difference in their ages, and that successive faunas in any one region of the earth (especially those nonmarine, and explicitly those in Australia and South America) tend to be more similar to each other than to those of widely different regions.

There could then be no reasonable inference from the fossil record other than the inference that it represents a history, in Darwin's words, of "descent with modification"—that is, of organic evolution. That has become even more evident as our knowledge has increased. The whole record of the history of life, so briefly summarized in Chapter 3 of this book, cannot be rationally interpreted in any other way. It demonstrates exactly what must necessarily have happened in the evolutionary sequence leading to the present state of the living world: first there were prokaryotic (nonnuclear) cells, then (in succession) eukaryotic protists and multicellular true plants and animals. Each kingdom of organisms radiated into many adaptive groups, each group with a separate progression, exemplified among vertebrates by jawless fishes, jawed fishes, amphibians, and reptiles, in that order, and then, separately, birds and mammals. Among many other groups of mammals were the primates, and among them (in succession) were monkeys, apes, and finally man. This is not the ladder of nature or *scala naturae* of ancient philosophers, but it is an ever-branching, diversifying, and continuing advance in the occupation of the possible world of life.

So much for one aspect of the relationship between fossils and evolution. Fossils demonstrate that evolution is a fact. On that point there is no dissent whatever among paleontologists. Darwin had already drawn not only that conclusion from the fossil record but also added that, with improbable exceptions, all the "great leading facts in paleontology" seemed to him "simply to follow on the theory of descent with modification through natural selection." From the latter part of that statement there was considerable dissension among paleontologists.

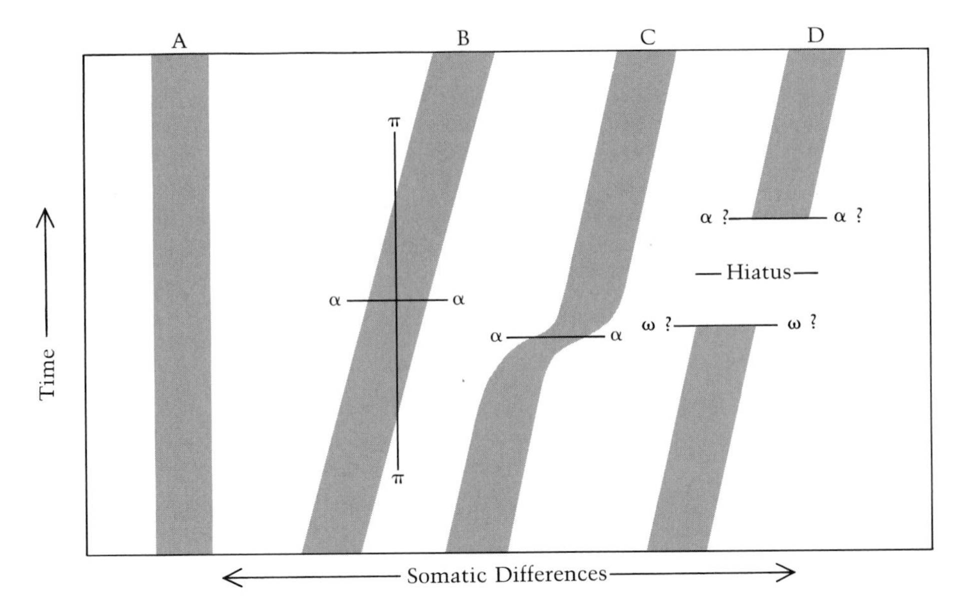

Diagrams of continuity and of pseudo-extinction (or, in G, of termination) in continuous or seemingly continuous successions of populations. The seven diagrams represent separate examples. They are not on the same absolute time scale, nor do they involve similar somatic characters and changes. The width of each graph at any given time symbolizes the amount of variation in the sequence of populations at that time. Actual populations and statistical inferences about them from samples in hand would be less regular than these simplified diagrams suggest.

A *represents a sequence of populations exhibiting no change in variation through a span of geological time. In reality, such completely unchanging sequences probably have never occurred over any considerable length of geological time, but variations from a straight line may be merely a sampling effect or may represent real oscillations around an almost steady mean. By any usable definition of species, all the members of such a sequence belong to just one species.*

B *represents a sequence of populations changing in what is here simplified as a single direction at a constant rate. After the time represented by the line marked* α *(a lower-case Greek alpha, to designate the "beginning"), the indicated somatic variation does not overlap that at the bottom of the diagram. Thus all the populations above the line differ in some respects from all those below the line, even though there is no break in their continuity. The later populations may be (and frequently are) given a specific name different from that below the line. The lower (earlier) species is thus pseudoextinct. If samples of fossils are taken from populations not much above or below the alpha line, it is possible to consider the populations as two species (or other taxa), one of which, here to the left, is dying out while the other is increasing and eventually replaces or relays the first. A separation of the species by the line marked* π *(a lower-case Greek pi, for* ptaisma, *"false step, mistake") is incorrect by any definition of species. With adequate sampling, the error is readily detected by the absence of any discontinuity between characters in specimens from the two sides of the pi line.*

It still continues but to a lesser extent and along somewhat different lines. The present dissent (and sometimes confusion) has to do not with whether evolution has occurred but with the evidence for, and opinions about, just how and why it occurred. The fossils are facts, but there are different possible interpretations of those facts. The problems arise from the incompleteness of the fossil record, not only in the sense that we do not come close to having specimens of all the species, genera, families, or even higher taxa at all times and all places but also because the known specimens give us only fragmentary knowledge of the whole anatomy, physiology, behavior, and other characteristics of the organisms when they were alive.

Much that bears on evolutionary theory depends on experimentation and on studies in increasing detail, with more advanced methods, on living organisms and on fossils. I cannot here adequately discuss evolutionary principles in general, except insofar as the fossil record—the present subject—adds to them, puts restraints on them, or is in turn restrained by them. Some of these aspects of the record will be considered first in this chapter under the general topics of survival, extinction, and faunal replacement or relays, then in the next chapter under the even broader topics of rates and patterns of evolution.

The first striking fact about the fossil record is that an overwhelming majority of known fossils belonged to groups of organisms that are now extinct. Because the word "extinct" is used in two different ways, these must be distinguished. In the course of many generations and over many years, the descendants of a population of organisms that constitutes a single species may (and eventually usually do) become so different that they are technically classified as a species distinct from

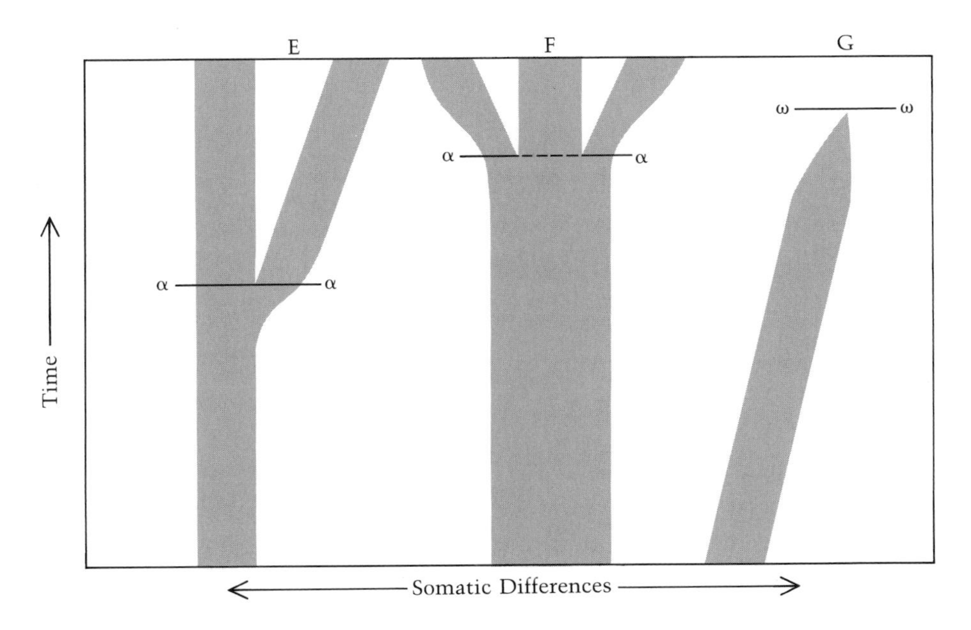

C represents a geologically rapid but continuous shift from one line of somatic change to another. This may, and probably usually does, occur in a relatively small or a marginal part of the ancestral population (compare also F *below). An alpha line across the segment of rapid change separates earlier and later populations that are distinctly different and may be so named; but, as in* B, *the earlier species is pseudoextinct, not terminally so.*

D *represent a more commonly encountered situation in the succession of similar but changing lineages of fossils. Here there is a hiatus in the sequence due either to the absence of sedimentation in the geographical area occupied by the fossil populations or to the nondiscovery of related fossils in this part of the sequence of sediments. The problem—often but not always soluble—is then to determine whether the earlier species became extinct at the line labeled ω? (a queried lower-case Greek omega, to designate tentatively the end) and a distinctly new species arose or came into the area, as indicated by the queried alpha line.*

E *represents the origin of a new species from an older one that continues without notable change. After the alpha line, there are two distinct species but one of these species is the same as the species ancestral to both. If both the species above the alpha line diverged instead of one continuing much as before, both would be considered as distinct from the ancestral species below the line, which would thus be pseudoextinct.*

F *represents the origin of two or more species from marginal populations (or subspecies, or demes, in technical usage) of a formerly more widespread and diverse ancestral species. The divergent populations may become separated at about the same time, geologically speaking, as shown here, or they may arise at geologically distinguishable times. Here there are three distinct species above the alpha line, one essentially the same, although somewhat diminished, as the one ancestral stock which may (and frequently does) eventually become terminally extinct.*

G *represents the simplest course of a moderately evolving species (or any other taxon) going extinct at its omega line.*

that ancestral species, or even as a new, higher-ranking taxon (in practical and usual classification). We then still speak of the ancestral species or higher taxon as extinct, but it did not die out—its descendants simply changed. On the other hand, a species may die out without leaving descendants, and it is then extinct in a different, more final sense. If and when the last species of a genus, family, or other higher taxon fails to have descendants, then the genus, family, or higher taxon is extinct in the final sense. When this distinction is to be clearly made, extinction in the first sense may be called "pseudoextinction," while extinction in the second sense may be called "termination" or "terminal extinction."

There are several million species of organisms still extant. No one knows their number more exactly. The birds and mammals, for example, have been fairly well sorted out, and the numbers of their species can be estimated, but that is not true of the far more abundant insects or of the many groups of more obscure organisms. Going back through geological time, the numbers of taxa ancestral to those still alive become fewer and fewer. The older they are, the more likely are those ancestors with still surviving descendants to be classified as extinct (or, more appropriately, pseudoextinct). However, you need not go back in time very far, geologically speaking, before you find terminally extinct taxa more commonly than pseudoextinct taxa. In the fossil record as a whole, terminal extinction greatly predominates over pseudoextinction. It seems strange, but it is true that the usual outcome of evolution is complete obliteration from the land of the living.

It would be expected theoretically, and it is substantiated by the known fossil record, that the incidence of extinction of both kinds would vary with the taxonomic level of the groups being considered. Species eventually all become extinct in one sense or the other. Genera and families usually include several or many species and do not become extinct until all their species do. Thus, on the average, they will outlast the average for species. Among the still higher levels of classification, it is fairly obvious that no group now known and classified as a kingdom has become extinct. There is no positively clear instance of a phylum becoming extinct; but there are possible exceptions, depending on one's opinion of the affinities and classifications of some peculiar groups of fossils. For example, the curious fossils of the group called Archaeocyatha, which were abundant in the Cambrian and unknown thereafter, have been classified in the phylum Porifera (sponges) and in the quite different phylum Coelenterata (corals and their kin) but are now frequently put aside in a phylum all by themselves, although that seems to be a Gordian solution resorted to when faced by a knot of ignorance as to what they were really like when they were alive.

The dinosaurs are the most striking and most widely known of the extinct animals. They might be called the prime exemplar of extinction. The known dinosaurs constitute two orders: Saurischia, with two suborders, about fifteen families, and at least 150 genera usually now recognized as valid; and Ornithischia, with four suborders, about ten to thirteen families, and more than 100 genera usually accepted as valid. The number of known species of the two orders is certainly well into the hundreds, but no really good estimate of the whole lot of them is available. Figures cannot be kept up to date because hitherto unknown genera and species of dinosaurs are still being discovered quite frequently. All of this tremendous and almost incredibly motley array is extinct. The extinction of the order Ornithischia at all taxonomic levels was unquestionably terminal. If, as may be true but is still open to some question, the birds (order Aves) evolved from some primitive saurischian dinosaur, then one family, probably a single genus, and possibly a single (as yet unknown or unidentified) species of that order is pseudoextinct, although even those single taxa are definitely extinct as that word is usually understood. In any case, the many other saurischian and all the ornithischian taxa have long been terminally extinct.

Even groups that are abundantly alive and well today have numerous extinct relatives. Few things are now more exuberantly alive than the corals in the reefs in warm seas, but (as noted in Chapter 3) all of the once equally exuberant known species, genera, and families of corals in the reefs of the Paleozoic have been terminally extinct since the end of that geological era. (No ancestors of the present corals are definitely known from the Paleozoic; this is ascribed to their then having had no fossilizable hard parts.) In spite of the depredations of mankind, living species and genera of ungulates (hoofed mammals) are still so numerous on earth that it may be hard to believe that they are enormously outnumbered by the known terminally extinct species and genera of ungulates, and even the living families are outnumbered by the terminally extinct ones by about four and a half to one and the living orders by about two to one. Terminal extinction is clearly not an exceptional event. It is by far the *usual* outcome of evolution.

The principal data for the study of extinction are the geological times of last occurrences of taxa in the known fossil record. These are then taken as times of extinction. It is never quite certain that a given taxon may not have survived for some time thereafter without being known in the incomplete record, but for the comparatively well-known Phanerozoic (from the Cambrian onward), multiple counts of last appearances are acceptable as reasonable approximations of the incidence of extinction at a given time. Another defect of such data is that it is rarely practicable to distinguish between pseudoextinctions and terminal extinctions. For most of the record, however, it is evident that, over an appreciable span of geological time, pseudoextinctions are so greatly outnumbered by terminal extinctions—at least at levels from species to families, and in some cases even up to orders—that the data will reasonably approximate actual patterns of terminal extinction.

At present, it is rarely practicable to compile such data for species, except within the limits of some larger taxon (such as an order) and for limited extents of geological time (such as the Pleistocene, for which the sampling is most intense and the time most accurately subdivided). For groups of large, fossilizable organisms in general, and for all or considerable stretches of Phanerozoic time, the useful data so far available include in some cases genera, usually families, and sometimes orders.

The simplest way in which to present such data and to show them as a pattern is to plot numbers of last appearances on the vertical axis of a graph and geological time (either successive or, preferably, in years before present) on the horizontal axis. The data thus entered as dots on the graph can then be connected by lines to give a historical pattern for the group or groups being studied. Many such graphs have been made, and two facts about them are evident. First, there has never been an appreciable or measurable extent of geological time in which there was not a considerable incidence of extinction, either overall or within almost any large group of fossils. That is clearly true of extinctions of genera and families, and it was almost certainly even more true of species, even though few useful data at that level have been compiled. The second point obvious from such graphs is that, although there has never been a geological time without many extinctions, the number of extinctions and, therefore, the rate of extinction have varied greatly over time.

There are several methods of measuring and comparing the incidence and rates of extinction. One, used especially by the American paleontologist Norman D. Newell, is to count the last known occurrences of taxa in a given part of geological time (such as the early, middle, or late part of a geological period), to estimate the length of such a segment of time in years, and to tabulate the number of last occurrences per million years. Newell also counted the total known taxa for such segments of geological time and tabulated the last occurrences among them as percentages of that total. In the following tables the data so treated by Newell for families of the main animal groups well represented in the fossil record have been recast as frequency distributions. Newell used 29 subdivisions of geological

Frequency distribution of numbers of last known occurrences of families of main groups of fossil animals per million years in 29 subdivisions of geological time from the early Cambrian onward.

Last occurrences per million years	Frequency in Newell's tabulation
2.00–2.24	2
1.75–1.99	1
1.50–1.74	2
1.25–1.49	0
1.00–1.24	3
0.75–0.99	5
0.50–0.74	8
0.25–0.49	8
0–0.24	0

Frequency distribution of percentage of last occurrences among total occurrences of main groups of fossil animals for 29 subdivisions of geological time from the early Cambrian onward.

Percentage of last occurrences	Frequency in Newell's tabulation
50–59	2
40–49	0
30–39	2
20–29	6
10–19	10
0–9	9

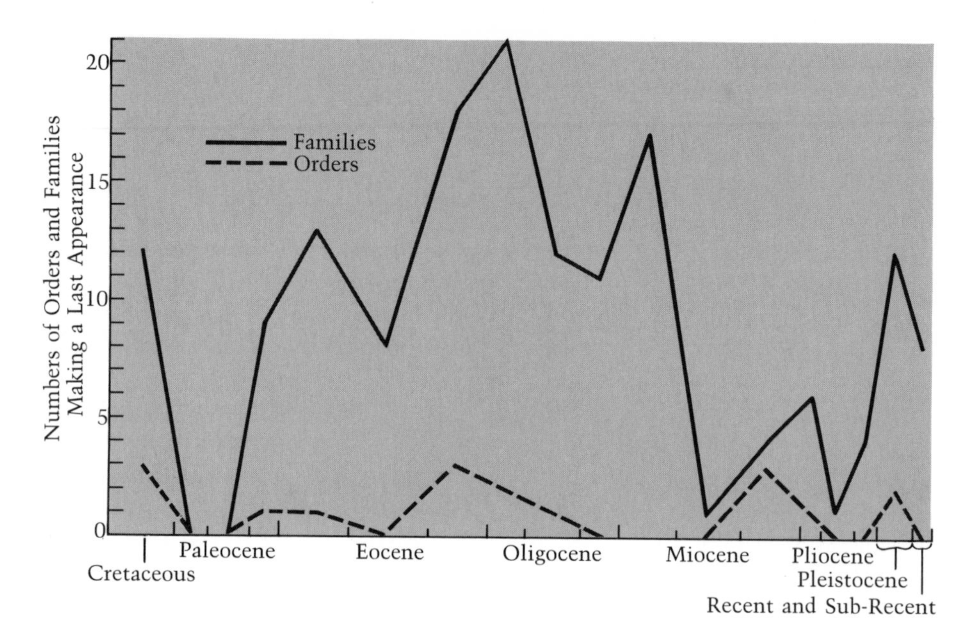

Last known appearances of orders and families of mammals from the latest Cretaceous to the Recent. The graph is in absolute numbers, not in rates per million years or in percentages of total known faunas. The apparent deep low around the early Paleocene is at least in part a sampling effect. Although there almost certainly were many more originations than extinctions in that time, early Paleocene mammals are at present less well known than those that lived later—or even, in some regions (western North America and Central Asia, for example), those that lived earlier. The Pleistocene peak has been recognized for quite a long time and it has been discussed at almost excessive length. A point of interest in this graph is that last appearances and therefore evident extinctions peaked much more highly in the early Eocene, early Oligocene, and early Miocene. Jason Lillegraven, who made this graph, pointed out that its highs and lows are probably correlated with changes in world climate and vegetation but that this relationship had not then (1972) been sufficiently studied. It still has not been. For these graphs, data on families of bats (a single order, Chiroptera, with a scanty fossil record) and that on most marine mammals (all the cetaceans except the relatively few and early archaeocetes) have been omitted. Therefore, the data involve almost entirely the strictly terrestrial mammals.

time from early Cambrian to Neogene. (Neogene, following the usage relevant to Newell's tabulation, is used as a subdivision of the Cenozoic including the Miocene, Pliocene, Pleistocene, and Recent epochs.) None of the 29 subdivisions had zero last occurrences, either per million years or as a percentage of total families. Last occurences vary from 0.30 to 2.11 per million years and from 3% to 52% of the total families.

Although Newell graphed his data by percentages, for several reasons not necessary to detail here I consider the distribution in last occurrences per million years to be more significant. A note-worthy point, to which I will return, is that the frequency distribution of last occurrences per million years is discontinuous. There is a strongly skewed total frequency of 24 from 0.25 to 1.24, zero frequency from 1.25 to 1.49, and a frequency of 5 at the top from 1.50 to 2.24 (more exactly, from 1.50 to 2.11). Those five times with exceptionally high extinction rates are

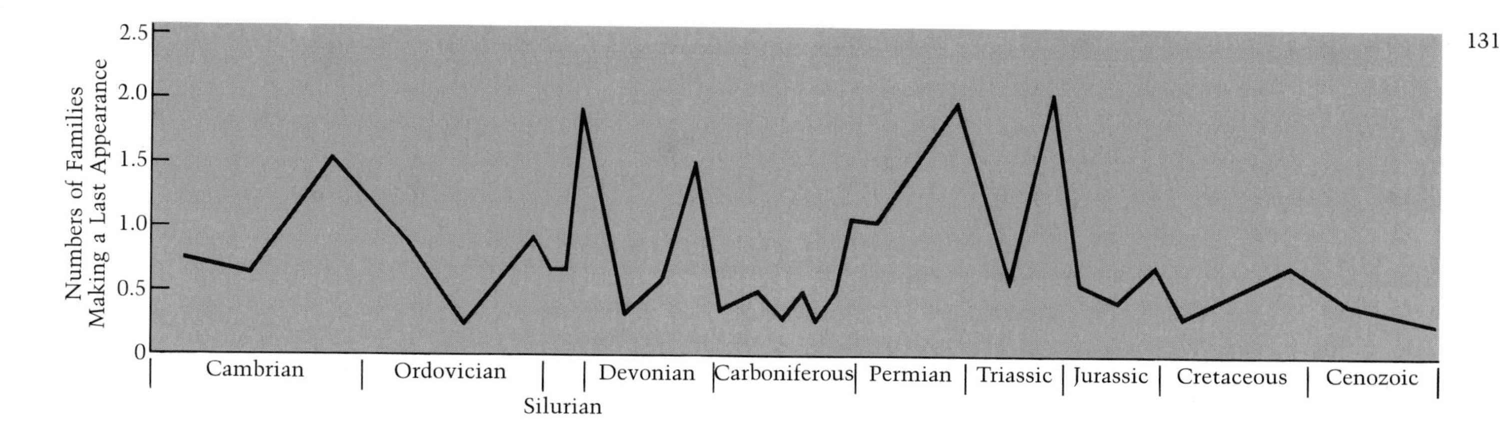

Graph of last known appearances, per million years, of families of the chief groups of fossil animals in Phanerozoic (Cambrian to Recent) time. There are noteworthy high points toward the ends of the Cambrian, Silurian, Devonian, Permian, and Triassic periods. For these groups of animals and in these terms, there are no high points toward the ends of the Jurassic and Cretaceous periods and the Cenozoic era, although there were markedly greater numbers of last appearances at those times in terms of the percentages for fossil vertebrates. It is a reasonable assumption that the patterns for last appearances per million years and for percentages of last appearances approximate rates of extinction. The peaks in this graph indicate last appearances in many different groups. The peak toward the end of the Cambrian is affected most by trilobites and sponges, probably too much so for the latter group, which does not have as consistent a fossil record as the others used in this tabulation. The late Devonian and late Permian peaks or Devonian–Silurian and Permian–Triassic turnovers involve most of the well-known groups of fossil invertebrates. That for the late Triassic, which is the highest of all by a small margin, largely involved ammonoids and brachiopods, but it may have been exaggerated by sampling effects in some other group. The data used here are slightly modified from Norman Newell (1967), who did not present them in graphic form. His estimates of relative lengths of successive periods, which were the basis for his tabulation of rates per million years, have been retained in this graph.

(in sequence from older to younger) the late Cambrian, late Silurian, late Devonian, late Permian, and late Triassic.

Another approach to the quantitative study of extinction and some related aspects of the fossil record is an adaptation to these subjects of what are usually called survivorship (or life) tables and curves. These have a long history dating from the third century A.D. at the latest. They have now been highly elaborated, mainly in applications to human populations—actuarial, in connection with life insurance, and demographic, in connection with sociology. The data may be the life spans of a sample from a defined population or cohort, in which case the analysis is called age-specific, or they may be the ages of all living members of such a sample at any one time, then called time-specific. It is also possible to combine the two approaches and make a composite life table.

These methods were devised for actuarial application to the species *Homo sapiens*, but they can also be applied to other species in which the life spans or the ages of individuals can be determined. This has been done extensively in population ecology, mostly of Recent animals, as is interestingly expounded and illustrated in the book by G. Evelyn Hutchinson cited at the end of this book. In some rather special cases, it is also possible to divide collections of fossils of a single species into successive age groups to which the actuarial methods can be directly applied. This has been done in a few instances, notably by the Finnish vertebrate paleontologist-paleobiologist Björn Kurtén, but it is surprising that it has not yet been more widely used.

The same methods have been adapted, and are in more general use, by paleontologists for the study of survivorship and extinction at specific and higher taxonomic levels in the fossil record. Here separate but usually related taxa—commonly species, genera, or families—are treated as if they were individuals in an actuarial study. The datum for each taxon is the geological time, usually in years, between its known first and last appearances in the fossil record. This is treated like an individual's lifespan in an actuarial study. When only extinct taxa are being considered, the analysis is usually age-specific. If the taxa under consideration all have living members (such studies have rarely been done as yet), analysis must necessarily be time-specific, and the data are the years before present of the first known appearance of each taxon in the fossil record. If some taxa are extinct and others are not, the analysis should be composite, but examples so far are even fewer. The data are usually presented graphically as a survivorship curve.

First and last known occurrences of families of the chief groups of animals in the fossil record as percentages of the whole fauna known for a given subdivision of geological time. Such graphs do not indicate rates of extinction, strictly speaking. They do indicate turnovers in the taxonomic makeup of world faunas to the extent that those faunas are represented in the known fossil record. As in almost all such records (or in correlated ones, particularly in terms of rates), the peaks of last appearances, which are indicative of extinction, precede those of first appearances, which are indicative of the evolution of new taxa. Thus there is an appearance of compensation, with ecological voids made by extinction being filled by evolutionary origins. However, it is indicated by other data on their fossil record that the peaks and troughs of first appearances of families of mammals tended nearly to coincide with those of their last appearances. For known orders of mammals, the all-time peak was in the late Paleocene and early Eocene, well before the major peaks for families.

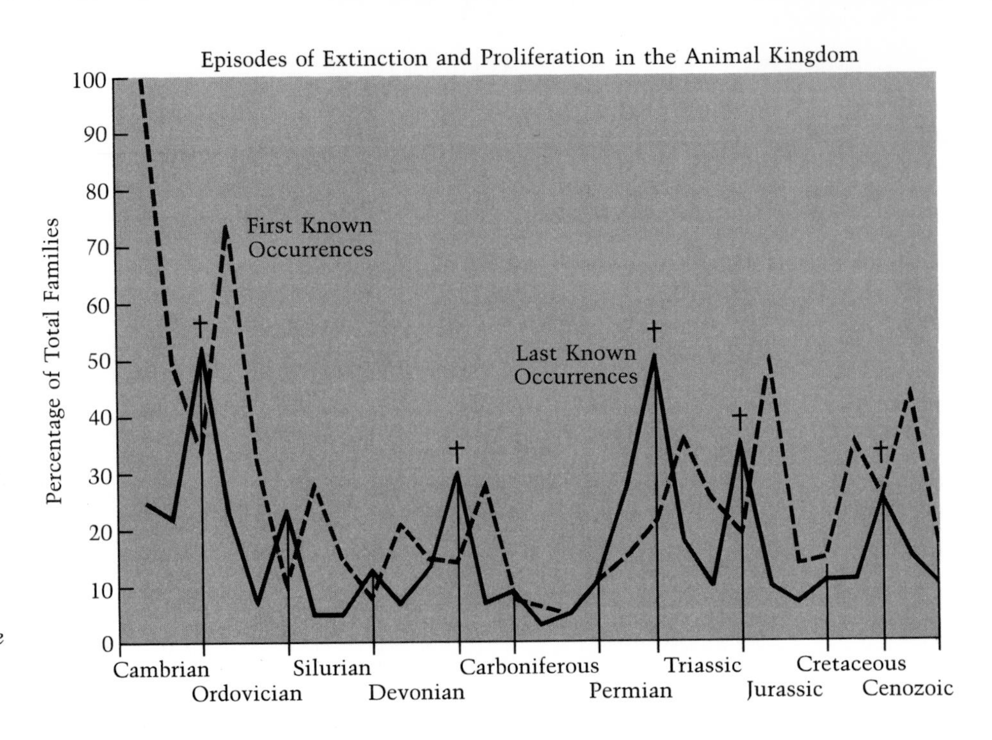

Formalized and idealized survivorship graphs to exemplify methods and relationships in interpretations. In each case, the graph is based on a cohort, either of individuals or of taxa. The length of survival is measured along the horizontal axis, beginning with zero at lower left: the individual at birth or the taxon at the time of evolutionary origin has not then survived any appreciable time. The point at the lower right is maximum time of survival, reached in theory by a single individual or taxon. The scale along the horizontal axis should be arithmetic in appropriate units—for instance in minutes, days, or years for individuals, or in tens of thousands or millions of years for taxa. The vertical scale measures percentages of the original cohort surviving. On an arithmetic scale, this runs from 0% at the bottom to 100% at the top. A particular graph will therefore start at the upper left corner and end at the lower right. The percentage scale may be arithmetic, in which case the graph is arithmetic. If the vertical scale is logarithmic, however, the graph is semilogarithmic. The slope of a semilogarithmic survivorship graph indicates the rate of loss by death or extinction. If this rate is constant throughout, the resulting "curve" is a straight line, as seen in graph A *of this figure. If, however, the vertical scale is arithmetic, the absolute number of deaths or extinctions becomes steadily less, even though the percentage of losses is constant, and the result is as shown by graph* B. *It is intuitive, however, that the rate of loss or of mortality would often be greater in youth and in old age than in the intermediate years, giving a curve more or less like graph* C. *Age-specific survivorship curves resembling this do indeed occur in some human populations and have also been found in some wild animals but other variant patterns also occur. Although (as noted on page 134) "Van Valen's law" requires that semilogarithmic survivorship graphs be straight lines, there are too many exceptions to make this a "law."*

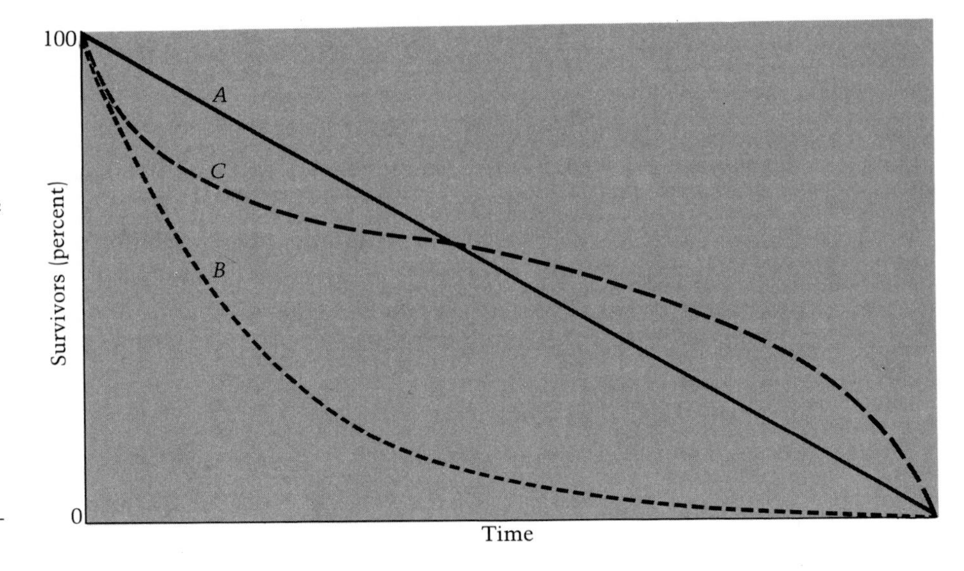

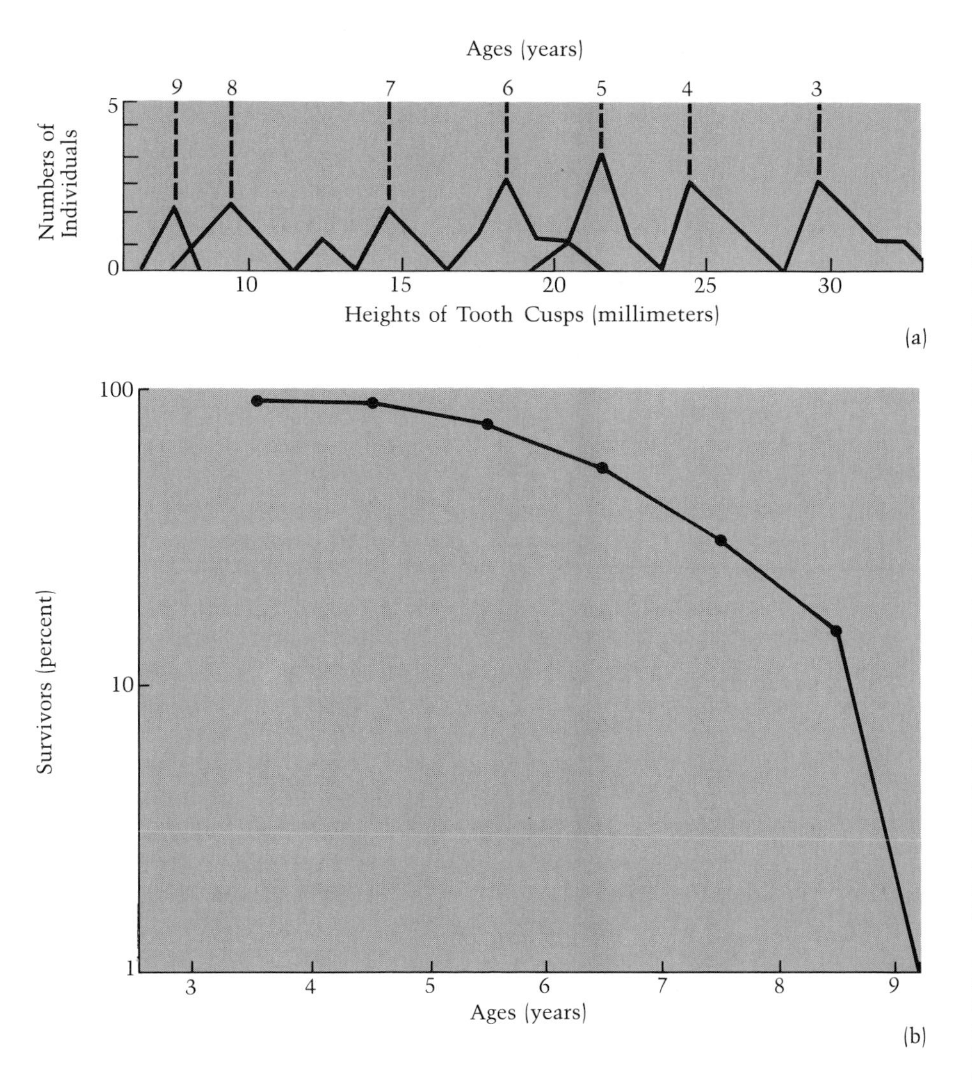

An example of survivorship in a single fossil species. For this purpose, it is necessary to have a medium to large sample of specimens all of one species, all from one locality or small area, and all of the same geological age. Next it is necessary to be able to measure (or reasonably estimate) the age in years of each individual at its time of death. Although good estimates of individual ages are not at present possible for many fossils, there are several available methods. Some animals (both invertebrates and vertebrates) that live in environments with annual changes develop annual rings of varying thickness or density in the hard parts that are preserved as fossils. Another interesting method, here shown in (a), *depends on the fact that grazing animals with high-crowned molar teeth wear those teeth down at a fairly constant rate. If, then, there is a seasonal time of birth, as there is in most animals in definitely seasonal climates, the animals in different yearly age classes will have separable peaks of frequencies for heights of their worn molars. Björn Kurtén found that this could be done for a fair sample of specimens all from a single fossil pocket in the early Pliocene of China. The results for the height of one cusp (the metacone) in one set of homologous teeth (the last upper molar, M^3) are shown in* (a) *with the inferred year groups as probable ages of the individuals. (These were also partly based on other evidence.)*

In a subsequent study, Kurtén derived from those data a semilogarithmic survivorship curve (b) *for* Plesiaddax depereti, *an extinct genus and species allied to the muskoxen. This does not entirely correspond with the whole idealized theoretical curve labeled* C *in the bottom figure on the facing page, but it is like the central (middle-age) and later (old-age) parts of that curve. As Kurtén's data do not include the first two to three years of these animals' lives, it is highly likely that those years did include much heavier mortality than the years from near 3 to about 6 or 7 years of age. In that case, the whole curve would be a simple variant of the generalized curve* C *in the aforementioned figure.*

There are sampling problems in such studies, especially at the level of species. It is also clear that the known duration of a taxon must usually be considered minimal because it may be quite likely that the taxon as such arose some time before it entered the known fossil record, and it may also, but probably less often, have continued in existence for an appreciable time after its last known presence in the record. Still, it is probable that the general form of a survivorship curve based on fairly well-known taxa usually is not seriously biased by those uncertainties. The precision with which the length of time of known occurrences is measured has increased with progress in methods of geological dating.

It is clear that the life tables and survivorship curves are determined by the times and rates of death in actuarial or population-ecological terms and by the times and rates of extinction in evolutionary terms. A graph of extinctions against time will slope down from left to right, and a steeper slope on the same scale will

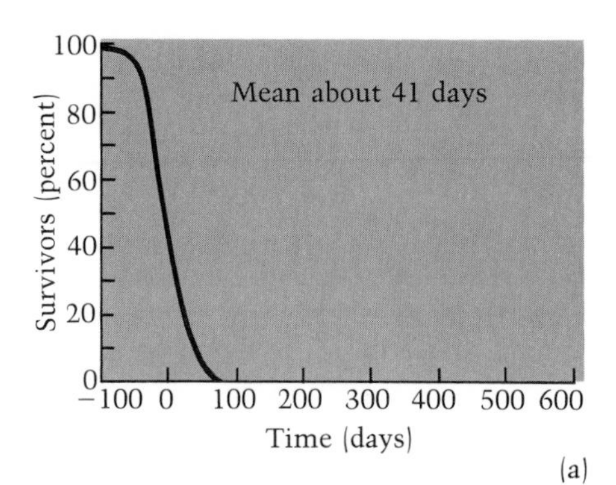

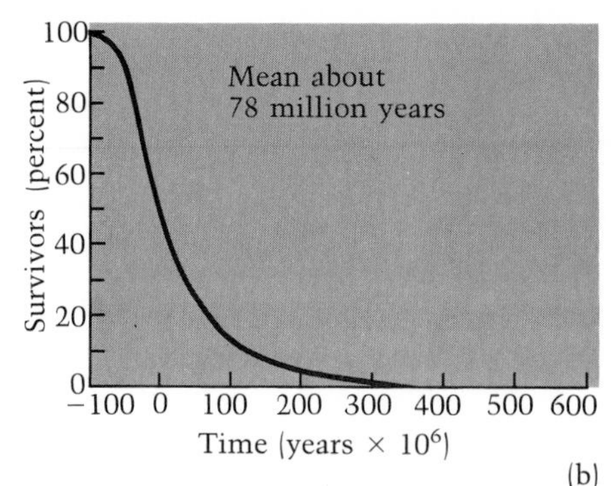

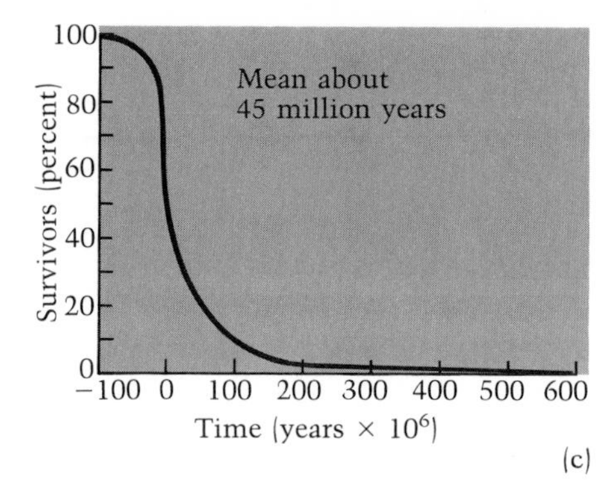

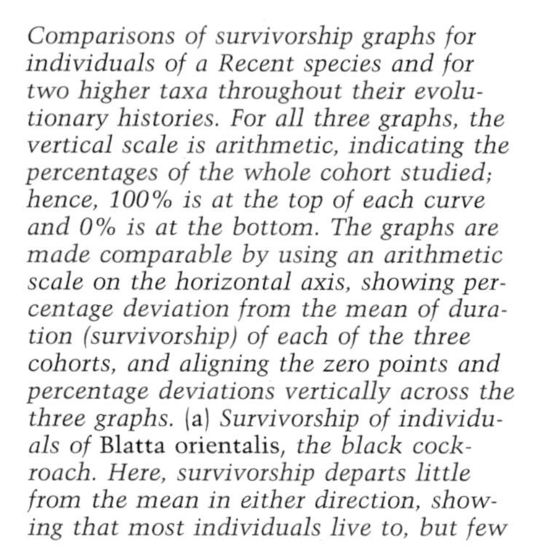

Comparisons of survivorship graphs for individuals of a Recent species and for two higher taxa throughout their evolutionary histories. For all three graphs, the vertical scale is arithmetic, indicating the percentages of the whole cohort studied; hence, 100% is at the top of each curve and 0% is at the bottom. The graphs are made comparable by using an arithmetic scale on the horizontal axis, showing percentage deviation from the mean of duration (survivorship) of each of the three cohorts, and aligning the zero points and percentage deviations vertically across the three graphs. (a) *Survivorship of individuals of* Blatta orientalis, *the black cockroach. Here, survivorship departs little from the mean in either direction, showing that most individuals live to, but few live beyond, a relatively short mature stage.* (b) *Survivorship of genera in the class Bivalvia of the phylum Mollusca. This graph, first calculated and drawn in the early 1940s, may have been the first application of survivorship curves to taxa rather than to individuals, and it is included partly for that reason. Increased knowledge of bivalves and increased precision in determining the length of existence of genera have changed the raw data, but the general shape of the survivorship graph seems to be about the same. Graph* (b) *differs from graph* (a) *principally in that it has a longer terminal segment, showing that more genera of bivalves survived past median age than do individual cockroaches.* (c) *A similar survivorship graph for genera of Brachiopoda, a phylum of marine shelled animals. This differs from graph* (b) *mainly in showing that an even larger percentage of genera reached ages around the mean but that the length of persistence of a small part of the whole group before extinction was longer relative to the mean than in* (b) *and especially more than in* (a), *where such survival is practically absent. It must again be recalled that the survivorship curves comparable to* (a), *on one hand, and to* (b) *and* (c), *on the other, are indicative of quite different things: in* (a), *the birth and death of individuals within a species or lesser group; in* (b) *and* (c), *the (always approximate) lengths of time between the first known appearances of whole taxa in the geological record and their last known appearances.*

indicate a higher extinction rate. Any change in slope within a single graph will, of course, indicate a change in the extinction rate.

In the 1970s and the early 1980s, there has been much discussion based on a publication by the American vertebrate paleontologist and evolutionary biologist Leigh Van Valen in 1973 illustrating and discussing survivorship curves for many different groups of organisms, including some protists and plants as well as many invertebrates and vertebrates well represented in the known fossil record. Van Valen concluded that, in all cases, the "curve" was in fact a straight line, and he based on it what he called a law (and others have since referred to as Van Valen's law). As stated by Van Valen, it is that "extinction in any adaptive zone occurs at a stochastically constant rate" or, in other words, if the adaptive characteristics of a group of organisms do not change much, any slight change in its rate of extinction will be random and probably only a sampling effect.

It is not possible here to give details either of Van Valen's discussion of his "law" or of criticisms of it. It has been suggested (especially by David Raup) that, if the survivorship curves for species are linear, those for supraspecific taxa, such as genera, almost necessarily are (and, in some tested instances, demonstrably are) concave. Van Valen's graphs are also biased by the separation of extinct and living organisms, which, by appropriate actuarial methods, can be combined to give a more realistic and valid indication of extinction even though—or rather because—living taxa are also included.

In view of the mass of data showing greatly different extinction rates in different taxa or in the same taxa at different times, it is incredible that extinction rates are constant in principle. The statement of Van Valen's "law" is applicable only within one constant adaptive zone, which is never true of the whole of any fauna or flora, and also there are admitted exceptions to the "law" when mass extinctions occur.

Another approach to the study of extinctions and faunal changes was devised and used by Björn Kurtén: faunal half-life. This is the length of time from the geological date of a first appearance of a given fauna to the time when half of its species (or taxa at other levels) last appear in the record and are presumed thereafter to be extinct. In these terms, the lower the half-life of a fauna, the higher the rate of extinction shortly thereafter, geologically speaking. Some of Kurtén's estimates of half-lives of faunas of mammalian species are given in the table shown here. In discussion of these, Kurtén concluded: "It is clear that additional evidence is necessary." The method is certainly interesting, but it has not yet been developed very far.

Some mean half-lives of faunas of mammalian species.

Geological age of faunas being averaged	Mean half-life (years)
Late Pleistocene	343,000
Middle Pleistocene	84,000
Miocene and Pliocene	1,800,000

That extinction has been a constant feature of at least the last seven hundred million years or so of the history of life and that this is among the dominant aspects of that history are facts. Until this was proved by the fossil record, there was no *a priori* reason to think that it should be so; and it was noted earlier (Chapter 1) that early students of the fossil record thought either that extinction never occurred or that it was exceptional, whereas we now know that it is the usual outcome of evolution. But why should it be?

Although Darwin was not fully aware of the extent to which extinction has been a dominant feature of life, it is not surprising that he considered its causes. He noted that, if the population of a species is rare, natural fluctuations in its numbers may reduce them to zero. He also noted that natural selection acts between species and not only within species—which, incidentally, has just recently been noticed by some other students of evolution and hailed as their own discovery. Thus, as another and principal reason for extinction, Darwin saw competition between species in which one, favored by natural selection, eventually caused the extinction of another not so favored. Although Darwin did not put it in just these words, we can say that positive natural selection in one species causes negative natural selection in the other.

Darwin also said that, when a species becomes rare and hence subject to extinction, "something is unfavorable in its conditions of life; but what that something is, we can hardly ever tell." There is now an enormous and sometimes polemic literature on the causes of extinction, but it seems to me that, like Darwin, we still "can hardly ever tell." Possible causes commonly listed include competition and chance changes in population size, the explicit Darwinian factors, but also other things "unfavorable in its [a species'] conditions of life," the general Darwinian factor, now itemized to include (among other unfavorable conditions) predation, diseases, or changes in the physical environment. In the most general way, extinction follows any changes in the population of a species, or in its whole environment, that tend toward fatal decrease in numbers of individuals (either immediately or over the course of generations) and that the species cannot evade (either behaviorally or by genetic change and selection).

That is all unsatisfactorily vague. What we really want to know is what exactly caused extinction in a particular instance, and this is just what even now we are hardly ever given to know. The efforts to supply such explicit explanations, characterized in *Principles of Paleontology* by David M. Raup and Steven M. Stanley as "some ingenious and some preposterous," have usually concentrated on one or another of the phenomena in the fossil record called mass extinctions. Extinction is constant in occurrence but variable in intensity. Peaks in intensity might then be explained as being within the range of essentially haphazard variation or as being the result of a chance coincidence of the effects of a number of different and disconnected causes. However, paleontologists have long agreed that these peaks constitute a phenomenon different from oscillations of the usual or background level of extinctions.

That is the reason for having called attention to the discontinuity in the frequency distribution shown in the first table on page 130 earlier in this chapter. The five times with frequencies of extinction between 1.50 and 2.24 per million years seem to belong to a different category from those below 1.24. As mentioned, these exceptional times are the late Cambrian, late Silurian, late Devonian, late Permian, and late Triassic. That indicates that mass extinctions occurred between the Cambrian and Ordovician, the Silurian and Devonian, the Devonian and Carboniferous, the Permian and Triassic, and the Triassic and Jurassic. It was perception of the faunal changes involved in these mass extinctions that caused designation of these times as boundaries between periods and eras even by preevolutionary geologists. Almost all geologists now recognize the Mesozoic–Cenozoic or Cretaceous–Paleocene boundary as marking the climax of another mass extinction, and some also so designate the Pleistocene–Recent boundary, but that is decidedly a special case. (Some question could also be raised about the Silurian–Devonian mass extinction.)

The obvious thing would be to look for some evidences about the physical environments that coincide with all accepted instances of mass extinction but are not found at other times. That has often been tried, but, in my opinion, with no clearly acceptable result. Such hypotheses as bursts of radiation from the sun or supernovae, fluctuation in the composition of the atmosphere or the oceans, changes in distribution of trace elements or in the productivity of sea or land, changes in worldwide climate, and others, seem to rest on inadequate (or no) evidence and are not shown to be present at all times of undoubted mass extinctions and absent at other times. Most persistent has been the idea that the pattern of lands and seas, with long cycles of flooding and regression, emergence and submergence, elevation and depression, somehow correlate with episodes of mass extinction, but there is not yet a clear consensus about just how these events bring about mass extinction, if they do. Perhaps more light will be cast on this as new knowledge is gained about plate tectonics.

Most of the attempts to explain mass extinctions are *ad hoc,* directed to particular instances and not to the repetitive phenomenon in general. These usually focus on the extinctions near the Cretaceous–Tertiary boundary and around the end of the Pleistocene and the early Recent. These subjects are popular because one involves the extinction of the last dinosaurs and the other the extinction of many large mammals, such as mammoths and mastodons.

The late Cretaceous extinctions involved not only dinosaurs but also many marine organisms, some of them large but many of them microscopically small. There is persuasive but perhaps not absolutely conclusive evidence that the extinctions of land and marine forms were not all closely simultaneous and that they usually also involved attenuation over an extended time and not a catastrophic or single geologically short episode. This makes it highly unlikely that the mass extinction resulted from one sudden extraterrestrial event, such as the flare of a distant nova, an old idea recently revived in slightly different form. Still less likely is a hypothesis that is the latest at the time of this writing: that a large asteroid or meteorite crashed into the earth and raised such a dust cloud that the sun was obscured and photosynthesis was stopped for an unstated length of time (but one so short that it must appear as instantaneous in the geological record). This has been forcefully advanced by Luis W. Alvarez, a physicist, but is viewed with doubt by most paleontologists. Another recent and probably untenable hypothesis is known as Arctic spillover. This involves the opening of a previously landlocked Arctic Ocean into the other oceans with complex, worldwide consequences. Apart from other dubious points, the timing is not right for terminal Cretaceous mass extinction. The opening of the Arctic Ocean to the Atlantic evidently did not occur until well into the Eocene, hence long after the mass extinction, and the way from the Arctic into the Pacific apparently has opened and closed repeatedly without any correlation with rates of extinction.

The summary of a recent (1979) conference among some two hundred students of the Cretaceous–Tertiary transition concludes about that mass extinction: "The patterns that are emerging are not simple. The theories advanced continue to grow in number and diversity. Are we approaching a state of maximal confusion, prior to clarity?" That clarity may be in the offing seems to be only a pious hope.

The extinctions of the late Pleistocene and earliest Recent epochs are a special case, and it may be argued that they were not mass extinction if that term correctly singles out phenomena unlike those of constant or background extinction. Extinctions at this time were far from general, being almost confined to land animals and among them mostly to mammals. These extinctions also predominantly affected the larger mammals, although by no means all of those became extinct and some small mammals did. The argument here has raged around the contention of one school of thought that these extinctions resulted mostly or entirely from human predation or "overkill" on game animals. The long controversy on this point has not produced agreement or even anything resembling a consensus. It seems relevant, first, that much more extensive episodes of extinction occurred repeatedly tens and hundreds of millions of years before the genus *Homo* existed and, second, that continuing predation by *Homo sapiens* for some ten thousand years since the Pleistocene ended is definitely known to have resulted in the extinction of few distinct mammalian species and even fewer genera. Moreover, in these cases, as seems clear for some birds, the species may have been on their way to extinction in any case, and man's intervention may only have determined the time, not the event. Also note that it is not known as a fact that extinctions in the earliest Recent, or in the New World before European settlement, were results of human predation, although some of them probably were.

Here again, after all the ingenious speculation, it appears that we still do not really know the proximate causes of mass extinction and that we very rarely know such causes for individual instances of extinction.

Despite the names used for them, life tables and survivorship curves are more strongly influenced by deaths than by births of individuals (in actuarial use) and by extinctions than by originations of taxa (in paleontological use). Evolutionists are especially interested in originations of new taxa, and for these also the fossil record provides the only direct evidence.

Frequency distribution of numbers of first occurrences per million years of main groups of fossil animals for 29 subdivisions of geological time from the early Cambrian onward.

First occurrences per million years	Frequency in Newell's tabulation
4.00–4.49	1
3.50–3.99	0
3.00–3.49	3
2.50–2.99	0
2.00–2.49	1
1.50–1.99	4
1.00–1.49	9
0.50–0.99	9
0–0.49	2

Here the most obvious approach is to tabulate times of first occurrences of taxa in the known fossil record and to put those in a graph with numbers of such occurrences on the vertical axis and geological time on the horizontal axis. This has been done for many groups of animals and a few other organisms. The first occurrences represent the latest possible dates for the evolutionary origins of the taxa involved, so that their actual origins probably were, on the average, somewhat earlier than these data indicate. However, it is a fair assumption that, for a reasonably good fossil record and for taxa above the species level, the difference is not great and that the pattern of first occurrences will approximate the actual pattern of origins. In order to quantify and compare these data, one can convert the figures to first occurrences per million years. This has been done by Newell for many groups of fossil animals, and the frequency distribution of some of his figures is given in the table shown here. Here again, as in the distribution in the first table on page 130 for last occurrences, although less clearly, the distribution is discontinuous, with most of the frequency clustered in the low values but four or five numbers somewhat dispersed among values greater than 2.00. (In the original data, the values ranged from 2.17 to 4.24.)

Just as in the case of last occurrences, here there are no appreciable lengths of geological time with no first occurrences; but there is a background level of fluctuating but moderate rates of first occurrences, and there are also a few exceptionally high levels. One might well speak of these as "mass originations," after the model of mass extinctions. The five of Newell's 29 rates of first occurrences per million years that have values greater than 2.00 are early Cambrian, early Ordovician, early Silurian, early Triassic, and early Jurassic. Except for the early Cambrian one, a special case, it is striking that each of these immediately follows an episode of mass extinction. Many compilations of data on first and last occurrences show that it is a common (or even usual) tendency for changes in the rates of last occurrences or extinctions to be followed at a geologically somewhat later time by comparable changes in rates of first occurrences or originations. Although the particular data embodied in the table shown here do not show this clearly, there was also an episode of mass originations in the Paleocene following the mass extinctions in the late Cretaceous. From what little we know of late Precambrian life and the very peculiar nature of the Ediacara fauna (see p. 49), it is also probable that there was an episode of mass extinction just before the early Cambrian. Newell's figure for first occurrences per million years in the early Cambrian is 3.00, which is high but is exceeded by the corresponding figures for the early Ordovician (3.04), the early Silurian (4.24), and the early Jurassic (3.33). Incidentally, the figure for the early Cambrian is in accord with other evidence that the new taxa that appeared in the Cambrian, in which practically all taxa at almost all levels were new to the record, did not appear together just at the nominal beginning of the Cambrian in an episode that was instantaneous in terms of geological time.

The late Pleistocene extinctions have not been followed by a rise in originations—not only because the extinctions were so limited in kind and extent but also because there clearly has not been enough time since then for the origination of distinctly new species in nature, let alone of genera or higher taxa.

Not only in the case of mass extinctions but also as a general rule (with some exceptions), there is some time lag between rises in numbers of extinctions and rises in numbers of originations. As previously noted, Darwin's most nearly explicit comment on a cause for extinction ascribed some extinctions to competition, and this is still regularly included among possible causes. There are indeed some instances of extinctions in the fossil record that can be reasonably (although only hypothetically) explained by competition. An example that strongly suggests this explanation is provided by the multituberculates, so called because their molars had many cusps. They constitute an extinct order of mammals (Multituberculata) whose first known occurrence (in Europe) was in the early part of the late Jurassic and whose last known occurrence (in North America) was in the early Oligocene. That is a time span of about 110,000,000 years, longer than is known for any other order of mammals. Although the early record is somewhat

Now extinct, the last Great Auk was killed in June 1844 on Eldey Island off the coast of Iceland by fishermen collecting bird specimens for an Icelandic bird collector. The penguin-like bird ranged from Newfoundland to as far as the coast of Maine. The Great Auk, which produced only one egg per season, was graceful only in water, unable to fly, clumsy on land, and totally defenseless. The bird's last major breeding ground was destroyed by a volcanic eruption.

The Takahé, Notornis mantelli, *was first known as a live bird, then thought to be extinct, and then found not to be extinct. That has been true of a number of other animals, especially in Australia with its sparse population and great extent. Today the Takahé is still in danger of extinction with only a few birds scattered in small groups over an area of 200 square miles.*

exiguous, it indicates that, through much of that history (approximately the first 85,000,000 years at least), the group was expanding in terms of numbers of species, genera, and families. In the late Cretaceous, it was dominant among the orders of mammals, at least in Asia and North America. (Fossils of late Cretaceous mammals are as yet extremely scanty in Europe and South America, and they are unknown from Africa and Australia.)

From the Paleocene onward, the multituberculates were declining, and the available evidence indicates that they became terminally extinct in the Oligocene. That is just the span of time during which maximum expansion of the marsupial and placental mammals was going on. Those groups, collectively known as the Theria (Greek for "beasts"), had a common ancestry in the early Cretaceous and are only very remotely related to the multituberculates. It is not a falsifiable hypothesis, but it is a reasonable one, that the adaptive radiations of the therians were bringing them into ecological niches and trophic roles in which they competed with, and gradually took over from, the multituberculates.

There are numerous other examples of probable or possible extinction caused by competition, but there are few on such a grand scale. If this were the usual or a dominant reason for extinction, it would seem probable that the rise in origination rates of the ultimately successful competitors would coincide with the rise in extinction rates of the losers (as it does in the example of Theria and Multituberculata) or that the former might even precede the latter rather than following it. As has been noted, a peak in origination rates more often follows one in extinction rates, which suggests that reoccupation of more diverse or narrower

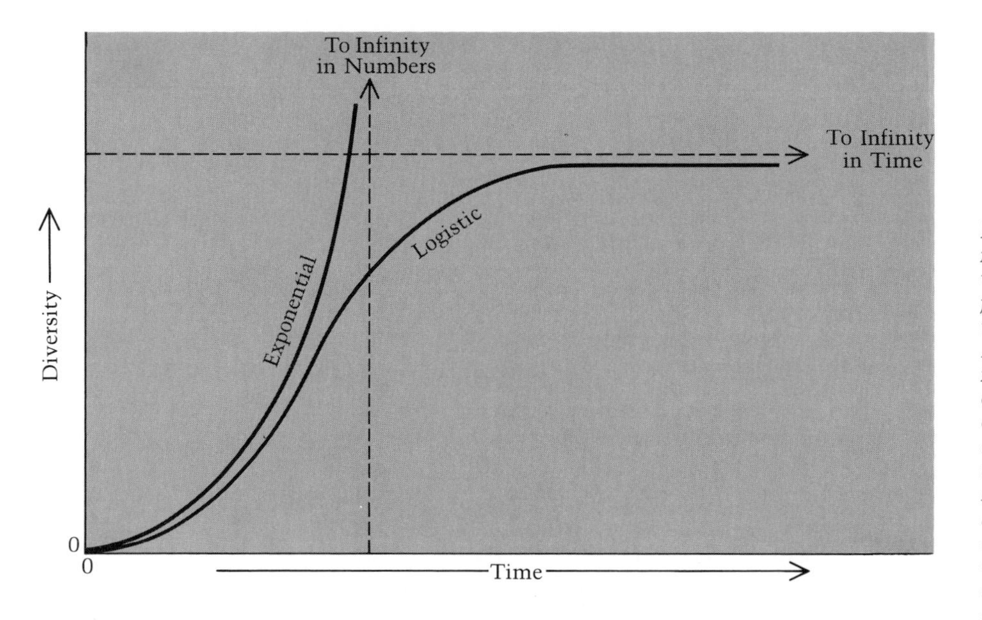

Exponential and logistic curves as mathematical models for the numbers of individuals or of taxa in the course of diversifying through time. The diversity at given times is scaled on the vertical axis. Elapsed time, which may be in terms of minutes for the shortest-lived individuals or in millions of years for taxa, is scaled on the horizontal axis. The dashed lines are asymptotes—that is, the values on the scales that are approached and limited by the variables (in this case, diversity and time) but never reached (except at infinity) and therefore, of course, never crossed. Since, to the best of our knowledge (and in accordance with common sense), neither diversity nor geological time can be infinite, it follows that neither model is possible in full for the history of life. However, as will be apparent later in the text and figures, these models do facilitate the interpretation and understanding of that history.

ecological niches or adaptive zones often (or usually) occurred after these were left unoccupied by the extinction of prior occupants.

Still thinking in terms of the proliferation of taxa, there are two particularly interesting mathematical and conceptual models of how this may occur. Both involve patterns of population growth, the growth here being that of numbers of taxa within a taxon of a higher category, such as of species within a genus or family, or of genera or families within an order or class, and so on. One of these models involves exponential increase in which the increase is constantly a fraction of the number of taxa existing at any one time, the equivalent of population size. The increase in absolute numbers thus is relative to the population size, and its rate constantly accelerates. With those numbers on the vertical axis and time on the horizontal axis, the corresponding graph is a concavely curved line becoming steeper as time goes on until it becomes vertical. The other model is a logistic curve, which accelerates to a maximum and then decelerates as it approaches a line called the asymptote, which is horizontal on the usual graph and represents the maximum size of the population under given (theoretical) conditions. For those mathematically inclined, the equations for these two models are given in the box on the following page.

In the exponential model, the number of taxa becomes infinite at a finite time; in the logistic model, the rate of change becomes zero at an infinite time. Obviously, neither model applies *in toto* to real proliferation of finite numbers of taxa in finite time, but either or both can approximate real events under some circumstances and at some times.

Paleontologist Steven M. Stanley has applied the exponential equation to eleven families of bivalves, in the class Bivalvia (clams and their relatives), and to seven families of placental mammals, Eutheria, belonging to three different orders (Primates, Rodentia, Artiodactyla). These were selected because the families have good fossil records and have known numbers of living species. Stanley has assumed that each family began with a single species at the time of its earliest

Mathematic models of increase in numbers of taxa.

Exponential increase

The differential equation for unlimited exponential increase at a constant rate is

$$\frac{dN}{dt} = RN$$

in which N is the size of the population, t is time, and R is a constant fractional change in the size of the population per unit of time.

Integration gives the equation for the resulting curve:

$$N_t = N_O\, e^{Rt}$$

in which N is the population at a given time, N_O is the initial population, e is the base of natural logarithms (2.71828 . . .), and R and t are as above.

Logistic curve

The differential equation for the logistic curve is

$$\frac{dN}{dt} = rN\frac{(K - N)}{K}$$

in which N and t are as above, r is the maximum rate of increase, and K is the asymptote.

Integration gives the equation for the resulting curve:

$$N = \frac{K}{1 + e} - rt$$

in which e is again the base of natural logarithms.

Increase through geological time in numbers of species based on the known number of living (Recent) species in selected families and on the hypothesis that increase of numbers of species since the family originated has been entirely exponential.

Selected families	Fractional increase in numbers of species per million years	Doubling rate*
Bivalves		
Donacidae	0.051	13.59
Semelidae	0.087	7.97
Mean for 11 families	0.061	11.36
Placental mammals		
Bovidae	0.15	4.62
Muridae	0.35	1.98
Mean for 7 families	0.22	3.15

*Calculated from equations for exponential increase by setting N/N_0 as 2. (At doubling time the number was twice as great as when N_0 was equal to 1.)

known occurrence and that the number of species has increased down to the present time at a constant exponential rate. Some of his calculated data are given in modified form in the table shown here. In each group, Bivalvia and Eutheria, the table gives just the lowest and highest exponential rate found by Stanley and the mean for all the rates given by him. Stanley also calculated what he calls a doubling rate, the time that it would take the number of species to double at a constant exponential rate, based on the mean exponential rate for the eleven families of mollusks and the seven of mammals. This table also gives doubling rates for the families with the lowest and highest exponential rates.

The doubling rates are arrived at in a different way, but they are analogous to the half-lives in survivorship data, previously mentioned. The exponential rate of increase in numbers of species, in this example, is an origination rate, which may be considered one kind of the numerous possible rates of evolution in general. As shown in the table, the Muridae (rat and mouse family) evolved in this sense more rapidly than the Bovidae (cattle and their numerous kin) and very much more rapidly than any of the mollusks in Stanley's table. The lower the doubling rate

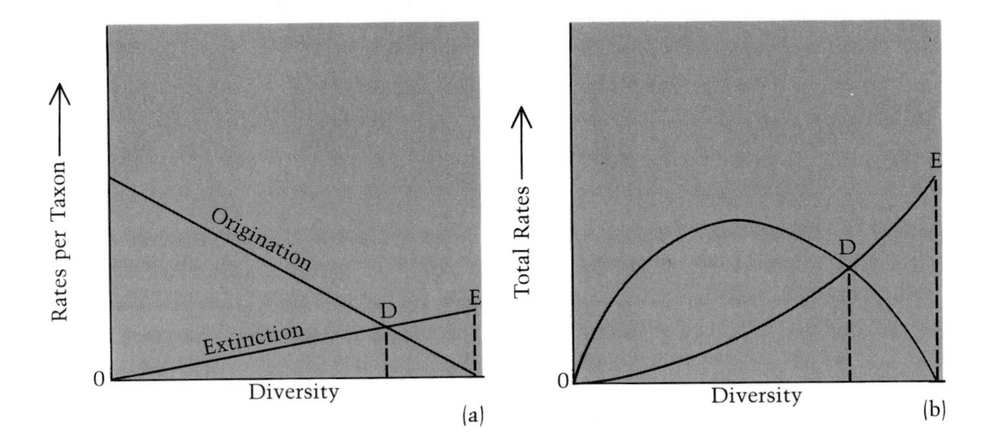

Mathematical models of the interaction of origination and extinction in the histories of individuals within species or lesser groups and, more especially, in the histories of taxa within higher taxa or in life as a whole in geological time. The curves in the figure on page 141 reflect only diversity, from births of individuals or evolutionary emergence of taxa. To put these in a more nearly realistic framework, it is necessary to relate them to the fact that individuals die and that taxa become extinct. In (a), *this is shown in linear models with origination rates decreasing and extinction rates increasing. When the lines intersect at point* D *in this figure, origination and extinction are in equilibrium and the diversity is neither decreasing nor increasing. This model becomes more realistic by conversion from taxon rates to total rates, which yields the intersecting parabolic curves shown in* (b). *At point* E *in both of these forms of the model, the origination rate becomes zero and all the individuals die or the taxa under consideration become terminally extinct. The extinction rate could then be considered infinite, as in the exponential curve in the figure on page 141, but that cannot be realistically shown in this graph.*

figures are, the more rapid the origination rates (or, in that sense, the rates of evolution) would be. That is also true of half-life figures and of mean survivorship figures.

In the 1940s, when survivorship curves were first being calculated from the data of the fossil record, it was found that some, at least, of the mammals had much shorter mean survivorship of genera, hence much higher origination rates, than some, at least, of the mollusks. (The first published data were for land carnivores among the mammals and bivalves among the mollusks.) There has now been much more study along these lines, and on the whole it supports the generalization that, with some exceptions, origination rates (and, as a corollary, taxonomic evolutionary rates) in vertebrates, and especially in mammals, have been more rapid than those in invertebrates, and especially in marine mollusks. There are some weaknesses in Stanley's exponential and doubling rates that need not be discussed here, but they do agree with the general finding about taxonomic rates of origination or of evolution in mammals and in mollusks. It has been suggested that this difference in rates may be an artifact resulting from the use of more characters in classifying vertebrates than are usually used in classifying invertebrates, but it has been demonstrated that, when characters similar in kind and in number are used, taxonomic rates are still, on the average, distinctly higher for vertebrates than for invertebrates.

Stanley notes that exponential expansion of numbers of taxa may be expected only in early phases of adaptive radiation and that thereafter an approximation of a logistic curve might occur. Recently (1978), J. John Sepkoski, Jr., has applied this concept to a theoretical interplay of origination rate and extinction rate. As shown in the figure above (modified from one by Sepkoski), the origination rate would be expected to increase at first and eventually to decrease, while the extinction rate would rise with continuous acceleration. Where the lines representing these two rates in a graph cross, there would be a point of equilibrium at which rates of origination and of extinction would be equal and (other things being equal) the size of a population, or the number of taxa present, would continue without further change.

That sequence is well represented in an idealized way by a logistic curve in which the rate of change at first accelerates (its slope increases) to a maximum. Up to this point, the graph closely resembles, but is not exactly the same as, the exponential curve for an early phase in the differentiation of a group becoming

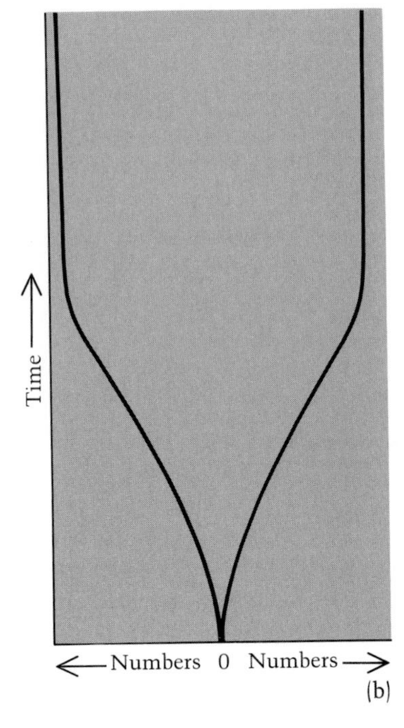

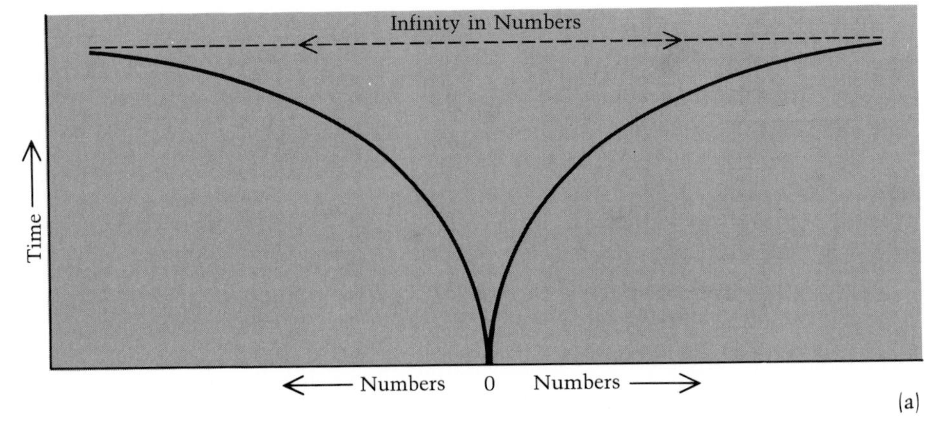

The increase of numbers of individuals within species, or of taxa within higher taxa, according to the exponential or logistic curves shown in the figure on page 141. (a) *According to the exponential model: Although the early part of this pattern matches well enough with many real examples of early phases of adaptive radiation, the subsequent unceasingly rapid expansion through long spans of geological time is not only unknown in the geological record but manifestly impossible.* (b) *According to the logistic model: The early part of this pattern is close to the early part of the pattern for the exponential model (also evident in the figure on page 143), but the two patterns then become increasingly different. In the later part of this model, increase in diversity becomes slower and eventually virtually ceases at or near the equilibrium point labeled* D *in the figure on page 143. This generalized diversity model closely approximates the logistic curve, which is also mathematically congruent with the graph* (b) *on page 143.*

taxonomically diversified. Thereafter, the rate of such diversification (the slope of the line in the graph) decreases, and it approaches zero as the equilibrium point is reached or, in the formalized logistic curve, as the asymptote (a maximum value of numbers but now a minimum rate of their change) is approached.

Sepkoski showed that the number of orders of marine animals does in fact approximate such a curve in the fossil record but that, instead of being mathematically constant on an asymptote, it wobbles randomly about such a line. From what has here been said previously, it seems clear that part of this wobbling arises from the lag between extinctions and following originations, nearly maintaining an overall average, and that the wobbling is random only in the sense that we do not know all the causal factors involved and so cannot reduce them to a (necessarily quite complex) adequate series of equations. It must further be mentioned that a graph of diversity of orders of marine animals previously published by James Valentine (1973) differs from that by Sepkoski and must have been based on other data.

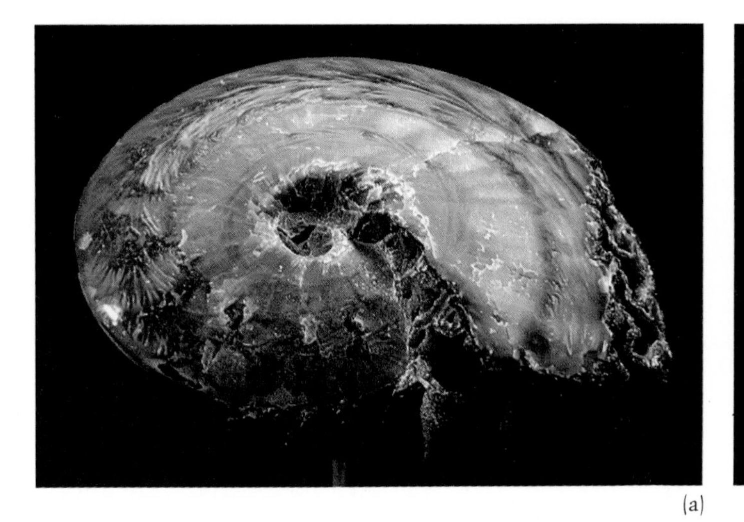
(a)

(b)

(a) *A late Cretaceous ammonoid* Placenticeras *approximately 80 million years old from the Pierre Shale, South Dakota. This is an external side view of the shell with the mother-of-pearl surface preserved. Tightly coiled in a single plane, this is a usual, often recurring shape for ammonoids.* (b) Pleuroceras, *from the lower Jurassic in Germany, is approximately 185 million years old. This specimen is sawed vertically across the middle of the spiral to show the internal structure. Growth started from the middle, and as size increased, a series of chambers was formed, separated by walls. The last, largest chamber at the upper and left part of this photograph had been occupied by the main part of the animal's body when it died and was buried. In this specimen the process of fossilization replaced the original, relatively soft and somewhat soluble shell material (a form of calcium carbonate) by the harder and less soluble mineral pyrite (a form of iron sulfide). The lumpy material outside the original shell is not part of that shell.*

The number of taxa does maintain a fairly constant average over long spans of geological time, whether this is from about the middle of the Ordovician onward, as in Sepkoski's graph, or only since the Triassic, as in Valentine's. However, this is true only in an approximate way and only within one fairly stable ecological situation. Such episodes as the mass extinctions are temporary from the long viewpoint of geological time, but they do cause rather more than slight wobbles in the total numbers of taxa. Spread into quite different environments, such as from aquatic to terrestrial environments first for plants and eventually for various animals, causes marked increases in numbers of taxa, not necessarily in any one environment but overall in the increasing number of different environments.

The relationship between extinction and origination rates in the fossil record strongly suggests that, once an environment has become populated by a diverse, balanced biota that essentially fills the available ecological roles or niches, it tends to remain so regardless of changes in the particular taxa present. Whatever the proximate cause of an extinction of a taxon may be, the extinction leaves unfilled an ecological role that may immediately become occupied by a different taxon, or such occupation may follow after a lapse of geological time.

An example of such relay among related but distinct groups of marine animals has already been mentioned: the extinction of Paleozoic reef corals and their replacement by quite different corals between the Mesozoic and the Recent. Another excellent example, among many preserved in the fossil record, is provided by the ammonoids. (Technically, the Ammonoidea are a subclass of the class Cephalopoda, which belongs to the phylum Mollusca.) Ammonoids as a whole are often called "ammonites," but that name is sometimes confined to the more complex and usually later ammonoids. These were relatives of the nautiloids, tentacled mollusks that were abundant for hundreds of millions of years but now

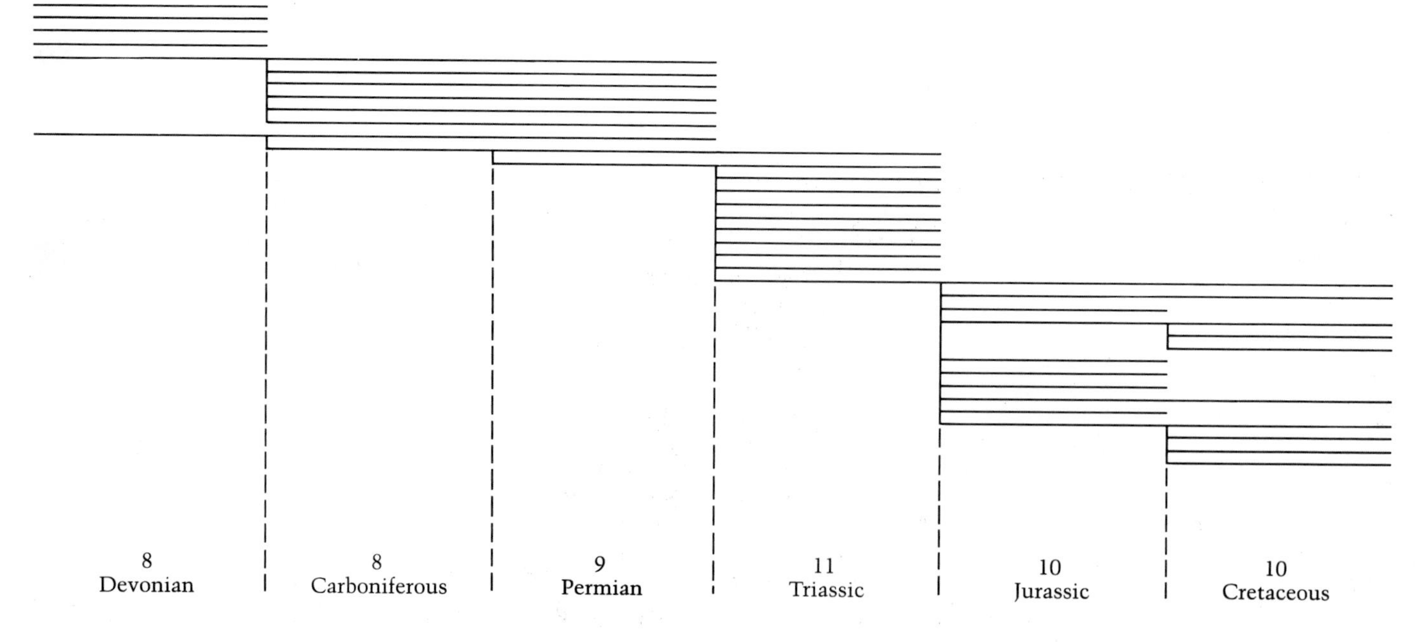

Extinction and replacement among superfamilies of ammonoids. In order to simplify the presentation and emphasize the points most relevant here, the periods are shown as if of equal length and the various superfamilies, each represented by a horizontal line, are represented as extending through the whole of each period in any part of which they occurred. The points to be made are as follows:

- *In the Devonian, there were eight superfamilies, but six of them were extinct by the end of that period. The other two Devonian superfamilies survived through the Carboniferous and into the Permian.*
- *The eight superfamilies in the Carboniferous all survived into the Permian, when one other superfamily evolved.*
- *Of the nine Permian superfamilies, only two survived into the Triassic, where one was ancestral to nine other superfamiles.*
- *Of the eleven Triassic superfamilies, only one survived into the Jurassic, where directly or indirectly it became ancestral to nine other superfamilies.*
- *Of the ten Jurassic superfamilies, five survived into the Cretaceous, where five more superfamilies arose directly or indirectly from two of the survivors from the Jurassic.*
- *All ten Cretaceous superfamilies were extinct by the end of that period.*

survive only in a single living species, the chambered or pearly nautilus. Like the nautiloids, the ammonoids also had chambered shells, but they differed in (among other characteristics) having less simple, and ultimately extremely complex, patterns of sutures, the lines of junction between the partitions of the chambers and the outer shell. Most ammonoids were tightly coiled in a single plane, as is the nautilus, but some were partly uncoiled, and others coiled in spirals or evolved more bizarre overall shapes.

Fossil ammonoids are extremely abundant worldwide, and their detailed study has suggested many theoretical principles of evolution, some now superseded but many still cogent. The aspect of their study most relevant in this chapter is the way ammonoids waxed and waned and eventually became extinct. They evolved from nautiloid ancestors early in the Devonian and initially diversified in that period. This diversity was markedly decreased when extinction exceeded origination around the Devonian–Carboniferous transition. Thereafter, the few lines that survived proliferated, became greatly divergent, and diversified throughout the Carboniferous and Permian. Then a crisis even more stringent than the one between late Devonian and early Carboniferous occurred between the late Permian and early Triassic. The whole group Ammonoidea came very near extinction; but then, through the Triassic, there was again proliferation into an extraordinarily large number of new families, genera, and species. Another severe crisis that nearly resulted in total extinction of the group occurred around the Triassic–Jurassic boundary, and again this was followed by relay and replacement within the Ammonoidea that continued through the Jurassic and Cretaceous. Another crisis of extinction came near the end of the Cretaceous, and this was final: the Ammonoidea as a whole became extinct.

It is noteworthy that the four crises of ammonoid extinction—three partial and one total for the group—coincide with the times of widespread mass extinctions specified earlier in this chapter. On that account, a student of ammonoids concluded that "no special theory" is needed to account for the ammonoid crises. The implication is that a single theory should hold for mass extinctions in general and that this should apply also to ammonoids in particular. The trouble is that there is no such theory that is based on adequate evidence and is impressively credible. There is one theory, better called a hypothesis, that might apply to the ammonoids and to some other marine animals: That the crises were caused by the regression of seas and the emergence of land, whereby marine ecology was markedly affected. That hypothesis is not acceptable for mass extinctions in general because those after the Devonian also involved land animals, and it would be expected that expansion of nonmarine habitats would have quite the opposite effect on them.

The fact remains that the Ammonoidea as a whole did—almost by chance, it seems—three times barely escape total extinction, and each time they were relayed, the older forms replaced from within the same broad taxon (subclass, in this case). Another cogent feature of this example, as pointed out (in 1977) by W. J. Kennedy, is that there was a "progressive reduction of ammonite diversity and abundance" during the millions of years of late Cretaceous time and that this indicates that their terminal extinction (and, by extrapolation, the previous crises) could not be explained by a catastrophic event. A final point for this example is that the interplay of extinction and origination in ammonoids follows what appears to be the general rule (with exceptions): Noteworthy increases in origination rates did not accompany but followed noteworthy increases in extinction rates.

The ammonoid example is unusually clear and well documented, but it is probable that similar relays by related but distinct groups of organisms within the same habitats were common (or even usual) in the history of life. There are also examples of such ecological replacements involving groups of markedly different ancestry and much longer lapses of geological time between the extinction of one group and the reoccupation of its ecological role by another. A striking example is provided by the ichthyosaurs and some cetaceans. The ichthyosaurs were marine reptiles, first known from the middle Triassic, extremely abundant and diverse in the Jurassic seas, waning in the Cretaceous, and becoming extinct several million years before the end of that period. (Incidentally, they are sometimes included among the terminal Cretaceous mass extinctions, although they died out long before some other marine reptiles and the terrestrial dinosaurs.) The ichthyosaurs were carnivores that fed on fish, squids, and some other medium-sized to large marine animals, including ammonoids at times.

The order Cetacea comprises the whales, dolphins, porpoises, and their many relatives, living and extinct. Cetaceans first appeared in the middle Eocene, and, from the late Eocene onward, some of them, similar to the living dolphins, came to resemble ichthyosaurs closely in external appearance. Modern dolphins also eat fishes, squids, and other aquatic animals, and their various ecological roles must widely overlap those of the ichthyosaurs, if they are not wholly identical.

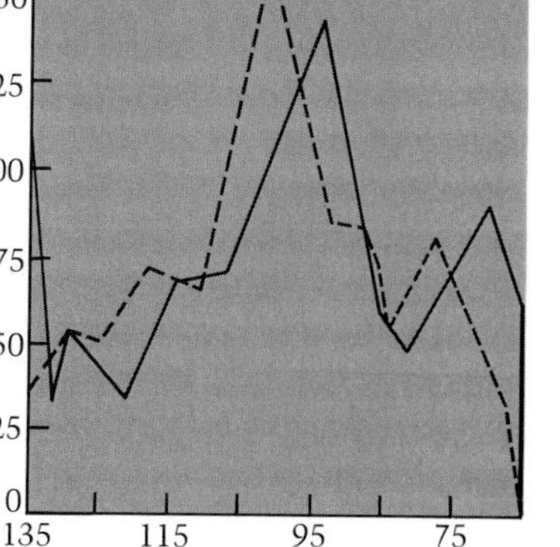

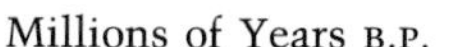

First and last appearances of ammonoids in the Cretaceous. The data are first appearances (solid line) *and last appearances* (dotted line) *of genera and subgenera. Time is scaled in years before present, with 135 million years* B.P. *as the beginning of the Cretaceous and 65 million years* B.P. *as the end. The preceding figure shows that ammonoids nearly died out between the Devonian and the Carboniferous, between the Permian and the Triassic, and between the Triassic and the Cretaceous. They completely died out between the Cretaceous and the Tertiary (the boundary also between the Mesozoic and Cenozoic eras), and this is often cited as simply part of mass the extinctions of that time. This more detailed study of their fluctuations during the Cretaceous shows that the extinction of ammonoid genera and subgenera peaked in about the middle of the Cretaceous, and the last, much lower peak of extinction was still well before the end of the Cretaceous. Thus, the ammonoids were not involved in the Mesozoic–Cenozoic episode of mass extinctions.*

The peaks of first appearances tend to follow peaks of last appearances by appreciable spans of geological time. The peak of total diversity, the highest for ammonoids at any time since the Triassic, occurred near the middle of the Cretaceous. Thereafter, diversity declined steeply and almost steadily, except for one much lower peak, coincident with the last rise in first appearances—not long, geologically speaking, before complete terminal extinction.

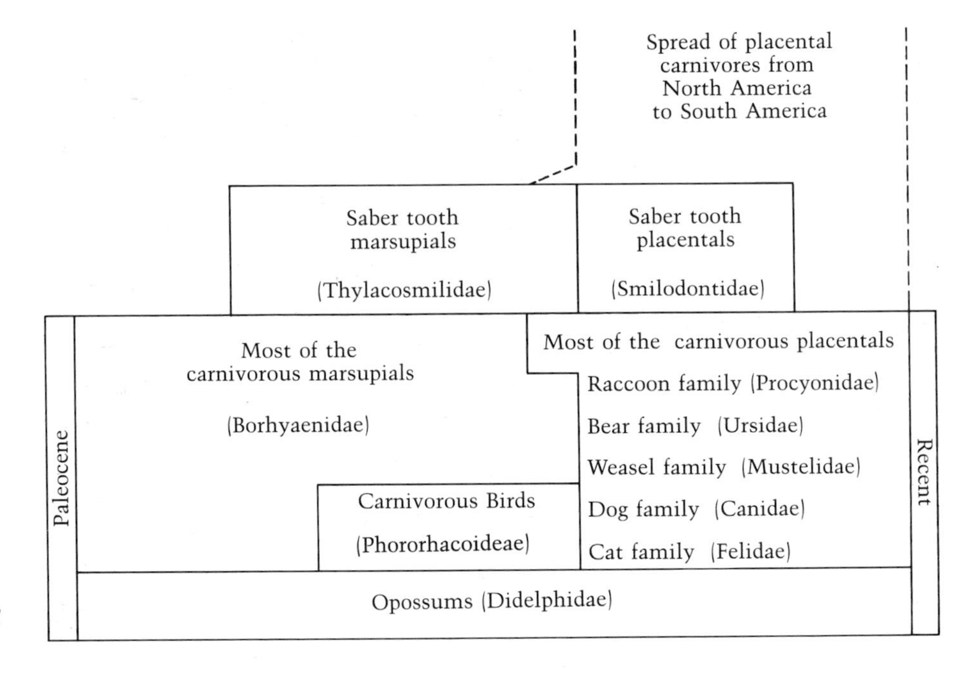

A highly simplified diagram of the relay or ecological replacement of most of the carnivorous land vertebrates in South America during the Cenozoic era. Geological time, somewhat more than 60 million years in this instance, runs from the Paleocene at the left to the Recent at the right. The intervening events are placed in their known sequence, but time lapses are not scaled. For example, for convenience of diagramming, the horizontal distance allotted to the spread of placental mammals from North America to South America is about two-fifths of the total width of the diagram, but the actual time elapsed was only about one-twentieth of the total time during which all those events occurred. There is no vertical scale, and again the allotment of height to the various compartments is only a diagrammatic convenience and not an indication of the abundance or diversity of the animals in question. For example, the carnivorous marsupials of the family Borhyaenidae were much more varied and abundant than either the carnivorous, largely predaceous, cursorial birds or the peculiarly distinct sabertooths, which included two highly convergent groups of quite different origin, one among marsupials and one among placentals.

The sabertooth marsupials and the carnivorous phororhacoid birds almost certainly originated in South America, and probably much earlier than indicated in this diagram, but their earlier histories are not yet known. The most striking feature of this evolutionary replacement is that the old native South American carnivores became terminally extinct with the sole exception of the opossums, smaller and less strictly predaceous than most of the other animals included here. It seems probable that extinction of the old natives in South America involved competitive ecological replacement by the newcomers, but this is not clear in all cases. The replacements clearly occurred, but the contributing factors were probably much more complex than can be suggested in so simple a diagram.

Their terrestrial ancestors were completely distinct from those of the reptilian ichthyosaurs, as is obvious from the internal skeletal characters of the two groups.

The time lapse between the extinction of the ichthyosaurs and the spread of cetaceans into similar ecological roles was at least thirty million years—a very delayed replacement, hardly to be called a "relay." It must, however, be noted that two other groups of carnivorous marine reptiles, the plesiosaurs and the mosasaurs, outlasted the ichthyosaurs and thus narrow the apparent ecological gap (although they, too, were extinct before what is technically regarded as the beginning of the Cenozoic era). Throughout the ichthyosaur–cetacean gap, there were also other marine predators, notably fish that ate other fish.

The examples of relay and replacement so far given were on a worldwide scale. Some final comments on the topics of relay and replacement also bring in the subject of biogeography. Early in the Cenozoic—the Age of Mammals—the South American land mammals included omnivorous to fully carnivorous forms, all marsupials, that preyed on an even greater variety of native herbivores. As time went on, various lineages of these marsupials became more narrowly adapted, and especially noteworthy was the evolution of a group of sabertoothed marsupials. Some of the South American marsupials continued to be relatively unspecialized small omnivores. Others became more specialized, including larger omnivores and predaceous carnivores. Also, from the earliest Cenozoic in South America,

A life-size restoration of one of the gigantic, flightless, rabidly carnivorous birds, the extinct South American phororhacoids. The artist, Leon L. Pray, is putting the last touches on the model, based on fossils of the genus Andalgalornis. *The fossils of this particular genus were collected by Elmer S. Riggs in 1926 and described and named by Bryan Patterson in 1960.*

there were terrestrial and semiaquatic snakes and crocodilians that preyed on terrestrial herbivorous mammals as well on various other land and water animals.

Around the middle of the Cenozoic, a group of large, flightless, running birds, some of them with large heads and enormous beaks, appeared in South America: the phororhacoids. It is inferred that they were predaceous carnivores, and Larry Marshall, an American paleontologist who has worked intensively on fossil marsupials, has speculated that their spread and competition contributed to the decline and eventual extinction of the large predaceous marsupial carnivores. If so, this would be an unusual case of ecological replacement of mammals by birds. It is not quite certain that the replacement was complete, and in any case it did not last long. The phororhacoids were themselves replaced and became extinct when members of the dog and cat families (Canidae and Felidae) spread from North America to South America. At the same time, the sabertooth marsupials (Thylacosmilidae) became extinct and were replaced by sabertooth placentals (Marchairodontinae, a subfamily of the Felidae). The sabertooth placentals themselves became extinct not much later, geologically speaking, and without relay or replacement. It has long been suggested that this extinction was related to the extinction of sabertooth prey animals, a plausible and acceptable hypothesis even though not a testable one. But that only moves the question to why those prey animals became extinct, a plausible answer for which, in my opinion, has not yet been proposed.

That same incursion of placental mammals from North America caused the replacement (and perhaps, but not demonstrably, caused the extinction) of other South American marsupials almost across the board, leaving alive only the omnivorous to small carnivorous opossums (Didelphidae) and a more obscure family, Caenolestidae, which is without a truly vernacular name. The other replacing North Americans were members of the weasel, raccoon, and bear families (Mustelidae, Procyonidae, and Ursidae). This event, known to paleontologists as the Great American Interchange, also brought into South America many new prey animals, which replaced all earlier South American hoofed mammals and some earlier South American rodents.

CHAPTER 6

RATES AND PATTERNS OF EVOLUTION

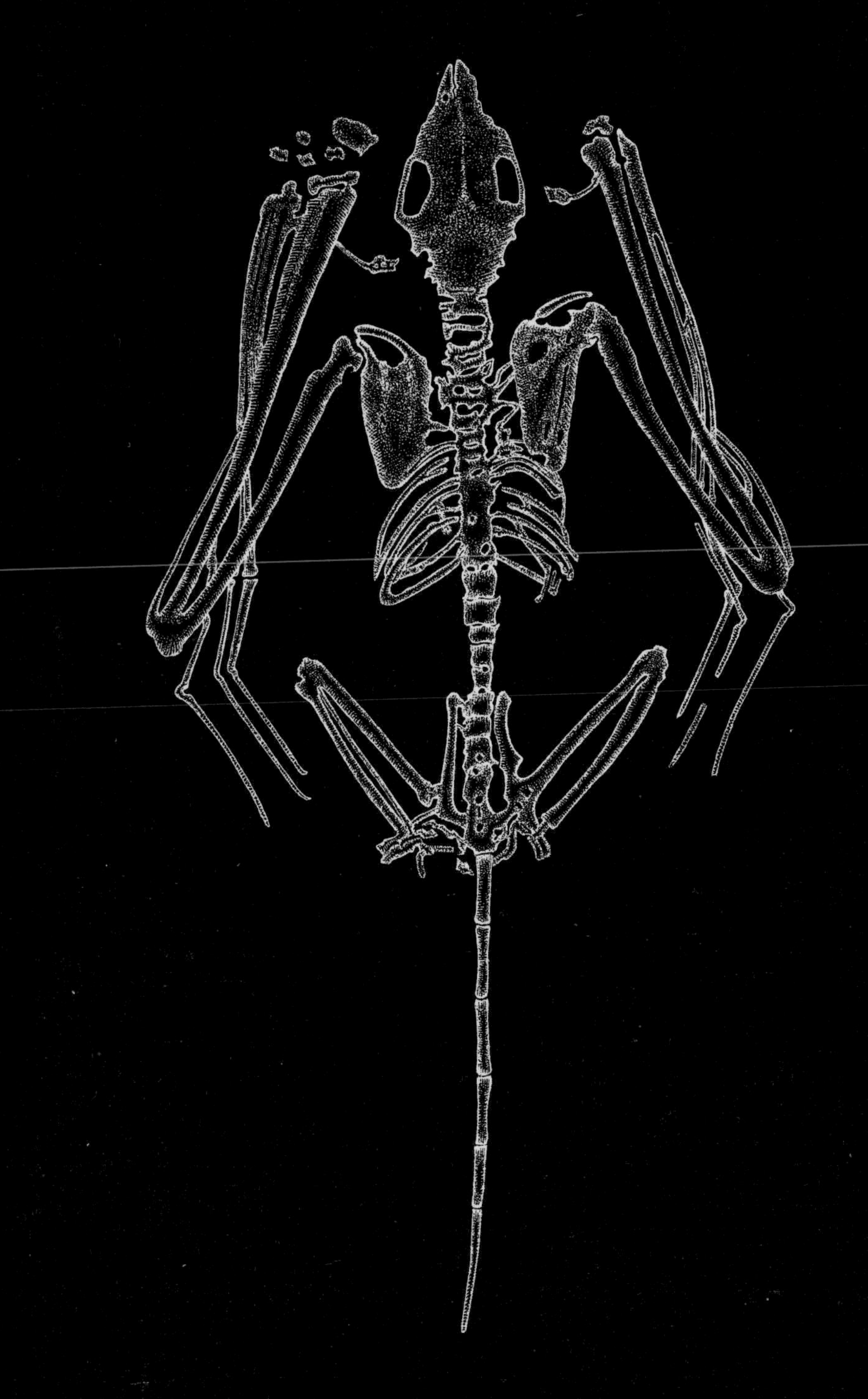

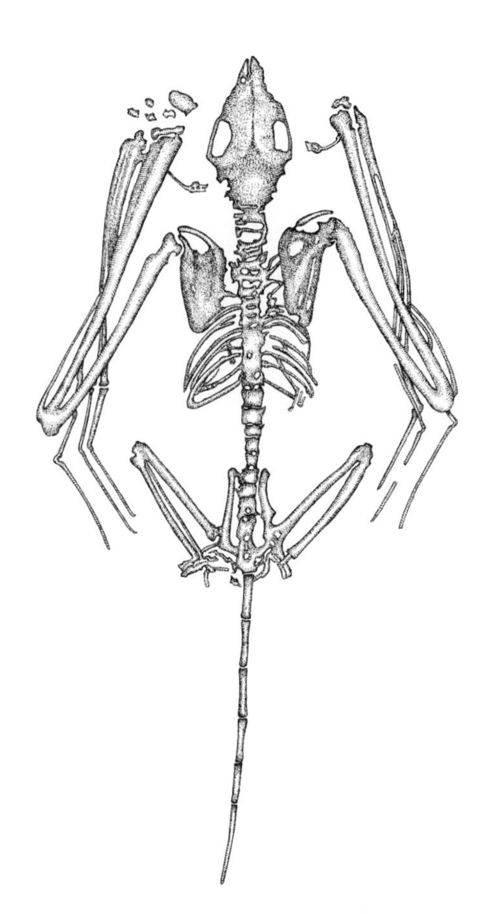

The complete skeleton of the oldest known bat. The name of the genus, Icaronycteris, *is derived from Icarus, the unfortunate human flier in an ancient Greek myth, and the Greek word for "bat." This individual was drowned or fell into a large lake about 50 million years ago in what is now southwestern Wyoming. It was rapidly buried whole in the limy sediment at the bottom of the lake. Time has converted the sediment to the Green River Formation of the geologists.* Icaronycteris *was already fully adapted to flight and thus was precocious in spite of having some primitive features. It was contemporaneous with little eohippus, the ancestor of modern horses, but the principal features of adaptation in bats had evolved more rapidly than those of horses.*

The preceding chapters have dealt, for the most part, with aspects of the evolutionary history of life that are elucidated primarily (or, in some instances, exclusively) by paleontology, the science of fossils. Inasmuch as this book is about fossils, the paleontological viewpoint will, of course, continue. It is, however, obvious (although biologists did not always think so) that acceptable general principles of evolution must take into account the factual data and the reasonable inferences in all the highly diverse branches of the study of organisms, living or dead. What is needed, and what has been widely pursued during the present century, is a synthesis of evolutionary theory involving all levels, from molecules through whole organisms and specific populations to multispecific biotas, at all times from the origin of life to now. Molecular biologists do not always agree with organismic biologists, nor do paleobiologists always agree with neobiologists, but a consensus has developed in what has come to be known as the synthetic theory of evolution. This is not a fixed or dogmatically maintained theory. It has itself evolved as more knowledge has been brought to bear. Certainly the theory is not complete or final, and there is some dissent from the consensus. Such is the nature of scientific theories and research in general. It bears repeating that there is no scientific dissent about the reality of evolution and that there is a consensus about its most important aspects.

This chapter will continue the discussion of rates of evolution, but rates of a different kind from those of changes in numbers of taxa and of the makeup of communities. Rates of evolution in different lineages, or at different times in a lineage sequence, or of different characters within an evolving taxon constitute different kinds of contributions from paleontology to evolutionary theory in general. The inferences on various rates and patterns of evolution from the fossil record combine and interact on the basis of occurrence in geological time, and beyond this, they also interact with studies of evolution in which geologic time is not involved. Some attention will also be given to apparently contradictory views that have recently generated much debate.

The direct and objective information derived from a fossil in itself is usually anatomical, a matter of the form and juxtaposition of parts actually preserved. There are instances in which relevant observational data are of other sorts, but they are exceptional. Rates of change of anatomical characteristics may be designated as somatic, bodily (from the Greek *soma,* "body", as opposed to soul), but in modern biology body as opposed to reproductive cells, or as phenetic (adapted from a Greek verb *phaino,* "to appear"). Note also the common biological term phenotype, what is directly visible in an organism as distinct from genotype, the heredity of an organism, not directly visible.

If the rates of change in such characters are to be expressed numerically and thus made simply comparable, the characters themselves must be measured. This is most readily done in terms of linear distances. Ideally, then, such measurements would be made on an ancestral organism at a determined geological time in the past and then on a descendant at a later geological date. One then need only divide the difference in a given dimension by the difference in time to get a rate per year or other unit of time. More useful than the rate of absolute change, however, is the rate of proportional change. This makes possible meaningful comparisons of rates in, for example, small rodents and large ungulates. If a given dimension in both sorts of animals increases 10 percent per million years, obviously the absolute change will be far greater in the larger animals. The relative rate is the same in both, however, and this certainly is a more significant comparison.

In 1949, J. B. S. Haldane—not a paleontologist but a sort of universal genius in evolutionary biology—pointed out that the relative rate is readily calculated by the following formula (here expressed in symbols different from those used by Haldane):

$$\text{relative rate of change} = \frac{\ln(\overline{X}_2) - \ln(\overline{X}_1)}{t},$$

in which ln means "natural logarithm" (that is, a logarithm to base $e =$ 2.71828. . .), $\overline{X}_1$ is the mean of a measurement in probably ancestral specimens all of the same geological age, $\overline{X}_2$ is the mean of the corresponding measurement in related, probably descendant specimens all of a geological age later than that of $\overline{X}_1$, and t is the difference in geological age between the two groups of specimens.

The time difference can be expressed in any units. Haldane used years, which intuitively seems suitable but is generally unsatisfactory for two reasons. First, in actual application, this gives figures that are always extremely small—a few millionths, as a rule. Second, measurements of geological time in years are never accurate to a year or even to a century, and they are accurate to a millenium only for the latest sequence of time. For most of geological time it is therefore handier and more realistic to express t in units of 100,000 or 1,000,000 years. For example, Haldane gave one rate calculated with t in years as 3.6×10^{-8}, and then explained that this means an average rate of change of 3.6% per million years. If t is taken in units of millions of years, the formula for the same data gives 0.036, which, as a relative rate, can of course be expressed as 3.6%. The percentage figure, simply 3.6 in this case, is an expression of evolutionary rate useful for comparisons.

One of the most interesting applications of this approach was made by Robert Bader in 1955. He calculated rates for 23 different linear measurements of the skulls, mandibles, and teeth of two approximately ancestral–descendant lineages of oreodonts. The oreodonts (which constituted the suborder or infraorder Oreodonta of the mammalian order Artiodactyla) were a somewhat piglike group of hoofed mammals once extremely numerous and widespread in North America, always confined to that continent, and now long extinct. The two lineages studied by Bader belonged to different subfamilies of the family Merycoidodontidae and were contemporaneous, mainly in the Miocene epoch, through much of their known ranges in time.

Some of Bader's results are summarized in the following table. The figures would probably be different if the study were done today, because more precise

Summary of relative rates of evolution of 23 linear measurements in two subfamilies of oreodonts.

Subfamily	Rate of change per million years (percent)		
	Highest rate	Lowest rate	Mean rate
Merycochoerinae	−8.03	−1.15	−2.25*
Merychyinae	+3.13	+0.30	+1.41

* This value would be 2.41 if only the relative amount of early change per million years, and not its direction (positive or negative, larger or smaller), were taken into account in the summation.

dating methods are available now than were known twenty-five years ago. Nevertheless, some points of general importance for evolutionary theory can confidently be inferred from this example. Although the two lineages were living in the same region and through almost the same time, one was evolving definitely more rapidly than the other. In only four of the 23 characters measured were the members of the subfamily Merychyinae evolving more rapidly than those of the subfamily Merycochoerinae. Within each lineage, different characters evolved at strikingly different rates. In one subfamily, one character was evolving almost eight times as fast as another. In the other subfamily, one character was evolving more than ten times as fast as another. In both subfamilies, the overall rate was appreciable. Evolution in these animals, which clearly had large specific populations, was not in stasis or at equilibrium. Some characters changed very little; others changed markedly.

Those are quite common features in evolution. A feature that is less general in animals is also clearly demonstrated in this example. In one lineage, the animals were rather steadily increasing in size: all of the measured rates of evolution are positive. That trend is so common that it has been called a law, sometimes specified as "Cope's law," after Edward Drinker Cope, a great nineteenth-century (1840–1897) vertebrate paleontologist. This is indeed the rule among most vertebrates and many invertebrates, but it is a rule with far too many exceptions to be a "law" in any proper sense of the word. It is clear that the subfamily Merycochoerinae did not obey the rule. In all but one of the 23 characters measured, the rate of evolution in this subfamily was negative—that is, the measurement became smaller in the course of its evolution. It may be more than incidental that the members of the subfamily (Merychinae) in which the animals became larger in the course of their evolution were from the start (and always remained) smaller in absolute size than those of the other subfamily (Merychochoerinae).

Among several other suggestions made by Haldane in his classic paper on rates of evolution was that the relative rate be measured per generation rather than per year (usually per million years, in later practice). Because evolution occurs in populations and not in individuals, it seems reasonable that its rate might depend on the mean time between generations, as the time of replacement of individuals in the population. Lengths of generations in fossil species can be rather confi-

dently inferred if they are related and similar to living species in which lengths of generations are known or reasonably estimated. Lengths of generations are correlated, although sometimes only loosely, with mean longevity of individuals in a species. This can be directly measured in some, but only a few, fossil species: those that have growth increments affected by lapse of time, such as the annual growth rings found in some invertebrates and also in the scales of fishes and the teeth of some vertebrates.

The most general approach to the study of the relationship between lengths of generations and rates of evolution, however, is quite indirect. In general, the length of generations is correlated with size, although the correlation is loose and there are some outstanding exceptions. For instance, most insects are quite small, as animals go, and they usually have short generations—often one year, in seasonal climates. Yet there are the seventeen-year cicadas (usually miscalled "locusts"). These insects live without breeding for seventeen years, which thus determines the succession of generations, a period longer than for most mammals of much greater size.

That leads us to a generalization derived from the fossil record. First in a monograph on some fossil insects (1931) and later in a book on "dating the past" (1946), now a classic, Frederick Zeuner concluded that, in general, rates of evolution are not determined or clearly influenced by lengths of generations. His definitive statement was based not only on insects but on animals in general and, in addition to insects, especially terrestrial mammals and marine mollusks. He then wrote, "There is apparently no directly proportional relation between the rate of succession of generations and the rate of evolution." This was, at the time, a conclusion unexpected by biologists, as witness Haldane's previously mentioned

Section of a mural by Jay H. Matternes showing animals and plant life from early in the Miocene Epoch. The animals at the lower left are Merychus, *a small even-toed hoofed mammal. The herd in the lower middle are mostly but not all horses. The most obvious animals are the two big ones to the left,* Moropus, *strange ungulates (chalicotheres) with claws instead of hoofs. The big animal to the middle right is* Dinohyus, *an enormous piglike animal but not in the pig family. The animals in the pool, left background, are* Promerycochoerus, *a piglike oreodont.*

assumption, and it could have been reached only from the fossil evidence. I and other paleontologists have continued to study this point and have found no reason to disagree with Zeuner. It is reasonable to suppose that lengths of generations set (or at least affect the upper limits of) rates of evolution, but the available evidence suggests that these limits have rarely been reached and that the effective rate has been largely or wholly determined by other factors. (This assumes that species do not usually arise by single "macromutations," a point to be discussed later in this chapter.)

The example of calculation of rates of evolution summed up in the table on page 154 incidentally also exemplifies changes in size, which are very common in evolutionary sequences. They are usually positive—that is, there is a tendency toward larger size overall—although the same example included one of many exceptions to that rule. A further point is now to be made: change in size, particularly among animals, is usually accompanied by other changes, especially in the magnitudes of various anatomical dimensions relative to each other or to the gross size of the whole organism. Thus an evolutionary rate in one dimension may entail (and indirectly measure) rates in other dimensions or in many characteristics of different sorts. This may also be called *allomorphosis* ("difference in form") or *allometry* ("difference in measurement"). It may also be called, in a more vernacular way, "relative growth." In its most general sense, it may also include not only morphological or metrical differences but also physiological and other characteristics. Study from this point of view is economical, insofar as it may relate a number of different changes to a single dimension or to overall size.

Interest in this subject has stemmed mostly from a heuristic book by Julian Huxley, *Problem of Relative Growth,* first published in 1932. Since then scores of articles and dozens of books bearing largely on this subject have appeared. The discussion has become complicated to a great (and often confusing) degree. The approach to the subject of size and associated changes in morphology and other characters has been applied to a minimum of five different kinds of comparisons. For present limited purposes, it is here necessary to designate only two of these: (1) changes during the growth of individuals, called *ontogenetic allometry, heterauxesis* (from the Greek roots for "differential" and "growth"), or *allometry of growth,* and (2) changes during evolution in lines (lineages) of descent, called *phylogenetic allometry, evolutionary allometry,* or *lineage allomorphosis.* As reflected in the title of his book, Julian Huxley wrote mostly about allometry in individuals, or about what amounts nearly (but not quite) to the same thing: allometry between individuals of the same species but of different ages. However, he did mention possible applications of much the same technique to evolutionary allometry. Both ontogenetic and phylogenetic allometry can sometimes be applied in various ways to fossils. It is evolutionary or lineage allometry that seems potentially more interesting in the present context.

For both those applications and certain others, Julian Huxley proposed the use of the following equation (with somewhat different symbols, but these are usual now):

$$y = bx^a.$$

(The a in this equation is often written as Greek lower-case alpha or replaced by k.)

In this equation y is any usable measurement, usually linear in practice; x is an analogous measurement being compared with y; b is the initial growth constant or the y intercept in a graph; and a is the equilibrium constant or (in the analogy with individual growth) the growth constant, determining the slope of the graph. If b and a are indeed constant, the graph of the equation is a straight line on logarithmic coordinates.

In the 1930s and 1940s, several studies of phylogenetic or evolutionary allometry, mostly by Huxley's equation, led to the suggestion that increase in size was the controlling factor, at least in some examples, and that other specified morphological changes were tied genetically to the overall size trend throughout the evolutionary history of the organisms in question. Among the examples was the fact that the proportions of face to skull length changed markedly from eohippus (*Hyracotherium*) to *Equus* in the evolution of the horse family. Cumming Robb's hypothesis (1935) was that the increase in skull length was primary or causal and that increase in the relative length of the face was genetically tied to skull length in an unchanging allometric relationship already present in eohippus. However, it was pointed out, especially by Reeve and Murray in 1945, that the hypothesis was probably invalid. Robb's method was statistically flawed, and some of his data were from species certainly not in or near the lineage ancestral to *Equus*. The values of b and a in Huxley's allometric equation may have been approximately constant for the length of the face relative to the length of the cranium in the Eocene and Oligocene (*Hyracotherium* to *Mesohippus*), but thereafter the values changed, both in the lineage leading to *Equus* and in collateral lineages leading elsewhere. It was found also that these values are not constant in the growth of living individuals of the genus *Equus*. After an initial period of allometry, the value of a tends to fall to 1—that is, the later growth is not allometric.

A review of the now fairly numerous studies of evolutionary allometry shows that, while simple or Huxleyan allometry may occur in some lineages and through some stretches of geological time, the relationship between size and other characters is often—or usually—more complex or downright erratic. Moreover, one cannot assume, in such two-sided comparisons, that one characteristic measured is the cause of the other or that both are the results of the same (genetic) cause. There is nevertheless great interest in the concurrent evolution of different characteristics. Although the reduction of such phenomena to quantitative terms is

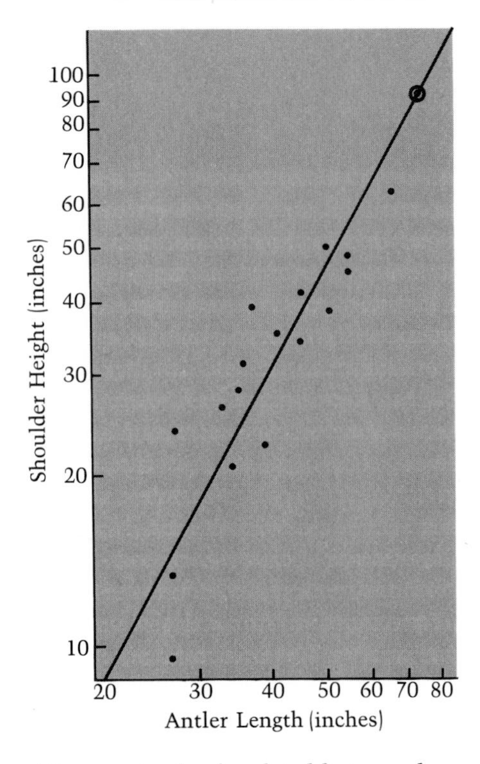

Allometry in closely related living and recently extinct species of deer. Each dot represents a single species, and the line is fitted to them on a logarithmic graph as the best fit of a reduced major axis. The data are maximal values of shoulder height and antler length (in inches) in the same individuals. In the allometric equation $y = b\,x^a$, *y is antler length and x is shoulder height. As calculated by S. J. Gould, from whom this figure is redrawn with some modification, the value of* b *is 0.0342 and that of* a *is 1.85. It is clear that species with larger adults generally have antlers not only positively bigger but also bigger in proportion to body size. The Irish elk* Megaloceros giganteus, *represented by the circled dot, has both the largest body size and the largest antler size, but the proportion between them is exactly that projected by the allometry of the rest of the subfamily to which it belongs. Thus, from this point of view, its enormous antlers were not unusually large for a deer with this body size. This example of interspecific allometry adds another to the two kinds of allometry explicitly mentioned in the text: ontogenetic and phylogenetic.*

not yet quite wholly satisfactory, some aspects will later be followed here in more descriptive terms—for instance, as related to the phenomena of convergence and of mosaic evolution.

There are just two more points about allometry that should be briefly mentioned here. One is that some allometric relationships evidently follow mechanical necessity rather than a predetermined growth pattern. A simple example is that the strength of a leg bone is approximately proportional to the area of its cross section, which varies more or less with the square of linear dimensions, while the weight of an animal varies approximately with the cube of linear dimensions. Thus, if body length becomes twice as great in the course of evolution, body weight will become about eight times as great. To bear such increase in weight most effectively, a bearing leg bone (such as the femur) should increase its cross-sectional area by considerably more than four times. In short, it should have positive allometry in relation to body size, and this is evident in the evolution of most large land vertebrates. If natural selection favors marked increase in size, as if often has, it will also (but independently) favor increase in the stoutness of limbs.

The other, and last, point about allometry to be mentioned here is that it has been implicated as a cause of extinction. If there were a constant allometric relationship between overall size and some other characteristics, it can be shown in many examples that projection of size beyond a certain limit would result first in monstrosity and finally in nonviability because of those allometric characteristics. Therefore, the argument goes, extinction ensues. That, however, is unlikely. As such inadaptive conditions were approached, natural selection would probably stop the trend toward greater size, or change the allometric constant, or both. The most famous supposed example is the misnamed "Irish elk," an extinct Old World deer that became the largest of all deer both in body and in antlers. Antlers are generally positively allometric in deer—that is, as body size increases, antler size increases at a relatively faster rate—and this has been found to be true also of the "Irish elk." For years, the usual hypothesis was that trend for larger body size went on so long that the inordinate increase in antler size became inadaptive and extinction of the species resulted. The alternative hypothesis, which now seems more probable, is that natural selection in these animals was primarily sexual selection, which led to an increase in antler size. With this as the primary effect, increase in body size would follow as a mechanical necessity, although at a slower rate and hence with negative allometry in relation to the antlers. Then, as usual, we do not really know why this species became extinct. Perhaps because of climatic change?

If a line of descent recognizable in the fossil record continued for an appreciable length of geological time in the same region and under similar ecological conditions, rates of evolution would be expected to be low (or perhaps even zero) for much of that record. Such populations would be likely to be affected by stabilizing selection—that is, natural selection would possibly slow down or even stop evolutionary change. Many lineage records of successive species and genera are

The Irish elk Megaloceros giganteus, *from the Pleistocene of Europe. This deer had an antler spread that could reach up to 11 feet.*

now known from fossils, although few were known in Darwin's day, and that troubled him. Thus we are now in a better position to check evolutionary rates in documented continuous lineages. (That these records commonly start and end abruptly is a different problem, and to some extent a more debatable one, which is discussed below.)

As was to be expected, rates of evolution in well-recorded lineages are usually rather slow on the average. Contrary to some recent theorizing, however, they are rarely if ever zero or simply static over any considerable length of geological time. They may here be adequately illustrated by three examples that cover several different points.

In 1975, I. Hayami and T. Ozawa published data on a species of fusulinids, *Lepidolina multiseptata,* that lived through much of the middle and late Permian. The fusulinids were a family of foraminifers, one-celled animallike organisms (protozoans), that were abundant in the Carboniferous and Permian but extinct thereafter. As a group, they tended to become larger as time went on and finally reached a length of about 60 millimeters (slightly less than 2½ inches),

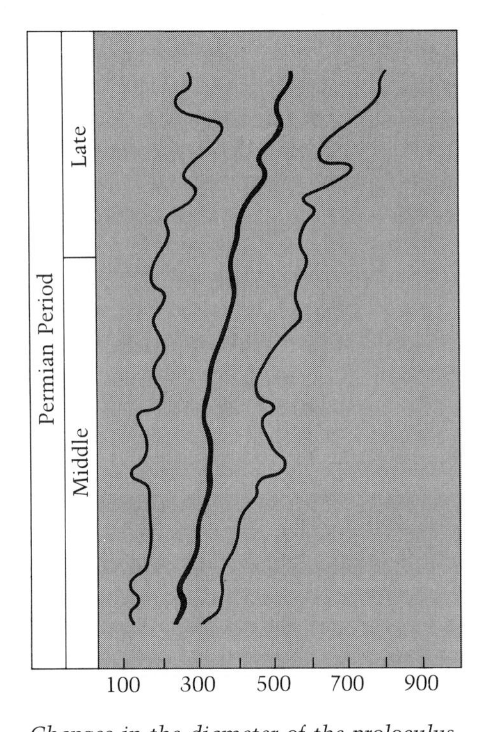

Changes in the diameter of the proloculus in the foraminifer (a protist) Lepidolina multiseptata. *The original data are from 34 successive samples, here smoothed out into curves. The heavier, central line connects the mean values for the 34 samples, and the lighter, outer lines connect points at two standard deviations from the mean for each sample. Most of the individuals in each population sampled would be within the outer lines of this diagram, but the total variation of each was certainly somewhat greater. The irregularity of these lines is largely, but not wholly, a sampling effect. The more even course of the mean is also affected by sampling, but it reliably indicates a moderate rate of evolutionary change toward increasing size.*

Differences in means of ratios of rib height to rib width in, and time spans of, thirteen samples of a lineage of the Silurian brachiopod *Eocoelia* and rates of evolution calculated from them.

Group	Approximate time from oldest to youngest sample in group (millions of years)	Range (from oldest to youngest in group) of means of ratios (expressed as percentages) of rib height to rib width	Rate of change in means of ratios (percent)
a: Five oldest samples	1.5	45–42	−4.6
b: Last sample in *a* through next two	1.0	42–28	−40.6
c: Last sample in *b* through next three	4.6	28–18.75	−8.8
d: Last sample in *c* through next three	2.25	18.75–7.5	−40.5
e: All thirteen successive samples	9.3	45–7.5	−19.3

which is enormous for protozoans. Their shells (tests) became remarkably complex for one-celled organisms, with the regular addition of chambers , the first of which is known as a proloculus. The data in this example are for the diameter of the proloculus in 34 successive populations through about 15 million years. The ranges of variation in the earliest and latest populations overlapped extensively, and all are therefore referred to a single species, but there was a clear and statistically significant increase in size. The rate of increase in mean size of the proloculus between the earliest and the latest samples was about 6.5% per million years. There was some wavering, but this could be a sampling effect, and the rate of change was at least approximately the same throughout the entire 15 million years. The rate is not notably high, but the species cannot be considered static through that length of time.

There is another example that is somewhat more complex and that adds an interesting point: The data, published by A. M. Ziegler in 1966, are statistics on thirteen successive samples of brachiopods (lamp shells) of the genus *Eocoelia* through nearly ten million years in the Silurian period. Rates of evolution calculated for the sample means and approximate ages from Ziegler are given in the table above. The character under consideration is the ratio of height to width of the external ribs on one valve of the shell. Because this is a ratio and is calculated as a percentage, its rates of change are not directly comparable with those of single dimensions calculated as such, but they are comparable with each other within this sequence. The relative rates as here calculated are negative: there was a trend for the ribs to become lower in proportion to their width. The shells ultimately became virtually smooth. For the first 1.5 million years, the calculated

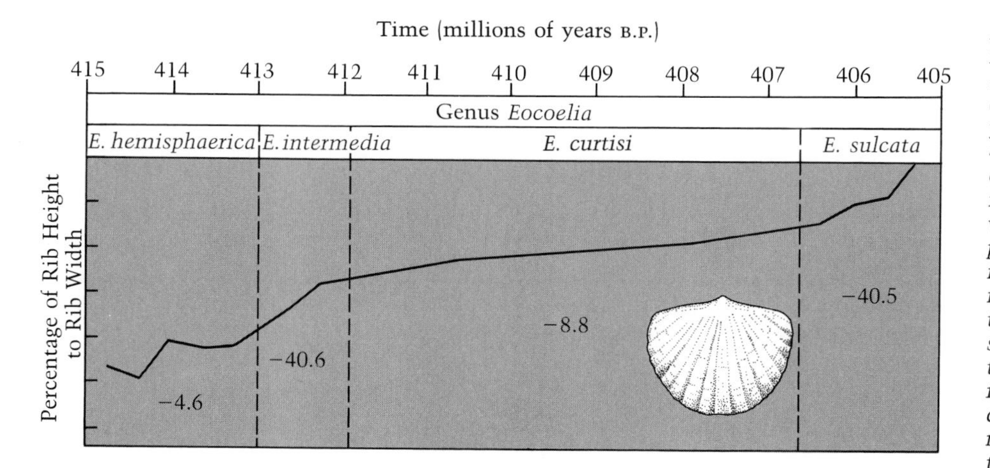

Evolution of one character, the ratio of rib height to rib width, in the Silurian brachiopod Eocoelia. *The geological time covered is approximately ten million years, from about 415 million to about 405 million years* B.P.*, as shown in scale on the horizontal axis. The vertical axis is scaled to percentage of rib height to width. Mean values from 14 samples were placed with respect to time and prominence of ribs. Successive means were connected by straight lines in order to make the trends more readily apparent. If the samples were closer together in time, there would doubtless be some incidental irregularity of slope, but the rates of change for each segment would not be materially affected. These rates, all negative, are entered for each of four unequal segments of the curve. (See also the text and table on page 160). The broken vertical lines separate segments of the evolutionary sequence to which different specific names have been given. It is significant that they also delimit times of less and of more rapid evolution of this character. The named species, if accepted as such, are chronospecies and accelerated evolution does not here represent a shift producing a new species as a branch from the lineage. The sketch gives an impression of the plicated appearance of shells of the genus. The shells became virtually smooth in the late (here right hand) stages of evolution.*

rate is relatively low and may represent only sampling error rather than a definite trend in the population. The differences in means of the five samples in this part of the sequence are not statistically significant. However, there ensued a relatively short period of time, about 1 million years, during which the rate of evolution was very rapid. That, in turn, was followed by about 4.6 million years with a significant but much lower rate of evolution and then, finally, in the last 2.25 million years or so, another phase of relatively very rapid change.

If only the first and last terms in the sequence are compared, there is a significant rate of evolution, but the intermediate samples disprove any assumption that this was a constant trend. There were two intervals of relatively slow change (in one of them, there may have been virtually no change) interspersed with two of very rapid evolutionary change. The specimens from these four distinct intervals have been classified as four successive species of a single lineage of ancestral and descendant populations. The end terms are significantly different and qualify as chronospecies, which are distinct in kind from contemporaneously existing species. Whether the intermediate samples are well classified as two other chronospecies is a matter of taxonomic usage or personal taste and, therefore, outside the scope of this discussion.

Another instructive example—or rather a combination of several examples with some general features in common—has been provided by Philip Gingerich (1976) in what he called a "stratophenetic approach to phylogeny reconstruction." He studied a large number of specimens of fossil mammals placed with good precision at successive levels in several thousand feet of sediments (middle Paleocene through early Eocene) in the Bighorn Basin of Wyoming. He found that in functionally similar mammals, the length of the first lower molar multiplied by its width is proportional to overall body size, and he took this as a key charac-

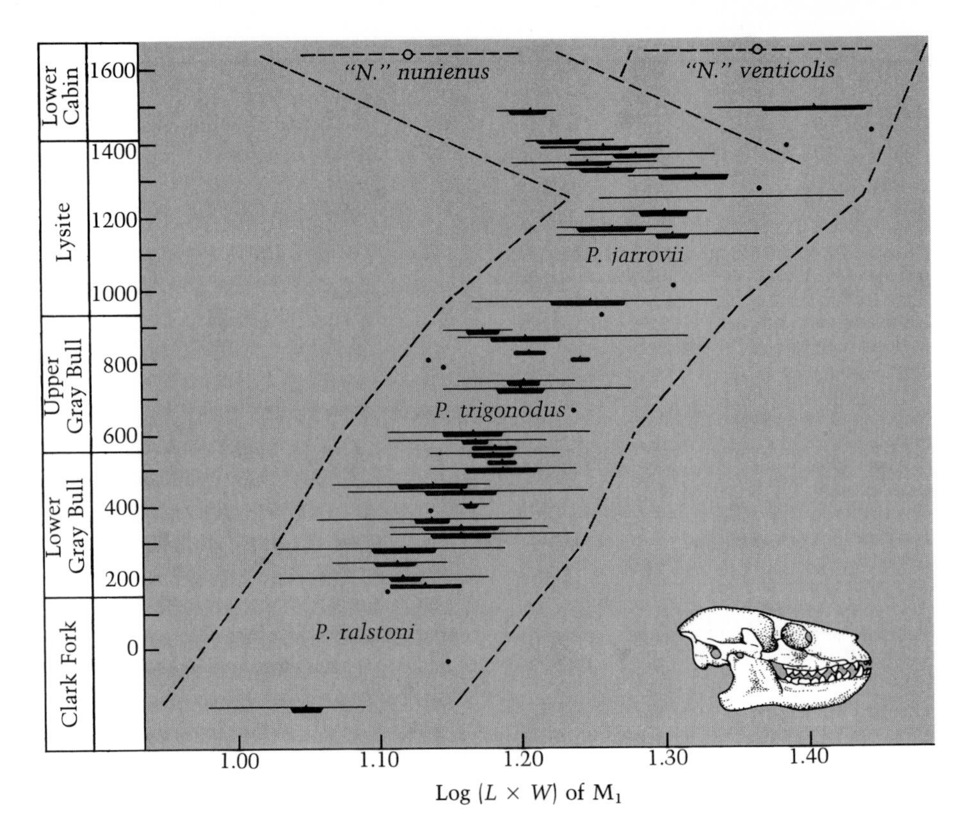

Part of the evolution of the genus Pelycodus, *primitive primates resembling the lemurs. The time represented is nearly the whole of the early Eocene, which, although not yet measured with close precision, lasted approximately 5 million years. (The names in the column to the left are those of stages of early Eocene nonmarine strata in North America.) The specimens used to make the graph came from samples at well-determined levels within a section measured in feet on the scale to the left. The values of the variate scaled on the horizontal axis are the logarithms of length times width of first lower molars. There is reasonable evidence that these values correlate well with body size. The transverse lines show the observed range, mean, and standard error of the mean. There is considerable sampling irregularity, but the data from the bottom to top left clearly suggest essential continuity of an ancestral–descendant lineage of populations. The broken lines are reasonable limits on the probable average variation within these populations. They were clearly evolving at a moderate rate and definitely not static. The main group was becoming larger up to about the 1300-foot level in the section and then, up to the top of this record (to about 1500 feet), they reversed that trend and started to become smaller. What is here called "the main group" can be divided into successive species or chronospecies, as Gingerich has done in this figure. Matthew already noted, some two generations ago (in 1915), that these populations were evolving more or less steadily, not only in size but also in other characters not clearly correlated with size, and this is confirmed by samples much longer and more exactly placed in the sequence now available.*

At or shortly after the time of reversal in direction of evolution of size in the main group, a second definitely different species of distinctly larger size appears in the known record. It has been suggested (and it is a reasonable hypothesis) that the reversal may have been adaptive in more definitely separating the ecological roles of the two species then in the same region. In the following middle Eocene, descendants of these two species became still more distinct—so much so that those descendants are now generally given distinct generic names, Smilodectes *for the descendants of the one to the left at the top in this graph and* Notharctus *for those of the one here to the right. (See also the figure on page 163.)*

There are three possible hypotheses for the apparently sudden appearance of the large species called "N." venticolis *in this graph:*

- *It may have split off gradually from the main group sympatrically (in the same area) and intermediates may simply not have been found. This is unlikely because wholly sympatric speciation is generally a rare event and, furthermore, fossils of this general group are so common in this area that intermediates would be likely to be found if they were there.*
- *It may have arisen instantaneously, that is, between one generation and the next. That is still less likely, as many studies have shown that such "macromutations," although not absolutely impossible, very rarely (if ever) produce distinctly new biological species.*
- *"N."* venticolis *may have evolved outside the area of the samples of the main group in this graph, either from marginal populations of the latter or from an earlier and geographically more distant offshoot of the common ancestry. This is by far the most probable explanation.*

ter obtainable from most of the available specimens. He gathered detailed data for three different sequences of related forms, one of a genus *(Hyopsodus)* of small primitive ungulates and two of early primates in different families (Plesiadapidae and Adapidae). For this example, there are at present no adequate applicable direct estimates of geological time in years (indirect estimates will probably be available later), so that quantitative figures for rates of evolution have not been calculated. The sequences, however, are exact as such, and most of the samples are large enough to give good estimates of statistical parameters.

The three groups studied are not closely related (the two families of primates were distinct from the start), but all three have some interesting features in common. All have long sequences that are gradual, in that the ranges of variation in successive samples overlap throughout. Gradual, in that sense, does not imply that the rate of evolution was slow, but simple inspection of the graphs suggests that the rates were moderate in these examples. It is, however, noteworthy in these cases (and usual in others) that there are no geologically perceptible spans of stasis—that is, periods with rates not clearly different from zero.

Another feature of all three, this one not usual in known sequences, is that each has one long sequence that can reasonably be interpreted as ancestral–descendant in which the direction of evolutionary change was reversed. In all three, the animals were at first becoming steadily larger and then, with apparent abruptness, the later members of the lineage began to become progressively smaller. The reversals occurred at different times in the three examples. A somewhat speculative explanation, but one that is reasonable and for which there is some evidence, is that the reversals are due to what is sometimes called character displacement. This phenomenon, deduced from study of recent animals and already known to Darwin, results when two related species closely similar in ecology come into contact. They then often tend to develop and to increase ecological and correlated somatic differences between them. In each of the groups studied by Gingerich, a second, related species does appear in the same area at or, geologically speaking, shortly after the reversal. The evidence also is compatible with another aspect of the synthetic theory: that the separation of an ancestral species into two (or more) contemporaneous descendant species often (but not always) occurs through the differentiation of local or marginal parts of populations within the ancestral range.

A final point in consideration of these examples of specific lineages in the fossil record is that, in Gingerich's examples, when the second lineage appears in the region it is at first closely similar to the resident species, and that divergence between them develops progressively thereafter in opposite directions, one positive and one negative, at rates apparently normal or not markedly accelerated. This is certainly not invariable, and it is probably not common in known records of specific lineages. When a second species appears in the record along with a related (and thereafter contemporaneous) species, the two are often or usually already distinct. This distinction probably arose elsewhere before the two species

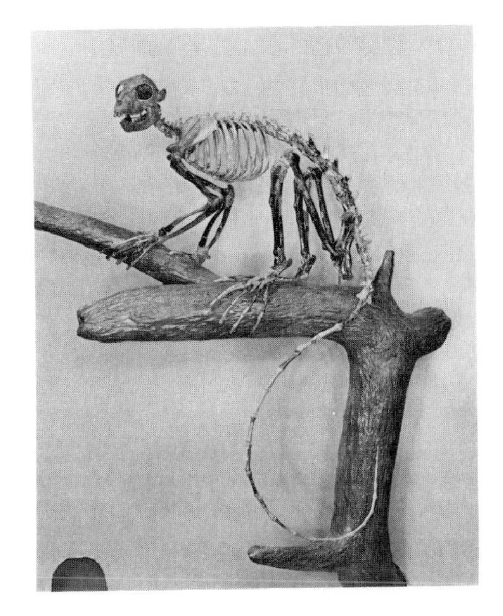

A fully reconstructed skeleton of a specimen of Notharctus, *a genus of early primates directly descended from* Pelycodus, *some species of which are referred to in the preceding figure. The middle Eocene specimen here shown most clearly resembles the species labeled "N."* venticolis *in the upper right of the preceding figure, and it is probable that* Notharctus *evolved directly from that species or another closely allied population in a somewhat different geographical area.* Notharctus *was most common in the Bridger Basin,* Pelycodus *in the Big Horn Basin, both in what is now Wyoming but some distance apart. The more completely known* Notharctus *differs only in details that are not apparent in this figure of its skeleton, which thus shows what the species referred to in the preceding figure and usually considered to be members of the genus* Pelycodus *were like.*

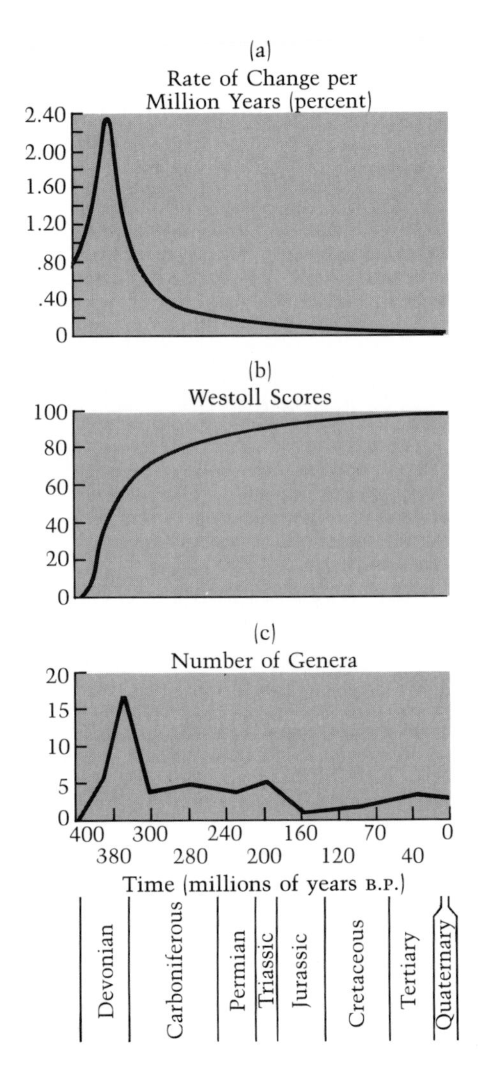

Aspects of the evolution of the lungfishes. For all three parts of this figure, time—from earliest (the early Devonian) to latest (the present)—is on the horizontal axis scaled in millions of years B.P. *with the names of geological periods below.* (a) *Rates of evolution, scaled on the vertical axis in terms of approximate percentage change per million years of the scores as graphed in* (b). *The height of the rate in any section of this curve is proportional to the slope of the curve of the scores in* (b). *Thus, the slope in* (b) *becomes steepest toward the end of the Devonian and is least steep in the Tertiary and Quaternary. Accordingly, the rate shown in* (a) *is highest toward the end of the Devonian and lowest in the Tertiary and Quaternary.* (b) *A graph of Westoll scores, but (as explained in the text) these have been essentially turned around: Westoll scored on the basis of the presence of primitive or ancestral characters, but, using the same characters and scores assigned, I have scored not for loss of the primitive conditions but for the acquisition of more advanced or derived conditions. In this form, the result resembles a logistic curve, although it is not identical with one.* (c) *A graph of the known numbers of genera in the various periods as listed in the last (1966) edition of Romer's* Vertebrate Paleontology. *Since 1966, quite a few new genera of early lungfishes have been discovered, and a full compilation of these (not yet available) would raise especially the Paleozoic part of the curve in* (c). *Nevertheless, the somewhat irregular but characteristic nature of that curve would probably be much the same. It bears a significant resemblance to curve* (a), *and that resemblance is probably being maintained (and possibly increased) by current discoveries.*

appear together. In most samples, there is no direct evidence in the fossil record about the rate of divergence between the species. However, as will be further discussed, there is evidence that, at times of especially marked proliferation of species, the rates of their evolution are often (perhaps even usually) exceptionally rapid.

Another instructive kind of evolutionary rate was exemplified in 1949 by Stanley Westoll in a study that has become classic. Westoll studied sixteen different morphological characters in the skulls, teeth, and bodies of fossil and living lungfishes (technically, of the subclass or order Dipnoi of the class Osteichthyes). He then gave numerical ratings to states of each character according to whether he judged the character state to be more primitive (that is, presumably present in the immediate ancestry of the lungfishes) or more specialized (that is, derived from, but to different degrees divergent, from the ancestral condition). The presumed ancestral condition was given a score of from 7 to 2 for the most primitive states and downward by integers to 0 for the more derived states. These scores were chosen in such a way that, for the presumed ancestor, they total 100 and, for the most specialized or most highly derived genera, they total 0. The scores for ten extinct genera and the three surviving genera were then graphed against a time scale in millions of years.

The graph, as Westoll drew it, indicates loss of ancestral characters. The development of new or more derived character complexes seems to me a somewhat more positive approach to evolutionary change. Therefore, in 1953, I took Westoll's scores and simply turned them around, for each character making 0 the presumed ancestral state and giving the highest scores to the most derived or modernized states of each character. As shown here in the graph, the curve begins at 0 at about 400 million years B.P. (before present)—Westoll used 350, but the difference does not affect the shapes of the curves—and rises with varying slope to 100 at 0 years B.P. (that is, the present time). The rate of evolution is well measured by the changing slope of such a curve. As seen in the figure, the rate begins at a moderate level in the early Devonian, rises very rapidly to a high peak in the late Devonian, and then drops at first rapidly and then increasingly slowly until it nearly levels out near 0 in the Cretaceous.

Another point also evident in Westoll's study, but not there shown in the same way as in the present figure, is that a graph of the number of genera against time somewhat approximates the curve of rate of acquisition of derived characters. The curve for numbers of genera is not as smooth as the rate curve, but it also rises rapidly from early through middle Devonian to a sharp peak in late Devonian and then falls off abruptly in the Carboniferous. One reason for this is that survivorship was much shorter in the Devonian than it later became. That could be either a cause or an effect of varying rates of morphological change, or it could quite possibly be a combination of the two in a sort of feedback.

Studies of taxonomic survivorship here exemplified in Chapter 5 were begun in the 1940s and have continued ever since. These studies suggested early on that most lineages in the fossil record had a mean or modal rate within any particular large taxonomic group and that this rate differs greatly from one group to another. It has already been mentioned that, in an early comparison, the modal survivorship for genera of bivalves among mollusks was found to be much longer than that for genera of carnivores among mammals. Within each group, the longevity for individual genera or species varies greatly; and, in graphs of the distribution of taxonomic longevity, there is commonly (but not invariably) a marked peak or modal group on the side of short longevity—hence, faster taxonomic turnover and, in that sense, more rapid evolution. In such distributions, the frequencies usually fall off rapidly on the short side (with the more rapid taxonomic rate) and more slowly on the long side (with the slower taxonomic rate). As similar distributions of longevity and of associated rates of evolution seem to be usual in the fossil record, I early suggested that they be called horotelic (from the Greek roots for "standard" and "tending toward an end").

When survivorship curves for extinct and living genera of bivalves and later for extinct and living species of centric diatoms (a group of one-celled, plantlike organisms) were compared, it was found that the living taxa had a markedly greater proportion of long-lived (and hence slowly evolving) taxa than would be expected from survivorship in the extinct taxa. It thus appears that the known fossil record of extinct taxa and the known fossil record of still extant taxa are sampling two different distributions of evolutionary rates. I therefore suggested that an excess of slow rates in one of these distributions might be called bradytely (from the Greek roots for "slow" and "tending toward an end"). It was found that, for mammalian carnivores, the survivorship curves for extinct and living genera are not significantly different and, therefore, that bradytely as originally defined does not occur in this particular group.

There is also evidence that there are groups and times in which evolution has occurred at rates so rapid that they are not clearly within the range of the horotelic rates usually evident in the fossil record. It is one of the biases or imperfections of the fossil record that direct evidence of such rates from fossil sequences are less numerous or less clear than records of horotelic rates. That brings up problems and opinions for some further discussion, but the distinction of a distribution of exceptionally rapid rates seemed so probable that I suggested calling it tachytelic (from the Greek roots for "fast" and "tending toward an end"). The terms horotely, bradytely, and tachytely are often used in the evolutionary literature, but perhaps now more commonly with bradytely and tachytely implied to be the slow and fast ends of otherwise horotelic distributions. This was not how they were originally defined, but the terms may nevertheless be useful in this somewhat different and somewhat less clear sense. It is not a postulate or a principle but a mathematical certainty that the shorter the mean longevity of the taxa involved, the faster the taxonomic turnover and hence the faster the taxonomic rate of evolution. Nevertheless, Steven Stanley has insisted that the obvious inverse relationship between such longevity and taxonomic turnover is wrong in principle.

Another concept and term that become relevant here are those of quantum evolution. The term quantum evolution was originally defined by me in 1944 as "the relatively rapid shift of a biotic population in disequilibrium to an equilibrium unlike an ancestral condition." It was noted that this could occur at any taxonomic level from subspecies upward but that its results, involving shifts in ecology or distinctive adaptive zones, became more evident at higher taxonomic levels, such as families, orders, or classes. It was thereafter (1953) stressed that quantum evolution was not the only mode of origin of new groups, but that it is probable that species often arise in this way and that genera or other groups above the species level certainly may do so.

In the fossil record, there is evidence—usually somewhat indirect, but nonetheless convincing—that exceptionally rapid rates of change have usually been involved when distinctly new kinds or levels of organization and of ecological occupation have arisen in evolving organisms. Many examples are provided by the records of almost all major groups of organisms known as fossils. Among the

(a)

(b)

The oldest bat surely identified as such is an absolutely complete skeleton from the early Eocene of Wyoming. This skeleton is drawn and described in detail at the opening of this chapter. The subsequent evolution of bats involved great proliferation of species, genera, and families, but even today they differ in structure only slightly from their earliest known ancestor. Two of the approximately 900 species in existence are pictured here: (a) Lonchorhina aurita *and* (b) Vampyrum spectrum. *The figure on page 168 indicates how little basic change has occurred since the early Eocene even though there was great proliferation of families, genera, and species of bats.* Vampyrum, *by the way, is not a vampire bat. The common vampire bat is* Desmodus.

most striking (but otherwise fairly typical) examples of this sort of evidence is provided by the bats, which constitute the order Chiroptera (from the Greek for "hand" and "wing"). There are some dubious older fossils that may possibly be bats, but the oldest bat surely identified as such is an absolutely complete skeleton from the early Eocene of Wyoming, about 50 million years old. (Other complete fossils of bats are also known from beds in Germany that are somewhat younger, about 45 to 48 million years old.) This skeleton does have some features more primitive than those of later bats, pointing back to ancestry in nonflying, ecologically shrewlike earlier mammals. Nevertheless, it was already fully batlike in essentials shared with all later and recent bats. Its anatomical adaptations to flying were complete and were *sui generis* for bats, radically unlike those of either flying reptiles (the extinct pterosaurs) or flying birds. The subsequent evolution of bats involved great proliferation of species, genera, and families. In this, bats compare with the rodents and exceed all other orders of mammals. Among these almost innumerable diverging lineages, evolution was far from static in other respects; but, if one takes adaptation to flight as the basic point of their entry into a new broad adaptive or ecological zone, it must be said that, since the early Eocene, the rate of evolution of the determinants of this vital adaptation has been extremely slow and has involved only a few minor or secondary details. Bats' wings have not progressed essentially over the last 50 million years or so, and I here iterate a conclusion I reached about forty years ago with respect to this point: "Extrapolation of this rate in an endeavor to estimate the time of origin [of a bat's wing] from a normal mammalian manus [front foot] might set that date before the origin of the earth." In fact, present knowledge of mammalian evolution in the late Cretaceous and Paleocene indicates that transformation of the bats' forelimb structure and function could hardly have begun earlier (and probably began somewhat later) than about 70 million years ago. This must then have been very much

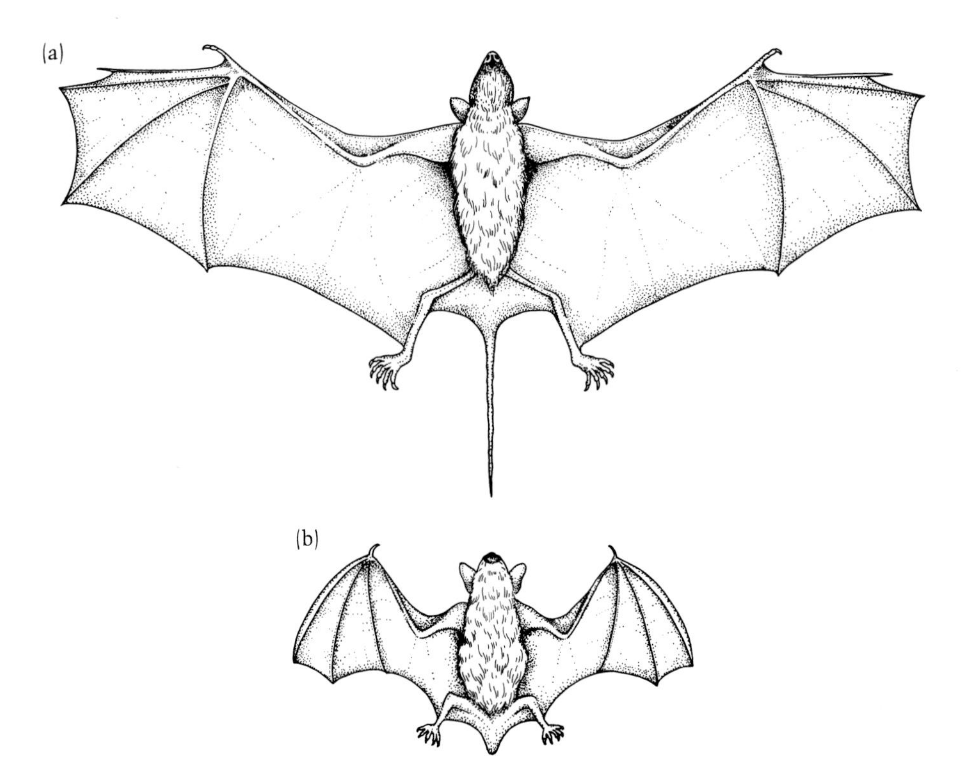

Comparison of an ancient and a living bat: (a) *A restoration of dorsal aspect of* Icaronycteris, *an early Eocene bat approximately 50,000,000 years old, based on a complete but distorted skeleton.* (b) *A sketch of a living brown bat (close to* Eptesicus*) for comparison with* Icaronycteris. *Most living bats have peculiar and diverse, sometimes fantastic, growths of the nose, face, and ears, related to their use of echolocation in flight. As these do not include bones, they are not visible in the fossil (if indeed it had them).* Icaronycteris *in flight was clearly completely batlike, and it is reasonable to infer that it also already had echolocation. Although bats have become extremely diverse in size, in dentition, and in many details, their basic distinction, the flying apparatus, has evolved hardly at all since the early Eocene. The diversification, an adaptive radiation, occurred at unusually rapid evolutionary rates. On the other hand, the further evolution of the peculiar, basic characters present in all bats (and, in fact, making them chiropterans and unlike the members of any other order of mammals) have hardly changed at all during the last 50,000,000 years or longer. It is impossible that the origin of these basic characters can have gone as slowly before that time as since then. That would have taken longer than the whole history of mammals, or even the whole history of life on earth. This does not mean that the chiropterans arose in one big step, instantaneously even in geological terms. It does indicate that their emergence occurred with unusual rapidity—in other words, that it must have been so highly tachytelic as to equal quantum evolution. It may have been, and in all probability was, nevertheless gradual in the correct etymological sense of the word—that is, it occurred small step by small step, even though the steps followed in sequence with unusual rapidity.*

more rapid than any later evolution in the resulting wing, and it is reasonable to infer that it involved quantum evolution—no matter which of the many somewhat varied definitions of that term is applied.

Adaptive radiation (which will be discussed later from a different point of view) usually involves quantum evolution. This is not so well exemplified by the bats because their fossil record, although fairly extensive in Europe, is still scanty elsewhere. When there is a breakthrough or shift from one adaptive or ecological zone to another, as in the origin of bats, this is frequently followed by the expansion of the zone and exploitation of its various subdivisions—such as niches, in ecological terms. This involves proliferations of separate lineages, and it is clear that, in many instances, the origins of the lineages are by quantum evolution.

Many theoretical studies of evolution concentrate on the origin of species, as Darwin did in his best-known work (although that work has much wider scope than his title suggests). As generally used in such studies, the term "speciation" is now assumed to mean the origin of species by separation of an ancestral species into two or more distinct species, one of which may or may not be considered a continuation of the ancestral species. At this level, quantum evolution becomes quantum speciation, a term now in general use but with varying definitions and concepts. In 1971, Verne Grant defined quantum speciation as "the budding

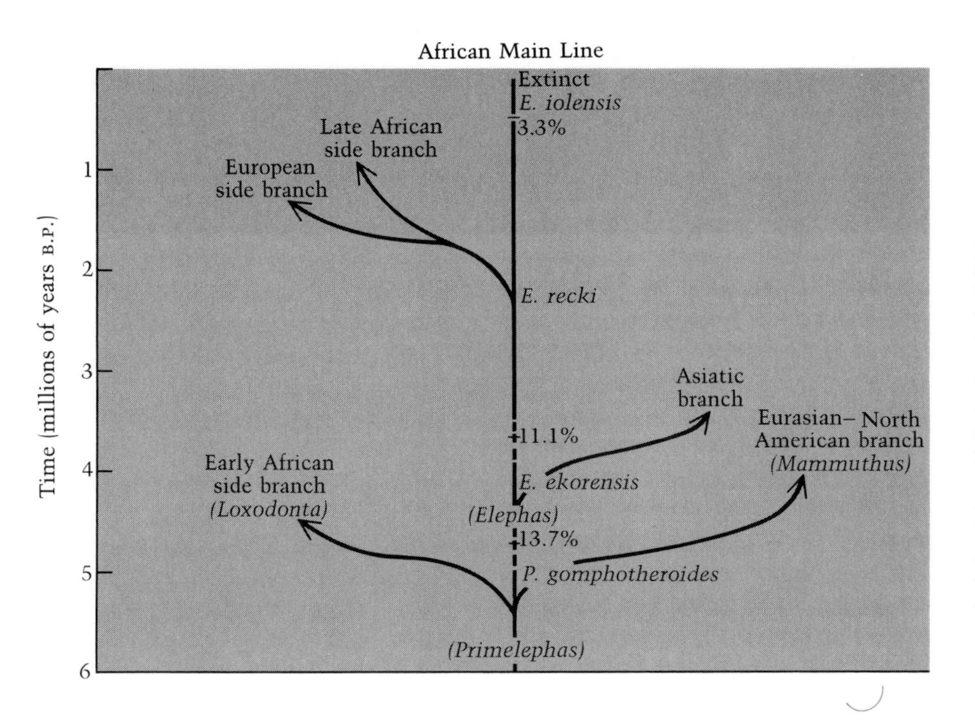

A simplified family tree of the elephant family (Elephantidae). This is primarily oriented on the most completely documented and most nearly complete record of the main line that evolved continuously in Africa, although it became extinct there in the Pleistocene. This is represented by the vertical line with its continuous sequence of chronospecies from Primelephas gomphotheroides *through* Elephas ekorensis *and* E. recki *to its terminal extinction in* E. iolensis. *The vertical scale in millions of years* B.P. *applies only to this line and to the approximate dating of offshoots from it. The lines with arrowheads indicate only the beginning of those offshoots, which themselves branched later. The two earliest of these offshoots became quite distinctive in a short time, geologically speaking. One, which remained in Africa, is still extant there as the African elephant,* Loxodonta africana. *The other early offshoot also originated in Africa, but it soon became extinct there after spreading first to Eurasia and thence to North America. These were the true mammoths (genus* Mammuthus*). They never reached Australia or South America. An Asiatic branch of somewhat later origin radiated to some extent, but it survives there in the only other living species of the family, the Asiatic elephant,* Elephas maximus *(whose specific name is an overstatement, inasmuch as it is usually smaller than the African elephant). The conservative classification by Vincent Maglio (1973) adapted here follows a phylogenetic reconstruction with eleven branches or subbranches, nine of which ended in terminal extinction. The figures on the right side of the central vertical line are placed at the somewhat arbitrary division points between chronospecies. They indicate rates of evolution of the molar teeth, as given in the table on page 170 and discussed in the text.*

off of a new and very different daughter species from a semi-isolated peripheral population of the ancestral species in a cross-fertilizing organism." Later (1977) he expatiated: "In geographical speciation, the pathway [leading to a new species] is: local race—geographical race—allopatric semispecies—species . . . . In quantum speciation by contrast, the pathway runs directly from local race to new species. Quantum speciation thus represents a shortcut method of species formation."

In 1979, Steven Stanley adversely criticized the general concept of quantum evolution, but he nevertheless defined and then extensively discussed quantum speciation in a way that makes it the application to the species level of the concept of quantum evolution: "We can define quantum speciation simply as speciation in which most evolution is concentrated within an initial interval of time that is very brief with respect to the total longevity of the new lineage."

An example also discussed by Stanley suggests that his descriptive definition may be somewhat ambiguous. This is the comparatively well-known history of the elephant family (Elephantidae) as authoritatively interpreted by Vincent Maglio in 1973. This family arose about 5.5 million years ago in the Pliocene and thereafter diversified rapidly into three genera and at least seven contemporaneous species, all but two of which, however, became extinct in the course of the last million years. Prior to those extinctions, the proliferation of species as distinct lineages, their cladogenesis (from the Greek *clados,* "branch," and *genesis,* "origin"), went on at a rate of about 33% per million years, as calculated by Stanley. That is a very high overall rate of cladogenetic speciation. In addition to cladogenesis, however, there are several nearly or quite continuous lineages that are known to have changed quite markedly over spans of from about 5.5 to 3.5 million years. The longest (and, in Maglio's phylogenetic pattern, the central) lineage has two successive chronogenera and four successive chronospecies. From oldest to youngest, they are *Primelephas gomphotheroides—Elephas*

(a)

(b)

Examples from the elaborate history of the order Proboscidea, consisting of the elephants, their ancestors, and relatives that evolved in distinct ways. (a) *A mural by Jay H. Matternes showing parts of an early Pliocene fauna in western North America. The line of large animals in the left middle distance is a group of mastodonts,* Ambelodon, *with shovel-like lower tusks.* (b) *A mounted skeleton of* Mammuthus columbi, *the Columbian mammoth with its enormous tusks. The ancestors of this species of mammoths, members of the elephant family, spread from north Asia (an Ice Age). In the late Pleistocene and early Recent they were hunted by Paleoindians, and some think that this caused their extinction, but others doubt this.*

Rates of change (in percentage changes per million years) in lamellar frequency (number of enamel plates in ten centimeters) for the last upper molar (M^3) in a direct lineage of elephantids (*Primelephas gomphotheroides–Elephas ekorensis–E. recki–E. iolensis*) from the origin of the family in the late Miocene to the late Pleistocene.

Species	
P. gomphotheroides– E. ekorensis	13.7
E. ekorensis– E. recki	11.1
E. recki– E. iolensis	3.3
Total change: *P. gomphotheroides– E. iolensis*	8.9

ekorensis—Elephas recki—Elephas iolensis. From a functional–adaptive–ecological point of view, the most important changing character of these species is the lamellar frequency of the third (last) upper molar, which is the largest grinding tooth and which, in maturity and old age of the animals, was the only upper cheek tooth (tooth posterior to the tusks) that was used for grinding food (in conjunction with the corresponding lower molar). These teeth in elephants have transverse enamel plates, lamellae, which, with anterior–posterior movement of the lower jaw, grind the food and are themselves worn down. The lamellar frequency is the number of such plates in a standard distance of ten centimeters. Increase in this number increased the durability and efficiency of the teeth. In all the various elephantid lineages the number increased steadily—but not at uniform rates. In the table shown here Maglio's data have been used to calculate the rate of change in the lineage here specified. The time intervals have been taken between the midpoints of the recorded durations of the species. The percentage change per million years is greatest between the first two species. This can reasonably be interpreted as a declining phase in a quantum change from their ancestry in the mastodont family Gomphotheriidae, in which this rapid evolution doubtless started but for which the known record is not yet complete. Thereafter, the rate declines to a minimum (but not to zero) between the last two species, after which the lineage became terminally extinct.

One point here is that quantum evolution can occur, or continue, between successive stages in a single line of descent. Another point is that this rapid phase here continues only slightly diminished for a time greater than the subsequent slower phase of the same lineage. Finally, the example also shows that the terminal phase can be seen as unusually rapid by another method of estimating evolutionary rates. The terminal species, *Elephas iolensis,* has the shortest duration (or, in terms of taxonomic survival rates, the shortest survival). This is taken by Stanley to indicate that this species has the highest evolutionary rate, although elsewhere he rejects the (mathematically necessary) conclusion that taxonomic survival and rates of faunal change are negatively correlated with longevity of species.

Niles Eldredge and Stephen Jay Gould, first in 1972, have discussed two phylogenetic patterns, one called by them "phyletic gradualism" and the other "punctuated equilibrium." They contrast these as follows:

Phyletic gradualism	Punctuated equilibrium
1. New species arise by the transformation of an ancestral population into its modified descendants.	1. New species arise by the splitting of lineages.
2. The transformation is even and slow.	2. New species develop rapidly.
3. The transformation involves large numbers, usually the entire ancestral population.	3. A small subpopulation of the ancestral form gives rise to the new species.
4. The transformation occurs over all or a large part of the ancestral species' geographic range.	4. The new species originates in a very small part of the ancestral species' geographic extent—in an isolated area at the periphery of the range.

The first paper on this subject by Eldredge and Gould and much of the subsequent discussion have been dialectical, maintaining that one or the other alternative, but not both and not any other alternative, must be correct. They equate "phyletic gradualism" with the synthetic theory and reject it, advancing "punctuated equilibrium" as the only valid alternative. One should always be wary of an "either–or" proposition, and this one is false. Both these patterns and a number of others occur in the fossil record. As strictly delimited, the two patterns concern different kinds of species. "Phyletic gradualism," by this definition, gives rise to species successive in time in one lineage—chronospecies—and "punctuated equilibrium" gives rise to two or more species—cladistic species—from a single ancestral species. All of the evolutionary processes ascribed to "phyletic gradualism" and to "punctuated equilibrium" were noted long before 1972 as valid parts of the synthetic theory. Neither one was (or is) considered as the only (or even as the usual) real phylogenetic pattern by synthesist evolutionists. Eldredge and Gould added as the "equilibrium" part of "punctuated equilibrium" that, after a new cladistic species arose by rapid development, both it and the now separate ancestral species would continue without further significant change through considerable stretches of geological time. That, too, occurs in the known fossil record and involves no contradiction of the synthetic theory, but it is unusual, and clearly not the rule, for *no* evolutionary change to occur in a geologically long record of a species.

Saying that new species develop rapidly, as they may but evidently do not always, leaves open the question of how fast is "rapidly." It is notorious that many new species and more taxa of higher categories—genera, families, and so on—appear suddenly in the fossil record without known direct ancestors. The pattern of "punctuated equilibrium" offers two stated alternative hypotheses to account for this observation: (1) new taxa evolve so rapidly that the elapsed time is not measurable in geological terms; (2) new taxa evolve in small geographic areas and do not enter the known record until they expand in numbers and in

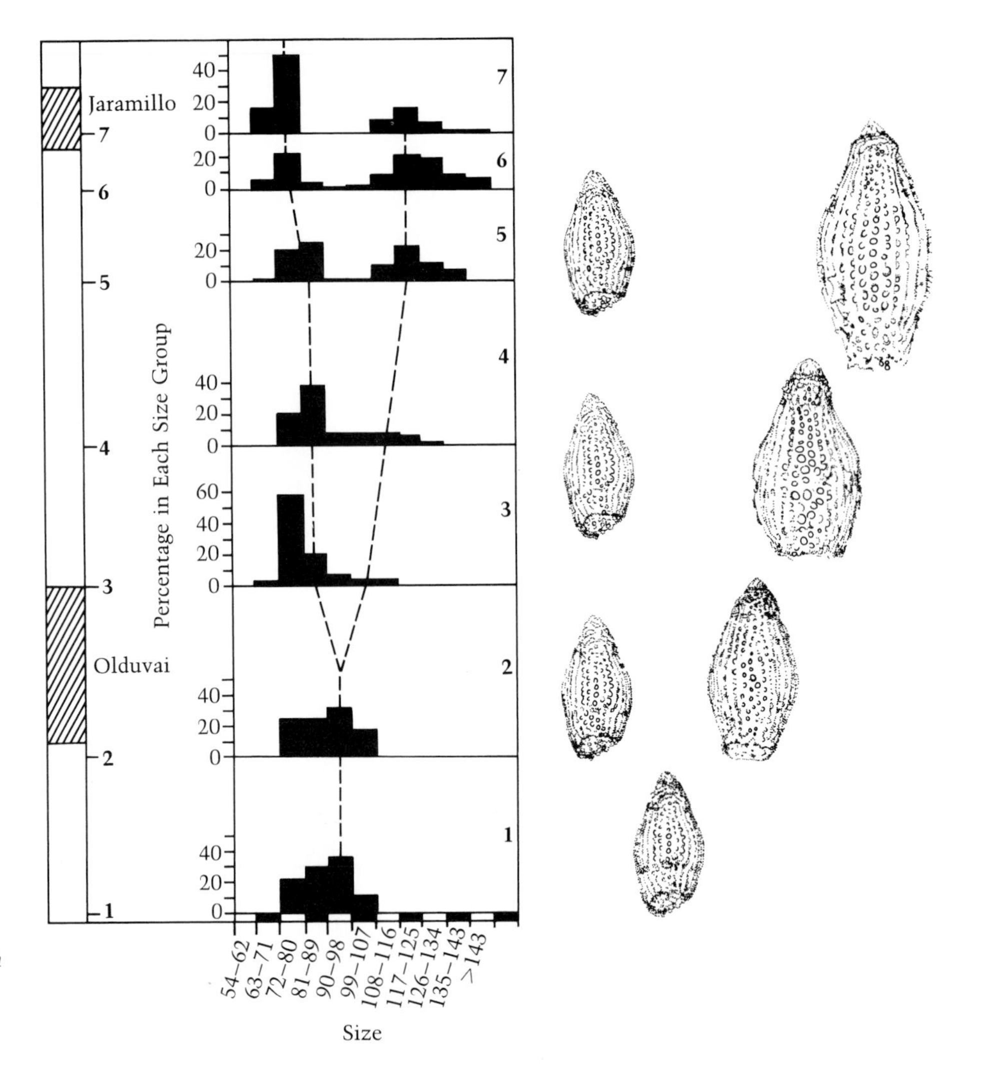

Rapid but gradual branching of a second species from a persisting ancestor. The ancestral species is a radiolarian (a small, one-celled organism with a siliceous skeleton), Eucyrtidium calvertense, *and the separate branch is an eventually larger species,* Eucyrtidium matuyamai. *Both are shown here to the right, greatly enlarged. The data are from a sea-floor core in the northern Pacific. The core has been dated paleomagnetically by the paleomagnetic episodes designated as Olduvai and Jaramillo, which are shown in measured positions in the core. The black histograms show the distributions of sizes of* Eucyrtidium *in samples from seven different levels in the core, numbered from the bottom up. The specimens were placed in ten different size groups, which are scaled horizontally at the bottom of the figure. The histograms are scaled by percentage in each sample of each size group.*

At the bottom of the figure, both sample 1 and sample 2 indicate a single species, the ancestral E. calvertense, *with some (but not great) variation in size. By sample 3, the indicated variation is markedly greater than is usual in single species, but there is as yet no clear indication of a division into two distinct parts. In samples 5 and 6, there is decidedly such a division, although there is still a very small number of intermediate specimens. In sample 7, there are no intermediates, and the two lineages clearly represent two quite distinct species. The average size of one (to the left) has become slightly smaller, but it is essentially stabilized and is still considered to be a surviving ancestral* E. calvertense. *The branch species,* E. matuyamai, *seems also more or less stabilized in samples 5, 6, and 7, but its later history is not followed in this particular core.*

space. The latter hypothesis invokes the incompleteness of the geological record—that is, the small area in which a species (or other taxon) actually evolved is rarely represented in the known record. In such a case, the rate at which the taxon evolved cannot be determined from the record, and the inference that it usually, or always, was especially rapid cannot be substantiated from observation. However so many fossils have now been obtained from so many places that there should be some known sequences for which rates can be determined. In fact there are, and examples were given earlier in this chapter. None of those follows the "punctuated equilibrium" pattern, but there is a recently published example that nearly does so, and this will now be added to the varied examples of phylogenetic patterns.

This example, published in 1980 by D. R. Prothero and D. B. Lazarus on the basis of an earlier study by J. D. Hays, involves the evolution of two species of one genus of radiolarians through much of the Pleistocene: *Eucyrtidium calvertense* and *Eucyrtidium matuyamai.* These are small, one-celled, drifting (nektonic), marine organisms with characteristic siliceous "skeletons" (tests) that were preserved in sediments that accumulated on the ocean bottoms. These sediments have been studied from a large number of cores obtained by oceanographers from the bottoms of practically all of the marine waters of the earth. Since the configuration of the seas has changed hardly at all since the Pliocene, it can be expected that the evolution of a species in a limited area of them would probably show up among the fossils in available cores, and so it did. *E. calvertense* was the first of the two species to appear, in the late Pliocene. It was clearly ancestral to *E. matuyamai,* which evolved from *E. calvertense* well along in the Pleistocene. Prothero and Lazarus did not publish measurements, but I have made them for the specimens they figured, drawn to the same scale. These show *E. matuyamai* gradually but rapidly diverging from *E. calvertense.* This occurred in a relatively limited part of the world's oceans, the north Pacific, to which *E. matuyamai* remained limited. I have calculated Haldane rates for length of the test. These are only approximate, but they do indicate a great difference for the two species while *E. matuyamai* was evolving. Its relative increase in length over a period of about 1 million years may have been as great as 55%, while that of ancestral *E. calvertense,* which continued to live elsewhere after *E. matuyamai* became a separate lineage, was only about 0.5% for the same span of time, a figure so small that its difference from zero, which is probably due to sampling, is not significant. Thus *E. calvertense* remained in equilibrium while *E. matuyamai* rapidly diverged, but by small steps and with the ranges of successive populations widely overlapping. This can be called a punctuation because it was rapid, but it did not occur by leaps and bounds (saltation). Whether, as in Eldredge and Gould's hypothetical model, this punctuation was followed by equilibrium in *E. matuyamai* does not appear in the published data.

Prothero and Lazarus ended their paper on speciation in *Eucyrtidium* with the statement that, "eventually, the fossils of these microplanktons may come to mean to paleontology what *Drosophila* has meant to the field of genetics: 'laboratory animals' for evolutionary study, whose evolution will provide the standard data upon which an original paleontologic theory of evolution may be based." That statement is excusably overenthusiastic. The study of marine microplankton can no more suffice alone for an original theory of evolution than did the study of *Drosophila* alone, and the cores for the "microplankton" study cover only a relatively short (and not necessarily typical) bit of paleontology's unique resource: the course of evolution in geological time. The cores include only a scant few millions of the more than 3 billion years of the history of life.

Another alternative hypothesis to explain the sudden appearance of taxa in the fossil record is that the new taxa evolved not merely rapidly or locally but immediately, in a single generation, by one radical leap or saltation in heredity. This hypothesis is not exactly and fully adopted—but it is to some extent promoted—by Gould's insistence that the incompleteness of the fossil record has been a millstone around the necks of paleontologists and that this can be corrected simply by taking the known fossil record at face value. But the incompleteness of the record will not go away just because some one chooses to ignore it. The fact that new kinds of fossils, new taxa at various levels, are being found practically every day shows incontrovertibly that the record was incomplete yesterday. Moreover, it is an evident fact that the record can never be really complete. That would require that fossils of all kinds of organisms be available to collectors for all geological ages in all parts of earth, which obviously is not true now and never can be. A good paleontologist will keep this in mind and will allow for it in his interpretations of the fossil record. Still, a great deal of information unavailable from any other source is obtainable from that record, as this book demonstrates within the limits of its size and scope.

These considerations lead to the related subjects of saltation in evolution and of the term and concept of macroevolution. The concept of saltation—literally, of a jump in the course of evolution—is pre-Darwinian. It was espoused anonymously in 1844 by Robert Chambers in *Vestiges of the Natural History of Creation,* which, despite the mention of "creation" in the title, was the most outspoken advocacy of evolution after Lamarck and before Darwin. That book was denounced deservedly by almost all the scientists of its time, but it so titillated the laity that it became a bestseller. Darwin believed that the saltatory appearance of organisms distinctly unlike their parents, which he called "sports," might play some part in evolution, but much less a part than natural selection. It is noteworthy that the "sports" actually known to Darwin occurred in domesticated plants and animals and not in wild populations. That is true still of the "sports" known to us. For example, the flat or pug-nosed faces of some breeds of dogs and some cattle were probably saltatory in origin, but these, too, are domesticated animals. Furthermore, that saltation did not produce a new species, and this characteristic does not appear in any wild species of the dog or cattle families (Canidae and Bovidae).

When Mendelism was rediscovered independently by three biologists around 1900, one of them, Hugo De Vries, proceeded experimentally to produce distinctly different forms of *Oenothera,* a genus of evening primroses. He interpreted these as due to genetic mutations with unusually large effects and held that these, and not Darwinian natural selection, have been the originating factors for the origin of species and higher taxa. It was subsequently established that his interpretations of the varieties in *Oenothera* were not in fact caused by Mendelian mutation. Nevertheless, through approximately the first three decades of the twentieth century, most geneticists and some naturalists supported the view that evolution has been caused for the most part by random saltations.

That situation became complicated as a distinction between "microevolution" and "macroevolution" was made. As far as I know, those terms were first published in 1929 by the Russian biologist Iurii A. Filipchenko in his book *Variation and the Methods of its Study.* He held that the evolution of Linnaean species (those recognized as species by most naturalists) is microevolution, largely explicable by Mendelian genetics, but that evolution beyond the specific level, macroevolution, "was and always will be only hypothetical, since species transformation is not one of the phenomena that can be actually observed" (English translation by Mark B. Adams from Filipchenko's Russian book on methods for the study of variation). His hypothesis was that macroevolution resulted from some unknown (and, by inference, unknowable) process within organisms themselves and quite separate from the known (or knowable) genetic factors.

In 1940, Richard Goldschmidt, an able German biologist who had early become acquainted with Russian biologists, adopted Filipchenko's terms "microevolution" and "macroevolution" and made essentially the same distinction between them. He also held that microevolution involves ordinary, Mendelizing mutations within species (Mendel's laws are the "law" of segregation, the "law" of independent combination, and the "law" of dominance), but that macroevolution requires purely hypothetical radical reorganizations of heredity that he called "organismic." This view of evolution by saltation was already anachronistic when Goldschmidt adopted it. In general, geneticists under the leadership of Dobzhansky and quite a number of others had adequately demonstrated that Devriesian saltation is not only unnecessary to explain evolution but is essentially ruled out by advances in increasingly detailed knowledge of genetics, both experimental and observational.

This very summary foray into the history of genetics has been necessary in a book about fossils because the terms "microevolution" and "macroevolution" have come back into use and have become entangled with the interpretation of the fossil record and the history of life. Genetics places some restraints on that interpretation. The further development of Mendelian genetics and increasingly plentiful and detailed biochemical studies of complex organic molecules that are ultimately determined by DNA or RNA in the genetic system have made it evident that most species (and probably all taxa of higher categories) differ by fairly complex rearrangements of multiple genes and much less often by one or a few Mendelian mutations. Thus we can agree with Goldschmidt to the extent that his macroevolution usually involves some remodeling of the genetic system. However, it is clear that a really systemic remodeling in a single step, as hypothesized by Goldschmidt, is highly improbable and must rarely, if ever, have occurred. This well-established restraint cancels the option of interpreting the frequent sudden appearance of new taxa in the known fossil record as usually due to saltation.

The universality of adaptation, a topic to which I will return in connection with adaptive radiation, clearly requires that there be some nonchance or antichance factor in evolution. That was long used (and is still used) by some pious but ill-informed dissenters as an argument against evolution. There clearly are such factors, and they explain how evolution can be directional without divine intervention. The demonstrable antichance factors are of three kinds. One is Darwin's great contribution: natural selection, now much closer to being completely understood than it could have been in Darwin's day. Another was also glimpsed by Darwin (but less clearly) and still is sometimes ignored even by well-informed evolutionists. This is that the possible directions of change for any group of organisms at any time in the history of life depend on the *previous* history of that group. Any change must occur on the basis of what evolution has already produced. A third antichance factor was clearly evident to Darwin and was discussed by him at some length, although in different terms from those now in use. This is the ecological factor. In order to survive, a species must remain adapted to the ecological situation in which it arose or must change in an adaptive way to another accessible ecological situation.

Those considerations bear on the resuscitation of the term and concept of macroevolution. In his book entitled *Macroevolution* (1979), Stanley distinguished this from microevolution mainly by saying that natural selection occurs between individuals in microevolution, whereas it occurs between already distinct species in macroevolution. He maintains that the two levels of evolution are thus "decoupled." His book includes informative insights, but on this (to him) crucial point he is, in my opinion, quite wrong. The synthetic concept of natural selection, which is not precisely that of Darwin or of some neo-Darwinians, is exactly the same within species as between them. This concept is that, if two kinds of organisms differ in some hereditary characteristics and one kind consistently produces more viable offspring than the other over a considerable sequence of generations, natural selection occurs in favor of the group more successful in reproduction. That process may act within a population *against* evolutionary change, the more modal or typical organisms being selected for and the more aberrant ones selected against. However, natural selection more obviously produces changes in a population. This may move an entire species in some evolutionary direction, or it may produce recognizably different subpopulations within the species—demes (local populations of any sort) or subspecies (taxa recognizable as such in formal classification). Precisely the same process may occur when a local population or a subspecies becomes a species, and natural selection may then ensue between separate species. The break (or the decoupling, if one chooses to use that word) is not a change in the occurrence of natural selection but comes about when, for any of many possible reasons, the interbreeding of an evolving subpopulation with the rest of a species becomes relatively insignificant or ceases altogether.

In D. J. Futuyama's generally excellent book on *Evolutionary Biology*, he defines macroevolution as "a vague term for the evolution of great phenotypic changes, usually great enough to allocate the changed lineage and its descendants to a distinct genus or higher taxon." If the term "macroevolution" should be used at all, which can certainly be questioned, it should be used in that rather vague sense. Evolution within and between species can be exemplified to some extent from the fossil record, as has been done in this chapter, but the greatest contribution of paleontology to the study of evolution is at the level of "macroevolution" in Futuyama's broad sense. This means the study in greater breadth, both in time and in space, of the tremendous complex of evolving life. It is what I have referred to in the title of a book: *The Major Features of Evolution.* Some of those will be further considered in the following chapter.

CHAPTER 7
OTHER MAJOR FEATURES OF EVOLUTION

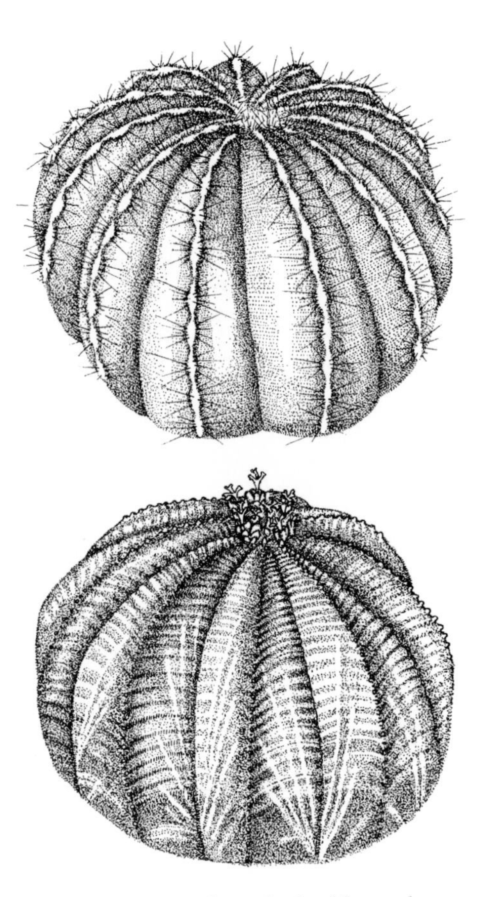

Although these plants look alike and have similar ecological adaptations, they are of very different ancestry. The upper drawing is a member of the Cactaceae or cactus family, which is native only in the Western Hemisphere. The lower drawing is one of the great numbers of Euphorbiaceae, which are native widely in both hemispheres and include such diverse plants as cassava, castor oil plants, poinsettias, spurges, and a large assortment of cactus-like plants especially in the African veld. The resemblances of the two plants shown here illustrate not only similar adaptations to similar environments but also the evolutionary principle of convergence, both involving Darwinian natural selection.

It has been suggested that there should be a theoretical independence of paleobiology and neobiology and that study of the fossil record, in itself, should produce a new evolutionary theory. This again brings in the dialectical, either–or, thesis–antithesis approach. As is recognized in dialectics, synthesis is the corrective for a misapplication of the thesis–antithesis dichotomy. Surely it is more sensible to assume that there is a relationship between the history of life, as far as it can be studied in the fossil record, and the results of that history as studied in organisms now alive. Then conclusions or even hypotheses on evolutionary theory from paleobiology and from neobiology should not be contradictory. Each approach has restraints that must be considered for consistency with the other approach. The preceding chapter closed with a constraint that neobiology places on paleobiology: It is prohibitively improbable that species or, still less probable, genera or taxa of even higher categories have usually, if ever, arisen by saltation. The famous saltationist remark that the first bird was hatched from a reptile's egg simply cannot be true.

The fossil record also puts constraints on some hypotheses that have been advanced by neobiologists. One neobiological view that meets with strong restraints from the fossil record is the so-called molecular evolutionary clock and the related theory of non-Darwinian evolution, which means, simply, evolution not involving natural selection. (That is not radically non-Darwinian and not at all anti-Darwinian, inasmuch as Darwin did not hold that all evolutionary events are guided by natural selection alone.) The basic hypothesis is that proteins, which determine so much of both form and function in all organisms, as well as the sequences of RNA (ribonucleic acid) and DNA (deoxyribonucleic acid) that determine the composition of proteins, have evolved at constant rates. Most (but not necessarily all) evolutionary changes in heredity have involved mutations in DNA, in RNA, or in both, and, by comparing the composition of proteins, DNA, or RNA in different species of organisms, it is possible to determine the minimum or the probable number of mutations necessary to have brought about the differences in their composition. If these differences arose from mutations occurring at a constant rate, they should be proportional to the geological time elapsed since the two organisms being compared had an ancestry in common.

If that hypothesis were correct, it would be possible to use such counts of mutational events as another method of determining geological ages in years. However, that would require calibrating the clock somehow, and the only evident way to do that would be to compare the number of required mutations with the geological age of a common ancestor. Early attempts to apply this method ran into trouble. For one thing, the procedure is circular: the clock is calibrated by one measure of geological time and then used as a different measure of geological time. The time used for calibration is open to considerable uncertainties: one must first estimate just when a common ancestor lived and then obtain its geological age in years by some method other than the molecular clock. Both determinations are open to definite errors. An item of chronology with special interest involves the dating of the common ancestry of the family that eventually included mankind (Hominidae) and the family to which the gorilla and chimpanzee belong (usually called Pongidae, but this name is open to question). The fossil record does not yet suffice to date this exactly by geological methods. Relatively recent discoveries tend to shift the date back by millions of years. They do show that the first applications of the hypothesis of the molecular clock to this date were almost absurdly off the mark.

The fossil record shows that the rates of morphological evolution have varied greatly both within and between lines of descent. Because morphology is largely determined by the DNA or, in some cases, the RNA in the reproductive cells, it follows that the rates of change in DNA and RNA, and therefore also the rates of change in proteins, cannot have been constant in the evolution of organisms in general. This paleontological fact thus refutes the simple, original form of the neobiological molecular-clock hypothesis. In fact, the early attempts to apply the simple hypothesis to comparisons of the compositions of one or a few proteins were questionable and did not substantiate the hypothesis.

Some biochemists do continue to support a somewhat similar hypothesis, but they do so by modifying it in at least two different ways. A. Thomas Vawter, Richard Rosenblatt, and George C. Gorman recently (1980) compared the compositions of proteins in fishes on the Atlantic and Pacific sides of the Isthmus of Panama. As was noted in Chapter 4, the rise of this isthmus separated parts of what had been a single marine biogeographic province. Thereafter, the faunas on the two sides of the isthmus barrier began to diverge. The authors of this study compared proteins in pairs of similar fishes in the Atlantic and the Pacific, and they also compared proteins of different individuals of a species from the same ocean. The assumption is that the populations paired from the two oceans descended from a single ancestral population or species before the isthmus separated them. These authors placed the date of that separation as sometime between 2 million and 5 million years ago, a considerable span of time. As would be expected, they found that the genetic differences inferred from differences in proteins between now separated pairs are almost ten times as great, on the average, as those within single populations confined to one ocean. In translating the differences between the pairs into years since the separation occurred, they obtained molecular-clock dates varying from 2 million to almost 6 million years. These differences for ten pairs give an average molecular date of 3.5 million years, which is not surprising since this figure, midway between 2 and 5, was used to calibrate the clock. The dates for individual pairs nevertheless vary greatly. The authors conclude that the molecular-clock hypothesis is not "an inviolate scientific law" but a "probabilistic statement," and they propose to avoid hostility to that hypothesis by calling this a "molecular divergence time estimator" rather than a "molecular clock."

Restoration of the skeletons of Archaeopteryx, *top, and a small coelurosaurian dinosaur. There are close resemblances between the two, although one is classified as a bird and the other as a reptile. It seems clear on this evidence that birds either arose from early dinosaurs or from somewhat earlier reptiles (thecodonts), which were the ancestors in common of birds and early bipedal saurischian (coelurosaurian) dinosaurs. R. T. Bakker, who published this figure, followed J. H. Ostrom in considering* Archaeopteryx *more dinosaurian than avian. Although the comparison clearly shows a relationship, it minimizes or omits altogether almost all the avian pieces of the mosaic. For example, the arm of* Archaeopteryx, *correctly shown as disproportionately long, had typical bird feathers, here omitted, that made it a wing and that would in this pose have impeded progress by dragging on the ground.*

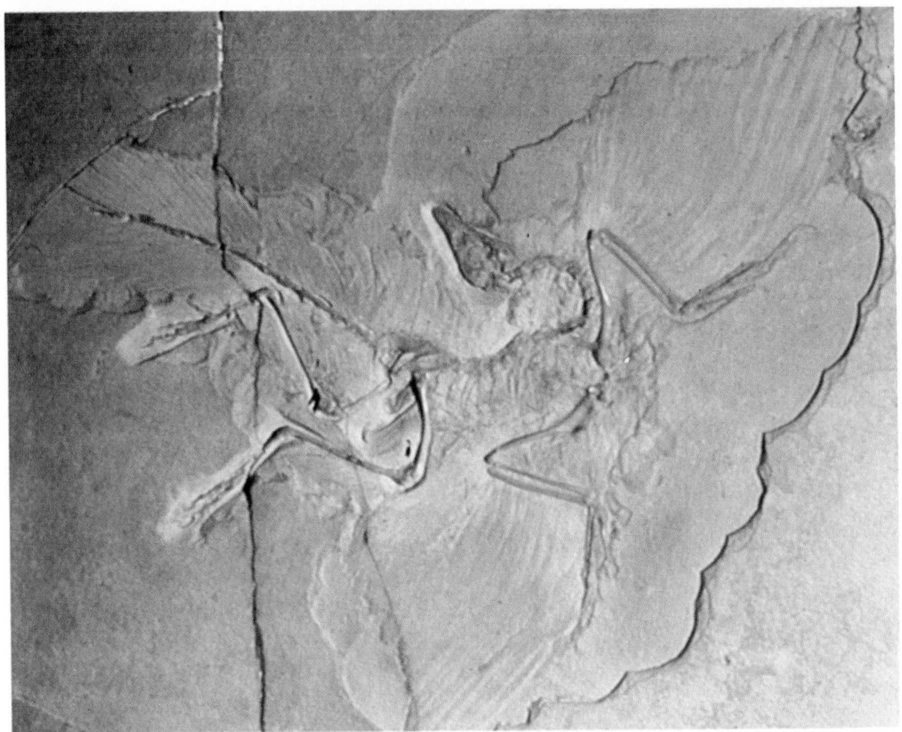

Archaeopteryx lithographica *is now generally accepted as the oldest known bird, although it is a mosaic of reptilian and avian characters, bearing witness to the derivation of one vertebrate class (Aves) from another (Reptilia). It is known from six specimens—three of them essentially complete skeletons, two of them less well preserved parts of skeletons, and one a single, completely birdlike feather. All are from a late Jurassic deposit of limestone in the vicinity of Eichstatt in Germany. This limestone is so extremely fine-grained that it has preserved imprints of even such usually perishable materials as feathers. These are clear and in place in what is generally called the Berlin specimen, here figured, and also in the equally complete London specimen. For years the Solnhofen and Eichstatt limestone was extensively quarried for use in lithography, and many extraordinary fossils were found incidental to that exploitation, which has now virtually ceased. The feathers on the wings were long and were arranged almost exactly as in most living flying birds. However, because* Archaeopteryx *did not have the bone attachments and arrangements for strong flight muscles that modern birds have, some paleontologists have questioned whether it could really fly. The consensus is that it could surely soar and could probably fly feebly.*

Another neobiological approach to this subject was summarized recently (1980) by Thomas Hughes Jukes, with numerous references to the previous literature. He points out that messenger RNA, which mediates between the DNA code and the molecular structure of proteins, contains numerous "silent substitutions"—that is, mutational changes in the DNA that do not change the protein sequences. It is therefore assumed (and does seem probable) that they are not usually, or not directly, subject to natural selection. (Hence the misleading name "non-Darwinian evolution" previously applied less clearly to selectionless evolution.) It is then postulated that such mutations would occur randomly, so that

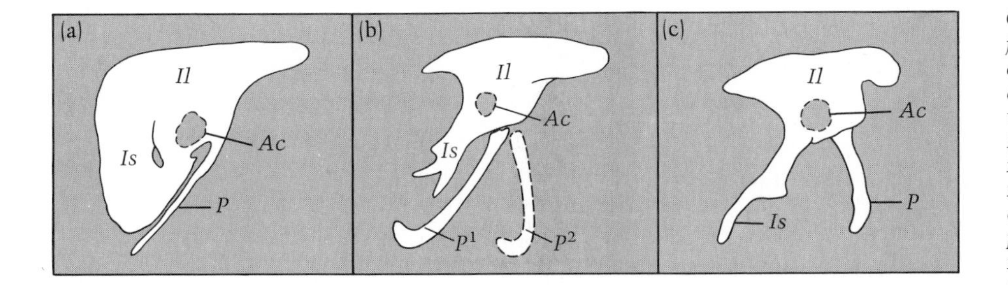

Comparison of the pelves of (a) *a modern flying bird,* (b) Archaeopteryx, *and* (c) *a coelurosaur (small, bipedal saurischian dinosaur). Ac, acetabulum (socket in which the head of the femur articulates); Il, ilium; Is, ischium; P, pubis (P^1 as seen in the Berlin* Archaeopteryx, *P^2 as Ostrom relocates it). Although there has obviously been considerable change in the pelvis from any reptilian ancestor to any modern bird, the position of the pubis in the reptile–bird mosaic is of special interest. In dinosaurs otherwise most like* Archaeopteryx, *the pubis was as shown here in* (c), *pointing widely away from the ischium. In modern birds, on the contrary, the pubis closely follows the edge of the ischium, and the two are often fused in part. Clearly in the Berlin* Archaeopteryx *and also (but less clearly) in the London specimen, the pubis has a more avian than reptilian position, as shown here in solid outline in* (b). *Enhancing resemblance to the coelurosaurs, Ostrom has suggested that the pubis somehow was shifted after death and had originally been in the position here shown in broken lines. This exemplifies the problems of interpreting an evolutionary mosaic even from superbly preserved specimens.*

their number would average out and be fairly constant over any considerable span of geological time. This seems to overlook the fact that there are mutagens in nature the presence or absence of which may influence rates of mutation, including those of "silent substitutions." It is suggested that such substitutions protect protein structure in the course of evolution because they leave the proteins more or less intact despite the frequent occurrence of mutations. Nevertheless, it is the other mutations, the nonsilent ones necessarily involved in the structures and functions of organisms, that must have provided variation on which natural selection does act. Indeed, if the "silent substitutions" do play a part in impeding changes in proteins, this might be thought of as a form of stabilizing selection and not as an absence of selection.

There can, then, be little doubt that the fossil record does put a definite restraint on any hypothesis of general (or even of average) constancy in rates of evolution through geological time.

Rates of evolution vary greatly not only within and between lineages of descent but also among the various characteristics, whether structural or functional, of any one lineage. General recognition of this fact may have been somewhat impeded by what might be called the missing-link fallacy. The so-called missing link in man's ancestry was conceived of as something in all respects simply halfway between an ancestral ape and the lord of the earth, *Homo sapiens.* But evolution does not necessarily (or even usually) proceed in that smoothly transitional way. A striking example is provided by *Archaeopteryx* from the middle Jurassic. This creature was certainly in or very near the transition between two major categories or taxa, the classes Reptilia and Aves among the vertebrates. Yet it was not in all respects intermediate between those classes. In some characteristics, such as its teeth and its (hind) legs, it was still quite like its reptilian ancestors; but in other features, such as its feathered wings and its furcula or wishbone, it was already quite like its avian descendants. In his sole excursion into paleontology, the distinguished embryologist Sir Gavin de Beer studied the British Museum specimen of *Archaeopteryx* and coined an apt expression for this sort of mingling of characteristics, some old and slow to evolve and some new and fast to evolve: mosaic evolution. This seems to have been quite a common phe-

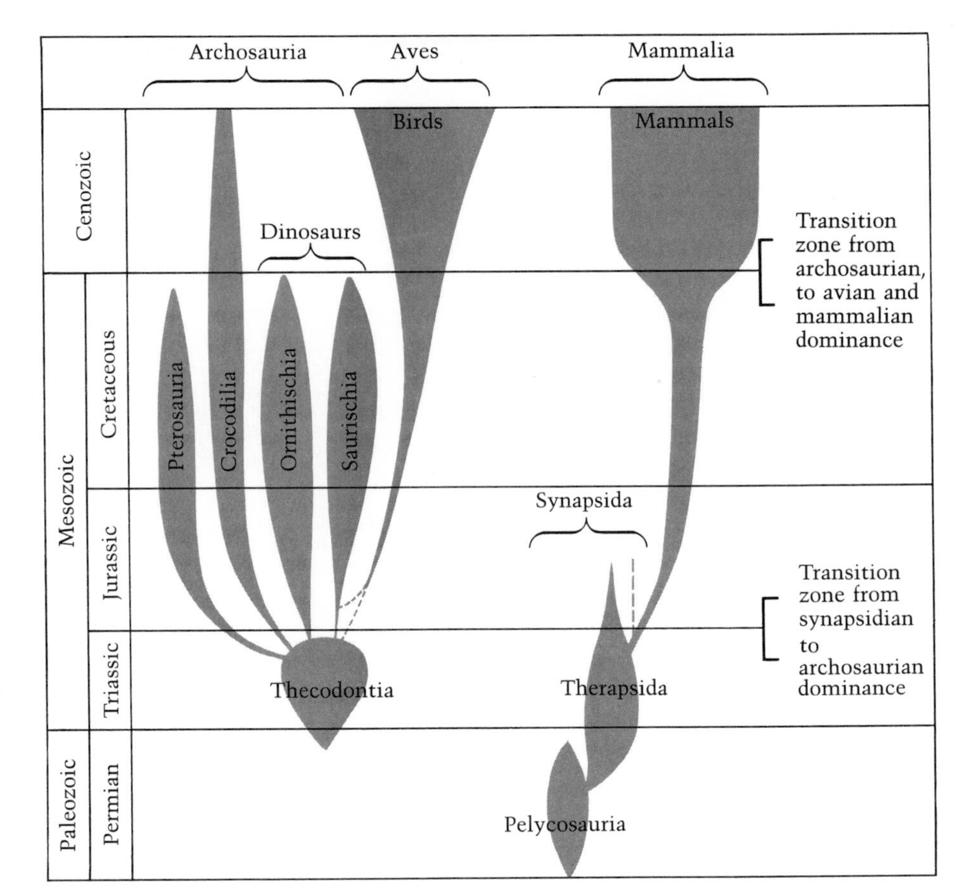

A diagram of adaptive radiations on a large scale. Among other reptiles, one group in particular—the mainly Triassic Thecodontia—gave rise to several other distinct subgroups also classified as reptiles. There are some others, but here only the four largest and most impressive are indicated: the pterosaurs, which flew with batlike wings; the crocodilians, all of which were semiaquatic and some extinct forms of which seem to have been completely aquatic; and the two orders of dinosaurs, so extremely varied in many ways, some of them wading or swimming but most of them fully terrestrial. The birds (Aves) were also derived from late thecodonts, either directly or by way of a somewhat more advanced group classified as coelurosaur dinosaurs. (The two possibilities are indicated by dotted lines.) The thecodonts and all their reptilian descendants are grouped in the subclass Archosauria of the class Reptilia. It has been suggested that the birds, as descendants of thecodonts, should also be classified as archosaurian reptiles or even as saurischian dinosaurs, but that is contrary not only to acceptable taxonomic principles but also to common sense.

The subclass Synapsida, a group of reptiles of quite different origin from the subclass Archosauria, includes two successive main groups: the Triassic pelycosaurs and their descendants, the Permian to Jurassic therapsids. Mammals originated from one (or perhaps two or three) of the lineages of therapsids. It has also been suggested that those reptiles should be classified as mammals, or that mammals should be classified as reptiles, but both alternatives are almost as silly as calling birds reptiles.

This diagram is broadly generalized and extremely simplifed. Within each of its divisions, there was a complex of lineages and taxa at lower levels of classification. Each higher taxon here shown had within it both successive and simultaneous adaptive radiations at lower taxonomic levels. The diagram also shows incidentally a sequence of relays or changeovers in the gross composition of faunas, in these examples predominantly nonaquatic vertebrate faunas.

nomenon in the evolution of major features or higher taxa in evolution. Evidence is now beginning to appear that the evolution of hominids from apish ancestry was also a mosaic—for example, humanoid bipedal locomotion evolved quickly, while the expansion of the brain still lagged behind.

The case of *Archaeopteryx* also bears on another major feature of evolution: adaptive radiation. Once an organism radically different from its own ancestors (and hence put in a different, higher category in most classifications) has evolved, it often tends to proliferate in species, genera, and families. A sort of breakthrough in morphology and function in primitive reptiles gave rise to what eventuated in the great subclass Archosauria sometime in the Permian. In the following Triassic, this group underwent an adaptive radiation by extensive proliferation of increasingly different lineages. A number of these, in turn, made breakthroughs and then gave rise to adaptive radiations somewhat more limited in scope. Notable among these was the order Crocodilia, which arose in the late Triassic and radiated markedly through the following Jurassic and Cretaceous. Another breakthrough gave rise to the flying reptiles, the order Pterosauria, probably also in the late Triassic, although this is not yet so well substantiated. In any case, the pterosaurs also proliferated in the Jurassic and Cretaceous and became extinct somewhat before the end of the latter. Two different archosaur lineages

Steneosaurus, *a member of the family Teleosauridae. The long, slender snout resembles that of the modern "needle-nosed" crocodile, the gavial, of southern Asia. Such slim snouts have developed in many unrelated groups of reptiles, as well as in some birds, that rely almost entirely on fish for food.*

gave rise to dinosaurs, the orders Saurischia and Ornithischia, which also arose in the Triassic, proliferated in the Jurassic and Cretaceous, regressed in variety and numbers in the late Cretaceous, and became totally extinct at the end of that period.

Another archosaur lineage, not precisely identified among fossils so far discovered, gave rise to *Archaeopteryx*, normally classified as the first known member of the class Aves. By the latter part of the Cretaceous, the archaic birds had undergone a marked radiation (which is not yet well known, although knowledge of it is increasing every year). Lesser radiations followed in the Cenozoic, the most extensive constituting the order Passeriformes, the so-called perching birds, which include most of the species of birds now living.

Another group of reptiles of even greater interest to us because they included our own ancestors arose in the late Carboniferous and proliferated enormously during the Permian and Triassic to form the subclass usually called Synapsida. Various of their lineages became more and more like mammals. The class Mammalia, as usually defined—including the living species of Monotremata (egg-laying mammals), Marsupialia (mostly pouched mammals), and Eutheria (all other or the placental mammals, including us)—had a single ancestry within the Reptilia, but the transition was so gradual that just where to draw the line in a classification is a matter of taste rather than of fact. As most students of this subject now draw the line, undoubted mammals classified as such (that is, in the

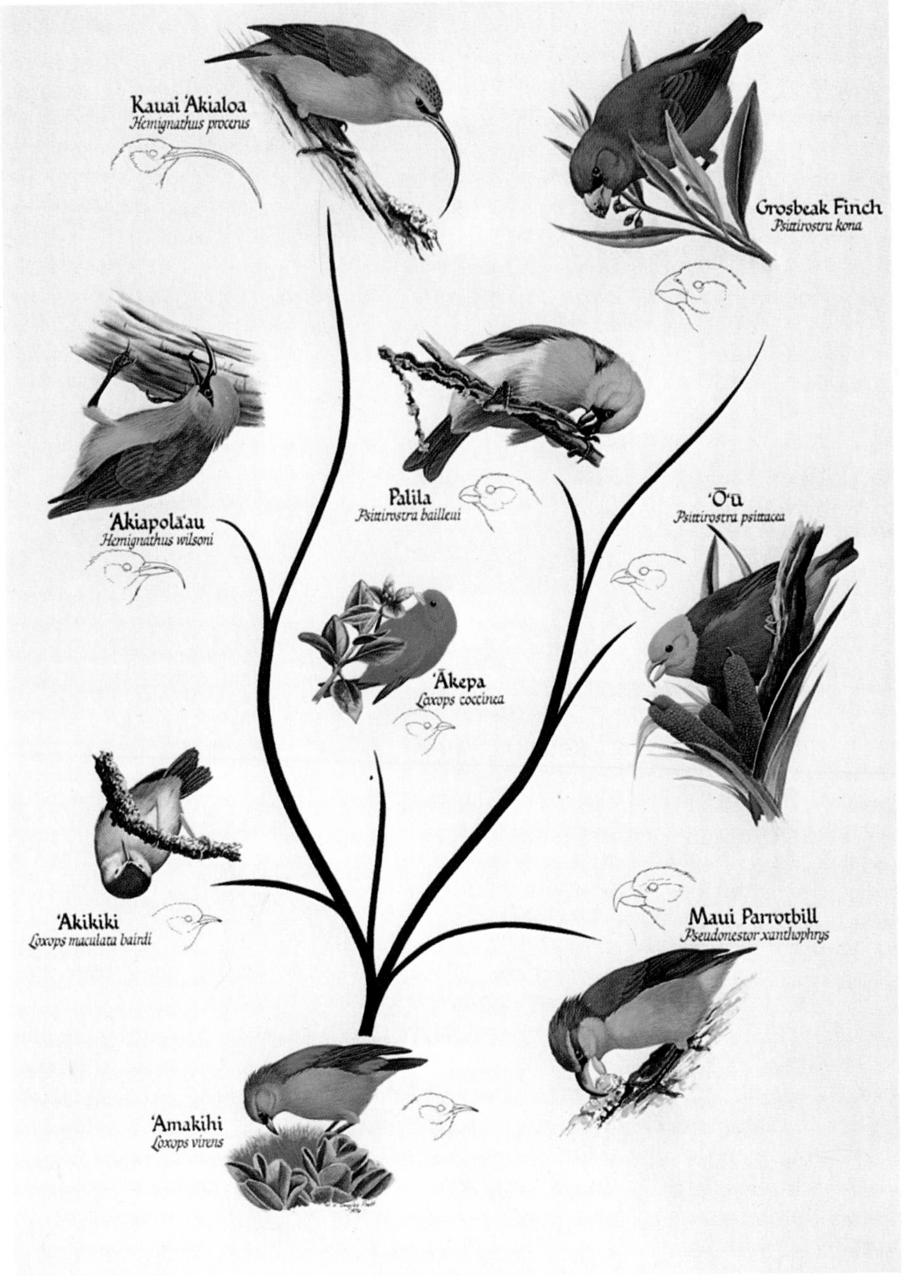

An example of adaptive radiation at the taxonomic levels of families, genera, and species. Many bird generations ago, a small landbird reached the Hawaiian Islands, which have never been connected to any continent. These were probably early North American songbirds ancestral or belonging to the family Fringillidae, which includes the finches. What ensued in the Hawaiian Islands is interestingly similar to the adaptive radiation of what are called "Darwin's finches" on the Galapagos Islands, but on a larger scale.

The descendants of the pioneers spread and eventually established isolated colonies on the larger of the numerous Hawaiian Islands. In the varied landscapes of some of the islands, local populations were further isolated or semi-isolated. Thus the descendants became so distinct as a group that they now constitute a separate family, Drepanididae, that is endemic to the Hawaiian Islands, that is, not present anywhere else. Within the family, the localization of populations and environments or ecological niches led to diversity of genera and species. The most authoritative classification now has two subfamilies, nine genera, and 22 species. Some species have become extinct since occupation of the islands by non-Polynesians, and introduction of so many birds, mammals, and plants foreign to the islands. Some now living became extinct before European discovery of the islands. As all the Hawaiian Islands are of volcanic origin and relatively late in geological time, there is little chance of finding fossils older than late Pleistocene and early Recent, and those so far found do include some of this family.

The selected genera and species shown in this figure are all contemporaneous. The lines branching out from the bottom thus do not have a dimension in time and cannot represent real lines of descent. They do indicate adaptive characteristics of different kinds and also in a general way from bottom to top the extent of adapting specialization. These nine selected species belong to four genera of formal Linnaean classification. In all but two the upper of the two names are in the Hawaiian language. In English all the birds of this family are usually called "honeycreepers." Some of them do creep on trees and eat nectar.

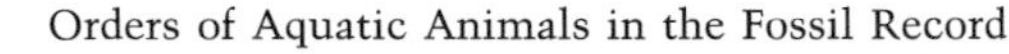

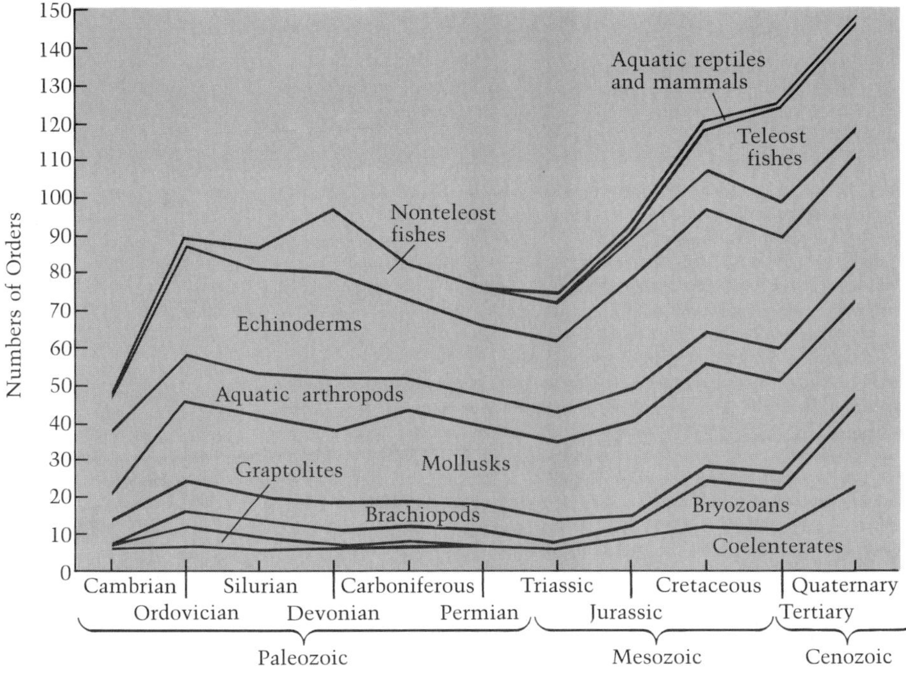

The numbers of orders of readily fossilizable ("skeletonized") aquatic animals in the known fossil record of the Phanerozoic (Cambrian to Recent). The numbers of orders are scaled on the vertical axis. The horizontal axis is not scaled in years but gives the sequence of geological periods, from Cambrian (far left) *to Quaternary (Pleistocene and Recent,* far right*).*

A marked rise in the number of known orders indicates a basic radiation at the taxonomic level of orders. The most radical radiation of all occurred between the late Precambrian (not well preserved in the fossil record and not shown here) and the Cambrian. However, there was a continuing radiation (or another basic radiation) evident here, especially among the mollusks and the echinoderms. Then, centering on the Devonian, there was a radiation of the nonteleost fishes (including the jawless "fishes," which are not fishes in the strict sense). In these broad terms, the overall makeup of marine faunas did not change radically in the later Paleozoic. From the late Mesozoic to the Recent, it did change markedly, mainly because of a tremendous radiation of the now dominant bony teleost fishes and also, to a lesser but distinct extent, the radiation of bryozoans.

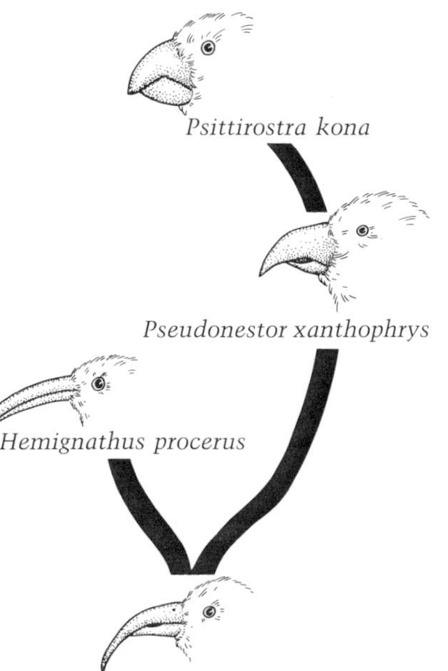

This figure shows specializations of the beaks of five of the species figured whole in the figure on the previous page. Again the connections indicated are not temporal or phyletic and only indicate the kinds and degrees of specialization. Loxops virens, *the "amakihi," has the least specialized beak in this subfamily and in that respect it may be most like the unknown North American colonists of these islands. It does eat some nectar, and hence may partly justify the name "honeycreeper," but it eats mostly insects with an occasional snack of berries. One extreme of specialization is seen in the very long, decidedly curved beak of* Hemignathus procerus, *the "akialoha." It does use the beak to get nectar from flowers, but it also snacks on insects. A different line of specialization, for short, stout beaks, is partly developed in* Pseudonestor xanthophrys *(Hawaiian name, if any, unknown) which lives almost entirely on insects obtained by tearing logs and branches with its beak.* Psittirostra kona, *one of the two birds called "palila" in Hawaiian, is champion of the strong-beak trend but it is more likely to use that beak to crack nuts, not so much for the nutmeats as for the maggots that infest them.*

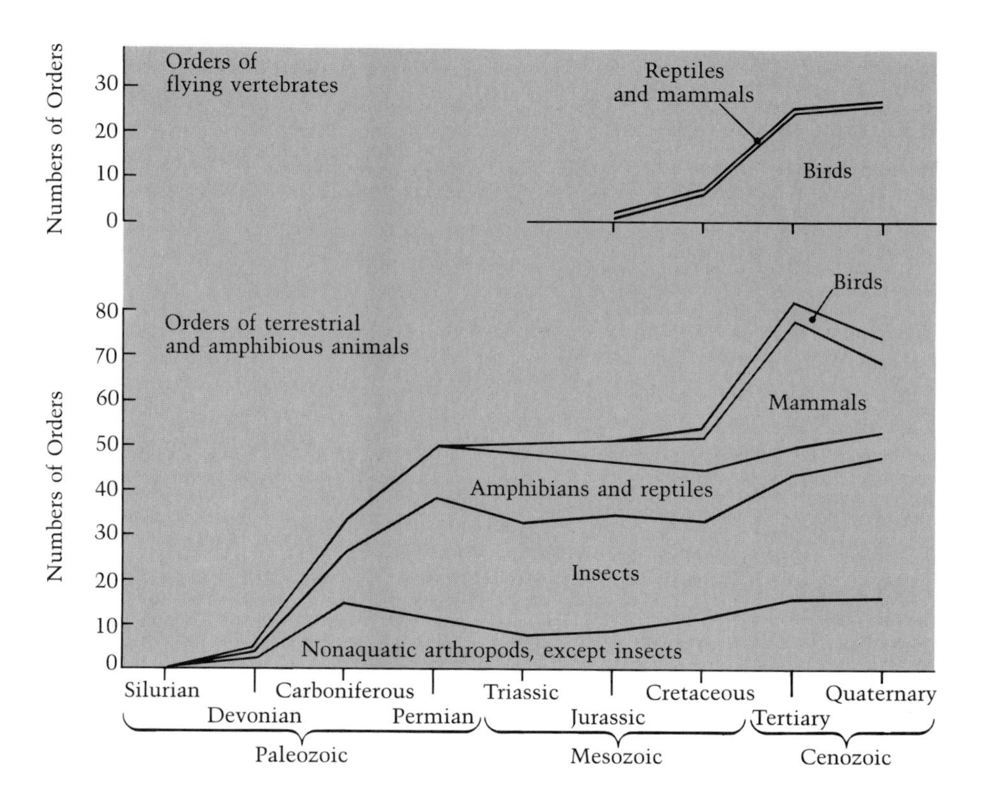

The numbers of orders of readily fossilizable ("skeletonized") terrestrial and amphibious animals (bottom) *and flying vertebrates* (top) *in the known fossil record. The scaling and arrangement are as in the preceding figure.*

The spread of life to land and into the air represents adaptive radiation on a tremendous scale, and there were many simultaneous and successive radiations within each of the orders. It is clear that the emergence of animals from the seas, and in large part also from fresh waters, did not get well under way until some time in the Silurian but that the really basic adaptive radiation associated with the emergence was very extensive in the later Paleozoic. For insects and for amphibians and reptiles among the vertebrates, it had already reached its height by the end of the Paleozoic. Insects are now the most abundant and most varied of all animals. The record is extensive and indicative, but it is difficult to interpret in some respects because there is no adequate recent compilation of it. (As I write this, the volume of the Treatise on Invertebrate Paleontology *on insects has not yet been published.) However, it appears that the dominance of insects, both in numbers and in basic (ordinal) diversity, was about as strong in the Permian as it is now. Some of the orders known from the Paleozoic—at least eight and probably more—became extinct well before the Recent, but most of them are still extant. There are five Recent orders without known fossils. For quite a few of the other Recent orders, the fossil record is confined to inclusions in Cenozoic amber, but these orders probably existed considerably earlier than the time in which the scattered and local deposits of amber were formed. Insects have certainly proliferated enormously in families, genera, and species throughout their history, but apparently much less so at the ordinal level since the Paleozoic.*

There was also a late Paleozoic radiation among amphibians, but, as already mentioned, there was an almost complete turnover or relay during the Triassic. Reptiles had their most basic radiation in the Permian and early Mesozoic, but most of the later Mesozoic groups evolved less radically, and many became extinct toward (or at) the end of the Cretaceous. That may be seen in the relatively moderate decline in orders of reptiles between the Cretaceous and the Tertiary. The striking radiation of mammals occurred in the early Cenozoic, and their ordinal diversity later declined radically.

Among flying vertebrates, the birds obviously dominate now. Their basic radiation reached a climax around the middle of the Tertiary, and the number of orders has been fairly stable since then.

When considered at the ordinal level and placed in a diagram like this one, the record of flying reptiles and mammals is misleading in some respects. For one thing, these may appear to be replacing groups, because no flying reptiles (pterosaurs) are known after the late Cretaceous and no flying mammals (bats) are known before the early Eocene, millions of years later. Their ranges may have overlapped somewhat, but it is not likely that they lived in the same or closely similar ecologies or that they competed. Another point is that, although each group comprises animals that are classified in a single order, their adaptive variety and importance in their biotas were much greater than is suggested by a graph based on orders only. The order Pterosauria has two suborders and at least seven families (all of them extinct), while the order Chiroptera, also with two suborders, is generally divided into nineteen families, of which only three are extinct.

class Mammalia) appear in the known record in the latest Triassic. It is not clear, or again is only a matter of taste, whether the arbitrary line was crossed by one, two, or three then separate lineages. These underwent what now looks like a moderate radiation in the Jurassic. However, that radiation may have been more radical than is yet known. The Jurassic mammals from North America and Europe are from a limited number of ecological situations, and extremely few Jurassic mammals have yet been found in either Africa or Asia. None have so far been found in Australia or South America, where nevertheless they must have existed.

The most extensive radiation within the class Mammalia was among the placental mammals (Eutheria). It began in a moderate way toward the very end of the Cretaceous period and rapidly, almost explosively, increased in the Paleocene epoch, which therefore ushered in what is popularly known as the Age of Mammals. The extent of this radiation was evidently increased by the spread of taxa of mammals, from species up to orders, in all directions among what are now the continents of North America, Europe, and Asia. There was an approximately simultaneous radiation of mammals in South America separate from that on the other land areas.

It is tempting to consider that the decline of the dinosaurs in the late Cretaceous, and their final extinction just at the end of that period, left vacant ecological niches into which the mammals radiated. Paleontologists have sometimes fallen for that temptation, but that hypothesis is not likely to be correct. Late Cretaceous and Paleocene mammals are, for the most part, smaller than even the relatively few smallest of Cretaceous dinosaurs, and all of them are structurally so different that they must also have been functionally different. Among the smaller Cretaceous and Paleocene mammals, some were probably arboreal and many were browsers, especially the Paleocene hoofed mammals that were not arboreal—some of them as large as (but not related to) relatively small modern browsing cows or many browsing antelopes. This suggests some relationship with a spread of forests and shrubby veldts. There was indeed some change in floras between the late Cretaceous and the Paleocene, but the basic radiation of flowering trees and shrubs had occurred long before that, not far from the Jurassic–Cretaceous turnover. The radical changes in faunas in the Mesozoic–Cenozoic turnover do seem to demand correlation with some worldwide ecological change, but more definite designation of its nature is one of the problems on which paleontologists must still work.

One of the adaptive radiations of mammals at lower taxonomic levels may here be addressed as particularly interesting and as controversial in its interpretation. Field mice of the family Cricetidae (distinct from the house mouse and rat family Muridae) are extremely abundant and varied in South America. Osvaldo Reig, an able student of fossil and recent South American mammals, says that living South American Cricetidae include 46 genera with 225 species. Those counts vary with personal opinions, and some other authorities consider Reig's figures inflated; but there is no doubt that these mice underwent a radical adapt-

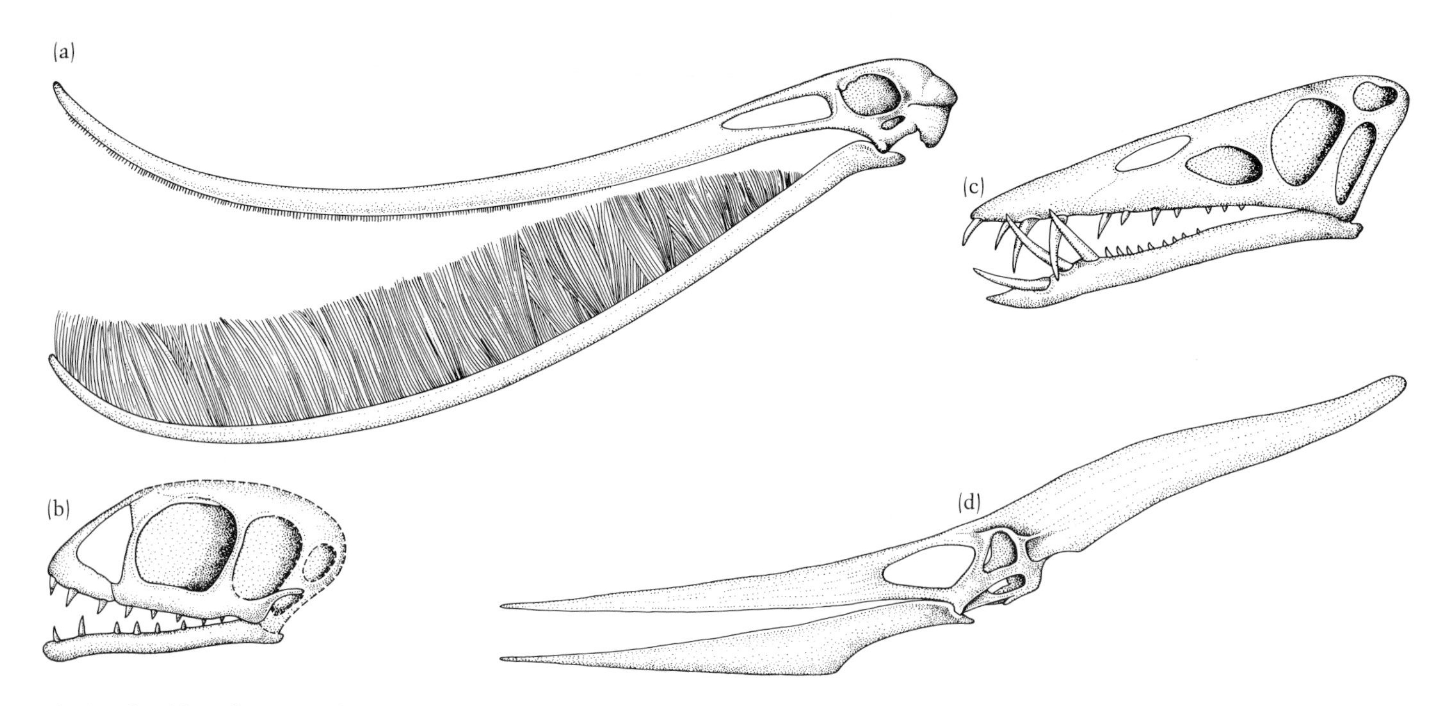

The heads of four flying reptiles (pterosaurs) illustrate the remarkably different forms that adaptive radiation may take within a single group, in this case an order of reptiles. Pteradaustro (a) *from the Jurassic of Argentina has greatly elongated and upcurved upper and lower jaws, the upper jaw toothless and the lower jaw with an enormous number of long, thin, almost hairlike teeth. These can only have served as a filter in which food, in the form of minute organisms, was caught. Filter feeding evolved in many animals, from small aquatic invertebrates to the enormous baleen whales, but* Pteradaustro *and one other pterosaur had what are so far the only known filters composed of true teeth. These may have served to capture insects as the pterosaurs flew through the air or small aquatic organisms skimmed from sea water, just as the baleen whales engulf and filter the tiny crustacean euphausiids.* Anurognathus (b) *from the late Jurassic of Europe is one of the smallest pterosaurs and has an unusually short face. Its jaws, upper and lower, have a few, well-separated, peglike teeth. Its food is uncertain, but it may have consisted of insects such as flying beetles, which were already abundant in the late Jurassic.* Dorygnathus (c), *one of the earliest pterosaurs, is from the early Jurassic of Europe. It has a long face, as do most pterosaurs, and a moderate quantity of upper and lower teeth, the most anterior of which are long, pointed, and well suited for seizing. There is evidence that the diet of the members of this genus consisted largely of fish. Another direction in this radiation is represented by* Pteranodon (d), *a large pterosaur with long and completely toothless jaws. It is a fairly common fossil in the late Cretaceous marine chalk beds of Kansas, and these animals must have died, or their sometimes intact remains must have drifted, many miles out to sea. They most certainly ate fish, for fish bones have been found within their skeletons, and it is probable that they sailed just above the water utilizing their long jaws to scoop up fish. Among their peculiar characteristics is a long, thin crest or vane on the back of the skull. Yet this is absent in some of their close relatives and sometimes perhaps even in the same genus or species. The crest must have had some aerodynamic effect, but its adaptive nature (if any) has been much debated.*

ive radiation in South America within a single family. The oldest known fossils of this family in South America are from the Monte Hermoso Formation in Argentina, which has been radiometrically dated as having been laid down in the middle Pliocene, about 3.5 million years before the present. Cricetids resembling the South American ones are known in North America from a much earlier date (radiometrically dated at 6.7 million years before the present). The ancestry of the South American cricetids is at least that old, and it may have originated earlier than 7 million years before the present. Reig, however, insists that 3.5 million years—or even 7 million years—is much too short a time for the origin of so many genera and species of South American cricetids. He concludes that their ancestors must have reached South America by island hopping or waif dispersal in the Miocene, perhaps the early Miocene, which would have given them time on the order of 20 million years or more to diversify in South America.

Reig noted that the cricetid teeth from the Monte Hermoso Formation are rather specialized, having high crowns and complex ridge patterns like those that occur in living pastoral (grass-eating) species. It was suggested that the long time between the hypothetical reaching of the northern extremity of South America and the appearance of these fossils in southern Buenos Aires Province was due to the long distance and slow geographic spread of the animals. Nevertheless, it borders on the incredible that these active, fast-breeding, and prolific animals would have taken at least 15 million years to spread some 5600 kilometers. That depends upon a rate of expansion of less than 4 meters per year. Bryan Patterson and Rosendo Pascual, both able students of fossil and recent rodents in South America, suggested that the basic radiation of the now South American cricetids had already occurred in Central America (tropical North America) and that, before they entered South America, they had already produced species as advanced as those found at Monte Hermoso. That is a surmise because no Miocene or Pliocene rodents have yet been discovered in Central America, although they were surely there. More recently (in 1979), Larry G. Marshall has proposed the hypothesis that cricetids island hopped to South America about 6 million years ago and then took about 2.5 million years to get to Argentina, having undergone an adaptive radiation while on the way. That does imply an unusually rapid multiplication of species once the cricetids were in South America, but not an impossible one. The fact that Miocene mammalian faunas are fairly well known both in Argentina and in Colombia and that no cricetids have been found in them gives this negative evidence some force. Following Marshall, it is reasonable to suggest that, as the evidence now stands, it does seem to exemplify especially rapid adaptive radiation at the specific and generic levels. It is relevant that, when the cricetids did reach South America, at least 3.5 million years ago and perhaps 6 million years or more, there were already great numbers of other rodents in South America, results of another adaptive radiation in the late Eocene and early Oligocene. These previous rodent inhabitants did not include any that were clearly similar to the cricetids in ecology and adaptation, so that when the cricetids arrived there were many empty ecological niches available to them.

The examples of faunal relays in ammonites and in corals, previously discussed from other points of view, can also be considered as involving adaptive radiation. Each time these groups of marine invertebrates were reduced by massive extinction, they were relayed by geologically rapid radiation from surviving relatives. Although the relaying groups were ecologically similar to the groups that became extinct, this was not simply a one-to-one replacement or reoccupation of precisely the same niches. Especially among the ammonites, some of those that evolved in later adaptive radiations were strikingly unlike the earlier forms in gross morphology.

(a)

(b)

(a) *During the Cretaceous, ammonites developed great diversity, and some, such as the* Ancyloceras gigas *shown here, developed loose spirals.* (b) *Two examples of the late Cretaceous ammonoid* Cirroceras nebraskense *found in marine shale in South Dakota. This is another example of the queerly distorted shells that evolved at times from the more usual, simply spiral form. Such unusual forms became more common toward the end of ammonoid history.*

"Adaptive radiation" has become a time-honored term for such episodes as have been exemplified here, but several objections to it have been made. Although I think these have little force, some attention should be given to them at this point.

Thomas Schopf, Stephen Jay Gould, Daniel Simberloff, and David Raup ran computer programs to determine whether patterns of taxonomic diversity through geological time, as observed in the fossil record, could be generated at random. Two complex computer runs produced patterns for 22 different clades (multiple lineages arising from one ancestral taxon). They found close resemblances of these with some taxonomic fossil records through geological time and concluded that these demonstrated randomness in the fossil record, including some patterns (with early diversity) of the sort that are usually called adaptive radiations. This conclusion has been controverted by several equally adept paleontologists and is not generally accepted. A strong objection is that the computer runs were not really random. They were set so that they involved more rapid origination of taxa at the beginning; thus, they were not random but had adaptive radiation built into the program (the authors of the concept of randomness so stated). Another objection is that the clades generated by their computer differ so much among themselves that it is not remarkable (and is not a proof of randomness) that some of them do resemble real-world sequences. If enough truly random sequences could be generated, they would doubtless include single clade patterns matching all those in the fossil record, but this is similar to the well-known remark that, if enough monkeys pounded enough typewriters at random for enough time, one of them would eventually rewrite all the works of Shakespeare. The original authors did note that their "random" program did not generate mass extinctions. The case for random evolution is not impressive.

Another objection sometimes made to the term "adaptive radiation" is that it confounds hypothesis with observed facts. The "radiation," a divergence among descendants from a common ancestry, is observed in the fossil record as morphological differences increasing in time among related taxa. That these differences are also "adaptive" is a hypothesis, or at least a theory, that is not directly observed. But hardly any student of evolution from Darwin onward has ever hypothesized or theorized that every detail of difference among related taxa is, *ipso facto,* adaptive. The consensus on this point is that the ensemble of such differences, the total divergence in morphology, is generally (or, at the strongest, always) adaptive. That the term and concept of "adaptive radiation" combine observation and interpretation is not contradictory.

That leads into another point. In their proposal of punctuated equilibrium, which was discussed in Chapter 6, Eldredge and Gould held that the theory it was intended to displace, essentially what is here called the "synthetic theory" (although they confounded it with "phyletic gradualism"), held as a tenet that all the separable characters of organisms, recent or fossil, were developed by natural selection. That would require that every observed feature of all organisms be adaptive—that is, be necessary (or at least useful) in the way of life of each group of organisms. That all organisms are in fact adapted to live where and how they do in fact live is obvious, even on the most casual observation. Criticizing the synthetic theory for maintaining that nothing in the structure and function of organisms has evolved unless it is adaptive is another phase of Eldredge and Gould's attack on a straw man.

It is clear that some such differences are nonadaptive if they are considered in isolation from the total of structure and function. An example particularly familiar to me is a comparison of the evolution of certain South American ungulates, now extinct, with the evolution of horses. In both certain notoungulates in South America and horses in North America, the premolars and molars became high-crowned, were coated with cementum, and evolved complex patterns of enamel ridges. In both cases, all those are plainly adaptations to grazing on coarse vegetation, such as siliceous grasses, and they almost surely arose by natural selection. The enamel ridges serve exactly the same use in the two groups. Nevertheless, the actual patterns of those ridges are quite different in the two groups. This difference cannot be considered adaptive and did not in itself arise by natural selection. Yet, its development was not random. It has already been noted here that, in addition to natural selection, there are other nonrandom factors in evolu-

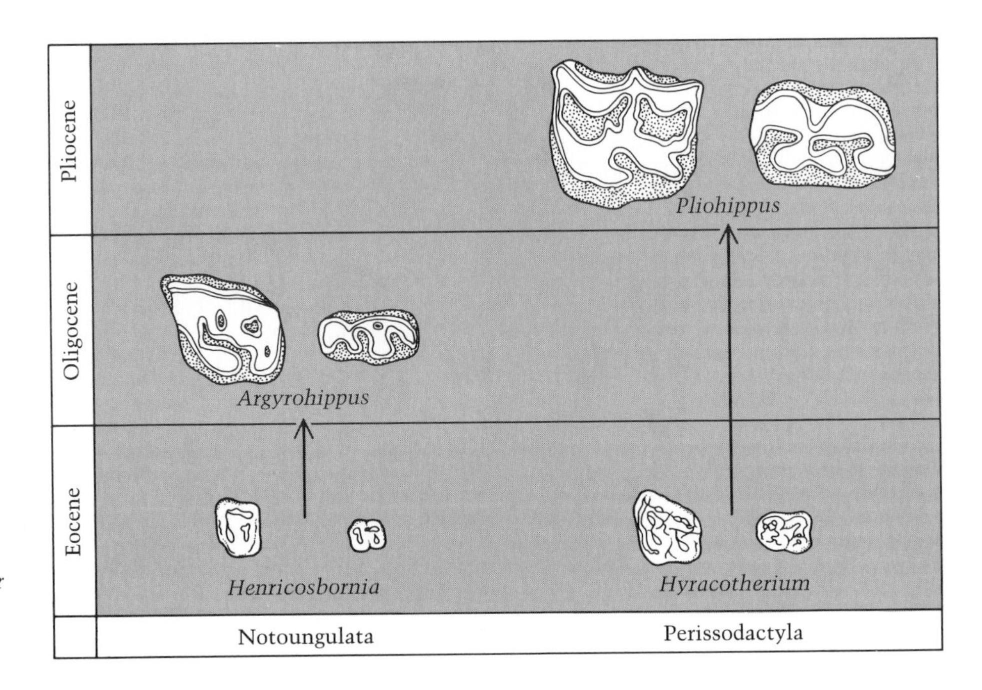

The evolution of functionally equivalent aspects of morphology may be quite different in ungulates evolving in isolation from each other. These notoungulates evolved in South America independent of the perissodactyls of North America, Europe, Asia, and Africa. Ancestral notoungulates had low-crowned molars with characteristic, simple ridges and cusps and no cementum. In subsequent adaptive radiation, some of them, including Argyrohippus, *evolved very high crowns with more extensive and somewhat complex enamel ridges (*double lines*), which, during wear, surrounded the exposed dentine (*white*) and were in turn surrounded by heavy cementum (*stippled*). In North America, the ancestral horse eohippus (*Hyracotherium*) had molars that had ridge and cusp patterns different from those of early notoungulates but that were similar in other respects. Its descendant* Pliohippus *(rather similar to the living* Equus*) had high-crowned molars with enamel grinding ridges and heavy cementum, as in* Argyrohippus, *but with markedly different enamel patterns. It is interesting that essentially similar adaptive functional arrangements evolved at different rates and times on the two continents. In the drawings, left upper molars are to the left in each case and the corresponding right lower molars are shown to the right.*

tion. One of these is the effect of prior history in the ancestry of different groups of organisms. It is this that caused the difference in the final enamel pattern in notoungulates and horses. The original basis of that difference was probably different mutations in the earliest members of the two groups. Those mutations may well have been random in one sense of that word and perhaps nonadaptive when they first occurred. However, they cannot have been truly antiadaptive, for in nature organisms with definitely antiadaptive characters are weeded out. That is another aspect of natural selection.

Thus one can be reasonably sure that a character well established in a population, whether fossil or recent, is not antiadaptive, but one cannot prove a negative. It is rarely possible to be sure that some characteristic is not merely nonadaptive, unlikely to be selected either for or against, or is not linked genetically with a balanced adaptive characteristic. The existence of balanced polymorphism and balanced selection is well established in some recent populations. In such cases, of which human sickle-cell anemia is one of the best known, a characteristic by itself may be antiadaptive, but its genetic balance with another character may be positively adaptive. In sickle-cell anemia, the balancing genes in the same individual are for normal blood, and the combination with the sickle-cell gene gives some immunity from malaria. Thus, in malarial regions, the continued presence of the sickle-cell gene is positively adaptive and has been selected for.

Such phenomena pose problems for paleontologists. When fossil populations have some characteristic that is not paralleled in living organisms and hence not available for experimentation or physiological study, it is often puzzling to explain what function, if any, they served when the fossil organisms were alive. A good example is provided by the crests of hadrosaurian dinosaurs discussed in Chapter 2. Structures as peculiar as these give ample scope for exercise of the imagination and conjecture by paleontologists. They also unavoidably give rise to a number of controversial and contradictory hypotheses.

Distinct but related groups of organisms may diverge, run parallel, or converge in the course of their evolution. All of these evolutionary patterns involve two or more separate lineages or clades and therefore must have a basis in splitting or cladistic speciation. As mentioned before, the crucial episode of speciation in this sense is the reduction and eventual cessation of interbreeding between parts of one ancestral population. There has been much discussion among geneticists, systematists, and naturalists as to whether this usually (or perhaps always) occurs between populations or subpopulations that are geographically separate, "allopatric" in technical terminology (from the Greek *allos*, "other," and *patrís*, "fatherland"). The alternative or antithesis usually specified is "sympatric" (from the Greek *syn*, "together," which becomes *sym-* before the labial *p*). This has become another unacceptable dialectical proposition. It now appears that splitting speciation may be allopatric, or sympatric, or not clearly either one. One of the other alternatives is now called "parapatric speciation" (from the Greek *para*, "beside" or "near")—that is, with the nascent species in geographic contact but not overlapping. Parapatric speciation may thus occur in what were originally marginal subpopulations or, in classification, subspecies of a more widely distributed parent species. Sympatric speciation may occur, despite more or less extensive overlap, through ecological or behavioral divergence of individuals within what had been a single population.

The consensus now is that allopatric, parapatric, and sympatric speciation have all occurred, each in various detailed ways, but that speciation has usually involved geographic factors, which is true of both allopatry and parapatry. This consensus is especially important for paleontology because it explains much of the incompleteness of the fossil record. As has been shown, the fossil record includes examples of speciation, but it is far less complete at this taxonomic level than it is for the more distinctly major features. Thus, paleontological studies of the principles of evolution are usually more fruitfully pursued at higher taxonomic levels, from genera to classes or even to phyla.

The speciation break in allopatry involves some sort of segmentation of an originally more unified population. This may occur (and, in some instances, quite clearly has occurred) simply by the extinction of a segment between geographic subpopulations that were earlier parts of a single extensive population. In other cases, the motility of the crust of the earth has been involved. This is clear in the previous example of the strictly marine vertebrates and invertebrates on the Atlantic and Pacific sides of the Isthmus of Panama, which rose in the Pliocene and formed an impassable barrier. Continental drift has also played a part by interposing a marine barrier between formerly adjacent lands.

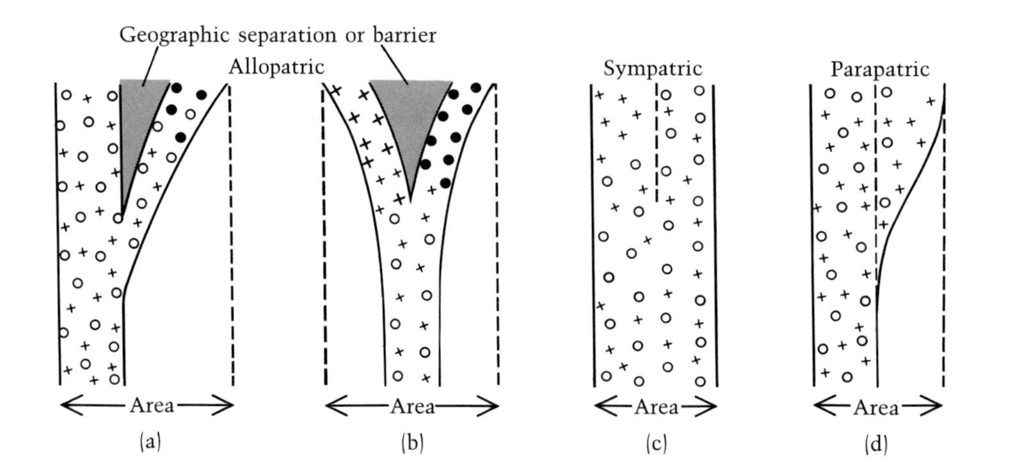

Spatial or distributional elements in speciation: In all four diagrams, time is indicated on the vertical axis, running from older, below, to younger, above. Space is shown on the horizontal axis, which indicates only whether the area in question is continuous or discontinuous. Neither time nor area is scaled. The use of circles and crosses is symbolic of variation in a population: the actual number of characteristics would, of course, be much greater than those indicated here. Darkening of the circles and crosses symbolizes evolutionary change in the variant characteristics of the species involved. (a) *Allopatric branching, in which the ancestral population remains essentially in stasis but a geographically separating branch becomes progressively more distinct from that ancestry.* (b) *Allopatric bifurcation, in which both of the geographically separate branches evolve characteristics distinct from their common ancestry.* (c) *Sympatric speciation, in which differential inheritance tends to sort out ancestral variation and to produce two distinct stocks (demes or local populations) within the same general area; such groups become distinct species when they cease to interbreed, and they eventually also tend to evolve new and different characteristics.* (d) *Parapatric speciation, which differs from sympatric speciation primarily in that the differentiating group, here more obviously a geographically definable deme, is marginal to the main body of the ancestral species. Here, too, interbreeding may cease and the differentiating formerly marginal group may also become geographically isolated.*

These microevolutionary events at or below the species level are of primary interest to geneticists and systematists dealing with living populations. Consideration of them is interesting also to paleontologists for several reasons, some negative and some positive. One is that, when related species reach clear distinction in different areas, as in (a) *and* (b) *and to a lesser extent in* (c), *it is rarely possible to follow their exact courses in geological time. That is because fossil-bearing strata of a precise age rarely are available over as large an area or for as long a time as speciation typically involves. That is a major element in the incompleteness of the fossil record. Another point is that, in a fossil sample of a population undergoing sympatric or parapatric speciation, it will usually be difficult and often impossible to determine objectively that speciation was in fact under way. A third (and, for paleontology, the most important) point is that any supraspecific group (a genus, a family, an order, and so on) for which the fossil record does often contain abundant and precise data almost certainly originated by simple speciation followed by long and frequent similar further speciational events. Thus the interpretation of the data that paleontologists have and the inferences about principles of evolution to be drawn from them should have a firm background in an understanding of speciation. Another point of special interest for paleontology is that species evolving sympatrically, or becoming sympatric after allopatric or parapatric evolution, generally are (or become) quite distinct without complete ecological duplication. Thus, if closely related fossils (such as those of organisms of the same genus) of the same age are found in the same local fauna, it is a reasonable assumption that they represent a single species unless two or more parts of the sample have definitely determinable distinctions not present in the other or others. This principle, called by the Argentinian paleontologist Angel Cabrera "the law of ecological incompatibility," has been repeatedly "discovered" and often applied by paleontologists and neozoologists alike.*

One of the clearest and most interesting cases involving continental drift is provided by the long-studied exemplars of evolution in action: the horse family and its relatives. In the early Eocene, what are now North America and Europe were essentially regions of a single continent. Little eohippus *(Hyracotherium)* then lived not only in North America but also in what is now western Europe, including especially Great Britain, where a specimen of this ancestral genus was first found. Specimens from the western United States and from England are so much alike that it is questionable whether they should be considered different species. (For a diagram of this in a different context, see figure on page 119.) At a time near what is usually considered the boundary between early and middle Eocene, the two regions broke apart and began drifting away from each other, with the North Atlantic and its marine extensions opening and forming a barrier between them. In North America, the horse family in the strict sense (Equidae) went on its complex evolutionary way, eventually becoming restricted by extinctions to a single living genus, *Equus,* with several living Old World species derived from immigrants there from North America via the land bridge that arose from time to time in the region now occupied by the Bering Sea. After the early Eocene in Europe, too, little eohippus had a somewhat complex mesh of descendants, going their own way in what had become nearly complete isolation. These included several distinct European genera in the later Eocene, such as *Pachynolophus* and *Lophiotherium,* and also probably the members of the short-lived Old World family Palaeotheriidae, which became extinct in the Oligocene.

Parenthetically, I should add that *Pachynolophus* and *Lophiotherium* are sometimes placed in the Equidae and sometimes in the Palaeotheriidae. The derivation of the latter family as a whole from *Hyracotherium* is not completely clear. The name *Hyracotherium* means "hyraxlike (or conylike) mammal," which was a blunder on the part of Richard Owen, who named it in 1840. *Pachynolophus* means "thick-crested" and *Lophiotherium* means "mammal with little crests," both names referring to the crested molars. *Palaeotherium,* the type of the family, was named by the great French paleontologist Cuvier in 1804 and means simply "ancient mammal." At that date, it was indeed among the most ancient mammals known, although now some that are more than three times as old have been discovered. The first known palaeotheres were found in the gypsum beds that form the Butte de Montmartre in Paris.

The acme of divergence is seen in adaptive radiation, examples of which have previously been discussed. Apart from such more or less episodic events, one has only to consider what may be seen in any landscape, and perhaps especially in an African veldt, to get some idea of the extremes of diversity among organisms. The number of species now living is so great that they have never been counted, only estimated at numbers into the millions. All these have arisen in the course of somewhat more than 3 billion years by divergence from what must have been at first a single group of the most primitive ancestors. Anyone who can consider this without a sense of awe must be lacking in imagination and insight. There will be more on that point in the next chapter.

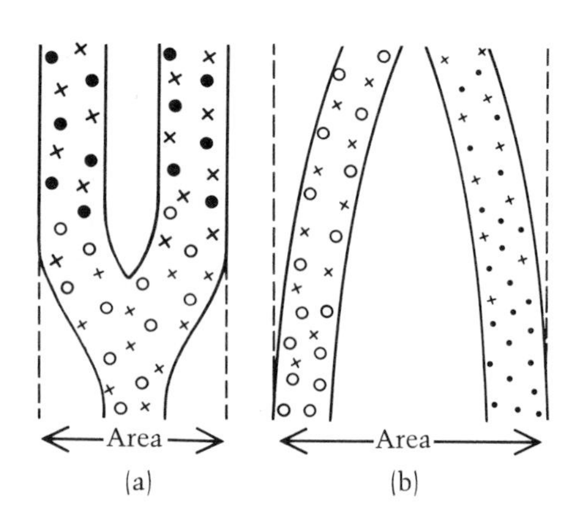

Parallelism and convergence: The axes (not to scale) are as in the preceeding figure and the simple symbolism of variation in characteristics and their evolutionary changes are also as in that figure. (a) *Parallelism following bifurcation and subsequent isolation of two taxa. They have the same ancestry and hence start evolving on their separate ways with much the same genetic, structural, and behavioral characteristics. As they become more specialized or evolve different ecological adaptations, if those adaptations are similar in both, their genetic and structural characteristics, although changing, tend to remain much the same in both descendant lines. These parallel changes are here simplistically symbolized by similar changes in the darkening of the ancestral circles and crosses.* (b) *Convergence of two lineages of different ancestry. The ancestry difference is here symbolized by the circles in the lower (older) part of the lineage to the left and the dots in that to the right. If the two lineages evolve in such a way as to adopt similar new behavioral and ecological adaptations, here symbolized by crosses appearing and increasing in both lineages, they resemble each other more and more. They will then usually (although not invariably and not in all ways) also become structurally and functionally more and more similar. There are no clear cases in the fossil record supporting the possibility that the increase in resemblance results in identity of organisms of different ancestry, and that probably has never occurred in the history of life. There are, however, numerous cases in which the convergent characters here symbolized by crosses can be taken to be ancestral characters in common. Then it may be inferred that two groups or taxa being compared are much more nearly related—that is, had a much more recent common ancestry—than was actually the case. The figure on page 192 illustrates such an error. Ameghino assumed the convergent characters of* Argyrohippus *and* Pliohippus *to have been derived from the same ancestry, although it is now clear that they evolved completely independently in the two lineages. (The error is immortalized in the name* Argyrohippus, *derived from Greek words for "silver"—referring to Plata, "silver" in Spanish as symbolic of Argentina—and for "horse".) Increased knowledge of the fossil record and of the problem of convergence has greatly lessened the errors caused by convergent evolution, but there is no doubt that some still persist. In fact, there are some systems of classification that almost inevitably fail to take sufficient account of convergence.*

It must be added that parallelism and convergence, which appear so distinct in this simple diagram, are the extremes of a continuum; along with many clear-cut instances, there are others that involve both and are correspondingly difficult to place in phylogenies or classifications. These matters are further discussed in the text.

In a broad sense, all organisms can be said to be mosaics, with some characteristics so ancient in origin that they have changed little and some so recent, geologically speaking, that they have changed more than a little. It rarely occurs to most of us that we share ancestral characters with such different organisms as, for example, a flowering shrub. We do at the biochemical level, although not at the anatomical level. All organisms have some conservative ancestral characters and some derived characters more special to each kind of organism. (In a jargon that I consider unnecessary and obfuscating but that is becoming too widely used to ignore entirely, the conservative characteristics are called "plesiomorphous" and the derived characteristics are called "apomorphous").

If two kinds of organisms have the same ancestry, it may usually be assumed that the resemblances between them are ancestral holdovers and the differences are separately derived. However, it also happens that organisms quite distinct in ancestry evolve derived characters that cause them to resemble one another. This is the phenomenon of evolutionary convergence, which has been a problem for evolutionists in general and for taxonomists or classifiers in particular. An outstanding (and, in retrospect, sad) example is provided by the voluminous work of Florentino Ameghino (1854–1911), especially that on the fossil mammals of Argentina. In most cases, he correctly recognized the general ancestry of those varied mammals, but also in most cases he was mistaken in considering coeval or later mammals on other continents as descendants of those he, or especially his brother Carlos, had found in Argentina. It was his misfortune that almost all the characteristics on which he relied for the latter supposed phylogenies were convergent. Convergence developed rankly, one might say, in South America just because it was an island continent during most of the Age of Mammals, although this was not clearly recognized until after Florentino Ameghino's death.

Convergence has occurred over and over again in the history of organisms, both animals and plants. The only reasonable explanation is that, when organisms of different ancestry become adapted to similar environments and ways of life, they often (but not always) tend to evolve similar structural, physiological, and behavioral characteristics. Natural selection is the reasonable explanation of this common phenomenon. Evolutionary relays and replacements, previously discussed, often involve convergence. For example, the corals in present reefs functionally resemble those in Paleozoic reefs but are of different origin. Among the ammonites, also previously mentioned, relays in successive adaptive radiation often produced convergent forms. Sometimes they also evolved quite different forms, but it has been shown that there were particular ones, called "morphotypes," that tended to evolve independently in different ammonite superfamilies.

Species living in the same biota, with similar ecological conditions, and at the same time have rarely become convergent. More often, they tend to diverge under those conditions. Convergence is more likely among groups separated in time, as in relays, or separated in space by geographic barriers. Thus, the extinct mammals in South America that converged on those of some other continents evolved in isolation there, and many of the marsupials that evolved in isolation in Australia converged toward placental mammals elsewhere. However, the later Cenozoic and living kangaroos are adaptively similar to grazing and browsing ungulates elsewhere, but they are anatomically very different. The adaptive similarity is extensive despite the anatomical differences. The dentition of kangaroos, like the dentition of most ungulates, includes cropping teeth in front and chopping or grinding teeth behind in the jaws; but, as in the previous example of notoungulates and horses, the patterns involved in these similar functions are not the same. That is also true of antipredator adaptation for rapid locomotion. Kangaroos and antelopes run very fast, but the kangaroos do so on two feet and the antelopes on four.

Examples of adaptive convergence can be found in almost any major group of animals and also in many plants. Visitors to semiarid parts of Africa are struck by the presence of plants that look quite like the cacti of North America and South America. The similarity is deceiving as regards relationship, for the large family Cactaceae is native only to the Americas and is quite different in origin from the pseudocactuses of Africa, which belong to the spurge family, Euphorbiaceae. Divergent evolution is also strikingly illustrated in the latter family, for the poinsettia, a plant native to tropical America, is not at all cactuslike, although it also belongs to the family Euphorbiaceae.

The fossil histories of those two groups is not well known, but there are some remarkable instances of convergence in the fossil record of plants. A particularly striking one is provided by the cycads, living and fossil, and their relatives. All are closely convergent, in general habit, to various palms, and nonbotanists often mistake the living ones for palms. The Mesozoic plants of the order Cycadeoidales had reproductive structures quite like flowers, and it was formerly even suggested that they were related to, or actually were themselves ancestors of, the flowering

(a)

(b)

(a) *This pseudocactus* Euphorbia hottentota *from South Africa looks very much like the cacti of North and South America but the similarity is deceiving in regard to relationship. The large family Cactaceae is native only to the Americas and is quite different from the pseudocactuses of Africa, which belong to the spurge family, Euphorbiaceae.* (b) *A remarkable instance of convergence, some cycades are closely convergent, in general habit, to various palms and is often mistaken for them.*

plants. However, it has become clear that they evolved early in the Mesozoic without any direct relationship to the ancestry of the palms or any other true flowering plants. They had a closer ancestry in common with the conifers.

Convergence carried to the conceivable extreme might be supposed to make some organisms of different ancestry indistinguishable from each other. A student of ammonites did once suggest that this had happened among members of that group. It eventuated, however, that he had been misled by the recurrence of a morphotype in different families of the protean ammonites, and that the supposedly identical results were quite distinguishable upon more thorough study. Even in rather simple organisms, genetic systems are extremely complex, and it is practically inconceivable that descendants with distinctly different ancestors would come to be identical in anatomical and functional characters determined genetically. There are no known and acceptable examples of such extreme convergence in the fossil record or, by deduction, for any living organisms. It is safe to say that convergence, although well attested as a real and fairly frequent phenomenon in the history of life, does not result in identity. Another good example is provided by the Australian thylacine, or "Tasmanian wolf." It does indeed, or did before its recent probable extinction, resemble a wolf in external appearance and in its behavior and ecological status, but any competent anatomist would know by even a bone or a tooth that this is due to convergence, not to a phylogenetic relationship. In fact, thylacines and wolves have had different ancestries ever since approximately 100 million years ago, when the progressing higher mammals split into marsupials and placentals.

If one pictures phylogenetic patterns in a graphic or geometric way, divergence may be represented by two lines literally diverging through time from an earlier connection. Convergence can be seen as two lines starting separately and angling toward each other without ever quite meeting. If one went back from their separate starts, one would indeed find them somewhere and at some time arising from a single ancestry and diverging until the much later descendants began to converge, but this would be true in comparing any two organisms if, as is probably the case, life arose only once on earth.

Now it will occur to anyone visualizing divergence and convergence in that way that the lines may converge or diverge at any angle to each other. Another aspect of the commonly mosaic nature of evolution is that some characteristics may have converged while others in the same lineages being compared were diverging. In the simplest case, comparing just two lineages, it is evidently possible that the geometric and graphic lines picturing the comparison might run in parallel. For two (or more) lineages to exist, there must have been some divergence from their common ancestry, but thereafter the overall difference between them might remain the same. This would be true if both went into stasis for a geologically significant length of time, but we have seen that such stasis, although possible, is not common in the fossil record. It is also possible that the degree of difference between them would remain the same if the lineages continued to

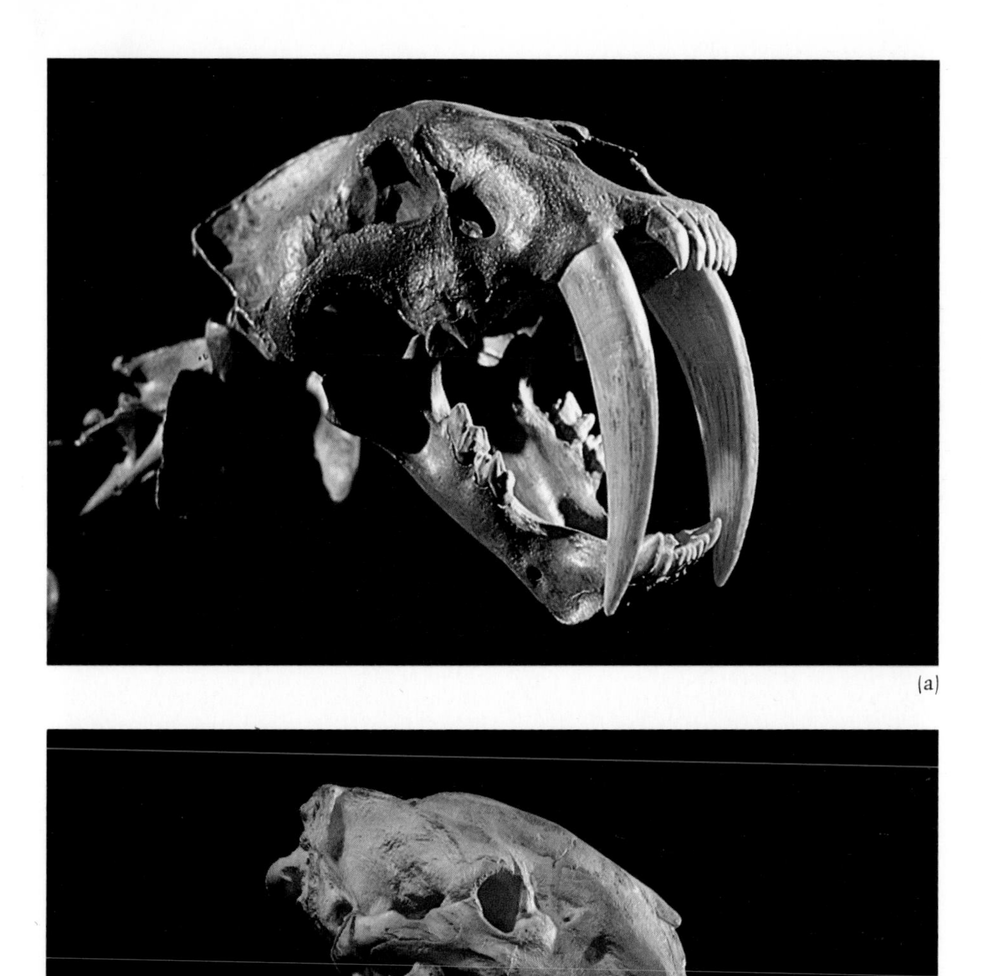

(a)

(b)

(a) *Skull and jaws of the extinct Pleistocene sabertooth cat* Smilodon *found at Rancho La Brea in Los Angeles. This genus also spread to South America in the Great Interchange from late Pliocene through the Pleistocene.* (b) *Skull and jaws of the marsupial sabertooth* Thylacosmilus. Smilodon *and* Thylacosmilus *constitute a striking example of convergence.*

change but both changed in the same way. Since stasis, if present, means that evolutionary change is not occurring, this latter sort of parallelism is what is usually taken as a model or pattern for parallel evolution.

Parallel evolution, thus defined, is unusual in the fossil record. Where it does seem to occur, there is usually some dissent about its interpretation, and there is also a semantic problem in distinguishing it from convergence or, for that matter,

*Examples of convergence and parallelism: (a) The true wolf (*Canis lupus*) of Eurasia and North America. (b) The thylacine or "Tasmanian wolf" (*Thylacinus cynocephalus*), formerly widespread in Australia, recently confined to Tasmania, and now probably extinct. (c) A borhyaenid (*Prothylacinus patagonicus*) from the Miocene of South America (the pattern of the coat represents only artist's licence; it could just as well have been like that of the thylacine). These three mammals look much alike, and two of them are known beyond reasonable doubt, and the third is inferred, to have acted much alike and to have played closely similar roles in the ecology of their places and times. Yet they evolved independently on three land masses that were isolated by broad seas while they were evolving. All of them were medium-sized, predatory carnivores that run down their herbivorous prey. The resemblance of the true wolf to the other two species in appearance and function is purely convergence. This is a placental mammal, and its ancestry diverged from that of the other two at a time on the order of 100,000,000 years ago. Their common ancestor, when the wolf's lineage diverged from that of the other two, did not look or act like any of them: it was a tiny, shrewlike mammal that probably lived on insects, grubs, and whatever else it could devour. The other two animals are marsupials, descendants of the other major division that separated from the placentals. The common ancestor of the thylacines and the borhyaenids, which may have lived as recently as 60 to 65 million years ago, probably resembled a small didelphid (like the American opossum, not the Australian "possum") or similar marsupials, such as those confusingly called "native cats" in Australia (although they are not related to the cat family, Felidae). Those primitive marsupials spread in one direction or the other between Australia and South America and underwent a complex, separate adaptive radiation on each continent. On each, the radiation included lineages leading to larger, predaceous carnivores by adaptation and specialization from the common marsupial origin. Thus, the thylacine–borhyaenid resemblance is at least partly due to parallel evolution, but it also involved convergence.*

from divergence. Nevertheless, there are some probably valid examples. Among these is a recent reinterpretation of data originally published by the German invertebrate paleontologist R. Brinkmann in 1929 on a large collection of some Jurassic ammonites through about 13 meters of fine-bedded shale. In these animals, the sexes differed in size and morphology. There are some not entirely clear complications but in both sexes there are two reasonably clear and distinct main lineages, and in each sex these changed in parallel through the geological time represented.

The most reasonable hypothesis to explain such examples of parallel evolution is that parallel lineages had separated from their common ancestry not long, geologically speaking, before the parallelism began. Both lineages, then, began with what were, overall, similar genetic systems. These systems would exert a similar nonrandom effect on the subsequent evolution in each of the lineages. The semantic problem persists because, for instance, in the case of the thylacine and the wolf, whose common ancestry is remote in geological time, the divergent characters of early marsupials and early placentals persist as differences while the characters usually designated as convergent evolved in the mosaic later and more or less in parallel. Here the dominant nonrandom factor evidently was natural selection more than the similarity of the genetic systems in remote ancestors.

The existence of sibling species poses problems for paleontologists somewhat similar to those of particularly close convergence or of parallel evolution with little divergence. There are species—well known in a wide variety of animal groups, especially in insects—that are reproductively isolated but that belong to the same genus and differ only in minor (or in no readily observed) traits or that are effectively identical in the features usually used by zoologists for identification. A considerable number of sibling species are known in *Drosophila,* the genus of flies so extensively used in genetic studies. Perhaps the most famous of these are *D. pseudoobscura* and *D. willistoni,* both common as laboratory animals as well as in the wild. Sometimes sibling species can be distinguished in one sex, usually the males, but not in the other. Generally, the sexes of one sibling species recognize each other and do not breed with members of the other sibling, at least not in the wild. On analysis, sibling species generally do prove to have some subtle, if perhaps only statistical, bodily differences, and they usually do differ genetically. The barriers to interbreeding may be directly genetic but are sometimes ecological or behavioral.

It is improbable that sibling species could be distinguished from each other in fossils. That is another incompleteness in the fossil record, but it is a relatively unimportant one. Although a moderate number of sibling species have been found among living organisms, these constitute an extremely small fraction of living species as a whole. Sibling species may have occurred more or less throughout geological history, but it is not likely that they have been abundant enough to distort the record for this reason alone. At worst, this may only be another (but a minor) reason why the record is already adequate for many major features of evolution—in taxonomic terms, above the specific level—but less adequate at interspecific and intraspecific levels. Yet, even at the latter levels, the known record is improving rather rapidly. This is due in considerable part to the use of mass collecting methods, which provide larger samples of ancient populations. This is particularly true of some protozoans, of small invertebrate and vertebrate animals, and of pollen and spores of plants, but also, to a lesser degree, of larger animals and other parts of some plants. The larger samples are important especially for making statistical estimates of variation in the populations from which they are drawn.

It was adumbrated by Darwin and more explicitly pointed out by William Diller Matthew, among others, early in the twentieth century that, when more than one species of a single genus is present in a fossil biota, the ranges of their variation in some of their anatomical characters usually will not overlap. Another way of putting this is that, if two related species are present, there will usually be a significantly different peak in the mean or mode of some characters in a frequency distribution that includes different species of a single genus. In some animals, this may indicate sexual bimodality in one species rather than the presence of two species, and this possibility must be considered by paleontologists. A favorite anecdote among paleontologists is one about Baron Francis Nopcsa, a Hungarian student of fossil reptiles, who wrote that, among the hadrosaurian dinosaurs (discussed in Chapter 2), those with crests were males and those without crests were females. The catch is that the two usually do not occur in the same faunas—perhaps another reason why they became extinct! The baron was an eccentric who, among other things, applied unsuccessfully for a position as king of Albania, was a spy for Austria in World War I, and finally committed suicide after murdering his secretary, who had been his homosexual lover. Most other paleontologists do not lead such colorful lives. Most of us are quietly devoted to our science and to our families. Something of what our science means to us and to the world will be discussed in the next and final chapter of this book.

CHAPTER 8
FOSSILS AND PEOPLE

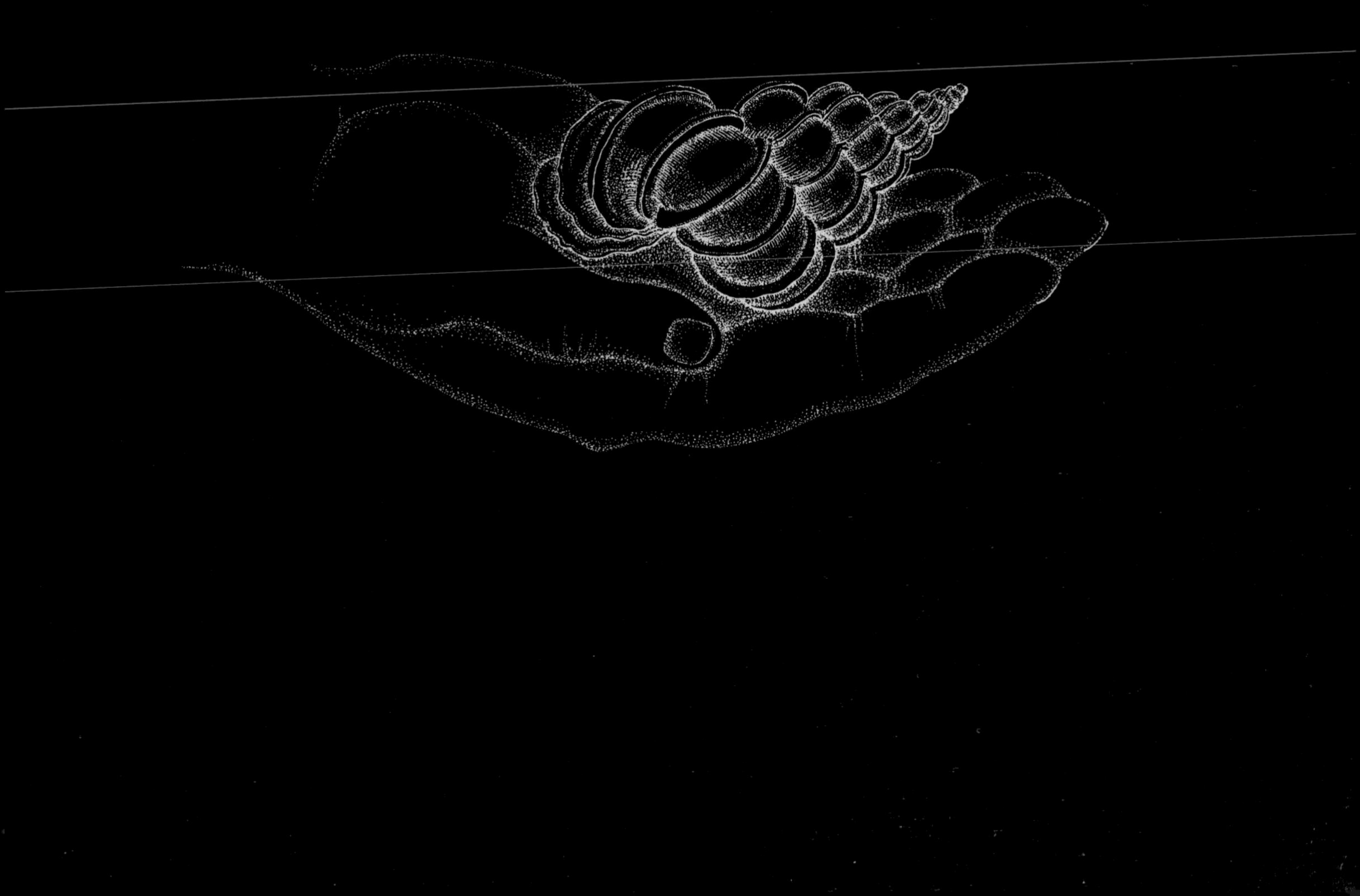

A child holding a snail. Both are members of the animal kingdom, and as such they are relatives. Their ancestral lines are of equal length. They both are descendants of one ancestral group that lived at least a billion (thousand million) years ago. They both still have many things in common, sharing physiological and chemical characteristics. They differ greatly in some respects, because their ancestral lineages began to evolve in different directions once they became separate. Both are also related, through ancestries even more ancient, with all the plants now living and awesomely even more distantly with the living organisms that are neither animals nor plants. Thus all living creatures are a tremendous unit, and the whole universe is an even greater unit.

Why do so many people, both men and women, devote their working lives to fossils—collecting them, studying them, pondering their meanings, writing about them? Each person starting a career as a paleontologist has his or her own answer to such questions. Those of us nearing the end of such a career also have answers, which may not be just the same as the answers we had at the start—at least, they will be better informed and affected by personal experience. To justify the profession, one must also ask what do (or should) fossils mean for people in general? Some version of this less personal question might be asked about a professional career in any field. This chapter will try to answer the question for paleontology in a necessarily summary way.

When people ask what good something is, they are often thinking in economic terms. Paleontology does have values in those terms, too. There is a Society of Economic Paleontology and Mineralogy. The identification of fossils and their placement in a time scale and in a stratigraphic context are necessary for much of the geological mapping of the world. That mapping, in turn, is an essential basis for the search for and the exploitation of mineral resources, including especially the fossil fuels, which are derived from fossils and usually occur in a paleontologically defined context. The location of such resources depends heavily on surface prospecting for fossils, among other things, and also has long involved identification of fossils in cores taken in exploratory drilling. Other methods now have supplemented this paleontological approach, but they have not entirely replaced it.

There is another economic value of fossils that is less direct and less obvious but not less important. Paleontology joins with the biological sciences to discover the way in which organisms have evolved in the history of life. It is greatly to our advantage, both as individuals and as nations, to emulate evolution in changing the characteristics of various economically important organisms. Our ability to do that involves correct understanding of how changes arose by evolution in nature. In *The Origin of Species,* the first chapter is devoted largely to artificial selection, such as is exercised by breeders of animals and by originators of varieties of plants. In the next chapter of *The Origin of Species,* a parallel is drawn between artificial selection and natural selection. Both involve differential breeding among the variants that arise spontaneously in populations of organisms and increase of the incidence of some variations and decrease of others as the populations reproduce. To that extent, the processes are closely analogous or even identical. They differ in that artificial selection has goals that are set by humans. Animal breeders aim for cows that give more milk or chickens that lay more eggs, and plant breeders aim for corn with a higher yield or a rose with a more attractive flower. Natural selection has nothing that can be called a goal, but, like artificial selection, it does have a direction. In natural selection, the trends are toward adaptation in accessible environments. In both kinds of selection, there are restraints that limit or determine the changes occurring or even counteract selection itself.

There is a horrifying example of the economic importance of understanding how evolution works. In the Soviet Union, Trofim Denisovich Lysenko, an agron-

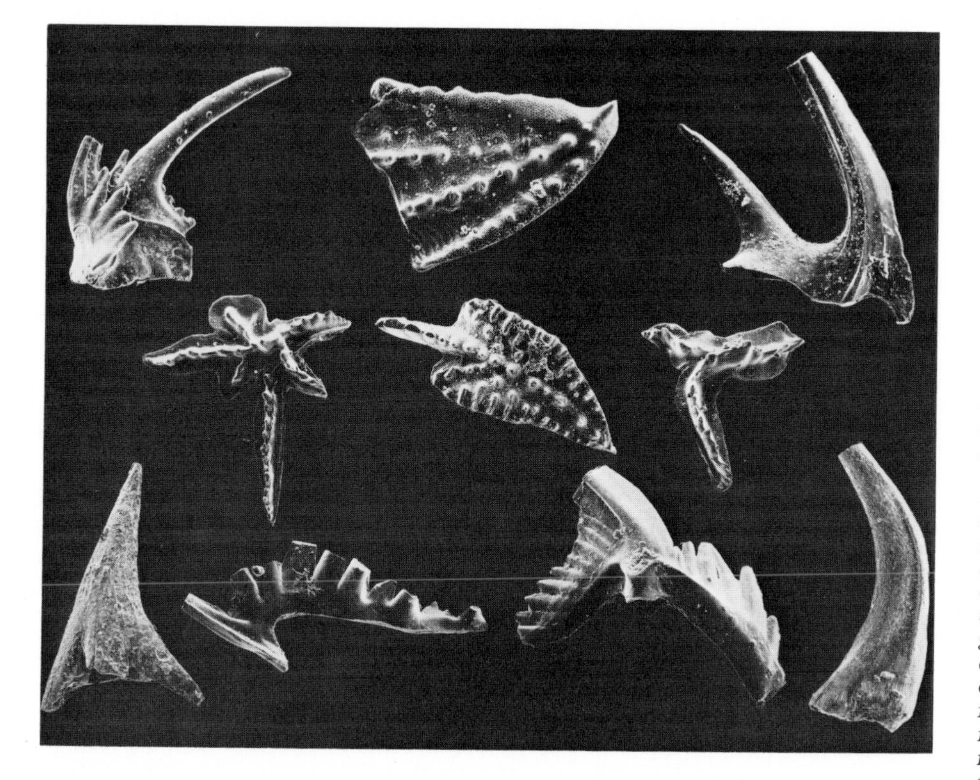

A variety of different microscopic fossils that have an economic application. They are called conodonts or Conodonta by paleontologists. These are the preserved hard parts of otherwise soft bodied marine organisms. The nature and classification of those organisms are unknown. Students of conodonts have argued or conjectured that they might be worms, mollusks, fishes, or a number of other kinds of organisms, even plants. They first appear in the fossil record in the Cambrian, about 550 million years ago, and they continued into the late Triassic about 190 million years ago. During that time they were diversifying and evolving so that assemblages of conodonts are characteristic of different geological ages during that span. This enables paleontologists to determine the sequential geological position of the strata in which they occur. They are thus among the most important index fossils that aid in exploration for oil, gas, or other resources in marine sedimentary rocks from Cambrian through Triassic in age. For those reasons thousands of publications devoted to them have appeared since 1856 and many hundreds of names have been applied to them.

omist and an astute Stalinist politician, espoused the neo-Lamarckian idea of the inheritance of acquired characters as scientific and political dogma and strongly opposed neo-Darwinian natural selection and neo-Mendelian genetics. He claimed that he had demonstrated the validity of his views, which eventually were officially adopted as the politically correct Marxist view. Some of his opponents among evolutionists and geneticists were exiled, and all had to discontinue their work. Lysenkoism was radically wrong, and its results almost ruined Soviet agriculture. Eventually, Lysenko was ousted from the presidency of the Academy of Agricultural Sciences and from the directorship of the Institute of Genetics. Since 1965, study of evolution in the USSR has slowly returned to what are essentially synthesist or neo-Darwinian approaches. The people of the Soviet Union learned the hard way that politicians cannot dictate how evolution works. The people of the United States need to know that politicians likewise cannot change the fact that evolution does indeed occur.

As a monitor of geological resources and an arbiter of evolutionary history, paleontology has played an essential and sometimes a crucial part in varied pursuits of great economic importance. It has even greater values in a more human and less strictly commercial sense. It helps us to understand the world in which we live and to understand ourselves, our origins, our relationships, and our natures.

First, as to time, it is an awe-inspiring abyss. In 1805, John Playfair, in a biographical account of the still earlier British geologist James Hutton, wrote that "the mind seemed to grow giddy by looking so far into the abyss of time." (The American historian and philosopher of geology Claude Albritton borrowed the expression *The Abyss of Time* as the title of his book, cited at the end of this book, on the history of concepts of geological time.)

In the "Discours préliminaire" of his great *Recherches sur les ossemens fossiles de Quadrupèdes*, published in 1812 and honored by vertebrate paleontologists as the foundation of a truly scientific approach to their subject, Cuvier urged that the remains of fossils should be carefully arranged in chronological sequence. He closed this preliminary discourse with this conclusion: "And man, to whom has been accorded only an instant on earth, would [thus] have the glory of restoring the history of the thousands of centuries that preceded his existence and of the thousands of beings that have not been his contemporaries." The statement that geological time would run into the hundreds of thousands of years was then daring, and Cuvier was taken to task for it by more orthodox geologists.

In the first edition of *The Origin of Species* (1859), Darwin estimated that erosion of the Weald, an early Cretaceous formation in England, probably took longer than 300 million years. He did not venture on a figure for the whole of geological time. He suggested that estimates based on rates of deposition of sedimentary rocks would give an inadequate idea of the time required. Physicists in Darwin's day (especially William Thomson, later Baron Kelvin, 1824–1907) were proceeding on the assumption, now known to be incorrect, that the earth started as a molten mass and had been cooling at an even rate ever since. Their calculations on that basis indicated that the age of the earth must be far too short for the now living species to have evolved according to Darwin's theory. Darwin's first figure for the erosion of the Weald was in fact too large, as we now know. In a later edition, he did back down to a more reasonable figure, on the order of 100 million to 150 million years, for that erosion, but Darwin continued stubbornly to insist that the physicists' estimates of the age of the earth were wrong.

We now know beyond doubt that Darwin was right on that point. As calculated by radioactive decay, the age of the Weald comes out as something under 135 million years, a figure bracketed by Darwin. As discussed in Chapter 2 of this book, we do not have an exact figure for the total age of the earth, but its order of magnitude must be approximated by 4.5 billion (or, in English style, 4.5 thousand million) years. The oldest organisms now known were found fossilized in rocks that are more than 3 billion years old. Those are dizzying figures, but the evidence for them is so clear that they can now be rejected only out of utter ignorance or, still worse, from terror. In *The Abyss of Time*, Albritton coined the word "chronophobiacs" for those who cringe in fear when pondering geological time. Incredible as it may seem, even today there are chronophobiacs who maintain that the age of the earth is only 10,000 years. Asked for evidence, they usually refer to Genesis, which in fact gives no such figure. If those who hold to 10,000 years advance any other "evidence," it is often simply fraudulent. As honest paleontologists, we are delighted to live on so mature a planet and honored that evolution took so many years to produce us.

That some people are frightened by geological time and more find it difficult to grasp its immensity may well be related to the sense of human mortality, to a fear of personal aging, and to the comparative brevity of our own lives. One of the great values of paleontology is that it enables us to live in our own complex minds not just a few score years but more than three billion years.

Paleontology has played a major role in forming our modern conception of geologic time. It was Cuvier's recognition of a long and elaborate succession of prehistoric animals that led him to believe in the hundreds of thousands of years. His fellow countryman Lamarck had come out with an evolutionary theory of a sort in 1809 (which, by a historic coincidence, was the year in which Darwin was born). Cuvier was then forty years old (he lived from 1769 to 1832; Lamarck, who lived from 1744 to 1829, was his elder by twenty-five years). Cuvier firmly rejected Larmack's view. In retrospect, we can see that he was right at the time.

Evolution for Lamarck depended mainly on two very ancient ideas: the *scala naturae* (the notion of a single succession of progressively "higher" organisms through time) and the inheritance of acquired characters. Both these ideas died hard, but it is now beyond serious doubt that both were wrong. Being right in that respect, Cuvier was wrong as to evolution, but he did in some other ways lay a basis for later developments of evolutionary theory. Fundamental for this was his demonstration that there really has been no single *scala naturae*. Ancient animals, many of them described by Cuvier, and recent animals as well simply do not fit into only one progression.

Pioneering geologists, and particularly the great Scot Charles Lyell (1797–1875), had already seen that, although there was no *scala naturae*, there was a definite and recognizable change of faunas, and later of floras, through time. Much of geological time therefore was partitioned and labeled sequentially by means of the known fossil record. The first edition of Lyell's major work, *The Principles of Geology*, was published in three volumes between 1830 and 1833. Darwin studied it assiduously during the voyage of the Beagle (1831–1836) and was already an accomplished geologist before he became an evolutionist. His own attempts to sound the abyss of time were based primarily on estimates of rates of erosion and of deposition of sedimentary rocks. However, his insistence that the earth must be abysmally old expressed his conviction that enormous expanses of time would be involved in the evolution of organisms up to now. That is indeed true, as the fossil record fully confirms.

So much (or so little) for the abyss of time. There are other aspects of special significance for us in the study of fossils. The great importance of *The Origin of Species* for human thought was that Darwin essentially established therein two fundamentals: the fact that evolution really has occurred and the fact that its nonrandom features can be explained without recourse to supernatural explana-

The traditional view of divine creation as portrayed in a sixteenth-century Flemish painting. This is an artist's version of the fifth day of creation showing only aquatic and winged animals, thus fishes (including a whale, then considered a fish) and birds. Reptiles, mammals, and man do not come into the story until the sixth day and are not in this picture of creation.

tions. In both of those essentials, the fossil record, much more incomplete in Darwin's day than in ours, gives crucial evidence. Although there were evolutionists of a sort before Darwin, the general opinion, even among learned people, was that the existence of so many and such diverse species of organisms was explicable only by divine creation and that this was most clearly proved by the apparent teleology or goal-centered nature of their adaptations. A whole series of popular books by then eminent scientists—the eight Bridgewater Treatises—was published in the 1830s to demonstrate "the Power, Wisdom and Goodness of God, as manifested in the Creation." The "demonstrations" included such old ideas as the analogy (now obviously false) between a watch and a human eye: the watch must have a maker, therefore the eye must have a Maker. Even before the Bridgewater Treatises, this specious analogy had been used in another extremely popular book: *Natural Theology* (first edition in 1802) by William Paley (1743–1805), an English theologian. It is extraordinary that, when William Berryman Scott (1858–1947) and Henry Fairfield Osborn (1857–1935) were in college in the 1870s, they were still reading Paley. Both these eminent paleontologists nevertheless became ardent evolutionists.

In the atmosphere of the time, it was thus necessary that Darwin should not only show that evolution is true but also provide an alternative, nonteleological and noncreationist explanation of the universality of adaptation. This he did mainly in his theory of natural selection. This theory could be applied to (but, for

Darwin, did not mainly derive from) the fossil record as then known. In the early 1940s, when Albert Eide Parr was appointed director of the American Museum of Natural History, he abolished the department of paleontology on the grounds that paleontology had been important only in demonstrating the fact of evolution and had no further contribution to make to science. It did soon appear even to him that paleontology still was alive and well and making contributions everywhere. I hope that the present book demonstrates, even though in a summary way, that paleontology does increase knowledge in many other ways than just demonstrating that evolution is factual.

There are today, even in this otherwise enlightened country, some people who deny that evolution is a fact. Those people have seen to it that their presence and their beliefs are well known. They hold that creationism, as set forth in the first two chapters of Genesis, is a science, and that evolution is "merely" a theory. That is a misrepresentation of the nature of science and of the significance of the term "theory" in science. There is no objective, scientific evidence that either of the two contradictory accounts of creation in those chapters of Genesis is factual, or was even meant to be taken as factual, in the literal sense of either the Hebrew words or of those words translated into English or other languages. Such literalism is strictly a religious tenet, and an illogical and unnecessary one, generally (but somewhat oddly) now called "fundamentalist." Those versions of creation can be understood and enjoyed as poetic parables, but there is no sense in which they can be considered science.

The vulgar, or at least fairly widespread, understanding of the word "theory" makes it nearly synonymous with "guess." In scientific usage, even a conditional hypothesis is more than a guess. It is a possible or partial explanation of some objectively observed facts. Lamarck's explanation of evolution was a hypothesis that eventually was found to be inacceptable because it was contrary to later factual observations. That evolution really has occurred—and is still occurring—is supported by an enormous number of scientific observations, especially, but far from solely, those of the fossil record, and it is not contradicted by any such observations. In the vernacular, then, evolution can be spoken of sensibly as an established fact. Darwin's natural selection was—and still is—only one theory about some of the events in the course of evolution.

It is one of the glories of Great Britain that in some British families through each of several generations there have been distinguished men and women. The Darwins are one such family, starting in the eighteenth century and continuing to our time. So are the Huxleys, who had a somewhat later start. Less well known but in their several ways also distinguished were three generations of Gosses, in which Philip Henry (1810–1888) begat Edmund William (1849–1928), who begat Philip (1879–1959). Edmund Gosse—Sir Edmund, as he became—was a poet, linguist, and general litterateur. The second Philip Gosse was a physician and also, oddly enough, an authority on pirates and the history of piracy. The first Philip Gosse was a naturalist. His works on the natural history of Jamaica were famous

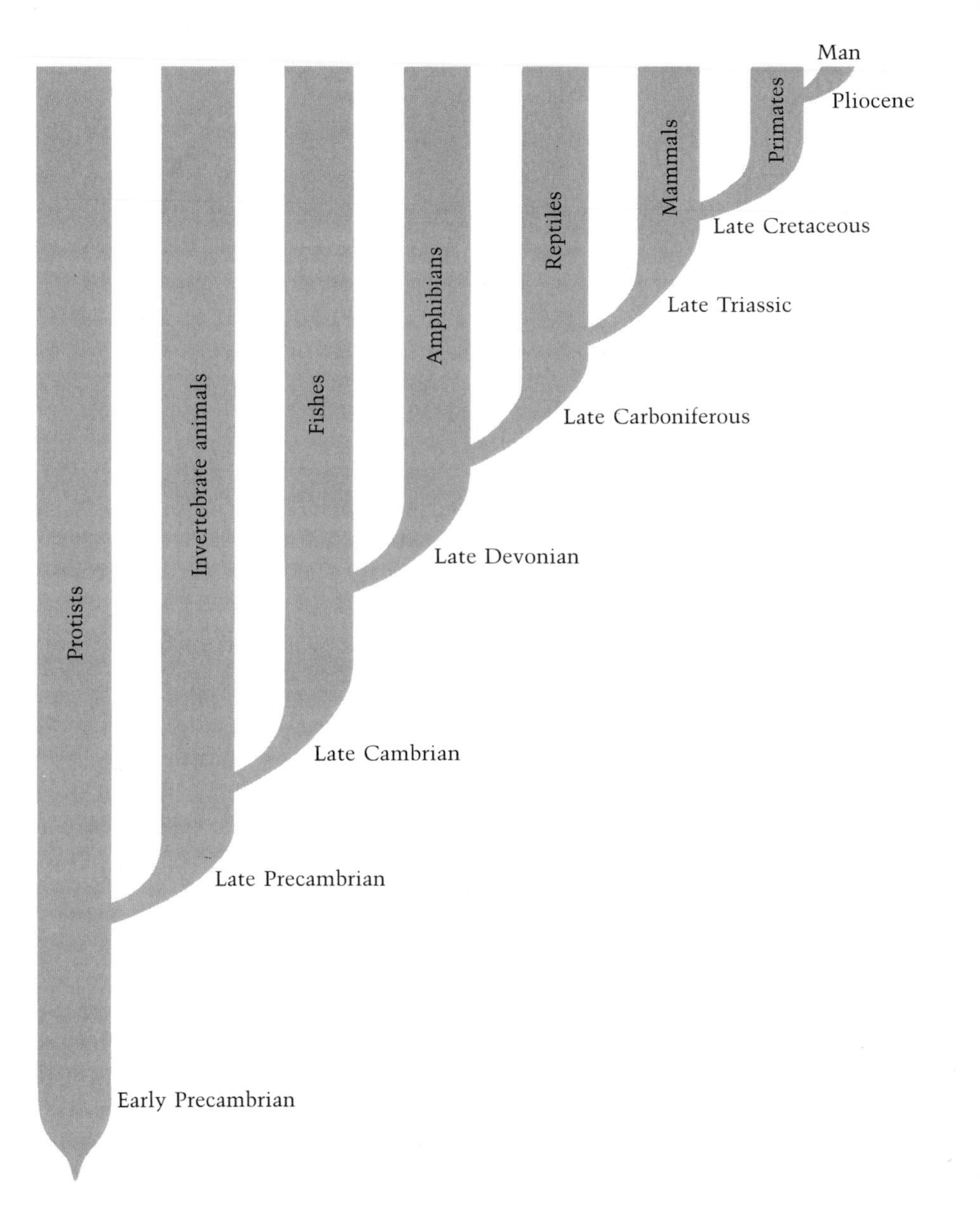

The long trail through earth history to ourselves. Although not to scale, the vertical dimension represents the sequence in geological time, from the origin of life at the bottom to the present time at the top. The vertical paths represent main groups of organisms successively involved in the eventual evolution of Homo sapiens. *The figure is wholly diagrammatic. Each vertical path had extremely diverse and complicated contents, eliminated here to keep the diagram as simple and clear as possible. Each had in fact (and as shown in its fossil record) an extremely complicated branching pattern of diverging (and sometimes converging) lineages or clades. These changed markedly in the course of geological time so that, in almost all cases, the still living members of a given group have evolved so extensively that they have become decidedly unlike their basic ancestry. Thus, taking a sequence (such as protists–invertebrate animals–fishes–amphibians–reptiles–mammals–primates–man) represented by species now living, as in studies of comparative anatomy, does not even roughly resemble the real lineage that led to* Homo sapiens. *Only the fossil record can give us evidence of how that lineage really went. For example, our ancestors among the amphibians were unrecognizably different from any amphibians now living. We did not descend from frogs, salamanders, or caecilians, all of which evolved long after our ancestors had gone on to become reptiles. And then our reptilian ancestry did not include or resemble lizards, snakes, turtles, crocodiles, or tuataras—and so it goes through all of this pattern. It is further worth noting (and for me, at least, it is a source of awe) that every one of the species now living—plants, animals, and all the rest—has an ancestry just as long as ours or as that of any other species.*

in their day, but he is now better remembered, and is relevant here, for a strange book titled *Omphalos* (a Greek word for the navel or umbilicus). The theme of that work was that the "higher" species of animals, at least, with *Homo sapiens* of course being the highest, were created just as they are now. He considered, but did not accept, the evidence for evolution—note that he was only one year younger than Darwin, whom he outlived by six years. He explained away that evidence by suggesting that God created the earth as a whole also just as it is now, complete with its fossil record and other evidence for evolution, which Gosse saw as all too convincing. In short, and in more modern terms than his, his thesis was that the Creator also created that conclusive evidence as a booby trap that caught Darwin and all the rest of the evolutionists. This, I think, still ranks as the most sacrilegious of all the creationist ploys. Present-day antievolutionists have not adopted Gosse's booby-trap hypothesis to do away with the evidence for evolution. Instead, they usually adopt the legendary ostrich method: if you don't look squarely at something, it ceases to exist.

There is no necessary conflict between religion and science. Among religions, only the bigoted fundamentalist sects have a dogma condemning evolution. Many religious teachers and laymen accept the fact of evolution. Many evolutionists are religious. Evolutionists may also be creationists, but in a very different and truer sense than that of those who call themselves creationists. If an ineffable entity that may be called God created the universe, a possibility that no evolutionist should deny, this creation was not in the fashion of the biblical parable, nor was it complete with the booby trap of *Omphalos.* It was the creation of a universe in which evolution could and did occur without supernatural intervention. It seemed necessary, in discussing fossils and people, to deal with this aspect of what fossils mean (or, in some cases, do not mean) to people, but the subject of creationism may now be dropped.

The concept of evolution suggests, and the fossil record confirms, that all organisms, past and present, are parts of one extremely long and extremely branching family tree. Life on earth is a single phenomenon with many millions of manifestations. From this widened point of view, *Homo sapiens* is just one small twig on the tree of life. One of the wise men of ancient Greece—some say that it might have been Thales, but no one seems to be quite sure—originated the saying *Gnothi seauton* ("Know thyself"). Certainly, the recognition that we are related to all other organisms is one of the greatest advances ever made in self-knowledge.

Our ancestry and phylogeny are included, with varying clarity, in most classifications of organisms, even those made before the fact of evolution was recognized. Obviously, we are animals, not plants, but animals and plants evidently had a common ancestry before their evolutionary paths diverged. Among animals, we are vertebrates, having backbones and other bones and a whole congeries of other characteristics that we share with fishes, amphibians, reptiles, and birds. We are mammals, as every mother attests. Among mammals, we are primates, a relationship sensed and named by Linnaeus in pre-evolutionary days. (However, Linnaeus' conception of the order Primates included the bats, which are now placed in a separate order of their own.) Among primates, our closest living relatives are unquestionably the gorillas and chimpanzees. Those two are closely related to each other, and it is clear that we share a common ancestry with both of them. The comparative evidence from the living species, at all levels from molecules upward, is irrefutable, and it is also in accord with the fossil record.

A book that had undeserved popularity some fifteen years ago designated *Homo sapiens* as "the naked ape." That is absurd zoology and even worse logic.

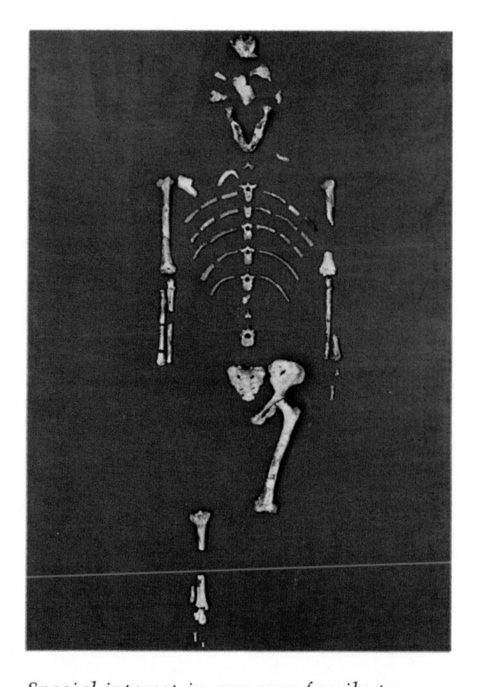

Special interest in our own family tree has led to increased effort and discovery of relevant fossils, especially in East Africa and southern and eastern Asia. Currently, there are lively (and at times objurgatory) discussions of various relevant points. Interesting as they may be, these are largely matters of detail, and they usually do not much affect the broader issues involved. For instance, it is argued pro and con whether the possible descendant from the dryopithecine radiation shown here is the forerunner of the Hominidae. This is the near complete skeleton of "Lucy," a four-foot tall 3.5 million-year-old Australopithecus afarensis, *discovered by Donald C. Johanson in the Hadar region of Ethiopia in 1974. The skeleton is probably female and walked fully erect. It may have been a descendant of earlier and more apelike* Ramapithecus.

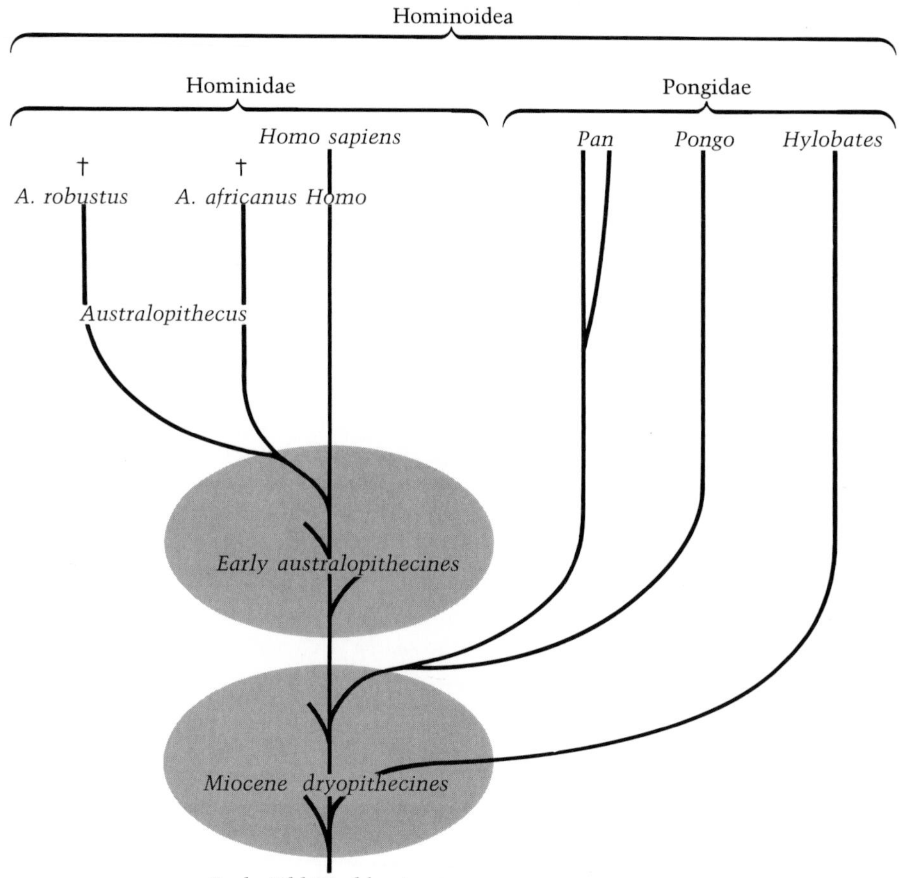

The family tree of the human species and its closest relatives. Time, although not here to scale, progresses from the bottom upward. In the classification here preferred, all the groups and lineages shown make up the superfamily Hominoidea, indicating that they are manlike in a broad sense, some more so than others. The lineages still living include, of course, our own genus Homo *and species* H. sapiens *and also the living apes, here put in three genera although they are often classified in five genera—an unimportant difference in subjective ranking, not a difference of fact. The genus* Pan, *as here used, includes the two living species of chimpanzees and also the one living species of gorilla, which is often given the generic name* Gorilla. *Chimpanzees and gorillas are closely related, and this is best expressed by placing* Gorilla *as a subgenus of the older generic name* Pan. Pan, *as a whole, comprises what are decidedly the closest living relatives of* Homo. Pongo, *which was used as a vernacular name for gorillas, orangutans, or both by early French naturalists, is supposed to have been a native name, but its tribal or linguistic origin is unknown. The genus* Pongo *includes only the one living species of orangutan (an erroneous anglicization of two Malay words, "orang hutan," meaning "forest people").* Hylobates, *as used here, includes all the gibbons, of which six living species are usually distinguished. One of these* (H. syndactylus) *is often put in the separate genus* Symphalangus, *but it is so closely related to* Hylobates *that it is here considered a subgenus. The gibbons as a group are quite distinct from* Pan *or* Pongo, *although they are generally included among the apes in a vernacular sense and are put in the family Pongidae.*

Australopithecus *is certainly the genus most closely related to* Homo *of all adequately defined and now universally recognized genera. It has been held that* Australopithecus *was directly ancestral to* Homo, *but this has become largely a matter of judgment and of how far back in their lineages one chooses to apply either or both of those generic names. It has become reasonably clear that the separation of the ancestral lineages occurred either in the Pliocene or possibly, but less likely on present evidence, in the Miocene. In any event, by early to middle Pleistocene time, there were two contemporaneous and then distinct groups best distinguished as genera under the names of* Australopithecus *and* Homo. *Many names, both generic and specific, have been applied to the varying specimens here grouped in* Australopithecus. *It is at least fairly clear that their lineage in the Pleistocene had bifurcated into a gracile species, for which the name* Australopithecus africanus *is available, and a robust species, which may reasonably be called* Australopithecus robustus. *Of the two, typical* A. africanus *is more like* Homo, *but the ancestry of the two Pleistocene lineages of* Australopithecus *had apparently already split from that of* Homo *before the later and final bifurcation of* Australopithecus *occurred.*

Before the australopithecine–hominine lineages became distinct, there evidently was a single lineage of hominids, much like the early australopithecines, that emerged from a Miocene adaptive radiation of the most primitive apes. These were the dryopithecines, which were widely distributed in Africa, Europe, and Asia. They became extinct in Europe, but various lineages from the radiation survived and became sufficiently grouped into local populations to give rise eventually to the orangutan, which originated in Asia but survives only in Borneo and Java (which were connected by land to Asia at times during the Pleistocene). Another Asiatic group gave rise, probably somewhat earlier, to the gibbons, which survive in southeastern Asia and also in East Indian islands that were once connected with Asia. In Africa—and only there, as far as we know—one branch of dryopithecines evolved into chimpanzees and gorillas, which are still confined to that continent. Finally, another branch of the dryopithecines gave rise to the australopithecines and to the hominines. Homo *almost certainly originated in Africa, but the tendency to specify a more restricted place of origin—Olduvai, for example—seems due only to chances of preservation and discovery.*

Four skulls illustrating three hominid lineages. They are: Homo erectus *(left), gracile* Australopithecus *(2nd left) and robus* Australopithecus *(right, male–unbroken–and female).*

People are no more "naked apes" than apes are "hairy people," although apes were sometimes so considered when first known to Europeans. To put the relationship of people and apes into a time sequence and to follow the history of *Homo sapiens* more precisely, the fossil record must be consulted. New discoveries of human fossils are now being made so frequently and in so many places that books cannot keep up with them. Many such finds have recently been made in East Africa and in southern and eastern Asia. The latest reports appear in newspapers and in such journals as *Science* in the United States and *Nature* in the United Kingdom. How to interpret the phylogeny in a classification is, as usual, subject to personal taste or even artistry, but the phylogeny itself is becoming clearer every year. The lineages leading, on the one hand, to modern apes and, on the other, to modern humans split sometime in the Miocene. Before the end of the shorter Pliocene epoch, the more human line had itself split into two or three lineages, only one of which eventuated in the still-living humans, who, despite a few conspicuous racial differences, all belong to a single species. In the Pliocene and into the early Pleistocene, there were at least two and probably more separate species in the human family (Hominidae)—or, by some usages, subfamily (Homininae). The members of the genus formerly separated as *Pithecanthropus,* including those commonly referred to as "Java man" and "Peking man" (some of them, obviously, were women), are now universally put in the living genus *Homo,* but usually as a separate ancestral species. The famous and once controversial genus *Australopithecus* is now usually considered to have ended in an

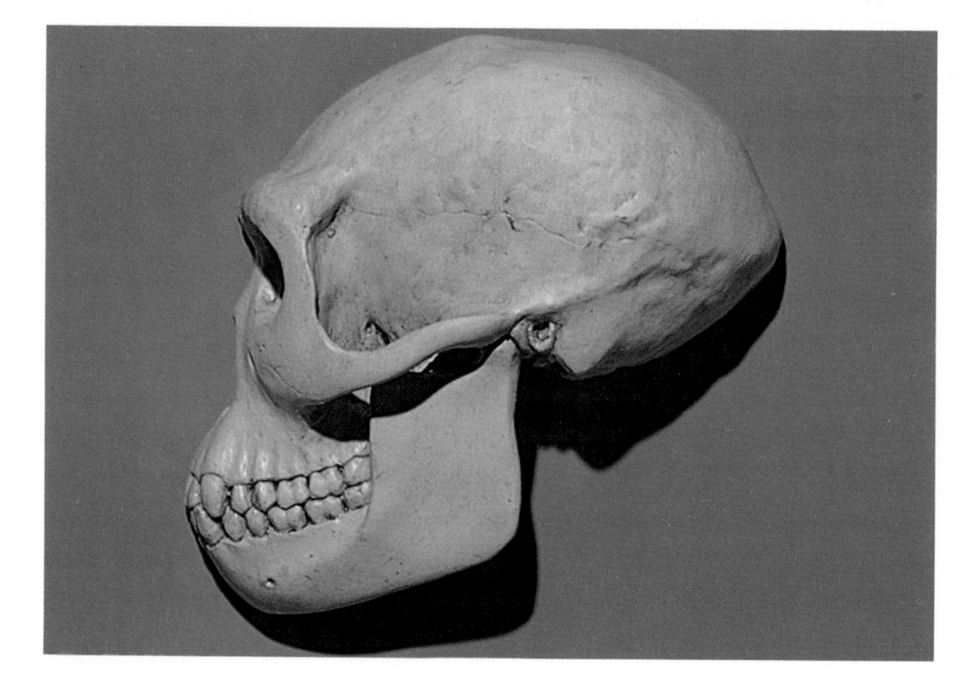

A reconstruction of the skull of an early Homo erectus. *The first remains of this species were found at Trinil on the island of Java by Eugène Dubois in 1891. Dubois named his find* Pithecanthropus erectus *(literally "ape-man [that stood] erect"). Since then, many other specimens have been found at older geological levels in Java and also at numerous different localities and levels in Asia (mostly in China), Africa, and Europe. It has been generally agreed that* Pithecanthropus *(and a number of other generic names based on specimens mostly of this same species) is not sufficiently distinct from* Homo *to be called a different genus. The species (also with large numbers of useless synonyms) is now usually called* Homo erectus. *It is the oldest species now generally referred to the genus, although some others have been somewhat dubiously distinguished from* H. erectus *and also placed tentatively in the genus* Homo.

As this figure shows, Homo erectus *had heavy brow ridges as well as other characters that distinguish it from* Homo sapiens*—notably, a smaller brain (on the average, it was about 950 cubic centimeters, compared with 1330 cubic centimeters for* Homo sapiens*).* Homo erectus *was the direct ancestor of* Homo sapiens, *and there are some specimens so nearly transitional between the two that calling them one or the other is merely arbitrary.* Homo erectus *spread over practically all of the habitable world that could be reached on foot, but apparently it never reached the New World, even though some contemporary animals did walk across on the Bering bridge. Specimens of* Homo erectus *from different localities are generally somewhat different in detail. Although there are not yet large enough samples of good specimens to make adequate statistical analyses, it is probable that populations so widespread were differentiated into different local subspecies. It has even been suggested, but it cannot at present be clearly established or refuted, that, when the whole species* Homo erectus *evolved into* Homo sapiens, *its subspecies (or some of them) passed on genetical differences, which became a basis for racial differentiation in* H. sapiens.

extinct sidebranch, but one hardly separable from the ancestry of *Homo* in the Pliocene.

That we are not descendants of any living species of apes would be too obvious to mention, were it not that representations of our ancestors as gorillas, both in popularizations and in antievolutionary religious tracts, are fairly common. As mentioned earlier (in Chapter 7), the idea of a missing link, half gorilla and half human, is a fallacy. Nevertheless, if we could see the Miocene ancestors of apes and humans as they were when they were alive, it is probable that we would think of them as apes rather than as humans.

From one point of view, it is correct to visualize the human species as a mere twig on the top (at the present time level) of the tree of life. That, however, is inadequate for evaluation of the special interest that the fossil record holds for the human species or for consideration of the status of the species. Our species is unique, but so are all species, whether they are amoebas, flowering plants, or mammals, once they have become reproductively isolated and thus have become established as separate species. On the likely assumption that life arose only once on earth—not as one individual but as the earliest animate populations of similar but already varying individuals—then every species now alive has an ancestry just as long in years as any other. Each living species is a survivor of an ancestor–descendant line through several eons of geological time. Within that ancestry, every ancestral species has coped with survival in its own environment, with adaptation to changes in that environment, and to life in other environments as the numbers of species expanded and the earth changed. In this respect, all species now living are the winners, the best of their kinds and champions in the history of life so far. The fossil record shows abundantly that many more species, although also champions at their own earlier points in time, have since lost and become terminally extinct. Clearly, there was an element of chance in which lost and which succeeded; but it is also clear that there were strong nonchance factors, shifting as time went on but not merely capricious or (in more formal jargon) purely stochastic.

Our species is a twig among others, but it is for us the most important twig. Self-importance can be considered as present in some way and to some degree in every other species-twig. One can imagine any one of them—let's say, for example, *Helix aspersa,* a common garden snail—being scornful of *Homo sapiens:* "Humans are too big and ugly. They move too fast and uncertainly on long projections from their bodies, not laying down a path as they go. Each person has only one sex, so their union is one-sided and imperfect. Only one of the sexes experiences gestation, which in this species is too long and too troublesome. They are covered with soft, vulnerable, drab skins, not with handsome, hard, protective shells. They eat all kinds of muck and not just clean, tasty leaves." And so on.

Obviously, one of the differences between *Homo sapiens* and *Helix aspersa* (or any other nonhuman species whatever) is that none except our species would think in such terms or could express such thoughts if they had them. Humans may not be the only self-conscious species, but they certainly are the most self-conscious. In some respects, almost all organisms guard against death, but most of them do so instinctively and probably with little or no awareness that they will die inevitably, however they may be able to avoid death on any one occasion. Certainly, humans are the only animals that know that they have evolved, even though some of them fearfully reject this knowledge. Above all, humans have the most intricate (even though not the largest) brains, and they alone have the natural ability of speech. A few captive chimpanzees have learned rudimentary, simple, and imperfect partial equivalents of human speech, but this was taught to them slowly and painfully by humans to whom speech is natural. No wild chimpanzees have any equivalent of human speech, but the experiments do suggest that the Miocene common ancestors of apes and humans did have the rudiments from which natural language evolved in humans but not in apes.

It is not anthropocentric but an obvious fact that humans have by far the most complex and extensive capacities and behaviors of all the existing species of organisms. Some writers have belonged to what the late Julian Huxley called "the 'nothing but' school." Perhaps they do so in order to amaze the common people. Certainly no common person is stupid enough to think that humans are nothing but animals or naked apes.

The status of humans as the most extraordinary of all existing organisms is manifest in all the arts and sciences. How this came about in the history of life is

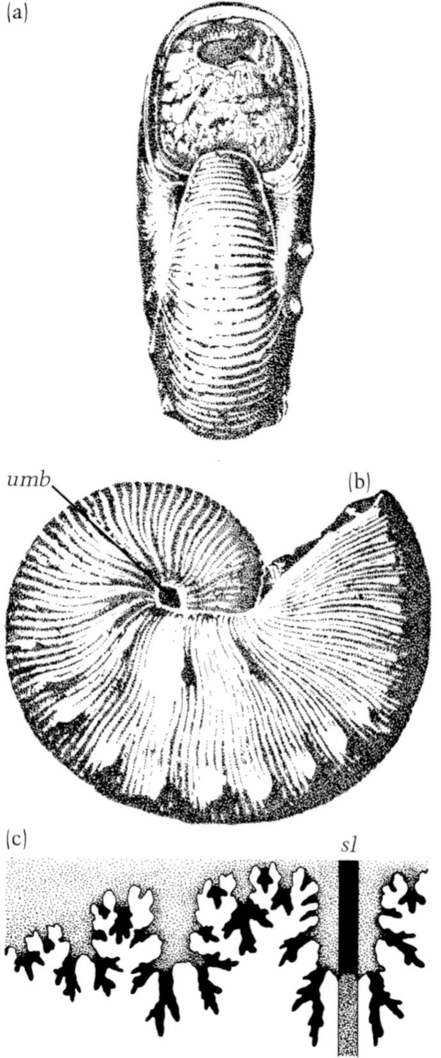

This ammonoid from the late Cretaceous species, Scaphites nodosus, *is abundant in the Pierre shale of the high plains east of the Rocky Mountains. A specimen of this species was one of the first fossils I collected. This figure is a copy of a lithograph published by Fielding Bradford Meek (1817–1876).* (a) *The opening of the living chamber, here choked with matrix.* (b) *The living chamber is below and to the right, its opening just below the letter* (b). *The umbilicus, the indentaton around which the older part of the shell is coiled, is indicated by* umb. (c) *The elaborate pattern formed by the ends of the partitions between successive chambers in the shell, revealed when the external shell covering is removed. The siphuncle, sl, is a tube just below the outer shell that extends from the body chamber to the center of the whole shell.*

evidenced largely and vividly by paleontology, although not solely by that science.

Frederick Dellenbaugh became the last survivor of the crews on the pioneering boat trips down the Green and Colorado rivers led by John Wesley Powell in the late 1860s and early 1870s. Dellenbaugh was only 17 when he started out with Powell in 1871. He died in 1935, but, in the meantime, he had written *A Canyon Voyage,* less well known than the several versions of Powell's own narrative but better written and even more interesting. Although both Powell and Dellenbaugh collected and mentioned fossils, *A Canyon Voyage* would not be relevant in the present book if it were not for a short passage in it: "The Colorado River teaches much that is not geology." Here, near the end of this book on fossils, there is an apt paraphrase of Dellenbaugh's simple but philosophically profound remark: Fossils teach much that is not paleontology.

Previous chapters have included mention of how fossils impinge upon subjects that are not, strictly speaking, paleontology, and they have suggested the synthesis of such subjects with those that fossils do teach. Now, in a lighter vein, we can turn to some mention of the interactions of fossils and people that are less profound and not obviously philosophical, that are even in some respects frivolous, but nevertheless are among the many reasons why fossils are important to people.

Almost any paleontologist will attest that, although of course he collects fossils to advance the science of paleontology, his personal drive also arises at least as much from the joy of the hunt and of outdoor life, often in remote camps and with some apparent hardships that are actually part of the pleasure. Until one becomes too old for them, these are the professional activities that are most enjoyable physically, even while subsequent research, writing, and teaching are equally enjoyable intellectually and become more so as time goes on. Besides the professionals of whom all this is true, there are quite a few amateur fossil hunters and collectors. They surely derive pleasure (and some of them also derive some money) from this occupation, but a professional paleontologist may view some of them as vandals who secrete, confuse, or destroy irrecoverable parts of the documentation of the history of life. Earlier in the history of paleontology, major discoveries were often made by amateurs while purposively searching for curious petrifications or serendipitously while hunting for something else. Amateurs can still be useful—if they take the trouble to learn how to collect fossils properly and to make full and exact field notes, which means that they become at least semiprofessional.

Fossil collecting is not for everyone, but looking at fossils and reading about them are widely available pursuits that can not only be simply instructive but also downright exciting. Fossils of various sorts are among the most popular exhibits in many museums of natural history. In the United States, the most extensive such exhibits are in three major public museums: the National Museum of Natural History (a division of the Smithsonian Institution) in Washington, the American Museum of Natural History in New York, and the Field Museum of

Enthusiastic amateurs display their finds—as well as the kind of careless digging which, in some cases, can render valuable sites worthless for careful scientific investigations.

Natural History in Chicago. Many universities from coast to coast have extensive fossil exhibits open to the public, and there are also many smaller museums with more local exhibits of fossils. At some localities, rich deposits of interesting fossils have been developed into exhibits displaying the fossils just as they occur in nature after the shielding matrix has been partially cleared away. That has been done with various dinosaur skeletons at Dinosaur National Monument near Vernal, Utah, and with rhinoceroses and other mammals at the Agate Fossil Beds in Nebraska, to mention only two of the most frequently visited such displays in the United States.

Picture books on paleontological subjects for preschool and grade-school children are so numerous and interesting that many a youngster can recognize and name such dinosaurs as *Tyrannosaurus, Brontosaurus, Triceratops,* or *Stegosaurus.* Other not strictly technical books about fossils include many that are more sophisticated and some that appeal to literate adults who have professions other than paleontology.

That fossils have recreational values is not as profound or as important as their philosophical implications but is another contribution to the richness of human life. Like other humans, paleontologists also enjoy the many cartoons about fossils and the comic strips with cave men and prehistoric animals. It is, however, sometimes distressing to find that some intelligent people, both young and old, become convinced that prehistoric humans had dinosaurs as pets and steeds and hunted wild dinosaurs for meat. A very successful team of musical-comedy writer and composer once planned to produce a musical about just such an association of cave men and dinosaurs, but they made the mistake of consulting a paleontologist. He told them that he thought the idea was great, but he let drop the information that cave men and dinosaurs never really existed at the same time. They then

The author on the 1930–31 expedition to Patagonia excavating the most nearly complete Eocene mammal skeleton ever found in South America. This is Thomashuxleya externa, *which had been named by the great Argentine paleontologist Florentino Ameghino in 1901 on the basis of just a fragment of a lower left jaw. (That was the year before I was born and thirty years before I found the skeleton.) You can* name *an animal from a fragment, but you cannot* restore *it without a nearly or quite whole skeleton.*

insisted on scrapping the whole project because they had intended it to be truthful as well as entertaining.

The fact that fossils are indeed entertaining is not to be underestimated as a part of their value to all of us. Being entertaining in these often confused and trying times is not trivial even if it is also not profound. The same may be said of the aesthetic interest of fossils, less widely appreciated but no less real. On this point, I will abbreviate and paraphrase something I wrote about thirty years ago in the lovely mountains of New Mexico, sitting where I could look out over a broad basin replete with fossils:

> *The symmetry of a Paleozoic lamp shell or the tracery of sutures in a coiled Mesozoic ammonite is beautiful in the same sense that a classic statuette or a great painting is beautiful. The skeleton of an Eocene mammal is also beautiful to a seeing eye, but not in quite the same sense. It is elegantly adapted to the motions and stresses of a creature once alive. It is to functional modern design what a beautiful ammonite is to a fine modern painting. Moreover, all fossils embody the inherent beauty, the mystery, and the great past of life.*

Surely no one can possibly contemplate the great sweep of time in which evolution has occurred, the endless vitality of organisms, the coming and going of their dynasties, their countless numbers and seemingly endless kinds, and their manifold intricate beauties without a feeling of awe that is in its own way truly religious. I can think of no better ending for this modest book than to quote the last sentence in the first edition of *The Origin of Species:*

> *There is grandeur in this view of life, with its several powers, having been originally breathed into a few forms or into one; and that, whilst this planet has gone cycling on according to the fixed law of gravity, from so simple a beginning endless forms most beautiful and most wonderful have been, and are being evolved.*

Introduction: The Fascination of Fossils

The following books are the sources of the two quotations in this introduction. Both have continuing relevance for the subjects in the rest of the present book.

Simpson, G. G., 1934. *Attending Marvels.* New York: Macmillan.
A slightly modified version with a preface by the new editors and a new foreword by L. M. Gould was published by Time Incorporated, New York, 1965. Another reprint with foreword by L. Marshall and afterword by G. G. Simpson was published by the University of Chicago Press in 1982.

Simpson, G. G., 1949. *The Meaning of Evolution.* New Haven: Yale University Press.
An extensively revised new edition was issued by the same publisher in 1967.

1. The Science of Paleontology

Behrensmeyer, A. K., and A. D. Hill, eds., 1980. *Fossils in the Making: Vertebrate Taphonomy and Paleoecology.* Chicago: University of Chicago Press.
A symposium volume in which taphonomy is studied mainly to determine what happens to the bones of recently dead animals.

Brouwer, A., 1967. *General Palaeontology.* Chicago: University of Chicago Press.
This unpretentious but thoroughly able and interesting study of the nature, rather than just the detailed contents, of the science of paleontology was translated from a 1959 edition in the Dutch language.

Kummel, B., and D. Raup, eds., 1965. *Handbook of Paleontological Techniques.* San Francisco: W. H. Freeman and Company.
Several new techniques have since been developed, but this is still the most complete authoritative work on methods in the preparation and study of fossils.

Müller, A. H., 1979. "Fossilization (Taphonomy)." In R. A. Robison and C. Teichert, eds., *Treatise on Invertebrate Paleontology,* part A, pp. A2–A78. Boulder, Colorado, and Lawrence, Kansas: Geological Society of America and University of Kansas.
A detailed, illustrated discussion of invertebrate taphonomy from death through diagenesis, but not including collecting and preparation.

Raup, D. M., and S. M. Stanley, 1978. *Principles of Paleontology* (second edition). San Francisco: W. H. Freeman and Company.
Unlike most textbooks of paleontology, this one is devoted to methods, principles, implications, applications, and deductions rather than to details of the classification and description of fossils. Like Brouwer's shorter and earlier book, also listed here, it is on general, not on systematic, paleontology.

Richardson, E. S., Jr., ed., 1971. "Extraordinary Fossils." In *Proceedings of the North American Paleontological Convention,* part I, p. 1153. Lawrence, Kansas: Allen Press.
These collected papers by various authors describe the preservation of fossils under unusual circumstances, two examples of which have been mentioned in this chapter.

Rudwick, M. J. S., 1972. *The Meaning of Fossils.* London: Macdonald (and New York: American Elsevier).
An episodic history of the origin and maturation of paleontology as a distinct science, approximately from the sixteenth to the nineteenth centuries.

Simpson, G. G., 1960. "The History of Life." In S. Tax, ed., *Evolution after Darwin,* vol. 1, pp. 117–180. Chicago: University of Chicago Press.
Includes an extended discussion of bias and sampling in the fossil record.

Swinnerton, H. H., 1960. *Fossils.* London: Collins.
This volume in the distinguished New Naturalist series is a simply but authoritatively and fascinatingly written intermingling of the human history of paleontology in Great Britain and the history of life as recorded in fossils there.

2. Fossils as Living Organisms

Ager, Derek V., 1963. *Principles of Paleoecology.* New York: McGraw-Hill.
A well-documented and well-organized treatment of the subject as a whole.

Charig, Alan, 1979. *A New Look at the Dinosaurs.* London: Heineman.
This clearly and interestingly written and profusely illustrated book is definitely the best of the many that have been written about dinosaurs.

Erban, H. K., J. Hoefs, and K. H. Wedepohl, 1979. "Paleobiological and Isotopic Studies of Eggshells from a Declining Dinosaur Species." *Paleobiology* 5(4):380–414.
The technical report that includes the results summarized in this chapter.

Ladd, H. S., ed., 1957. "Treatise on Marine Ecology and Paleoecology. Volume 2: Paleoecology." *Geological Society of America Memoir* 67(2):i–x, 1–1077.
This voluminous classic, which firmly established paleoecology as a geological and paleontological discipline, has not been outdated.

Laporte, Léo F., 1979. *Ancient Environments* (second edition). Englewood Cliffs, N.J.: Prentice-Hall.
An excellent, relatively brief treatment not only of ancient environments but also of the communities in them.

McLoughlin, John C., 1979. *Archosauria: A New Look at the Old Dinosaur.* New York: Viking.
This book is cited only as proof that there are indeed popular works in print that insist that birds are dinosaurs. The author is a competent illustrator, but he is neither a paleontologist nor a systematist.

Simpson, G. G., 1961. *Principles of Animal Taxonomy.* New York: Columbia University Press.
This is a fairly simple approach to taxonomy that I still consider valid, although now reinforced by more complex (especially mathematical) methods.

Sneath, Peter H. A., and Robert R. Sokal, 1973. *Numerical Taxonomy: The Principles and Practice of Numerical Classification.* San Francisco: W. H. Freeman and Company.

This is an extension of what is usually called phenetic taxonomy, which was originally expounded with fervor as excluding phylogenetic considerations from classification. The authors here go far beyond their original intentions in complexity and in including phylogeny in the discussions.

Thomas, Roger D. K., and Everett C. Olson, eds., 1980. *A Cold Look at the Warm-blooded Dinosaurs.* Boulder, Colorado: Westview.

This symposium volume, with twelve chapters by sixteen authors and an introduction by the two editors, is largely technical but not always burdensomely so. Its 43-page bibliography includes almost all the serious literature of its subject. The longest chapter, by R. T. Bakker, who has been most active in promoting discussion of this subject, is uncompromisingly positive that dinosaurs were endothermic. The other authors either express some doubts or oppose Bakker's views.

Valentine, James W., 1973. *Evolutionary Paleoecology of the Marine Biosphere.* Englewood Cliffs, N.J.: Prentice-Hall.

A full treatment of the paleoecology of marine invertebrates in its evolutionary aspects.

3. Fossils and Time

Dunbar, C. O., and J. Rodgers, 1957. *Principles of Stratigraphy.* New York: Wiley.

Biostratigraphy is included in this now classic but not outdated work.

Easton, W. H., 1960. *Invertebrate Paleontology.* New York: Harper.

A good example of the conventional treatment of the subject, dealing with the anatomy, classification, and distribution in time of the groups of invertebrates known as fossils.

Eicher, D. L., 1976. *Geologic Time.* Englewood Cliffs, N.J.: Prentice-Hall.

Another concise treatment, this one covering geological time in general.

Faul, H., 1966. *Ages of Rocks, Planets, and Stars.* New York: McGraw-Hill.

This book covers most of the radiometric dating methods in a brief, reasonably thorough, and understandable way.

Fenton, C. L., and M. A. Fenton, 1958. *The Fossil Book.* Garden City, N.Y.: Doubleday.

A richly illustrated and well-informed popular book.

Hedberg, H. D., ed., 1976. *International Stratigraphic Guide.* New York: Wiley.

This is the most authoritative formulation of the classification and terminology not so much of geological time as such but of stratified rocks classified in various ways, including by time.

Laporte, L. F., ed., 1978. *Evolution and the Fossil Record.* San Francisco: W. H. Freeman and Company.

This is a collection of twenty articles that originally appeared in the magazine *Scientific American.* Here there are added a preface and five useful introductions to the main topics by the editor. All the articles are interesting and well-written, but the two on Precambrian fossils by Barghoorn and Glaessner and the introduction to them by Laporte are especially relevant to this chapter of the present book.

Romer, A. S., 1966. *Vertebrate Paleontology* (third edition). Chicago: University of Chicago Press.

This is the standard work on its subject in English. A further revised edition is being prepared by a former student of the late Professor Romer.

Shaw, A. B., 1964. *Time in Stratigraphy.* New York: McGraw-Hill.

A treatise on determination of geological time, emphasizing biostratigraphic methods.

Simpson, G. G., 1969. "The First Three Billion Years of Community Evolution." *Brookhaven Symposia in Biology* (22):162–177.

An ambitious attempt to give a brief long-distance view of the whole fossil record of animals and to exemplify some of the most important phenomena that it reveals.

Wilmarth, M. G., 1925. "The Geologic Time Classification of the United States Geological Survey Compared with Other Classifications Accompanied by the Original Definitions of Era, Period and Epoch Terms." *U.S. Geological Survey Bulletin* 769:i–vi, 1–138.

Although the U.S.G.S. has changed some of its own usages in the many years since this bulletin was written, it remains the best and most nearly complete source book for the history of many geological time terms and names.

4. Fossils and Geography

Cox, C. B., and P. O. Moore, 1980. *Biogeography: An Ecological and Evolutionary Approach* (third edition). New York: Halstead.

This pre-drift book is deservedly a classic. Its subject, thoroughly treated, is the zoogeography of fresh-water and land vertebrates, not of animals in general. Formerly out-of-print, it has recently been reissued without change by the Robert E. Krieges Publishing Co., Huntington, New York.

Ekman, S., 1953. *Zoogeography of the Sea.* London: Sidgwick and Jackson.

The historical discussions are now out of date, but I know of no equally good treatment in English of the distribution and characters of the living marine faunas of the world.

Gray, J., and A. J. Boucot, eds., 1979. *Historical Biogeography, Plate Tectonics, and the Changing Environment.* Corvallis, Oregon: Oregon State University Press.

This huge symposium volume is devoted largely to fossil marine invertebrates, but it also includes some plants and some vertebrates, marine and nonmarine, as well as some treatment of the plate-tectonics approach to biogeography. Although technical, much of it is comprehensible to anyone with some background in biogeography.

Hallam, A., 1973. *Atlas of Paleobiogeography.* edited by A. Hallam. Amsterdam: Elsevier.
This large symposium volume contains more text than the title "Atlas" may suggest. It provides maps mainly of the distribution of fossil marine invertebrates on the geography of the present world, but it includes some paleogeographic maps as well. Some plants and nonmarine vertebrates are also included. Although technical, it is the best source for usually reliable and detailed data.

MacArthur, R. H., and E. O. Wilson, 1967. *The Theory of Island Biogeography.* Princeton, N.J.: Princeton University Press.
This small volume is largely mathematical and is hard going even for biogeographers, but it is cited because it has recently had a particularly strong influence on biogeography in general.

Marvin, U. B., 1973. *Continental Drift: The Evolution of a Concept.* Washington, D.C.: Smithsonian Institution Press.
A clear, thorough, and fascinating account of the inception and history of an idea and the resulting eventual revolution of a field of thought. There are other histories of plate tectonics, but this is the best.

Neill, W. T., 1969. *The Geography of Life.* New York: Columbia University Press.
An unusually broad (but not historical) popularization of both plant and animal biogeography.

5. Extinction, Origination, and Replacement

Hutchinson, G. Evelyn, 1978. *An Introduction to Population Ecology.* New Haven: Yale University Press.
Life tables and survivorship curves, mainly of Recent animals but also of some fossil animals, are clearly and interestingly treated in Chapter 2 of this excellent book.

Kennedy, W. J., 1977. "Ammonite Evolution." In A. Hallam, ed., *Patterns of Evolution as Illustrated in the Fossil Record,* pp. 251–304. Amsterdam: Elsevier.
A rather technical but excellent and understandable treatment of an example used in this chapter.

Kurtén, Björn, 1968. *Pleistocene Mammals of Europe.* Chicago: Aldine.
This popularization includes a short discussion of faunal turnover, with references to Kurtén's earlier technical work on that subject.

Martin, P. S., and H. E. Wright, Jr., eds., 1967. *Pleistocene Extinctions: The Search for a Cause.* New Haven: Yale University Press.
This book is centered on the hypothesis of overkill, but it gives cons as well as pros.

Newell, Norman D., 1967. "Revolutions in the History of Life." *Geological Society of America Special Paper* 89:63–91.
A classic on rates and patterns of origination and extinction in the fossil record.

Russell, D. A., 1979. "The Enigma of the Extinction of the Dinosaurs." *Annual Review of Earth and Planetary Sciences* 7:163–182.
Although Russell inclines toward the supernova hypothesis of mass extinction, he gives a balanced summary of other views.

Simpson, G. G., 1980. *Splendid Isolation: The Curious History of South American Mammals.* New Haven: Yale University Press.
Chapters 14 and 15, pages 179–239, treat the Great American Interchange, discussed in the final part of the present chapter.

6. Rates and Patterns of Evolution

Bader, Robert S., 1955. "Variability and Evolutionary Rate in the Oreodonts." *Evolution* 9(2):119–140.
The now classic study, somehow overlooked in Gould's review of allometry, discussed in the present chapter.

Dobzhansky, Th., F. J. Ayala, G. L. Stebbins, and J. W. Valentine, 1977. *Evolution.* San Francisco: W. H. Freeman and Company.
A highly authoritative and fairly comprehensive statement of the synthetic theory of evolution. The late Theodosius Dobzhansky was one of the founders of genetic aspects of the theory. One of the authors, James Valentine, is a paleontologist and has summarized some of the contributions of the fossil record to the theory.

Eldredge, N., and S. J. Gould, 1972. "Punctuated Equilibria: An Alternative to Phyletic Gradualism." In T. J. M. Schopf, ed., *Models in Paleobiology,* pp. 82–115. San Francisco: Freeman, Cooper.
This is the first statement of "punctuated equilibrium" by its two authors. Each provides one example of paleontological evidence for their views. It is curious that neither example involves speciation by their own interpretations.

Futuyama, D. J., 1979. *Evolutionary Biology.* Sunderland, Massachusetts: Sinauer.
A good addition to the general works on evolution already cited. Some fossil evidence is briefly summarized but not stressed.

Gould, S. J., 1966. "Allometry and Size in Ontogeny and Phylogeny." *Biological Reviews* 41:587–640.
The most nearly comprehensive review of this subject, as well as an original contribution to it.

Grant, Verne, 1977. *Organismic Evolution.* San Francisco: W. H. Freeman and Company.
A fairly concise statement of the synthetic theory by an eminent botanist who is also a general authority on evolutionary biology.

Haldane, J. B. S., 1949. "Suggestions As to the Quantitative Measurement of Rates of Evolution." *Evolution* 3(1):51–56.
Haldane's classic paper, referred to in the text of this chapter.

Levinton, J. S., and C. M. Simon, 1980. "A Critique of the Punctuated Equilibria Model and Implications for the Detection of Speciation in the Fossil Record." *Systematic Zoology* 29(2):130–142.

This well-reasoned rejection of the thesis of punctuated equilibrium should be read by anyone who also reads Eldredge and Gould on that topic.

Simpson, G. G., 1953. *The Major Features of Evolution.* New York: Columbia University Press.

Although now of course outdated in some respects, this book includes what is still a reasonable classification and discussion of rates of evolution and expounds some other contributions of paleontology to the synthetic theory. The present chapter and the next update some of the points made.

7. Other Major Features of Evolution

Colbert, E. H., 1968. *Men and Dinosaurs.* New York: Dutton.

Full of anecdotes and historical records of collectors and students of dinosaurs, including the eccentric Baron Nopcsa.

Hallam, A., ed., 1977. *Patterns of Evolution As Illustrated in the Fossil Record.* Amsterdam: Elsevier.

This symposium volume begins with a historical account by Stephen Jay Gould, which, I believe, is cast incorrectly and illogically in a dialectical mold. Thereafter, however, it deals with the data of paleontology and with the evolutionary patterns that they indicate.

LeCam, L. M., J. Neyman, and E. L. Scott, eds., 1972. *Darwinian, Neo-Darwinian and Non-Darwinian Evolution.* (Proceedings of the Fifth Berkeley Symposium on Mathematical Statistics and Probability, volume 5). Berkeley and Los Angeles: University of California Press.

Despite the title of the series in which it was published, this symposium is not much concerned with statistics or probability but mainly with molecular evolution. A synthesist botanist and a synthesist geneticist also took part. There was no discussion of the fossil record and its restraints.

Mayr, Ernst, 1970. *Populations, Species, and Evolution.* Cambridge, Massachusetts: Harvard University Press.

This is a condensation (and, to some extent, a simplification) of a previous book on the general principles and patterns of evolution, as seen by a leading systematic zoologist, who is also one of the founding synthesists. There is some, but not much, consideration of the fossil record in connection with major (or, as the author puts it, "transpecific") features of evolution.

Simpson, G. G., 1953. *The Major Features of Evolution.* New York: Columbia University Press.

This relatively technical work has become the most cited of my books in later studies of evolution. Some of its ideas are updated in the present book.

Simpson, G. G., 1964. *The View of Life.* New York: Harcourt Brace Jovanovich.

This book, which is at least semipopular, is my own favorite and has several chapters that are relevant to the discussions in this book.

(Previously cited books on evolutionary and paleontological principles are of course also relevant for this chapter.)

8. Fossils and People

Albritton, Claude C., Jr., 1980. *The Abyss of Time.* San Francisco, Freeman, Cooper.

A delightful history of the development of conceptions of geological time from the seventeenth century onward. Especially recommended to chronophobiacs.

Darwin, Charles, 1859. *On the Origin of Species by Means of Natural Selection, or the Preservation of Favoured Races in the Struggle for Life.* London: John Murray.

Everyone should read this book, especially those who discuss Darwinism without having read it. It is now generally called simply *The Origin of Species.* There were six editions from 1859 to 1872. It has never gone out of print. The reprints most widely available today are of the sixth edition, but many students of evolution prefer the first edition. There were only 1,250 copies of that edition, and these are difficult to find and expensive to buy now. It was, however, reprinted in Great Britain and sold here by the Philosophical Library in 1951, and a facsimile was issued by Harvard University Press in 1964. A variorum covering all six editions and some later minor corrections by the original publisher was compiled by Morse Peckham and published by the University of Pennsylvania Press for the United States and Oxford University Press for Great Britain, India, and Pakistan in 1959.

Dobzhansky, Theodosius, 1955. *Evolution, Genetics, and Man.* New York: Wiley.

The author, a geneticist who worked mainly with wild and laboratory *Drosophila,* was also a leading student of evolution in general and of human evolution in particular. In those fields, this is a classic, and it remains one of the best treatments of its subjects.

Ruse, Michael, 1979. *The Darwinian Revolution: Science Red in Tooth and Claw.* Chicago: University of Chicago Press.

The title of this book is misleading. It is really an interesting and recommended exposition of the relevant scientific milieu in which Darwin grew up and eventually wrote *The Origin of Species.*

Simons, Elwyn L., 1972. *Primate Evolution: An Introduction to Man's Place in Nature.* New York: Macmillan.

Parts of this book are already (inevitably) out of date, but it is still, on the whole, the best treatment of its subject for most readers.

Szalay, F. S., and E. Delson, 1979. *Evolutionary History of the Primates.* New York: Academic.

Although some of its interpretations are not generally accepted, this is (as of the time of this writing) the most recent compilation on the primates as a whole. The fossil genera and species are profoundly and beautifully illustrated.

CREDITS

Chapter 1

pages 3 and 4
Adapted from a photograph taken by the University of Arizona's Audio Visual Service of specimens in the Department of Geoscience at the University of Arizona.

page 5 (top)
Historia Animalium, Konrad Gesner, 1558. By permission of The Houghton Library, Harvard University.

page 5 (middle)
De omni rerum fossilium genere, Konrad Gesner, 1565. By permission of The Houghton Library, Harvard University.

page 5 (bottom)
Ibid.

page 6 (top)
Musaeum Franc. Calceolari, Andrea Chiocco, 1622. By permission of The Houghton Library, Harvard University.

page 6 (bottom)
Museum National d'Histoire Naturelle.

page 7
Black Star

page 8 (top)
The Monthly Magazine and British Register, v.II, 1976, p. 637. Harvard College Library.

page 8 (bottom)
Courtesy American Museum of Natural History.

page 9 (bottom)
Australian Information Service.

page 10 (top)
Courtesy Senckenbergische Naturforschende Gesellschaft.

page 10 (bottom)
Redrawn from Dr. Gerhard Storch, *Senckenbergiana lethaea,* **59** (4/6): 503–529 (1978).

page 12 (top)
Adapted from Richard Swann Lull, 1953.

page 12 (bottom)
Smithsonian Institution Photo No. 18267.

page 13 (top)
Field Museum of Natural History.

page 13 (bottom)
Courtesy American Museum of Natural History.

page 14
The SEM photographs were taken by Hazel Parish, Paul Martin, and Charles Drew in the Department of Geosciences, University of Arizona.

page 15 (top left)
Bill Ratcliffe

page 15 (top right)
Charles Palek/Tom Stack and Associates.

page 15 (bottom)
University of Arizona Audio Visual Services.

page 17 (left)
Museum of Natural History, Princeton University.

page 17 (right)
University of Arizona Audio Visual Services.

page 21 (top)
Harald Sund/Image Bank.

page 21 (bottom)
George Sheng.

page 22–23
Fritz Goro.

page 24
Richard E. Grant/Smithsonian Institution.

page 25
Courtesy American Museum of Natural History.

Chapter 2

page 29 (left)
American Heritage Center, University of Wyoming.

page 29 (right)
Yale Peabody Museum of Natural History.

page 30
British Museum (Natural History).

page 31
Photographs from Institute Royal des Sciences Naturelles de Belgique. Restoration based on skeletons on display at the same institution.

page 33
Courtesy American Museum of Natural History.

page 34
Adapted from H. F. Osborn (a) and L. M. Lambe (b).

page 35
Adapted from Richard Swann Lull and Nelda Wright (a) and John Ostrom (b).

page 36
Courtesy American Museum of Natural History.

page 37
Tyrrell Museum of Paleontology.

page 38
Adapted from Richard Swann Lull and Nelda E. Wright.

page 39
Adapted from John Ostrom.

page 40
Compiled and arranged from several sources.

page 48
Dr. Elso Barghoorn.

page 49
Redrawn from "Pre-Cambrian Animals" by Martin F. Glaessner. Copyright © 1975 by Scientific American, Inc. All rights reserved.

page 52
Adapted from Everett Olson.

page 54 (top)
Data generalized and rearranged from K. R. Walker and L. Laporte (1970).

page 54 (bottom)
Bruce Coleman Inc.

page 55
Peter Parks/Oxford Scientific Films.

Chapter 3

page 61
Jay Matternes/Smithsonian Institution.

page 64 (top)
John Shelton.

page 64 (bottom)
Based, with considerable modification, mainly on data from L. F. Noble.

page 68
From *Principles of Geology,* by Gilluly, Waters and Woodford.

page 69
Adapted from several sources, especially L. G. Marshall, R. F. Butler, and G. H. Curtis.

page 70 (top)
Dr. Elso Barghoorn.

page 70 (middle and bottom)
Dr. S. M. Awramik.

page 71
Adapted, but considerably modified, from a diagram by Elso Barghoorn.

page 72 (top left and right)
Neville Pledge/The South Australia Museum.

page 72 (bottom left)
Chip Clark.

page 72 (bottom right)
Fritz Goro.

page 76 (left)
(a) redrawn from Dunbar; (b) redrawn from Hall and Clarke; (c) redrawn from R. Bedford and J. Bedford; (d) redrawn from Holm; (e) redrawn from a report of the Missouri Geological Survey.

page 76 (right)
(a) redrawn from Canu and Bassler; (b) compiled from various sources, mainly from Davidson; (c) redrawn from Bather; (d) compiled from various sources; (e) redrawn from Bather; (f) redrawn from Oakley and Muir-Wood; (g) redrawn from Clark; (h) redrawn from Cronesis.

page 77 (top)
(a) redrawn from Hall; (b) redrawn from Heilprin; (c) redrawn from Hall; (d) redrawn from Hall with modifications; (e) and (e') redrawn from Reeside with some modifications.

page 77 (bottom)
(a) redrawn from Walcott; (b) redrawn from Ulrich and Bassler; (c) redrawn from Clark and Ruedemann; (d) redrawn from after Handlirsch.

page 79
S. Conway Morris.

page 80
Raw data mainly from the *Treatise on Invertebrate Paleontology.*

page 81
(a) redrawn from Grabau; (b) redrawn from Hirmer; (c) redrawn from Kidston and Long; (d) redrawn from Hirmer; (e) redrawn from Lesquereux; (f) redrawn from Lesquereux; (g) redrawn from Grand'Eury; (h) redrawn from Thomas and Edwards; (i) redrawn from Sahni.

page 83
Field Museum of Natural History.

page 83 (right)
Else Marie Friis.

page 84 (left)
Walter Lietz/Field Museum of Natural History.

page 84 (right)
Kjell Sandved/Smithsonian Institution.

page 87 (top)
Academy of Natural Sciences of Philadelphia.

page 87 (bottom)
Field Museum of Natural History.

page 89 (top)
Staatliches Museum für Naturkunde.

page 89 (bottom)
E. R. Degginger/Earth Scenes.

page 90
(a) redrawn from White; (b) restored from a partial reconstruction by Watson; (c) redrawn from Dean; (d) restored from a skeletal reconstruction by Gregory and Raven; (e) restored from a skeleton in the American Museum of Natural History; (f) restored from a skeleton reconstruction by Williston.

page 91
(a) restored from a skeletal reconstruction by von Huene; (b) from Gregory and a skeletal restoration by Heilman; (c) restored from a skeletal reconstruction by Colbert; (d) from Gregory.

Chapter 4

page 93 and 94
Redrawn from a photograph from the Field Museum of Natural History.

page 98
Courtesy American Museum of Natural History.

page 103
David Houston/Bruce Coleman Inc.

page 104
Field Museum of Natural History.

page 107
Paintings by H. Douglas Pratt/Bernice P. Bishop Museum.

page 108
Modified from data from W. P. Woodring.

page 111 (top)
Museum of Comparative Zoology, Harvard University.

page 111 (bottom)
Vince Abromitis photo, Carnegie Museum of Natural History.

page 112
Redrawn and modified from studies by several stratigraphers and paleontologists, including A. R. Palmer.

page 113
Redrawn and modified from numerous sources.

page 114
Redrawn and modified from many sources.

page 115
Smithsonian Institution.

page 116
From *Fossil Land Mammal from Antarctica,* Woodburne, M. O., and Zinsmeister, W. J., *Science,* v.218, pp. 284–286, fig. 2, 15 October 1982. Copyright 1982 by the American Association for the Advancement of Science.

page 119
Outline restorations of *Hyracotherium* and *Epihippus* from skeletons mostly in the American Museum of Natural History, New York; that of *Paleotherium*

from specimens in the Museum National d'Histoire Naturelle, Paris. A reconstruction of *Paleotherium* was published in 1812 by Curvier.

Chapter 5

page 123
Discours sur les revolutions de la surface du globe, George Curvier, 1825. Courtesy National Library of Medicine.

page 124
Buffalo Museum of Science.

page 125
Chuck Nicklin/Ocean Films, Ltd.

page 131 (graph)
After Jason Lillegraven, 1972.

page 131 (tables)
Based on data by Norman D. Newell, 1967.

page 132 (top)
Adapted from Norman D. Newell, 1967.

page 134
The data for (a), here modified and redrawn, are from Raymond Pearl, who also devised the method of comparing groups of quite different average ages of survival by graphing each group by percentages of differences from the mean. The data for (c), also modified and redrawn, are from A. Williams and J. M. Hurst.

page 135 (table)
Estimated by Björn Kurtén.

page 138 (table)
Based on data published by Norman D. Newell, 1967.

page 139 (left)
National Audubon Society.

page 139 (right)
Painting by James Fenwick Lansdowne, from *Rails of the World* by S. Dillion Ripley, courtesy of M. F. Feheley Arts Limited.

page 142 (lower table)
Based on the equation for exponential increase in the table on page 142 and modified from exponential rates given by Steven M. Stanley.

page 143
Both graphs redrawn with some modification from figures by J. John Sepkoski, Jr.

page 145
Chip Clark.

page 146
The data are from the *Treatise on Invertebrate Paleontology.*

page 147
Redrawn, with slight change, from part of a figure by W. J. Kennedy.

page 149
Field Museum of Natural History.

Chapter 6

page 151 and 152
Redrawn from a photograph by Donald Baird at the Museum of Natural History, Princeton University.

page 154 (table)
Data from R. S. Bader (1955).

page 155
Jay Matternes/Smithsonian Institution.

page 159 (photo)
Fritz Goro.

page 159 (graph)
Data from T. Ozawa, but here modified and redrawn in a distinctly different form.

page 160 (table)
Data from A. M. Zeigler (1966).

page 161
Based on data from A. M. Ziegler, but in highly modified form and with rates of evolution calculated and added.

page 162
This figure is copied directly from Gingerich's first publication on the subject in 1976. He later published other versions, bringing in data from other regions and changing the names of various of the species, these complicate the picture but do not change the basic data or the probable significance of Gingerich's first version.

page 163
Courtesy American Museum of Natural History.

page 164
Sources of data are acknowledged in the caption. The three parts of this figure are original, redrawn, and updated here.

page 167
Dr. Merlin Tuttle.

page 169
Data for this figure are based on a monograph by Vincent J. Maglio published in 1973, but he did not put them in this form.

page 170 (top left)
J. Matternes/Smithsonian Institution.

page 170 (top right)
George C. Page Museum.

page 170 (table)
Calculated from data by V. J. Maglio.

page 172
This figure is part of one from a paper by D. R. Prothero and D. B. Lazarus, who were using and interpreting primary data from an earlier publication by J. D. Hays.

Chapter 7

page 180 (left)
Redrawn from "Dinosaur Renaissance" by Robert T. Bakker. Copyright © 1975 by Scientific American, Inc. All rights reserved.

page 180 (right)
John Ostrom.

page 183
Vince Abromitis photo, Carnegie Museum of Natural History.

page 184
Painting by H. Douglas Pratt/Bernice P. Bishop Museum.

page 185 (top)
Data from *The Treatise On Invertebrate Paleontology,* A. S. Romer's *Vertebrate Paleontology,* and various more limited sources.

page 185 (bottom)
Data from Dean Amadon, 1950, and W. J. Bock, 1970, but not given by them in this form.

page 186
Data collected from many sources.

page 188
Redrawn from "Pterosaurs" by Wann Langston, Jr. Copyright © 1981 by Scientific American, Inc. All rights reserved.

page 190 (left)
Vince Abromitis photo, Carnegie Museum of Natural History.

page 190 (right)
Black Hills Institute of Geological Research.

page 197 (top)
Chip Clark.

page 197 (bottom)
Field Museum of Natural History.

page 198 (top)
Danny Brass/Photo Researchers.

page 198 (bottom)
E. Tanson/Tom Stack and Associates.

Chapter 8

page 205
Anita Harris, USGS.

page 208
Scala.

page 211
Institute for Human Origins.

page 213
John Reader.

page 214
Tom McHugh/Photo Researchers. Specimen Field Museum of Natural History.

page 217
Courtesy American Museum of Natural History.

page 218
George Gaylord Simpson.

INDEX/GLOSSARY

References to illustrations are printed in boldface type.
The lower case "t" indicates reference to a table.